THE PURCELL COMPANION

THE
PURCELL
COMPANION

edited by

Michael Burden

faber and faber

LONDON · BOSTON

First published in 1995
by Faber and Faber Limited
3 Queen Square, London, WC1N 3AU

Phototypeset by Intype, London
Printed in England by Clays Ltd, St Ives Plc

A CIP record for this book is available from the
British Library

ISBN 0–571–16325–4
0–571–16670–9 (pbk)

2 4 6 8 10 9 7 5 3 1

528·580

In memory of
Michael Tilmouth

Contents

IV   Purcell and the Theatre

V   Purcell in Performance

List of Illustrations

Preface

The idea of a *Purcell Companion* was one originally advanced some years ago by the dedicatee of this volume, Michael Tilmouth, Tovey Professor in the University of Edinburgh from 1971 until his death in 1987. Although he had remarkably eclectic tastes both as a scholar and as a performer, he remained devoted to the music of Purcell. As Chairman of the Purcell Society, he presided over the production of this important collection and produced his own memorable editions. Given Michael Tilmouth's dry remarks on *Festschriften* it was inappropriate that one should be produced in his honour, but it seemed a fitting tribute to revive this lapsed project of his own. However, some years had passed since the table of contents had been prepared and no text had been written either by himself or by the proposed contributors; as editor of the volume, I must, therefore, take responsibility for its new layout and organization.

I should like to express my gratitude to Helen Sprott, then music editor of Faber and Faber, who was inspired to revive the idea of a *Purcell Companion*, to her successor Andrew Clements for his support during the final stages of the project, and to Jane Feaver and Michael Durnin without whom we should all be lost. John Wagstaff showed exemplary patience with my endless questions of detail. Finally, I owe its completion to the interest of Martin Williams, Fellow in Engineering, who suffered it from commissioning to publication, only leaving for Vancouver before the proofs arrived.

Michael Burden
New College, Oxford
1994

Bibliographical Note

The following bibliographical abbreviations are used:

Evelyn: *The Diary of John Evelyn*, ed. E. S. de Beer (London, 1955); the initial citation is followed by the date, the volume in the edition and the page number.

Grove VI: *The New Grove*, ed. Stanley Sadie (London, 1980).

Pepys: *The Diary of Samuel Pepys*, ed. R. Latham and W. Matthews (London, 1970–83); the initial citation is followed by the date, the volume in the edition and the page number.

Works I: *The Works of Henry Purcell* started in 1876 by the Purcell Society and completed in 1965.

Works II: The revised edition of *The Works of Henry Purcell*.

Zimmerman I: Franklin B. Zimmerman, *Henry Purcell 1659–1695: an Analytical Catalogue of his Music* (London, 1963).

Zimmerman II: Franklin B. Zimmerman, *Henry Purcell 1659–1695: his Life and Times* (Philadelphia, 1983).

Acknowledgements

The Editor and Contributors wish to acknowledge the assistance of the staff of the reading rooms of the Bodleian Library, Oxford, the British Library, the British Museum, the Guildhall Library, London, and the Public Record Office, and of the following individuals: Elizabeth Agate, Andrew Ashbee, Donald Burrows, Ian Cheverton, Francesca Franchi, Nicholas Kenyon, Tess Knighton, Margaret Laurie, Robert Manning, E-J. Milner-Gulland, W. J. Oxenbury, Curtis Price, Robert Shay.

The musical examples in this volume are not always new editions; where appropriate they have been drawn from *The Works of Henry Purcell*, with the permission of Novello and Co. for the Purcell Society. In Chapter 4, examples 2 (copyright 1972), 3 (copyright 1972) and 5 (copyright 1986) are copyright by the Musica Britannica Trust and are reproduced by permission of Stainer & Bell Ltd; example 4(b) (copyright 1958, 1968, 1969) is copyright by Stainer & Bell Ltd and is reproduced by permission; and example 9 is reproduced by permission of Schott & Co. Ltd.

I
INTRODUCTION

I

The Purcell Phenomenon

ANDREW PINNOCK

Three hundred years on, we look back to Purcell through a long tunnel. It's easy to forget that the 'early music' composer viewed from this end was a very modern one in his own day, and is famous now because he managed unwittingly to supply generation after generation of performers and listeners, critics and scholars with material adaptable to a range of purposes, all 'modern' in their turn. How he acquired his reputation in the first place, and why his musical heirs took such trouble to preserve it, are the questions briefly considered in this essay.[1]

He was born at a lucky time, only a year before Charles II's 'Happy Restoration' to the English throne; the son of a London musician much in demand when the royal establishment re-opened for business. Purcell senior was quick to recognize Henry's potential, and to steer him towards a musical career – into the Choir of the Chapel Royal, where he obtained a thorough, practically based musical education at the King's expense. The choristers learned to sing of course, to play, to copy parts, maintain instruments, and to compose. Purcell probably joined at the age of 7 or 8 and stayed on the court payroll for the rest of his life. There he was at the centre of things, aware of every new musical development, taking part in every important performance, learning from the older men, growing up among friends who were to become his professional colleagues in adult life. Better training for a natural talent could hardly have been arranged, nor a better way to control the jealous instincts of possible rivals. It was clear to everyone that Purcell did well because he deserved to.

It would be wrong to think that the Restoration in 1660 blew away a cultural dam, freeing people to carry on just where the Civil War had forced them to stop eighteen years earlier. Musical development continued during the Commonwealth period. Though Charles II smiled on the 'growth . . . of Arts'[2] (good news for artists in that 'Happy Age'), Cromwell had winked at least. And abroad, where the English courtiers went into temporary exile, they acquired spicy tastes – a liking for French and Italian musical fare which Cooke back home did his best to cater for. (Henry Cooke, that is: Master of the Children at the Chapel Royal from 1660 to 1672.) Charles II set up a private string band modelled on his cousin Louis XIV's Vingt-Quatre Violons du Roi; brought Louis Grabu to London to train them in French-style playing; paid for the English violinist John Banister and young Pelham Humfrey to study in France. Foreign influence on English musical style is a subject too involved to deal with here, but there can be no doubt about either the provenance or the importance of imported musical hardware. In the 1670s and 1680s newly developed French woodwind instruments arrived, oboes, bassoons and three-piece recorders, with French specialists to play them; the Italian violin virtuoso Nicola Matteis settled in London (his teaching brought about 'no small reformation' in English violin-playing[3]); and English trumpeters mastered the clarino technique.

Here were the ingredients of a new thing: the Baroque orchestra, unavailable to any of Purcell's predecessors, and the skill with which he came to grips with it is hugely impressive. From 1690, the year of *Dioclesian*, *The Yorkshire Feast Song* and 'Arise, my Muse', to his death in 1695, Purcell was unchallenged as England's leading orchestral composer; a point worth stressing, for the man put in charge of a brand new and very expensive music machine is bound to attract attention. Henry Playford may have praised his 'peculiar Genius to express the Energy of English Words, whereby he mov'd the Passions of all his Auditors', in the preface to *Orpheus Britannicus*, 'A Collection of all the Choicest Songs . . . Compos'd by Mr. Henry Purcell', first published in 1698. But contemporaries may have admired Purcell's orchestral writing quite as much. For some time his were the only all-stops-out orchestral numbers regularly played to paying customers in the commercial theatre. Odes, welcome songs and anthems by other composers featured the full orchestra, to be sure – Blow's were notably successful – but these were occasional pieces performed once or twice only, which only a few hundred people would ever be able to hear. Purcell, the 'pride and darling of the stage',[4] had cornered the operatic market with four widely admired dramatic opera scores written between 1690 and 1695 (*Dioclesian, King Arthur, The Fairy-Queen, The Indian Queen*), and provided incidental music for another forty play productions 'operatized' to a greater or lesser extent. Not only were the shows revived, meaning that Purcell was performed more often: success in the theatre ensured a brisk sale for his songs and instrumental music in printed form, which spread his name further afield. The accessibility of music he had written already fuelled demand for more. Higher and higher, the commercial snowball lifted him up: perhaps Purcell is the first example in English musical history of a phenomenon very familiar now, though difficult to object to in his case, considering the quality of the product.

Purcell had become a public figure, and his death was mourned as a public loss. No one waited for the mysterious 'test of time' to pass judgment: it was clear to his contemporaries that 'a greater musicall genius England never had'.[5] They were right about Dryden too – the best English poet of the late seventeenth century – and about Wren, and about Newton. Leaving time to do what ought to be the critics' job is a twentieth-century evasion, it seems to me: a sign of cultural insecurity from which the seventeenth century did not suffer. A sound basis for Purcell's lasting fame had been established during his lifetime, his varied output providing music for the church, the theatre and domestic markets (product diversity, we might say), and his reputation riding high (brand awareness). Grove's *Dictionary* described a 'more or less continuous stream of editions of [Purcell's] works' from 1695 onwards, which seemed to be an 'exception to the usual course of composers' reputations'.[6] But Purcell's music had monetary as well as artistic value: soon the stream of editions turned into a busy commercial waterway.

The commercial analogy will stretch to tedious lengths before it breaks. Changing fashion serves commercial interests in music as in everything else (clothes, curtains, car upholstery or whatever); and musical fashion was reformed 'al'Italliana' within ten years of Purcell's death.[7] Italian opera stars – proto-Pavarottis with whom the English singing actors could not compete – may have been more of an attraction than Italian opera itself, in the early stages of the invasion; but really the two went together. Alongside the latest Italian arias Purcell's English songs sounded very old-fashioned; but there was still a use for them. Purcell had defined a musical sterling standard against which all the foreign notes in circulation could be compared. Thus Dr Burney in 1789, writing on the songs in *Orpheus Britannicus* after eighty years of Italian domination:

> [A Purcell melody] will at first seem to many uncouth and antiquated; but by a little allowance and examination, any one possessed of a great love for Music, and a knowledge of our language, will feel, at certain places of almost every song, his superior felicity and passion for expressing the poet's sentiments which he had to translate into melody ... there is a latent power and force in his expression of English words, whatever be the subject, that will make an unprejudiced native of this island feel more than all the elegance, grace, and refinement of modern Music less happily applied can do. And this pleasure is communicated to us, not by the symmetry or rhythm of modern melody, but by his having fortified, lengthened, and tuned, the true accents of our mother tongue; those notes of passion, which an inhabitant of this island would breathe, in such situations as the words he has to set, describe ... These remarks are addressed to none but Englishmen: for the expression of words can be felt only by the natives of any country, who seldom extend their admiration of foreign vocal Music, farther than to the general effect of its melody and harmony on the ear ... [8]

Burney was bound to object to the 'uncouth and antiquated' traits he had detected in Purcell's music, so upsetting to refined ears, to the 'crudities' which he hoped 'the organists of our cathedrals [would] scruple not to change for better harmony'; and probably to underrate Purcell's orchestral writing when he compared it with the latest Haydn and Mozart: '. . . the colouring and effects of an orchestra were then but little known'.[9] But pangs of conscience, as one by one he exposed 'defects' in the work of 'our musical Shakespeare' – note the comparison: he upon whom the nation's musical pride depended – set the influential Burney looking for a proof of Purcell's genius which time and changing taste would never erase. The proof he settled on was this: an 'exquisite expression of [English] words' for which 'Purcell is still admirable, and will continue so among Englishmen, as long as the present language ... still remain[s] intelligible'.[10] As 'exquisite expression of words' is the Purcellian characteristic most widely praised from Burney's day to the present, it is worth going a little further into.

English is said to be an unmusical language, and that may be true if all we mean by 'music' is a big tune, one to hum at idle moments, one to set the foot tapping, or a sort of aural mudbath to wallow in. Words fitted to a 'big tune' are like citizens in an authoritarian state, all conforming meekly to the grand plan which government imposes on them. In Purcell's music, though, power is devolved to the words instead, and the composer is free to meet every expressive demand at a local level. Dennis Arundell explains:

> Living at the time he did, when the dramatic in music was being shaped, Purcell ... could mould his heightened naturalism of speech into a musical shape that was also tuneful. One generation later still had formalized both tune and shape, and music in the larger forms such as opera and oratorio moved in jerks with well-defined barriers between the conventionalized speech of the recitative and the *da capo* format of the melodic aria ...[11]

If we imagine a graph showing increasing melodiousness from about 1670 to 1770, flat at the beginning, with airs 'as unformed and misshapen, as if they had been made of notes scattered about by chance, instead of being cast in an elegant mold',[12] climbing to Purcell, whose compositions 'seemed to speak a new language',[13] rising further through Handel to level off at Arne, Purcell's very fortunate placing in the lower-to-middle, tuneful but not tune-bound reaches will become clear. For what are the characteristics of spoken English, characteristics which English song should properly reflect, not try to hide?

Assuredly not the 'elegance, grace and refinement' which Burney so admired. According to Otto Jespersen, the Danish philologist to whom we turn for an impartial view:

> The English language is a methodical, energetic, business-like and sober language, that does not much care for finery and elegance, but does care for logical consistency and is opposed to any attempt to narrow-in life by police regulations and strict rules either of grammar or of the lexicon.[14]

Purcell's musical technique and English itself – 'so noble, so rich, so pliant, so expressive'[15] – are so exactly matched, that the same thumbnail characterization might serve for either.

Christopher Smart, 'arguably the greatest English poet between Pope and Wordsworth',[16] anticipated Jespersen on the 'manliness' of the language by nearly two centuries:

> But hark! the temple's hollow'd roof resounds,
> And Purcell lives among the solemn sounds. –
>   Mellifluous, yet manly too,
>   He pours his strains along,
>   As from the lion Samson slew,
>   Comes sweetness from the strong.
>   Not like the soft Italian swains,
>   He trills the weak enervate strains,
>   Where sense and music are at strife;
>   His vigorous notes with meaning teem,
>   With fire, and force explain the theme,
>   And sing the subject into life.

When Smart's poem was set to music by William Russell 'about 1800',[17] Purcell performances were still fairly frequent[18] – of the church music especially. And by then Purcell had been canonized by the arbiters of musical taste, fixed as if a set of bells to Shakespeare's harness. Wherever Shakespeare went, pulling the whole English cultural bandwagon behind him, Purcell was bound to follow. In the nineteenth century we can point to a Purcell Club and, later, to the Purcell Society, like the Shakespeare Society and New Shakspere Society; to their respective centennial jamborees; to increasing interest in the biographies and work-chronologies of their respective subjects; even to the start of an 'authentic' performance movement affecting both.[19]

But, although the Purcell and Shakespeare industries were organized along similar lines, one very regrettable difference stands out. Whereas Shakespeare-worship seems to have stimulated interest in other poets and playwrights who had been active around the same time, whose works were reprinted to 'illustrate' Shakespeare, as possible Shakespeare sources and so on, Purcell's contemporaries were pointedly ignored.

By about 1890 modern editions of the complete works of practically every important seventeenth-century English playwright were easily available; and the cheap Mermaid series put representative plays by some quite obscure authors into public circulation. But a publishing effort in any way comparable had yet to be made for seventeenth-century music. William Barclay Squire complained in 1921 that:

> ... in cases like these ... the need for an English publication along the lines of the German 'Denkmäler' is so much felt. Locke's 'Psyche', the Shadwell 'Tempest' music, Eccles' 'Macbeth' and 'Semele', the operas of Daniel Purcell and Godfrey Finger, the 'Macbeth' music before it was tinkered with by Boyce – these ought all to be available to students of the history of English music. But a country which owns Purcell and yet has not succeeded in completing the edition of his works begun forty-five years ago cannot be expected to take any interest in the music of its minor composers.[20]

And Ralph Vaughan Williams, thirty years later still:

> The Purcell Society has, I believe, at last almost completed its labours, carried on by the devotion of a few experts who gave their scanty leisure to the work and were entirely neglected by the State or the public. Meantime, Austria, Germany, Italy and France have all produced at the public expense complete and critical editions, not only of their great masters, but also of their lesser lights. In this country we have too long allowed one of the greatest geniuses of music to languish unwept, unhonoured and almost unsung.[21]

Matters have improved somewhat: the 'old' Purcell Society edition was completed in 1965, and *Psyche* finally appeared with all the surviving *Tempest* music in Michael Tilmouth's

1986 Musica Britannica edition. But there are still some alarming gaps to be filled.

Put another way: although Purcell's genius was recognized in his own lifetime, by fellow musicians (the public, even) who knew and valued the work of his abler competitors, today it is founded upon eighteenth-century judgments – Burney's above all; and is maintained *uncritically*, in ignorance of much of the best music by composers he himself admired. Burney may be to blame for this too, damning poor Blow – 'Master to the famous Mr. Henry Purcell', 'his name venerable among the musicians of our country' before Burney set to work – as 'barbarous'; a man who 'threw notes about at random . . . [and] insulted the ear with lawless discords', of whose *'faults* in counterpoint . . . it may, in general, be said . . . that there are *unaccounted millions* of them in his works'.[22] So much for the composer who had once been considered very nearly Purcell's equal. What point could there be in looking at the rest of the field?

Burney's *General History* served as the standard textbook on English music history until Ernest Walker's *History of Music in England* appeared in 1907; and Walker did little to set the record straight. Not surprisingly, Purcell remained in his sainted isolation throughout the nineteenth century.

In 1828 Vincent Novello 'began the publication of the master's sacred music, and carried it on with such energy that in 1832 he had given the world what was then thought to be a complete collection' (five volumes).[23] Then in 1836 the Purcell Club was founded 'for the cultivation of Purcell's works'. Its forty members met twice a year, in February for a formal dinner, and in July to perform his music: they were allowed to 'assist' at morning service in Westminster Abbey (Purcell anthems and settings were chosen for the occasion), and in the evening tackled a secular programme with the help of boy choristers from the Abbey, the Chapel Royal and St Paul's Cathedral.[24] The 'words of the several Pieces intended for performance at each Anniversary' were printed for members to keep.[25]

Edward Taylor – Professor of Music in Gresham College and, significantly, an editor for the Musical Antiquarian Society founded in 1840 – became club president in 1842. Four of the

Musical Antiquarian Society's nineteen published volumes were of music by Purcell: his Ode for St Cecilia's Day, 1692 ('Hail! Bright Cecilia!'), *Bonduca* and *King Arthur* (both fine patriotic pieces: 'Britons strike home!' in *Bonduca*, 'St George, the patron of our isle' in *King Arthur*), and *Dido and Aeneas* – the first printed edition. Professor Taylor and Purcell Club members were much in evidence during celebrations to mark the 'bicentenary' of Purcell's birth, held in London – rather too early – on 30 January 1858; but the club disbanded shortly afterwards.

Its successor, the Purcell Society, still going strong, was founded in February 1876 'for the purpose of doing justice to the memory of Henry Purcell; firstly, by the publication of his works, most of which exist only in manuscript; and secondly, by meeting for the study and performance of his various compositions'.[26] Founder-members aimed to extend the publishing activities of the Musical Antiquarian Society, at least as far as Purcell was concerned, and to promote performances of the new editions; but the performing part of the scheme 'was soon given up'.[27] The list of prominent English musicians who served their turn as Purcell Society committee members or editors or both is impressive – to name a few: Sir Frederick Gore Ousley, Sir George MacFarren, Sir J. F. Bridge, Dr William H. Cummings, Ebenezer Prout, Sir John Stainer, Sir Hubert Parry, Sir Charles Stanford, Ralph Vaughan Williams, Sir Michael Tippett. And it is far from a coincidence that Purcellian committee work should have united so many key musical figures in the 'English Musical Renaissance'.[28] Purcell was the only earlier English composer for whose works the entire musical community had assumed a proud, collective responsibility; the only one honoured with a complete edition in progress, until Fellowes set to work on Byrd in the 1930s.

As the Purcell Society edition slowly progressed and a pattern of dots began to emerge, so the biographers set to work joining them up and colouring bits in. William H. Cummings first and foremost: a Purcell Society stalwart, editor of the Society's *Dido and Aeneas* volume, and owner of a large private collection of prints and manuscripts on which he was able to draw for musical background information and biographical raw material. His

Purcell appeared in 1881, in Sampson, Lowe, Marston, & Co.'s 'Great Musicians' series. J. F. Runciman's *Purcell* followed in 1909, a well-researched French *Purcell* (by Henri Dupré) and Dennis Arundell's *Henry Purcell* both in 1927, A. K. Holland's *Henry Purcell* in 1932, and J. A. Westrup's *Purcell* in 1937 – this last the most authoritative of the pioneer studies, in print until recently. But the facts available to Purcell biographers are very few: 'A life of Henry Purcell is of necessity a slender record', Westrup had to admit in his opening sentence.[29] Biographies from Cummings's on have been filled out with musical value judgments and, alongside the Purcell life story, pages of disapproving comment on the times in which he lived. Much of his output could be written off because it offended the Victorian sense of propriety:

> Purcell's secular music undoubtedly frequently suffered from the worthless trash he had to accept as poetry; too often it was not only devoid of literary merit, but still worse, indecent; that was, however, the fault of the age, and pervaded most of the dramatic literature then in vogue.[30]

Would-be performers were not encouraged to stray beyond *Dido and Aeneas* (a chaste little piece for schoolgirls, it used to be thought), *The Fairy Queen* (attractive as a 'Shakespeare/ Purcell collaboration'), *King Arthur* (for its solid patriotic sentiments), the grandly titled 'Golden Sonata' and a few well-worn songs. Some notable performances stand out: bicentenary celebrations in 1895 (including *Dido and Aeneas* given by students from the Royal College of Music – Stanford himself conducting), Fuller-Maitland's *King Arthur* at the Birmingham Festival in 1897, Holst's concert performance of *The Fairy Queen* in 1911, *The Fairy Queen* and *King Arthur* staged in Cambridge (1920, 1927, 1928, 1931: Edward J. Dent and Dennis Arundell the driving forces here), the dance-inspired *Fairy Queen* which opened Covent Garden's first season of opera in English after the Second World War (1946),[31] eight concerts of Henry Purcell's music presented by the Arts Council of Great Britain and the Purcell Society in the 1951 Festival of Britain, *Dido* and *The Fairy Queen* staged by the English Opera

Group that year, the tercentenary of Purcell's birth marked in 1959 with an exhibition in the British Museum, concerts, lectures and radio broadcasts, and a *Tempest* production staged at the Old Vic. Purcell was clear favourite for a national celebration, especially one to mark the end of war with one or other of our culturally dominant neighbours. 'A national festival without some celebration of Purcell would be a monument of national ineptitude.'[32] On anniversaries connected with the 'Orpheus Britannicus' the great and the good in English music threw a party in his honour; while in churches up and down the country Purcell went about his daily service noticed only by a few devout who gathered together behind the choir-screens. For the rest he remained a 'famous' composer more written and read about than listened to. On through the 1960s, 1970s and 1980s . . . *Dido*, *The Fairy Queen* and *King Arthur* staged again at intervals, concerts here and there, broadcasts and recordings increasingly frequent as the new technology caught on. No need to name names, when record catalogues and record reviews tell the story; especially the reviews in *Early Music* – 1973 onwards – which are fully indexed.

And now, predictably, our tercenturions are on the move again: authors lone and companionable, editors, performers, record companies, TV and film producers all heading for the festival campsite, marching along to the boom-boom of 'early music' drums[33] – promising a bigger crowd than ever before. What's new is not the idea that early music exists ('early' music as opposed to new/new-ish: the adjectival 'early/ancient' has a long pedigree), but the thought that 'earliness' confers a special value on music old enough to qualify. *Antique* value. Old music, like old paintings, old furniture, old teaspoons, is worth more on account of its age. The listener has turned collector: snapping up each new release to build his complete set of this or that, putting the silver discs on show at home. Only 'authentic' performances interest him, as if other approaches to music were somehow 'fake'.

It would be foolish to mistake this publishing revolution for a genuine 'Purcell revival'. Records, tapes and CDs supply a mass market which was beyond reach till recently; and the music-canneries are working overtime to meet demand. Purcell Society editions a hundred years old and dangerously frail (hence the Society's decision to replace them) are solemnly recorded on period instruments; when *obbligato* parts are recorded on quite the wrong instrument no one seems to notice; and no one minds either when whole odes and anthems are recorded at the wrong pitch. Modern scholarship feeds into the recording process haphazardly and often too late – only when the discs arrive for review are the scholar/critics' opinions sought, leaving them to huff and puff about what *might* have been.

Record companies have backed the 'period' approach for sound business reasons: because 'authenticity' commands a premium price (like the stoneground flour in expensive bread), because collectors converted to the healthy-listening lifestyle will pay to replace stodgy old recordings as fast as they can afford to, and because the authentic sales-pitch has created new demands for some very improbable repertoire. Musical interest was always there (experiments go back a hundred years at least); but players have an added professional incentive to master period instruments, now that studio work provides the bulk of their living. I don't mean for a moment to underrate the achievements of period-instrument specialists. Indeed, without harpsichord and lute players able to realize the continuo lines imaginatively, nimble 'early music' voices trilling out his incredible graces and more or less historical strings, woodwind and brass pleasantly balanced both in tone and volume, I doubt whether much of the Purcell we listen to with such pleasure on record would sound like music at all. The critics in earlier generations were not so fortunate, having a comparatively narrow (and sometimes actively misleading) experience of Purcell in performance on which to base their opinions. In fairness we should remember this: '. . . hands apt, drugs fit, and time agreeing' – it took all three to bring about the 'early music' revolution.

Purcell studies, like most others, grow increasingly specialized from year to year, and to the general reader less and less appealing. Where Westrup covered Purcell's life and times and all his music in one volume, now there are books devoted to his theatre music, his trio sonatas, his cadences (a thin one, to be fair), to single works raked over minutely; even a book about Purcell books which spares me the need to comment further – Professor Zimmerman's *Henry Purcell: A Guide to Research*, published in 1989.[34] (Zimmerman is the 'Z' behind Purcell numbering: author of the *Analytical Catalogue* which everyone refers to, and of the only 'modern' Purcell biography.[35]) For the future – who can tell? Armchair travel is easier than ever, now there are maps to guide us (the Purcell Society volumes), records and CDs to feed the imagination like colour photos in a holiday brochure. But no one can claim to know Purcell country who hasn't been to live there for a while. Well run, the tercentenary celebrations will offer plenty of opportunity to hear Purcell *live* in appropriate settings: his operas in the opera house, his anthems in church, his chamber music where it belongs, in domestic surroundings. Some who pass through in the tercentenary tour parties will like what they hear, will pluck up courage to return on their own – and journey further with any luck, into the wider world of English Restoration music. 'The greatest Genius we ever had',[36] no doubt; but Purcell isn't quite the only one.

NOTES

1 For more on the 'fate of Henry Purcell's works and reputation in the eighteenth century' see Richard Luckett's splendid essay 'Or rather our musical Shakespeare: Charles Burney's Purcell', in Christopher Hogwood and Richard Luckett, eds., *Music in Eighteenth-century England: Essays in Memory of Charles Cudworth* (Cambridge, 1983). And a lot of what Gary Taylor has to say in *Reinventing Shakespeare: A Cultural History from the Restoration to the Present* (London, 1990) applies equally to Purcell and the Purcellians busily 'reinventing' *him*.

2 John Dryden, in *Astrea Redux. A Poem on the Happy Restoration & Return of His Sacred Majesty Charles the Second*. See John Sargeaunt, ed., *The Poems of John Dryden* (Oxford, 1910), 10.

3 Roger North, in John Wilson, ed., *Roger North on Music* (London, 1959), 309.

4 Anon., *A Poem Occasioned on the Death of Mr. Henry Purcell . . . By a Lover of Music* (London, 1695); quoted in Zimmerman II, 297.

5 *Roger North on Music*, op. cit., 307.

6   Quoted in Frank Howes, *The English Musical Renaissance* (London, 1966), 90.

7   *Roger North on Music*, op. cit., 307.

8   Charles Burney, *A General History of Music From the Earliest Ages to the Present Period (1789)*, Frank Mercer, ed., II (London, 1935), 392, 404–5.

9   Ibid., 385, 383.

10   Ibid., 393, 387.

11   Dennis Arundell, 'Purcell and Natural Speech', *The Musical Times*, c (1959), 323.

12   *A General History of Music . . .* op. cit., II, 390.

13   Ibid., 382.

14   Otto Jespersen, *Growth and Structure of the English Language* (Oxford, 9/1956), 16.

15   Ibid., 234.

16   Richard Luckett, op. cit., 77.

17   See W. H. Husk, *An Account of the Musical Celebrations on St. Cecilia's Day in the Sixteenth, Seventeenth and Eighteenth Centuries* (London, 1857), 227–33.

18   For eighteenth-century Purcell performances see Richard Luckett, op. cit., and Parts 2–5 of *The London Stage 1660–1800* (Carbondale, Ill., 1960–68).

19   See for instance Robert Speaight, *William Poel and the Elizabethan Revival* (London, 1954); Margaret Campbell, *Dolmetsch: the Man and his Work* (London, 1975); and Harry Haskell, *The Early Music Revival: a History* (London, 1988).

20   W. Barclay Squire, 'The Music of Shadwell's "Tempest" ', *The Musical Quarterly*, vii (1921), 572.

21   Foreword to *Eight Concerts of Henry Purcell's Music: [a] Commemorative Book of Programmes, Notes and Texts . . . Published by the Arts Council of Great Britain* (London, 1951), 7.

22   *A General History of Music . . .*, op. cit., II, 382, 351–2.

23   *Works I*, i, 2.

24   See W. H. Cummings, 'Purcell Club', reprinted from the first *Grove* (London, 1879–89) in Eric Blom, ed., *Grove's Dictionary of Music and Musicians* (London, 5/1954).

25   A book collecting together 'The Words of Henry Purcell's Vocal Music', compiled by Edward Taylor and including Taylor's 'Historical Introduction . . . to the Principal Operas', was privately printed and presented to members in January 1863 – just before the club disbanded. Its valuable library was deposited at Westminster Abbey.

26   *Works I*, i, 1.

27   Footnote to H. C. Colles, 'Purcell Society', *Grove's Dictionary . . .*, op. cit., (London, 5/1954).

28   See Frank Howes, op. cit.

29   J. A. Westrup, *Purcell* (London, 1937), 1.

30   W. H. Cummings, *Purcell* (London, 1881), 90.

31   See *Purcell's The Fairy Queen as presented by The Sadler's Wells Ballet*

and *The Covent Garden Opera: A Photographic Record by Edward Mandinian* . . . (London, 1948).

32 *Musical Britain 1951 Compiled by the Music Critic of 'The Times'* (published for *The Times* by Oxford University Press, London, 1951), 141.

33 See Jeremy Montagu, *Making Early Percussion Instruments* (Oxford, 1976).

34 Franklin B. Zimmerman, *Henry Purcell: A Guide to Research* (New York, 1989).

35 Zimmerman I and Franklin B. Zimmerman, *Henry Purcell 1659–1695: his Life and Times* (London, 1967).

36 Thomas Tudway's verdict. See Christopher Hogwood, 'Thomas Tudway's History of Music', in Christopher Hogwood and Richard Luckett, eds, op. cit., 44.

II
BACKGROUNDS

2

Purcell and the English Baroque

JONATHAN P. WAINWRIGHT

Henry Purcell was born into one of the most turbulent centuries in English history: by the time of his birth – some time in the summer or autumn of 1659 – there had already been a bloody Civil War, the trial and execution of the King, and the establishment of a Commonwealth; during the composer's lifetime the monarchy would be restored – Charles II (1660) – and a Catholic king – James II – would accede to the throne (1685), only to be peacefully removed by the Protestant William of Orange at the Glorious Revolution (1688). Christopher Hill observed in a recent essay that, 'It does not seem possible . . . to understand the history of seventeenth-century England without understanding its literature, any more than it is possible fully to appreciate the literature without understanding the history.'[1] A historian might possibly consider a study of England in the seventeenth century without mentioning music, but no music historian of the period could possibly ignore the political, religious or indeed literary background and hope to do his subject justice. This chapter attempts to provide the general historical and musical background to Purcell's career and compositions in the context of the court, church and theatre.

Charles II's return to England in May 1660 created a mood of euphoria and expectation among a populace who were weary of Puritan rule. Charles had spent much of the interregnum at the French Court of Louis XIV where he had witnessed a stable monarchy which patronized the finest artists, writers and musicians in Europe. It is not surprising that on his return to England Charles sought to emulate the French Court both politically and culturally. The King quickly became the acknowledged arbiter of taste and fashion in a society which, after eleven years of puritanical restraint, sought every kind of entertainment – from the sophisticated to the lewd.[2] The theatres, which had officially been closed since the beginning of the Civil War, were authorized to re-open, and the King surrounded himself with music, both sacred and secular, in emulation of the magnificent French Court. One of the most important records of Restoration musical taste is the diary of Samuel Pepys. As well as his daily reports on women, fashion, food and drink, Pepys vividly describes musical gatherings, theatre-going, and church services enlivened by the most up-to-date music.[3] On 23 April 1661 Pepys reports that, at Charles II's coronation festivities, he 'took a great deal of pleasure to go up and down and look upon the ladies – and to hear the Musique of all sorts; but above all, the 24 viollins'.[4] The King's violin band (in reality a string orchestra) had been reformed in emulation of the 'grande bande des vingt-quatre violons de la Chambre du roi' to play when the King dined in state and at court balls.[5] By September 1662 violinists were being used in Chapel Royal services whenever the King was present, and in 1664 they were used in the theatres (twelve players assigned to each house). In fact the full complement of instrumentalists were rarely used together, even at Court, for in May 1662 John Banister the elder had been asked to form a select group of twelve players from the twenty-four. This was probably a direct result of Banister's visit(s) to France the previous year where he would have heard the Petits Violons directed by Jean-Baptiste Lully.

At the Restoration the music of the re-established Chapel Royal[6] was entrusted to Captain Henry Cooke, who had himself been a chorister in the Chapel Royal of Charles I before his war service – firstly as a lieutenant and then as a captain – on the Royalists' side. Cooke's task in rebuilding the Chapel Royal choir was not an easy one; although he could ensure a degree of continuity with the past by re-appointing a number of Gentlemen who had been members of Charles I's Chapel, the sixteen-year break meant that the boys' section of the choir had to be rebuilt from scratch. Cooke went about his task with a vengeance and revived the 'pressing system' whereby a promising chorister could be removed from a provincial cathedral for service in the Chapel Royal. By the end of 1660 Cooke had a full complement of twelve boys, and over the next ten years – due no doubt to Cooke's ear for natural talent – many of the best musicians of the next generation were trained in the Chapel: Pelham Humfrey, John Blow, Michael Wise, William Turner, Thomas Tudway and Henry Purcell were all Children of the Chapel Royal in the 1660s.

The most precociously talented of Cooke's first batch of choirboys was Pelham Humfrey,[7] who was a chorister from the early 1660s until his voice broke and he was forced to leave the choir on Christmas Day 1664. By this time a number of his anthems had been performed by the Chapel Royal choir – the texts of five of these works were published in the second edition of James Clifford's *The Divine Services and Anthems* (London, 1664) – and he had collaborated on 'The Club Anthem' ('I will always give thanks') with two fellow choristers, William Turner and John Blow. Humfrey's talent was such that between 1664 and 1666 he was granted £450 from the secret service fund 'to defray the charge of his journey into France and Italy'.[8] Presumably the trip was undertaken in order to study the latest musical styles of composers such as Lully and Carissimi, and it is therefore unfortunate that no details survive concerning Humfrey's experiences abroad. He certainly came back an 'absolute Monsieur' according to Pepys,[9] but just how much he learned abroad is difficult to assess. The question of foreign influence on English musicians at this time is a thorny one; awkward questions have to be asked, such as: when do foreign influences end and personal style begin, and when do foreign elements become assimilated into the native English idiom? Nor can the issue of influence be divorced from that of the dissemination of foreign music in England in the seventeenth century. Many of these questions are examined, in relation to Purcell's music, in the forthcoming chapters; thus the following comments are intended only to provide the background information without pre-empting their conclusions.

Although much has been made of the French influence on musical life at the Restoration Court, it was not the only, nor

even the chief influence on English music. Underpinning English
– and indeed French[10] – 'Baroque' music are Italian methods.
English musicians, collectors and patrons had been interested in
Italian music from the early years of the sixteenth century;
Italian instrumentalists appear in the lists of Henry VIII's
musicians,[11] and from then on Italian music had frequently been
imported and copied into English manuscripts. The prestige and
circulation of the Italian madrigal and its effect on the English
madrigalists in Elizabeth I's reign are well known and have been
thoroughly examined,[12] but the continued interest in Italian
music in England throughout the seventeenth century has been
comparatively neglected. Italian monodies were available in
England from about 1610 onwards through publications such
as Robert Dowland's *Musicall Banquet* (London, 1610) and
Angelo Notari's *Prime Musiche Nuove* (London, c1613),[13] and
although the precise relationship between Italian monody and
the English declamatory style is difficult to assess, owing to the
different characteristics of the Italian and English languages, it
must have provided the underlying principles for the development of an English recitative.[14] In certain circles the interest in
Italian music continued unabated into the 1630s: the published
catalogues of the London bookseller Robert Martin indicate
that the most up-to-date Venetian music was easily obtainable
in London.[15] One of Robert Martin's main customers was Sir
Christopher Hatton III – later First Baron Hatton – who was
Charles I's Comptroller of Household during the Civil War years
when the Court was based in Oxford (1643–6). Hatton appears
to have collected a large library of Italian music (the bulk of
which survives today in Christ Church, Oxford)[16] from which
his musicians made manuscript copies, probably for performance at the Oxford Court.[17] The most important musician in
Hatton's employ was the organist and composer George
Jeffreys. It was undoubtedly exposure to the Italian music in
the Hatton collection – particularly the small-scale *concertato*
motets written by contemporaries of Monteverdi such as Alessandro Grandi – which inspired Jeffreys's most successful compositions; his Latin motets (many written before 1646) show a
complete assimilation of the Italian *seconda prattica* style.[18] The

political situation (Civil War and Commonwealth) and the circumstances in which Jeffreys worked (as steward to the impecunious Hatton family) assured that his music was not widely disseminated and that he had little influence on either his contemporaries or the succeeding generation of English composers. However, some of the Italian music which Jeffreys copied from the Hatton collection appears to have been rather more influential: music by Egidio Trabattone, Giovanni Felice Sances and Tarquinio Merula, in particular, was widely disseminated and was frequently copied into Restoration manuscripts.

Another English composer who is known to have been interested in Italian music in the mid-seventeenth century is the composer Matthew Locke. Towards the end of the 1640s Locke visited the Netherlands (perhaps as part of Queen Henrietta Maria and Prince Charles's exiled retinue), and while he was there he copied various Latin motets by Francesco Costanzo, Giovanni Rovetta and Galeazzo Sabbatini.[19] It seems that while he was in the Low Countries Locke converted to Catholicism, and his own Latin motets, which were clearly influenced by Italianate idioms, may have been written for the Roman Catholic chapel of Charles II's Queen, Catherine of Braganza.[20] His English anthems and instrumental pieces, however, are rather more conservative in style and, in these works, Locke must be regarded as a standard bearer of an 'English style' in the face of ever increasing foreign influence.[21] Perhaps the greatest advocate of 'the Italian way' was the aforementioned Captain Henry Cooke. The diarist John Evelyn described him as 'the best singer after the *Italian* manner of any in *England*',[22] and in the 1664 edition of *A Brief Introduction to the Skill of Musick* – which includes an abridged translation of Caccini's treatise on Italian vocal practice[23] – John Playford considered that the Italian manner of singing 'is now come to the Excellency and Perfection . . . , by the Skill and furtherance of that Orpheus of our time Henry Cook'. Sir Jack Westrup suggested that Cooke's knowledge of 'the Italian manner' implied 'residence in Italy or at least study with Italian masters';[24] while this is a possibility, it seems more likely that Cooke's experience of Italian music was gained at home from imported publications.[25] During the Commonwealth, like many Royalist musicians, Cooke earned his living as a teacher,[26] and was employed by Lady Hatton of Kirby Hall, Northamptonshire, to teach her children.[27] It has already been noted that Lady Hatton's husband, Baron Hatton, owned a substantial amount of Italian music,[28] and it is therefore not unreasonable to suggest that it was at Kirby Hall, in the 1650s, that Cooke learned 'the Italian manner'.

One of the most popular Italian composers in England in the mid-seventeenth century was Giacomo Carissimi. His motets and cantatas were widely disseminated, and at least one of the former was known in England as early as 1645/6.[29] Carissimi's music was certainly popular after the Restoration; in 1664 Pepys wrote of an evening spent 'singing the best piece of musique, counted of all hands in the world, made by Seignor Charissimi the famous master in Rome'.[30] The presence of Italian musicians (such as Vincenzo Albrici, a pupil of Carissimi's) in London in the 1660s undoubtedly contributed to the dissemination of his motets and cantatas,[31] and over the next four decades George Jeffreys, Henry Aldrich, Henry Bowman, Charles Morgan and Richard Goodson the elder all included music by Carissimi in their manuscripts.[32] He was so popular that pieces by other Italian composers – such as Trabattone, Rovetta, F. M. Marini, Cazzati, Monferrato and Graziani – were often incorrectly attributed to Carissimi by English copyists.[33] A thorough examination of the manuscripts reveals that Carissimi was only one of many Italian composers whose music was readily available in England.

The two surviving examples of Italian pieces copied by Purcell himself are an indication of the chronological range of this interest in Italian music: an autograph score of Purcell's *Benedicite* in B flat (z 230m/3) contains a correction slip[34] on the reverse of which, in Purcell's handwriting, is a fragment of a score of Monteverdi's five-voice madrigal 'Cruda Amarilli',[35] and another of his autograph manuscripts[36] includes a copy of a two-voice motet, 'Crucior in hac flamma', by Maurizio Cazzati.[37] Purcell's interest in Italian music is further demonstrated in his contribution to the twelfth edition of Playford's *Introduction to the Skill of Musick* (London, 1694), in which he quotes a few bars from a trio sonata by 'the famous Lelio Colista' (although the piece is actually by Carlo Ambrogio Lonati).[38] By the early 1680s the most up-to-date Italian instrumental music was available in London, and Purcell very probably knew sonatas by Bassani, Cazzati, Colista (or Lonati),[39] Legrenzi, Vitali, and possibly even Corelli's *Sonate a Tre*, op. 1 (Rome, 1681).[40] It is not surprising that Purcell – who was keenly aware of the latest market trends – stated in the preface of his *Sonnatas of III Parts* (London, 1683) that 'he has faithfully endeavour'd a just imitation of the fam'd Italian Masters'; he was less flattering about the French and warned that his 'Country-men . . . should begin to loath the levity, and balladry of our neighbours'.

This extended examination of foreign influences on music in England in the seventeenth century should not be allowed to disguise the importance of the indigenous musical tradition. Purcell's fantasias and In nomines and the 'full' anthems are the most obvious examples of his reverence for the older English traditions, but even his fashionable trio sonatas were, according to Roger North, 'clog'd with somewhat of an English vein'.[41] Purcell's musical style is, in fact, a synthesis of English, French and Italian elements and, in the words of Lorenzo Bianconi, is 'voraciously heterogeneous and versatile, to the point at which the strength of the composer's own personal imprint of melodic and harmonic invention becomes the only truly recognizable factor'.[42]

In the above discussion of Italian influence in England no mention was made of Italy's greatest musical export: opera. The development of opera in Florence, Mantua, Rome and Venice in the first half of the seventeenth century was to have far-reaching effects in the rest of Europe and – if we follow the line taken by many opera-centric music historians – would improve beyond measure any indigenous stage traditions. What then of English opera in the seventeenth century, and why are there only three surviving all-sung English operas from the period (*Albion and Albanius* by the French-trained Spanish composer Louis Grabu, *Venus and Adonis* by John Blow and *Dido and Aeneas* by Purcell)?[43] The fact that England did not fully embrace all-sung Italianate opera until the eighteenth century was something of an embarrassment to many music historians who judged English dramatic music purely by continental standards.[44] More recent commentators, notably Richard Luckett and Curtis Price,[45] have written about the 'dramatick operas', 'semi-operas' or 'ambigue entertainments' – the contemporary names for the English musical dramas produced after 1670 – in the context of the English stage tradition, and without any sense of apology for the fact that England did not develop all-sung opera during the seventeenth century. The English tradition was one of spoken drama in which music played an important, but subsidiary, role and, despite various operatic experiments, it was a tradition which satisfied playwrights, composers, actors, musicians and audiences alike.[46]

The first 'operatic experiment' in England was Sir William Davenant's *The Siege of Rhodes*, which was performed in the spring of 1659.[47] The opera was apparently sung throughout, mostly to 'Recitative Musick' composed by Henry Lawes, Henry Cooke and Matthew Locke, and the instrumental music was by Charles Coleman and George Hudson; unfortunately all the music to this, 'the first Opera we ever had in England',[48] is lost. On Charles II's return to London in 1660 the theatres, which had been officially closed since the beginning of the Civil War (1642),[49] were authorized to re-open. Two licensed theatre companies were established under the patronage of the King and his brother, James, Duke of York, and together they had a monopoly of all theatrical performances in London. The Duke's Company, based at Lincoln's Inn Fields, was directed by Sir William Davenant, who had been trained in the pre-Commonwealth theatre and in the production of Caroline masques; his productions were noted for their use of music, lavish scenery, and stage effects (although he appears to have lost interest in opera proper after the Restoration). Following Davenant's death in 1668, his widow, together with the two new managers, Thomas Betterton and Henry Harris, made plans to build a new theatre.[50] The Dorset Garden theatre, designed by Christopher Wren, was finally opened in November 1671, and it was in this theatre that all Purcell's major stage works were produced.[51] The King's Company, headed by Thomas Killigrew, occupied a

theatre in Vere Street until 7 May 1663 when they moved to the
Theatre Royal, Bridges Street. The Theatre Royal was destroyed
by fire in January 1672 and the company occupied the Lincoln's
Inn Fields theatre, recently vacated by the Duke's Company,
until March 1674 when they moved to their new theatre in
Drury Lane.[52] The two licensed companies combined to form
the United Company in November 1682 and Drury Lane
became the main house; Dorset Garden was used only for large-
scale presentations which required extensive scenery and stage
room (such as Purcell's semi-operas). The situation remained the
same until March 1695 when, following an actors' rebellion,
Betterton obtained a licence to set up a rival company which
performed in the refurbished theatre in Lincoln's Inn Fields.
Purcell remained with the Patent Company, now under the man-
agement of the notorious Christopher Rich, despite the fact that
all the best actors and singers had sided with Betterton;[53] he
endured this situation for only eight months, for by the end of
November 1695 Purcell was dead.

The musical productions which took place in the Restoration
theatres were a fusion of two pre-war traditions: firstly the
spoken play – the favourite repertoire being plays by Shakespeare, Jonson, Beaumont and Fletcher – and secondly the
masque with its elaborate staging, mythological scenes and
extensive use of music. Restoration theatre music consisted of
overtures, act tunes, dances, and songs or airs which were performed at certain points in the play, usually by subsidiary
characters (supernatural beings, their worshippers or servants),
and were rarely essential – and often quite irrelevant – to the
main action, which was reserved for the spoken dialogue. All-
sung Italianate opera was not welcomed and, despite a number
of experiments and a few performances of imported operas, it
was the genre of 'semi-opera' which dominated stage music in
England until the early eighteenth century. However, it should
not be forgotten that in October 1660 a privilege was granted to
Giulio Gentileschi to establish an Italian opera in London; that
this was never implemented was probably due both to a lack of
financial support and to representations made by Davenant and
Killigrew.[54] Although Davenant appears to have lost interest in

full-blown opera after the Restoration, Killigrew did have definite operatic ambitions and, according to Pepys, had plans to
mount four operas each year, for six weeks at a time, with 'the
best Scenes and Machines, the best Musique, and everything as
Magnificent as is in Christendome; and to that end hath sent for
voices and painters and other persons from Italy'.[55] Again
nothing came of this, but Killigrew appears to have been instrumental in persuading Charles II to establish the King's 'Italian
Musick'. This was complete by 1666 and included the Albrici
brothers (Vincenzo and Bartolomeo) and 'Seignor Baptista'
Draghi;[56] as well as providing musical entertainments for the
King and Queen in their chambers, the Italian musicians were
also employed in the Queen's Roman Catholic Chapel. The
'Italian Opera in musique, the first that had be[e]n in England'
reported by Evelyn[57] was most likely a rehearsal of the French –
not Italian – opera *Ariane ou Le Mariage de Bacchus* by Robert
Cambert with additions by Louis Grabu, which was performed
by a visiting French troupe at Drury Lane on 30 March 1674 to
celebrate the marriage of James, Duke of York, to Mary of
Modena. In fact French stage works fared rather better than
Italian in London in the seventeenth century: one other French
opera was performed, Lully's *Cadmus et Hermione*, again by a
French company, at the Dorset Garden theatre in February
1686, as was Mme La Roche Guilhen's *Rare en tout*, a *comédie-
ballet* performed at Court in May 1677. All this happened
despite the fact that the 'French Musick' – a chamber group of
French musicians established after the Restoration – had been
disbanded late in 1666 following the rise of the 'Italian
Musick'.[58]

A number of French musicians did, however, find employment
in the English establishment; the most successful was Louis
Grabu[59] who, in quick succession, was appointed Master of the
King's Musick (24 November 1666), director of the Twenty-
four Violins (24 December 1666), and director of the select band
of twelve violins (14 March 1667).[60] Grabu's meteoric rise was
matched by an abrupt fall: in 1674 he was dismissed from his
Court posts because of his religion, and following the Popish
Plot of 1679 he was, along with a number of Catholics, forced

to flee the country.[61] He returned to France, but by the autumn of 1683 he was back in England and again active in the theatre.[62] Grabu is chiefly remembered today for his collaboration with Dryden on the first surviving full-length, all-sung English opera *Albion and Albanius*, which was produced at the Dorset Garden theatre on 3 June 1685. Dryden's original plans had been to produce an English 'Dramatick Opera' or 'semi-opera' with a French-style prologue but, for political reasons, he was forced to defer his planned entertainment; the project finally came to fruition in 1691 when Dryden revised the text and, in collaboration with Purcell, produced the semi-opera *King Arthur* (z 628).[63] In 1685, however, in order to satisfy Charles II's demand for an allegorical entertainment celebrating the Restoration, Dryden had expanded the prologue of his semi-opera into the three-act opera *Albion and Albanius*. The opera was doomed to failure even before its première, not because of the quality of Grabu's music[64] but because of unfortunate timing: Charles II died and the Catholic James II acceded to the throne while the opera was still in rehearsal, and the opera's première coincided with the rebellion led by the Protestant Duke of Monmouth, Charles II's illegitimate son.

The two other contemporary English operas, John Blow's *Venus and Adonis* (c1682) and Purcell's *Dido and Aeneas* (z 626; 1689?),[65] although revered by present-day audiences, were – like *Albion and Albanius* – not a great success in the seventeenth century.[66] The first recorded performances of the two operas took place not, as one would perhaps expect, in the public theatres but at Court (*Venus and Adonis*) and at a girls' boarding school in Chelsea (*Dido and Aeneas*). The school, which was run by the dancer and choreographer Josias Priest, appears to have had close connections with the Court (probably because it catered for the daughters of noblemen); thus it is not inconceivable that *Dido and Aeneas* – like *Venus and Adonis* – was originally a court entertainment.[67] Purcell's first successful major composition for the London stage was *Dioclesian* (z 627), which was performed by the United Company at the Dorset Garden theatre in June 1690. In the five years between *Dioclesian* and Purcell's death, in November 1695, he composed the music for about forty stage productions, although only four – *Dioclesian, King Arthur, The Fairy Queen* (z 629; 1692) and *The Indian Queen* (z 630; 1695) – can be considered as full-scale semi-operas. The semi-operas represent the summit of Purcell's career as a composer for the stage, and through them the genre of semi-opera or dramatick opera can be assessed, not as a hybrid poor relation to opera-proper or as a halfway stage to the development of the 'perfect' all-sung English opera, but as a dramatic form in its own right. Dryden's opinion that in 'Mr. Purcell . . . we have at length found an Englishman equal with the best abroad' is surely correct.[68]

NOTES

1 Christopher Hill, ed., 'The Pre-Revolutionary Decades', in *The Collected Essays of Christopher Hill* (Brighton, 1985), I, 3.

2 It should be stressed that the Puritans were not opposed to music *per se*; see Percy Scholes, *The Puritans and Music in England and New England* (New York, 1934). It is true that the musical profession suffered great hardships during the Commonwealth as a result of the disbandment of the main musical establishments – i.e. Court, Church of England, and theatres – but the Puritans did not object to domestic or devotional music. Cromwell had an organ at Hampton Court (removed from the chapel of Magdalen College, Oxford), employed the organist John Hingeston, and apparently enjoyed listening to Richard Dering's Latin motets. In fact Puritan rule positively aided the cultivation of domestic music and created a market which the publisher and bookseller John Playford successfully exploited.

3 For a commentary on the musical references in Pepys's diary, see Richard Luckett, 'Music', *Pepys*, X, 258–82.

4 *Pepys*, 23 April 1661; II, 86.

5 It should be noted that the violin band was not a new concept in England; the violin had been brought to the English Court as early as 1540, although until the early 1620s it was used only for dance music. For full details see Peter Holman, *'Four and Twenty Fiddlers': The Violin at the English Court 1540–1690* (Oxford, 1993).

6 It should be remembered that the Chapel Royal is not a single building but a body of persons within the Royal Household responsible for the ordering and performance of divine service in the sovereign's presence.

7 Humfrey's life and works are examined in detail in Peter Dennison, *Pelham Humfrey* (Oxford, 1986).

8 Cited in E. F. Rimbault, *The Old Cheque-Book or Book of Remembrance*

of the Chapel Royal from 1561 to 1744 (London, 1872), 213, but the location of the original manuscript is unknown; see Andrew Ashbee, ed., *Records of English Court Music* (Aldershot, 1991), V, 270–71.

9 *Pepys*, 15 November 1667; VIII, 529.

10 We should remember that Lully – the leading composer in France in the mid-seventeenth century – was actually born in Florence and did not move to France until 1646, and that this was the period when Cardinal Mazarin was striving to promote Italian entertainments at the French Court; see James R. Anthony, *French Baroque Music from Beaujoyeulx to Rameau* (London, rev. 2/1978), 40–53.

11 See John Izon, 'Italian Musicians at the Tudor Court', *Musical Quarterly*, xliv (1958), 329–37.

12 See Alfredo Obertello, *Madrigali Italiani in Inghilterra* (Milan, 1949); Alfred Einstein, 'The Elizabethan Madrigal and *Musica Transalpina*', *Music and Letters*, xxv (1944), 66–77, and ibid., xxvii (1946), 273–4; Everett B. Helm, 'Italian Traits in the English Madrigal', *Music Review*, vii (1946), 26–34; Joseph Kerman, 'Elizabethan Anthologies of Italian Madrigals', *Journal of the American Musicological Society*, iv (1951), 122–38; Joseph Kerman, 'Master Alfonso and the English Madrigal', *Musical Quarterly*, xxxviii (1952), 222–44; and Joseph Kerman, *The Elizabethan Madrigal* (New York, 1962).

13 See Ian Spink, 'Angelo Notari and his *Prime Musiche Nuove*', *Monthly Musical Record*, lxxxvii (1957), 168–77.

14 For a full examination of this issue, see Peter Walls, 'The Origins of English Recitative', *Proceedings of the Royal Musical Association*, cx (1983–4), 25–40.

15 See Donald W. Krummel, 'Venetian Baroque Music in a London Bookshop', in Oliver Neighbour, ed., *Music and Bibliography: Essays in Honor of Alec Hyatt King* (London, 1980), 1–27.

16 See David Pinto, 'The Music of the Hattons', *Research Chronicle [of] The Royal Musical Association*, xxiii (1990), 79–108; and Jonathan P. Wainwright, 'The Musical Patronage of Christopher, First Baron Hutton (1605–70)' (Ph. D. diss., U. of Cambridge, 1992).

17 See Jonathan P. Wainwright, 'George Jeffreys' Copies of Italian Music', *Research Chronicle [of] The Royal Musical Association*, xxiii (1990), 109–24.

18 Another English composer who contributed to the genre of the small-scale *concertato* motet was Richard Dering, organist to Queen Henrietta Maria 1625–30. Dering's Latin motets for two and three voices and basso continuo remained popular long after his death in 1630; their appeal was such that John Playford published a substantial number of them in two pubications entitled *Cantica Sacra* (1662 and 1674). For full details concerning Jeffreys, see Peter Aston, 'George Jeffreys', *Musical Times*, cx (1969), 772–6; Peter Aston, 'Tradition and Experiment in the Devotional Music of George Jeffreys', *Proceedings of the Royal Musical Association*, xcix (1972–3), 105–15; and Robert Thompson, 'George Jeffreys and the

Stile Nuovo in English Sacred Music: a New Date for his Autograph Score, British Library Add. MS 10338', *Music and Letters*, lxx (1989), 317–41.

19 *GB-Lbl* Add. MS 31437 ff. 29–43: 'Collection of Songs [made] when I was in the Low Countreys 1648'.

20 Locke was organist to Catherine of Braganza's chapel in St James's Palace from 1662 to 1671, and then at Somerset House from 1671 to his death in 1677 (the King's mother, Queen Henrietta Maria, had occupied Somerset House until her death in 1669); alternatively, Locke's Latin motets may have been written for Oxford Music Meetings as most of the works survive in manuscripts connected with the University Music School.

21 See Peter Dennison, 'The Sacred Music of Matthew Locke', *Music and Letters*, lx (1979), 60–75.

22 *Evelyn*, 28 October 1654; III, 144.

23 Originally the preface to *Le Nuove Musiche* (Florence, 1601/2).

24 J. A. Westrup, *Purcell* (London, rev. 4/1980), 20.

25 Cooke's first exposure to Italian music may have been as a chorister in the Chapel Royal in the late 1620s at the time when Walter Porter – the self-styled pupil of Monteverdi – was a Gentleman. Two copies of Porter's *Mottets of Two Voyces* (London, 1657) at Christ Church, Oxford (Mus. 818–23 and 877–80), include the manuscript addition 'Monteverde' in Porter's handwriting in the preface after the words 'my good Friend and Maestro'. This is the only evidence to suggest that Porter was a pupil of Monteverdi's; it would have been quite possible for Porter to be well acquainted with the works of Monteverdi without having left England.

26 Cooke's name occurs in a list of 'excellent and able masters' in the Rules and Directions prefixed to John Playford's *A Musicall Banquet* (London, 1651); his name is given under the heading for 'Voyce or Viol'.

27 This is indicated in a letter dated 11 December 1656 from George Jeffreys to Lady Hatton (*GB-Lbl* Add. MS 29550 f. 275): '. . . My Sweet Mistresses have been to ask Blessing and are very well, Capt: Cooke came into the lodgings yesterday to teach them, when he promised to do his utmost for them . . .'.

28 See David Pinto, op. cit.; and Jonathan P. Wainwright, 'The Musical Patronage of Christopher, First Baron Hutton (1605–70), op. cit.

29 Evelyn MS 211 (deposited at Christ Church, Oxford, by the trustees of the will of Major Peter George Evelyn), a copy – in an Italian hand – of Carissimi's motet 'Si linguis hominum', bears Evelyn's annotation: 'Coll: Evelynus: Romæ Aprilis: 11: 1645'; for details of Evelyn's visit to Rome, 7 February–4 May 1645, see *Evelyn*, II, 355–91.

30 *Pepys*, 22 July 1664; V, 217. Pepys was a bass and one is therefore tempted to speculate that this 'best piece of musique' was Carissimi's solo bass motet, 'Lucifer caelestis olim' (but see below p. 45). The piece was later transcribed for Pepys by Cesare Morelli, who was his household musician between 1675 and 1693; the MS is preserved in the Pepys Library (*GB-Cmc* MS 2803, ff. 80v–87v).

31 See J. A. Westrup, 'Foreign Musicians in Stuart England', *Musical Quar-*

terly, xxvii (1941), 70–89; and Margaret Mabbett, 'Italian Musicians in Restoration England (1660–90)', *Music and Letters*, lxvii (1986), 237–47.

32 For details, see Andrew V. Jones, *The Motets of Carissimi* (Ann Arbor, 1982), 2 vols, *passim*.

33 For full details of Latin motets attributed (both correctly and incorrectly) to Carissimi in English manuscripts, see ibid., *passim*.

34 *GB-Ob* MS Mus. a. 1. The MS fragment is reproduced in Imogen Holst, ed., *Henry Purcell 1659–1695: Essays on his Music* (London, 1959), Plate II, and *Zimmerman I*, 53.

35 *Il Quinto Libro de Madrigali a Cinque Voci* (Venice, 1605).

36 *GB-Lbl* R.M. MS 20.H.8, ff. 127–125*v* reversed.

37 *Tributo di Sagri Concerti*, op. 23 (Bologna, 1660). The motet is unattributed in the MS.

38 See Peter Allsop, 'Problems of Ascription in the Roman *Simfonia* of the late Seventeenth Century: Colista and Lonati', *Music Review*, l (1989), 34–44.

39 Ibid.

40 See, for example, *GB-Lbl* Add. MS 31431 (dated 1680) and *GB-Lbl* Add. MS 33236 (early 1680s); these and other instrumental manuscripts of the period are discussed in Robert Thompson, 'Some Early English Sources of Italian Sonatas', Chapter XI of 'English Music Manuscripts and the Fine Paper Trade, 1648–1688' (Ph.D. diss., U. of London, 1988), 431–67. See also Peter Walls, 'The Influence of the Italian Violin School in 17th-Century England', *Early Music*, xviii (1990), 575–87.

41 Roger North, 'An Essay of Musicall Ayre', *GB-Lbl* Add. MS 32536 f. 78*v*.

42 Lorenzo Bianconi, *Music in the Seventeenth Century* (Cambridge, 1987), 252.

43 I use the term 'opera' in the modern sense to mean an all-sung music drama, and thus ignore the fact that Blow's *Venus and Adonis* is described as a 'Masque' in the earliest surviving manuscript source (*GB-Lbl* Add. MS 22100). The words 'masque' and 'opera' were used very loosely in England in the seventeenth century; see Richard Luckett, 'Exotick but Rational Entertainments: The English Dramatick Operas', in Marie Axton and Raymond Williams, eds, *English Drama: Forms and Development* (Cambridge, 1977), 130–32.

44 See, for example, Charles Burney, *A General History of Music*, Frank Mercer, ed., (London, 1789), IV, Chapter 5; and Edward J. Dent, *Foundations of English Opera* (Cambridge, 1928), 230–34.

45 Richard Luckett, 'Exotick but Rational Entertainments', op. cit., 123–41, 232–4; and Curtis A. Price, *Henry Purcell and the London Stage* (Cambridge, 1984).

46 Roger North's opinion that 'some [of the audience] come for the play and hate the musick, others come only for the musick, and the drama is pennance to them, and scarce any are well reconciled to both' (John Wilson, ed., *Roger North on Music* (London, 1959), 307) is not supported by the financial successes noted by John Downes in his *Roscius Anglicanus*

(London, 1708); see Richard Luckett, 'Exotick but Rational Entertainments', op. cit., 125.

47 See John Buttrey, 'The Evolution of English Opera between 1656 and 1695: A Re-investigation' (Ph.D. diss., U. of Cambridge, 1967), 22–47. *The Siege of Rhodes* had first been prepared – apparently as a spoken play – for semi-private performance in the hall of Rutland House, London, in 1656, but was postponed until 1659 because of political events. It was revived after the Restoration in the standard form of theatrical entertainments: as a spoken play with some music; see Edward J. Dent, op. cit., 43–77.

48 As described in the preface to the play-book of *The Fairy Queen* (London, 1692).

49 Graham Parry points out that the 'common notion that the theatres were closed and acting suppressed from 1642 onwards is . . . only a half-truth, for there are many records of plays being performed during the 1640s, even though play-acting had become illegal'; *The Seventeenth Century: The Intellectual and Cultural Context of English Literature, 1603–1700* (Harlow, 1989), 95.

50 Davenant had been granted a royal patent in 1639 to build a new theatre for 'plays, musical entertainments, scenes or the like presentments' but it had come to nothing.

51 During the period when Purcell was connected with the Dorset Garden theatre it was known as the Queen's Theatre as a compliment to Queen Mary.

52 See Peter Holland, 'Theatre', *Pepys*, X, 434–8.

53 See Curtis A. Price, op. cit., 16–17.

54 Richard Luckett, 'Exotick but Rational Entertainments', op. cit., 126.

55 *Pepys*, 2 August 1664; V, 230.

56 Richard Luckett, 'Exotick but Rational Entertainments', op. cit., 127, 233.

57 *Evelyn*, 17 January 1674; IV, 30.

58 *Pepys*, X, 266.

59 Grabu was actually a French-trained Spaniard.

60 Andrew Ashbee, ed., *Records of English Court Music* (Snodland, 1986), I, 74–5.

61 See *Zimmerman I*, 54–69.

62 Thomas Betterton, who had been sent to Paris by the King 'to endeavour to carry over the opera', appears to have been instrumental in bringing Grabu back to London; see Curtis A. Price, op. cit., 289.

63 The complex background and the allegorical designs to both *Albion and Albanius* and *King Arthur* are examined in detail in Curtis A. Price, op. cit., 289–97, and Curtis A. Price, 'Political Allegory in Late-Seventeenth-Century English Opera', in Nigel Fortune, ed., *Music and Theatre: Essays in Honour of Winton Dean* (Cambridge, 1987), 1–29.

64 Although Grabu's music has been subjected to severe criticism – see, for example, Edward J. Dent, op. cit., 165–7, and Robert E. Moore, *Henry Purcell and the Restoration Theatre* (Cambridge, Mass., 1961), 71 – 'there

is not the slightest hint in contemporary documents that the failure of *Albion and Albanius* was its composer's fault' (Curtis A. Price, *Henry Purcell and the London Stage*, op. cit., 266–7).

65 The first known performance of *Dido and Aeneas* was at a girls' boarding school in Chelsea in the spring of 1689 (see John Buttrey, 'Dating Purcell's *Dido and Aeneas*', *Proceedings of the Royal Musical Association*, xciv (1967–8), 51–62); it is, however, possible that the opera was written earlier (see Bruce Wood and Andrew Pinnock, '*Unscarr'd by Turning Times?*: The Dating of Purcell's *Dido and Aeneas*', *Early Music*, xx (1992), 372–90; and, for an alternative view, see Martin Adams, 'More on Dating Dido', correspondence published in *Early Music*, xxi (1993), 510; and Curtis Price, '*Dido and Aeneas*: Questions of Style and Evidence', *Early Music*, xxii (1994), 115–25).

66 Concerning the allegorical implications of *Dido and Aeneas* and possible reasons for the lack of public performances during the composer's lifetime, see Curtis A. Price, *Henry Purcell and the London Stage*, op. cit., 225–62.

67 See Richard Luckett, 'A New Source for *Venus and Adonis*', *Musical Times*, cxxx (1989), 76–9.

68 John Dryden, *Amphitryon* (London, 1690), Epistle Dedicatory.

3

Purcell's Italianate Circle

GRAHAM DIXON

It has commonly been supposed that French music set the standard for the re-establishment of English Court music after
Charles II's return from exile in France. We read about his founding a band of twenty-four violins, to mirror the *Vingt-Quatre
Violons* on the other side of the channel, and indeed the composers John Banister and Pelham Humfrey were sent on the
equivalent of fact-finding missions to the Continent.[1] In consequence, Purcell has been viewed as the product of a French
musical environment, and French traits in his music have
accordingly been discerned.

It is not my primary purpose to discuss Italianate hallmarks in
Purcell's work; rather, I should like to examine how Italianate
were his surroundings, and leave others to draw their own conclusions. And one thing is certain: however musically eclectic the
Stuart Court was when it arrived from France in 1660, it
returned to exile in France some three decades later to establish
an entirely Italian musical culture in the Paris suburb of St Germain-en-Laye. This acquisition of Italian musical style as the
Stuart Court vernacular covers not only Purcell's formative
period in London, but most of his life. It is clearly worth considering which Italian musicians Purcell would have come into
contact with, either in person or through their compositions.

Purcell would certainly have seen one particular volume of
Italian music. *Scelta di canzonette italiane de piu autori. dedi-
cate a gli amatori della musica*, published in London in 1679,
contains secular pieces by up-to-date composers and a preface
which, even allowing for the exigencies of marketing, makes
impressive reading:

Observing how favourably Italian compositions are received by lovers of music in this city, I resolved to print this volume, and to make it as admirable as possible, I have selected the most beautiful songs by the most excellent composers of our century, to the end that the variety of style may render it more pleasurable and no less useful. Some of these have been composed in London specially for your pleasure by persons whose ability you fully recognize, and I trust that your approval and praise will repay their efforts on my behalf. I refrain from dedicating these volumes to many people of great merit and nobility, only in order that each one of these virtuosi may be able to elect his own patron. I know that I shall be ridiculed for having inserted my name among such an illustrious catalogue, but one cannot drown in a sea of virtue, and any one who is not bold and rather timid clings to the shore and can never carry cargo. Dear Reader, I know you understand me: Adieu, and live well.

GIROLAMO PIGNANI[2]

Unfortunately, no information about this enthusiast for the propagation of Italian culture in England has yet been found, but Pignani must have been quite influential to build a relationship with the important publishers Godbid and Playford, and to convince some Italian musicians of the period, living in London, to write a *canzonetta* for his anthology. It is interesting to note which of the musicians included in the volume were resident in London, at least for some time at the period. But initially it is more valuable to examine a list of those who are represented, but are not recorded as having resided in England: Giovanni Antonio Boretti; Carlo Caproli; Iacomo Carissimi; Antonio Cesti; Carlo Ambrogio Lonati; Bernardo Pasquini; Luigi Rossi; Alessandro Stradella.

When a certain amount of biographical material has shed its light on the list, it emerges that we are not dealing with a disparate group of composers, but with a fairly well-defined school of musicians, around a central nucleus. All of them were associated with Rome, and all except one achieved a good measure of success in the city; the sole exception to this is Boretti who, though Roman by birth, achieved prestige away from the city in the opera houses of Venice. The careers of the remainder were centred on a limited number of focal points, and as a circle of musicians the father-figure would have been Carissimi, who by the mid-century was established as the leading musician in Rome, and acclaimed as such by Athanasius Kircher.[3] Carissimi's career centred on three main fields of activity: he was *maestro* at the Jesuit German College from 1629; from the mid-century onwards he participated in the music at the Oratorio di San Marcello; and from 1656 he was in charge of chamber music for the exiled Queen of Sweden.[4] His activity defines an institutional orbit within which the other musicians seem largely to have functioned: Caproli was, in his youth, second organist at the German College and was later associated with the Oratorio; Cesti's opera *L'Argia* was performed for Queen Christina in Innsbruck, and it would seem certain that she did not ignore him on his arrival in Rome some two years later; Lonati was a 'virtuoso' in the household of the Queen, and sang at San Marcello, as well as in the Teatro Tordinona, a theatre which reopened under her patronage; Stradella was also patronized by her at an early stage, and received a number of commissions, as well as being appointed her *servitore di camera*; Pasquini combined the same spheres of activity, being associated with San Marcello, as well as enjoying the patronage of the Queen as a keyboard player. In 1687 Pasquini composed a cantata for the accession of James II of England, which was performed at the palace of the Queen of Sweden as part of the reception for the English Ambassador to Pope Innocent XI.[5] Luigi Rossi stands slightly apart from this immediate area of activity, working for the French at S Luigi dei Francesi, as well as in Paris itself; however, his inclusion is no surprise, since – alongside Carissimi – he was the most highly regarded musician in Rome at the time.

Why, then, did this particular sphere of composers attract the attention of the London musical public at the time? To answer this we must compile another list, namely of the composers who arrived in England in the years leading up to the publication of Pignani's volume of *Canzonette* for one and two voices: Bartolomeo Albrici; Giovanni Battista Draghi; Nicola Matteis; Girolamo Pignani.

As mentioned above, nothing is yet known about Pignani, and

information on the early lives of both Draghi and Matteis is sadly lacking; though disappointing, this lacuna is not insuperable, since it would seem that it is Bartolomeo Albrici, or at least his family, who provides the solution to the problem. Before we consider Bartolomeo, it is worth examining the biography of his elder brother, Vincenzo. The musical career of the elder boy had begun at the German College in Rome, where he was a boy soprano from 1641, and organist from 1646.[6] Clearly, all his early training had been carried out under the supervision of Carissimi. From 1652 he was among the Italian musicians engaged by Christina of Sweden in Stockholm, and he once again joined her establishment around the year 1660. In the mid-1660s he was in London at the Court of Charles II, who also employed his brother Bartolomeo from 1666 at the latest. Vincenzo, the restless member of the family, soon left London for Dresden, Leipzig and Prague, while Bartolomeo stayed on in England until his death, which probably took place in the late 1680s. Bartolomeo was also employed in Stockholm at the same time as his brother, so could have brought works of the Roman school to London sooner; in this he may have been assisted by the German violinist Thomas Baltzar, who had worked in Sweden before coming to England shortly after Christina's abdication in the mid-1650s.

I would suggest that the works in the *Canzonette* come from a source close to the composers, since it is possible to state with some confidence that the pieces by Rossi, Stradella, Caproli and Cesti are unique to this source; of the two cantatas by Carissimi, one is found elsewhere, *La mia fede altrui giurata*, and it is consistently attributed to him.[7] This is not an anthology of Roman music whose content is based on Roman printed sources, a practice found, for instance, in the production of Jan van Geertsom in Rotterdam in the same period.[8]

In following the progress of the Albrici family we have at least one clear scheme of connections between a capable musician familiar in the Carissimi circle in Rome, who must have brought some Italian repertoire to London during the period in question. It is probable that Vincenzo was a more dynamic character than his brother, Bartolomeo, even though the latter – as the one who remained in London – contributed to the collection of *Canzonette*. And it is notable in this connection that it is only at the time around Vincenzo's arrival that the diarists Evelyn and Pepys begin to mention the presence of Italian music in London. Both other sources are also possible: in 1667 Pepys met Philip Thomas Howard, later Cardinal Protector of England and Scotland, who 'discoursed much of the goodness of the Musique in Rome', in which city he had entered the Dominican order.[9] North also recalls in his autobiography that he had a brother who 'loved the Italian songs and recitatives to fondness',[10] and that he had first been introduced to them through some books lent him by a certain Mr Willis; the books 'came from Rome, and were of Ricilli and others'.[11] Presumably here we are dealing with music by Giovanni Bicilli, at the time *maestro* at the Chiesa Nuova, whose motets appear in several anthologies from 1650 onwards, and whose cantatas survive in manuscript.[12] The attraction of Roman music for the English is again underlined in a conversation Pepys had with Thomas Killigrew in February 1667, in which Killigrew, manager of the Theatre Royal and groom of the King's Bedchamber, tells Pepys that he 'hath gone several times, eight or ten times he tells me, hence to Rome to hear good music; so much he loves it . . .'.[13]

Another musician, employed by Christina until her abdication, arrived in England in the early 1660s: Pietro Reggio, a singer and player of lute and guitar. At least for a while during 1664, Reggio seems to have had a weekly appointment to visit Pepys's house in order to sing for him, and to instruct him and two acquaintances in singing.[14] Both Reggio and Bartolomeo seem to have taught music to Evelyn's daughter, Mary. When she died tragically of smallpox in 1685 he wrote an obituary in his diary, noting that she had been the best pupil of 'Two famous Masters, Signor *Pietro* and *Bartolomeo*'; the diary also tells us that Bartolomeo had taught her for three years.[15]

Others may have played their part in making this repertoire known: Giovanni Sebenico can be excluded because of his primarily Venetian background, but the French violinist Michel Farinel, who visited England in the late 1670s, had studied with Carissimi in Rome in the previous decade. In any case, we can be

sure that by the end of the 1670s there was a sufficient market
for Italian vocal music, or at least sufficient hope of creating
one, to make the publication of the *Canzonette* a worthwhile
project. And it contains a Roman rather than a Venetian repertoire, reflecting the way that musical taste had developed
through the various visitors.

Whatever groundwork Pignani and Italians from Queen
Christina's circle had done, interest in Italian music in London
blossomed in the late 1680s with the visit of the famous castrato
Giovanni Francesco Grossi, known as Siface. One short harpsichord piece by Purcell establishes his awareness of the visit,
Siface's Farewell (z 656). Whatever the precise motivation for
the composition of this piece, one thing is clear: Purcell joined in
some measure in commemorating the departure of the great
singer from these shores. Siface spent only six months in
England, during the first half of 1687, but his visit was not
quickly forgotten. Shortly after his arrival in London he sang at
James II's private chapel to what must have felt like a packed
house, rather than a large congregation.[16] John Evelyn recorded
the occasion, presumably the service of Vespers, which would
explain both the hour and the dominance of music:

> I heard the famous *Cifeccio* (Eunuch) sing, in the popish chapell
> this afternoon, which was indeede very rare, & with greate skill:
> He came over from Rome, esteemed one of the best voices in *Italy*,
> much crowding, little devotion . . . [17]

Evelyn, who had heard a considerable amount of Roman
music during his stay there, again admired Siface's performance
at Pepys's house in April:

> I heard the famous Singer the Eunuch *Cifacca*, esteemed the best in
> *Europe* & indeede his holding out & delicatenesse in extending &
> loosing a note with that incomparable softnesse, & sweeteness
> was admirable . . . this was before a select number of some par-
> ticular persons whom Mr. Pepys . . . invited to his house.[18]

Siface may well have impressed the musical populace with his
high standard of singing, yet the cultural baggage which he
brought with him was probably far more interesting and influential than the voice itself, remarkable though that clearly was.

Few singers in Europe, and none in England, could boast a cosmopolitan career to rival that of Siface: he had gained his sobriquet for his performance of the part of Siface in Cavalli's *Scipione affricano*; he was a member of the papal chapel; and had sung in the Venetian opera, as well as in Naples for Alessandro Scarlatti. From 1679 until his death he was in the service of Francesco II d'Este, Duke of Modena, and it was in this capacity that he visited England, in order to entertain Maria Beatrice d'Este, the Duke's sister and wife of James II.

While in Rome, creating the initial sensation of a highly successful career, Siface had attracted the attention of the exiled Queen of Sweden, Christina, whose director of chamber music was still the ageing Carissimi. Indeed, Siface's initial success in *Scipione affricano* had taken place at the Teatro Tordinona under Christina's patronage. During the 1670s he lived in Rome, and it would be extremely unlikely that he broke his close connections with the Christina circle. The music of Carissimi was held in the highest esteem after the composer's death in 1674, and it was no doubt still regularly performed. When eventually Siface left Rome, it was in favour of a position at Modena, where one of the most important sources for the music of Carissimi is the library of the d'Este Court.[19] It seems that the collection was well under way before Maria left for England in 1673, since the covers of an entire collection of manuscripts, including important Carissimi sources, bear the date 1662. I would also suggest that, whatever their provenance, these are sources with an exceptionally good stemma, since they provide more details about the poets than almost all others, as well as giving titles independent from the texts of the first lines. It seems certain that Siface contributed to Carissimi's growing reputation in England. Indeed, it was probably in England rather than in Rome that Handel learnt of Carissimi's music, from which, on occasion, he borrowed.

Certainly Roman rather than Venetian music typified the Italian style for the English, even during the reign of Charles II. Roger North reports that the monarch wished to hold a trial of musical works from the various nations, and Carissimi's trio 'Amante che dite' from the cantata *Sciolto havean dall'alte sponde* was chosen on this occasion to represent Italian music.[20] This section of the cantata must have subsequently enjoyed wide popularity, since it survives in a remarkable number of English manuscript sources, and is also the only extended musical example which North chooses to include in his *Musicall Grammarian*.[21]

This shows North to have had a high estimation of the Roman style in general, and of Carissimi's music in particular, but even more abundant praise is lavished on his works by Pepys as early as 1664. The diarist spent the evening of 22 July in the company of two acquaintances and the singer Pietro Reggio, 'singing the best piece of musique, counted of all hands in the world, made by Seignor Charissimi the famous master in Rome' – high praise indeed![22] It is an interesting exercise to attempt to narrow down the various candidates for the accolade of the 'best piece of music'. In my estimation there are two possibilities: the first is the cantata mentioned above, and the second is the closing chorus from Carissimi's oratorio *Jephte*, which also survives in a remarkable number of sources.[23] One of the copies of the latter is in the hand of William Gostling, the son of a famous bass associated not only with the Court circle of Charles II, but also directly with Purcell through the Chapel Royal.[24] And Henry Aldrich, Dean of Christ Church, who died in 1710, adapted this movement to English words, 'Haste thee, O Lord, my God'.[25] Purcell grew up in a city where a group of amateur musicians could reckon a work by Carissimi to be the best music in the world.

But the interest in Italian music was no sudden occurrence; it had developed slowly and steadily since the Restoration. Even Pepys, who was eventually a great supporter of Italian music, was rather indifferent the first time he visited the Queen's Catholic chapel in September 1662: 'I heard their Musique too; which may be good, but it did not appear so to me, neither as to their manner of singing nor was it good Concord to my eares, whatever the matter was.'[26] It took until April 1666 for his view to be modified: '. . . to the Queen's chapel – where I do not so dislike the music'.[27] A fortnight later we read: '. . . to the Queen's chapel and there heard a good deal of their mass and some of their Musique, which is not so contemptible ...',[28] and by Midnight Mass of Christmas in the following year, he states: 'Their music very good endeed ...'.[29] In the following years his reactions were to be consistently positive. Once established, then, Pepys's enthusiasm for Italian music did not wane over time: for seven years, from 1675, Pepys maintained in his service an Italian singer called Cesare Morelli. The manuscripts copied by Morelli, now in the Pepys Library at Magdalene College, Cambridge,[30] contain Italian songs by the same circle of composers as represented in the *Canzonette* of 1679, including Stradella, Draghi, Cesti, as well as numerous pieces of Morelli's own, and some to English texts by Pepys himself. The predominant scoring in these volumes is for bass voice with guitar thorough-bass accompaniment, suggesting that in a domestic setting Pepys and his household musician would have performed these works together. It would be unfair were I not to mention the presence of French and English songs, but I would also suggest that Morelli's nationality reflects Pepys's own strong musical preferences by this stage.

Morelli may have been influential outside Pepys's immediate sphere of influence: Roger North reports in his autobiography that a girl who took his fancy (probably before 1676) had 'mastered that puzzling instrument the lute, and having a good voice, and the instruction of an Italian, one Signor Morelli, she acquired to sing exceeding well, after the Italian manner, to her own playing upon the lute or guitar'.[31]

Pepys is at least a valuable indicator of musical taste in the early Restoration period, but with the accession of James II it looked as if the Italian style would become even more popular. Italians already in the country found a new source of employment at the opening of the Catholic royal chapel on Christmas Day in 1686;[32] new musicians were imported, such as Innocenzo Fede, who had previously been in the papal choir and, like so many musicians who had crossed the channel in the previous decades, had worked for Queen Christina. Fede probably came to the attention of the English, presumably through the Ambassador, having sung in the *Accademia di musica* mentioned above which was commissioned by the Queen of Sweden for the Roman celebrations of the accession of James II. But the King was soon in exile, and it was his Court which was to propagate Italian music in France. Fede, only recently arrived in London, left with the Stuarts for Paris, where he came to take a leading part in their Court music, which even in France was predominantly Italianate.[33]

However, even the expulsion of the Stuarts with their Italianate tastes could not extinguish the Italian musical culture. It was now so deeply rooted as to be almost indigenous, and although England had lost many of its Italian musicians, their music proved durable. Indeed, writing in his *Memoires of Musick*, Roger North states that 'most of the yong nobillity and gentry that have travelled into Italy affected to learne of Corelli, and brought home with them such favour for the Itallian musick, as hath given it possession of our Pernassus'.[34] Thus Roman music remained popular well after 1700.

Having noted the presence of a distinct Rome–London cultural axis as the background to Purcell's music, it is perhaps helpful in conclusion to suggest a few ways in which Purcell fits into the picture. Clearly, he must have been aware of the growing interest in Italian music during his lifetime, as anyone in cultured circles in the capital would have been. Pepys emerges through the 1660s as a clear supporter of the Italian style, and it is interesting to note that he was personally acquainted not only with Matthew Locke, but with one member of the Purcell family, perhaps Henry, the composer's father, or Thomas, probably an uncle. Pepys records meeting Locke and a member of the Purcell family in congenial circumstances in February 1660.[35] It would be extremely surprising, then, if the paths taken by Purcell did not cross with members of the circle defined by Pepys and Evelyn. And we know that Purcell had at least encountered Siface.

Given the vogue that Italian music enjoyed in the 1680s, one is prompted to question the real intention of Purcell's preface to his *Sonnatas of III Parts* (z 790–801), published in 1683. Many debates have attempted to reveal the identity of the 'fam'd Italian Masters', whom Purcell was imitating. Perhaps, in the light of the vogue for Italian music, Purcell, or his publisher, decided that such a reference to the Italian taste might make a good marketing tactic. After all, the original intention was to issue them without continuo, and the style is not actually strikingly Italian. Perhaps this is a later example of what one might dub 'the Coprario syndrome', since Purcell appears to be issuing normal English music, while claiming that an eye-catching and fashionable influence has contributed to the style. Even North, who must have had a shrewd idea of what Italian and English music sounded like, says – as a contemporary – that the sonatas are 'clog'd with somewhat of an English vein'.[36]

Whatever Purcell may have been thinking in 1683, his sincerity seems beyond doubt in the 1691 preface to *Dioclesian* (z 627), where he claims that music is still in its infancy in this country; the infant 'is now learning Italian, which is its best Master, and studying a little of the French Air, to give it somewhat more Gayety and Fashion. [We must be] . . . content to shake off our Barbarity by degrees.' By this stage the Stuarts with their Italianisms had been banished and there no longer existed the Queen's chapel with its alternative musical and liturgical practice.

But the cultural orientation remained the same. Indeed, if the two volumes of *Harmonia sacra* are anything to judge by, the vogue for the Italianate became more pronounced, at least as far as Purcell was concerned. Purcell clearly had a considerable role in the compilation of these volumes of spiritual music, published in 1688 and 1693. In Book One Purcell contents himself with a selection of his own works, together with those of Blow, Locke and Humfrey, but in the second volume the choice is far more wide-ranging. Purcell included music by himself, his brother Daniel, Blow, one Barrincloe, Robert King, and Jeremiah Clarke. But the table of contents does not finish there: motets in Latin are also included by Carissimi and Bonifazio Graziani, who was *maestro di cappella* at the Gesù, the major Jesuit church in Rome, until 1664. As Playford explains in the preface to the second volume of *Harmonia sacra*, addressing himself to Henry Aldrich, the adaptor of Carissimi to English texts:

To make the Collection Compleat, and that it might consist of some of the best Foreign Hands as well as our own, I have at the End inserted some of Gratiano's and Carissime's Compositions, which you, with the rest of the just Judges of Musick, so much Esteem.

In this volume, Purcell and Playford acknowledged the importance of Roman compositions as a potent strand within London musical life, in the expectation that a receptive market awaits such pieces. The publication of the second book of *Harmonia sacra* unites Purcell's own music to a rich seam of music which remained in favour throughout his lifetime, despite its foreign origins. Like any stylistic study, an assessment of the interaction between Purcell and the Roman aspect of his musical environment is a daunting and complex task. What is certain, however, is that Carissimi and other Roman composers and performers were an inescapable influence on any musician raised in London during the period of the Restoration.

NOTES

1   *Pepys*, 15 November 1667; VIII, 529.
2   Havendo osservato, quanto favorevolmente sono ricevute le Composizioni Italiane dagli amatori della Musica, in cotesta Città mi fece risolvere imprimere il presente Volume, & per renderlo più stimabile, hò scielto le più belle Canzoni de più Eccellenti Autori del nostro secolo, accio che la varietà dello stile, lo rendi più dilettevole, non meno utile. Alcune di esse sono state composte in Londra espressamente per compiacerti, da Persone, la di cui virtù, ti è molto ben nota, è spero che la tua approbazione, e lode, ricompenseranno per me loro fatica. Io ne consacro gli esemplari a più Persone di gran merito, è Nobiltà solo a fine, di procurare a ciascheduno di cotesti Virtuosi il suo Protettore. Io so bene che sarò biasimato, d'havere inserito il mio nome fra un Catalago [*sic*] si degno, ma pure nel mare della Virtù non può ingolfarsi, chi non è audace chi è timido rade le sponde, non si carica mai de merce pellegrine. Caro Lettore so che m'intendi Addio, e vivi sano.

                                                    GIROLAMO PIGNANI
    Preface to Anthology *RISM* 1679[6], author's translation in text.
3   *Musurgia universalis* (Rome, 1650), I, 603.
4   On Carissimi, his music and career in general, see Graham Dixon, *Carissimi* (Oxford, 1986).
5   Alberto Cametti, *Il teatro di Tordinona poi di Apollo* (Tivoli, 1938), I, 9.

6   On Albrici's association with the College, see T. D. Culley, *A Study of the Musicians connected with the German College in Rome during the 17th century and of their activities in Northern Europe*, Jesuits and Music, i (Rome, St Louis, 1970), 216–18, 271–2.

7   See Gloria Rose, *Giacomo Carissimi*, The Wellesley Edition Cantata Series (Wellesley College, 1966), no pagination.

8   On this printer, another Northern compiler of Roman music prints, see Graham Dixon, 'Jan van Geertsom, a Seventeenth-century Dutch Printer, and the Dissemination of Roman Music', *Tijdschrift van de Vereniging voor Nederlandse Muziekgeschiedenis*, xxxii (1982), 116–25.

9   *Pepys*, 23 January 1667; VIII, 26.

10   A. Jessopp, ed., *The Autobiography of the Hon. Roger North* (London, 1887), 85.

11   Ibid.

12   Motets by Bicilli appear in the anthologies *RISM* 1650[1]; 1655[1]; 1664[1]; 1668[1]; 1672[1].

13   *Pepys*, 12 February 1667; VIII, 26.

14   Ibid., 22 July 1664; V, 217. See also 29 July 1664; V, 226, and for Pepys's abandonment of the project, 12 August 1664; V, 239.

15   *Evelyn*, 14 March 1685; IV, 421.

16   *Works I*, VI, 32.

17   *Evelyn*, 30 January 1687; IV, 537.

18   *Evelyn*, 19 April 1687; IV, 547.

19   For a precise documentation of the presence of Carissimi in these manuscripts, cf. Rose, op. cit.

20   Mary Chan and Jamie C. Kassler, eds, *Roger North's The Musicall Grammarian 1728* (Cambridge, 1990), 262.

21   Ibid., 273–8.

22   *Pepys*, 22 July 1664; V, 217.

23   See C. Sartori, ed., *Giacomo Carissimi: catalogo delle opere attribuite* (Milan, 1975), 105. For a different candidate see above p. 34, n. 30.

24   *GB-Lbl* Add. MS 31477.

25   *GB-Lbl* Harley 7338, f. 177.

26   *Pepys*, 21 September 1662; III, 202.

27   Ibid., 1 April 1666; VII, 87.

28   Ibid., 15 April 1666; VII, 99.

29   Ibid., 24 December 1667, VIII, 588.

30   MSS Pepys 2591, 2802–4.

31   *The Autobiography of the Hon. Roger North*, op. cit., 29.

32   See Margaret Mabbett, 'Italian Musicians in Restoration England (1660–90)', *Music and Letters*, lxvii (1986), 237–47, 242.

33   Material in Paris had recently been identified as belonging to the Stuart Court, and Jean Lionnet was kind enough to supply a note on this discovery which I include in full in the Endnote to this article.

34   *Roger North's The Musicall Grammarian 1728*, op. cit., 272.

35   *Pepys*, 21 February 1660; I, 62–3.

36   John Wilson, ed., *Roger North on Music* (London, 1969), 48, 301.

ENDNOTE

When James II founded his Catholic chapel, inaugurated at Christmas 1686, he already showed a very clear preference for Italian Music. The new director of music, Innocenzo Fede, came from Rome, and the organist and several of the singers were Italians. We should not forget that the Queen, Maria Beatrice d'Este, was Italian and that she came from the Court at Modena where music was held in very high esteem. When the sovereigns fled England, Fede followed them into their exile at the castle of Saint Germain-en-Laye which Louis XIV put at his cousin's disposal – Queen Henrietta, mother of Charles II and James II, was Louis XIII's sister. Apart from being the King's Master of Music, Fede was also music teacher to the princes. Certainly compiled for his circle, and probably for the needs of the Court at Saint Germain, are the seven volumes which contain some of his compositions, held today at the Bibliothèque Nationale in Paris, call-mark H659.

This is a collection of cantatas and Italian airs, regrouped into alphabetical order according to the beginning of the text, each 'letter' separated from the next by one or two instrumental pieces. Finger and Paisible are the only non-Italian composers in this collection of compositions by the best Italian composers: Alessandro Scarlatti, Stradella, Perti, Bononcini, Corelli and Pasquini. Among the great names and many anonymous, there are also some Bolognese composers, probably recommended by the Marquise Vittoria Davia, who travelled with the Queen, and who came originally from that town. Several compositions, anonymous and attributed, have similarities with pieces in the Chigi collection, which suggests that Fede had stayed in contact with his uncle Giuseppe, the famous castrato at the pontifical chapel, who had also worked for Cardinal Flavio Chigi. His contacts with Rome are also demonstrated by the presence of several compositions by Pietro Paolo Bencini, who had never left Rome and whose works had never been published. All this seems to indicate that the English Court at Saint Germain was one of the means of dissemination of Italian music in France.

Jean Lionnet

4

Purcell and his Contemporaries

MICHAEL BURDEN

Perhaps characteristically, George Bernard Shaw had no doubts about the relative merits of Purcell's music and that of his contemporaries. When reviewing a concert of music by the seventeenth-century English composers William and Henry Lawes in 1894, he expressed the opinion that it was 'very charming music':

> ... inferior to that of Purcell and Handel only because Purcell and Handel happened to be much abler than the Lawes brothers, and not at all on account of any inferiority of the art of music in their time – rather the contrary, perhaps.[1]

That Shaw saw Purcell as a figure of greater musical stature than those around him comes as no surprise. It is less expected that the composer's talent was appreciated at the time to the extent that his master, John Blow, had the generosity to resign in his favour the post of Organist of Westminster, only to resume it after the younger man's death. As the anonymous author wrote 'To his esteemed friend, Dr. Blow, upon publishing his book of songs, *Amphion Anglicus*':

> Thus has our isle been long ablig'd by Blow
> Who first with decent modesty did show
> In blooming Purcell what himself cou'd do.[2]

Apart from a small amount of music by Blow and Matthew Locke, and some anthems of Pelham Humfrey, what music do we really know from this period? Further, is that about which we know nothing worth troubling over anyway? Clearly Shaw, to name only one, would have us believe it is. Yet in some senses it is not. It would be a foolish and pointless exercise to attempt to make a case for the inclusion in a cathedral repertoire on a regular basis of the anthems of, say, Henry Cooke, or the frequent performance in recitals of the songs of Jeffery Hart. Equally pointless here would be a series of potted assessments of the music of Purcell's contemporaries, each one concluding that the composer in question was a lesser figure than Purcell. This approach, in any case, is not the one that Shaw is suggesting, since the thrust of his argument is that Purcell wrote music of great merit because he was surrounded by more than competent composers. It is, therefore, through an examination of the points at which they came into contact with Purcell that the context for his development as a performer, a composer and a *bon vivant* emerges.

So, who were Purcell's contemporaries? 'Contemporaries' is, perhaps, a slightly misleading term here, since composers such as William Child, whose composing career overlapped that of Purcell's, were not of Purcell's generation. As in theatre history, the period of the Commonwealth provides a *terminus ad quem* in the discussion; the suspension of services in the Chapel Royal in 1644 saw the end of a particular type of musical education, an education through which many seventeenth-century English composers passed. Indigenous composers who worked contemporaneously with Purcell can be divided fairly neatly into several groups. Firstly, there were the pre-Commonwealth composers, many trained in the Chapel Royal, who returned to Court at the Restoration. These included William Child, Matthew Locke, Henry Cooke, Charles Coleman, John Wilson and Henry Lawes, whose brother William, a prolific composer and a gifted musician, was killed fighting at the siege of Chester in 1645. An exception to this pattern was George Jeffreys, who claimed to have spent some time in Italy before the Commonwealth. He appears in the records of the Chapel Royal before 1643, at which date he became organist to Charles I while the Court was in Oxford. After the Restoration followed those who were approximately of Purcell's own generation, including John Blow, Henry Hall, Pelham Humfrey, Jeffery Hart, Robert Smith, Thomas Tudway and Michael Wise, men who were trained

during the years immediately following the re-establishment of
the Chapel Royal. Humfrey, Wise and Blow constituted what
Boyce was to call 'the three Great Geniuses produced from this
first set of Children'. Humfrey and Wise died at a relatively early
age, but Blow 'lived many Years after his School-fellows, to
cultivate with Success his uncommon Talent of Modulation'.[3]
The generations which succeeded Purcell included his brother
Daniel, William Croft, Francis Pigott, John Barratt, Jeremiah
Clarke, John Lenton and John Eccles. Their education was less
centred on the Chapel Royal, for although the first five were
choristers, musicians such as John Lenton joined it only as men,
while John Eccles, William Corbett and foreigners such as
Gottfried Finger, Nicola Matteis and James Paisible were never
part of it. The later generations of Purcell's contemporaries saw
the Chapel Royal decline steadily and lose its pre-eminent position in the musical life of the country as William and Mary made
substantial retrenchments in their support of its activities.

This was not merely through the desire for financial savings.
As a Calvinist, William had handed down an edict which disal-
lowed the use of the 'Musick' except on certain days, effectively
finishing off the symphony anthem.[4] After 1690, Purcell's *Te
Deum* and *Jubilate* (z 232) is his only substantial sacred piece.[5]
This edict and retrenchment were reflected in Purcell's works for
the theatre, since 1690 saw the beginning of an intensive period
of composition which included all the multi-media spectaculars.

It is a truism to say that a composer's output reflects his
circumstances, and it is hardly significant that Purcell and
his contemporaries all wrote in the same genres. As Thomas
Brown penned in the character of Blow writing to Purcell:

> You know Men of our Profession hang between the Church and
> the Play-house, as *Mahomet's* Tomb does between the two Load-
> Stones, and must equally incline to both, because by both we are
> equally supported.[6]

However, it is striking that their compositional activity in
each of those genres is, proportionally, almost the same. All
concentrated on the anthem and all wrote some service music,
although no one composer wrote terribly much of it. All work

lists include some instrumental pieces and, with the exception of Blow who contributed a number of important organ and harpsichord works, all wrote a few relatively insignificant keyboard compositions. The one major exception is the amount of theatrical music written by Purcell. The composer with the next most significant output is Matthew Locke, whose music for *The Tempest*, for *Psyche* and for *The Mask of Orpheus* constituted the first flowering of dramatick opera. After Locke, there is Blow's *Venus and Adonis* and some theatrical songs by almost every composer, but there is nothing approaching Purcell's Herculean efforts of *The Fairy Queen* (z 629) or the integrated sophistication of *King Arthur* (z 628). It was only after Purcell's death in 1695 that those composers already mentioned – Clarke, Eccles, Finger and Daniel Purcell – began to write dramatick operas, providing at least one in almost every season until 1702.

Purcell's relationships with men such as these can only be guessed at, for scholarship is hampered by an almost total lack of contemporary documentation. Without suggesting that the laudatory poems published by them in *Orpheus Britannicus* are simply empty praise, they convey little or nothing about the authors' relationship with the man. It is possible to surmise – but not to recount – what Purcell's views were on the music of his colleagues which was performed at the coronation of James II, or how he reacted to the teaching offered him by successive Masters of the Children of the Chapel Royal.

It was the energies of the flamboyant Henry Cooke (c1615–1672), appointed as a bass to the King's Private Musick in the first entry in the Lord Chamberlain's records after the Restoration, which did much to restore the glories of the Chapel Royal in time for Purcell to become a chorister in the later 1660s, possibly as early as 1666. Cooke's rapid establishment of the Chapel Royal owed much to his being 'bred up in the Chapel' of Charles I, to his energy, and to his ruthless but efficient selection of choristers. Wainwright mentions the 'pressing' system, a method whereby Cooke obtained promising boys from the provincial cathedrals and chapels.[7] 'Poaching' rather than 'pressing' would seem to have been Cooke's style on these occasions, as a querulous minute referring to 'the insolencys of

Mr. Cooke (Mr. of the King's boys) ... in stealing away two of our choristers without any special warrant' suggests.[8] Cooke's teaching of the choristers appears to have been as rigorous as his selection of them was inspired. He was paid to instruct them on the organ, lute and theorbo, and also taught harpsichord and violin. Further, those who were 'ye forwardest & brightest Children of the Chapell' were encouraged 'by indulging their youthfull fancys, so that ev'ry Month at least, & afterwards oft'ner, they produc'd something New of this Kind; In a few years more, Severall others, Educated in the Chapell, produc'd their Compositions in this Style, for otherwise, it was in vain to hope to please his Majesty'.[9] One probable result of these 'youthfull fancys' is considered to be Henry Purcell's earliest composition, the song 'Sweet Tyraness' (z 567) published in 1667.

Like Thomas Purcell, Cooke gathered royal and public appointments like nuts in May, becoming a bass and lutenist in 1660, Master of the Boys in the Private Musick in June of that year, and 'composer in his Majestys private Musick for voyces in Ordinary' in 1664. His activities outside the Court saw his election in 1662 as an assistant of the Corporation of Music, becoming a deputy marshal and finally marshal in 1670. As a singer he was clearly remarkable, being credited by Evelyn as being 'esteem'd the best singer after the *Italian* manner of any in *England*'.[10] Pepys heard him sing several times, and had at least one altercation with him on musical technicalities.[11] The diarist, however, thought Cooke a fine composer, a judgment not sustained by posterity. However, to pontificate at this point on the stature of Cooke's compositions is to ignore the role they played in the development of the English anthem. The form of the verse anthem – solo voices, ensembles and a chorus – can be found in early, isolated, pre-Commonwealth instances such as William Lawes's 'The Lord is my Light', but it was Cooke's own anthems and the newer ones of Matthew Locke with their separate continuo parts allowing interplay between these three elements that clinched the form. According to Tudway, the appearance of symphonies and ritornellos between the anthem verses on Sundays and Festivals was the result of the intervention of Charles

II, who must have been inspired by his experiences at the French Court during his years of exile.[12]

Among the music that Purcell must have heard and sung at this time was that by the man whose name appears alongside Purcell's throughout his life, William Child (1606/7–97). Not only heard and sung; Child's anthem 'Sing we Merrily' appears in Purcell's hand in a collection of music associated with the Chapel Royal in Fitzwilliam 88.[13] Nearly all of Child's music dates from before the Restoration, and what there is suggests, not unnaturally perhaps, a conservative approach.[14] However, he had previously acknowledged the appearance of the earlier Italian style by adding 'newly composed after the Italian way' to the title page of his *Choice Musick to the Psalmes*, first published in 1639. Child did not join the Chapel Royal until after the Restoration, when he succeeded Alfonso Ferrabosco – Child's earlier royal appointment had been to St George's Chapel, Windsor, a post to which he was returned when the Chapel was re-opened. Child was also a friend of Pepys's, setting music for him on several occasions and taking the diarist with him to rehearsals. Pepys records a number of meetings, including a fascinating visit to Windsor in February 1666.[15] He gives the following account of the scene he discovered in 1663 when calling at the house of his patron, the Earl of Sandwich, whom he found:

> . . . within with Captain Cooke and his boys, Dr. Childe, Mr. Mage, and Mallard, playing and singing over my Lord's Anthemne which he hath made to sing in the King's Chappell . . . And after that was done, Captain Cooke and his two boys did sing some Italian songs, which I must in a word say I think was fully the best Musique that I ever heard yet in all my life – and it was a very great pleasure to hear them.[16]

Pepys had already heard some measures of this untraced anthem when calling on Lord Sandwich earlier in the month.[17] As part of his long association with the Chapel Royal, Child participated as an organist in the three later seventeenth-century coronations, those of Charles II, James II and William and Mary. Purcell was only about a year old when Charles II was crowned, although Thomas Purcell took part as a Gentleman of the Chapel. However, in James II's coronation procession Purcell is listed among the basses as 'organist of Westminster', and Child, listed as the same voice, is billed as 'Dr. in music, Eldest Gentleman of the Chapel'.

Among those boys singing at Lord Sandwich's house was possibly one of those talented pupils Cooke is known to have pushed forward, Pelham Humfrey (1647?–1674). Pepys had heard his 'Have Mercy on me, O God' at the Chapel Royal on 22 November 1663, recording that 'the Anthemne was good after the sermon, being the 51 Psalme – made for five voices by one of Captain Cookes boys, a pretty boy'.[18] This anthem is Humfrey's first recorded composition. Humfrey was dubbed once and for all by Pepys an 'absolute Monsieur', whose arrogant criticisms and extravagant name-dropping were enough 'to make a man piss'.[19] Humfrey, returning from a sojourn in France, apparently to absorb the French style after his voice had broken, seems to have acquired a number of personal affectations and a camp style that, to the British, was unacceptable. Sadly, Pepys's colourful language obscures the fact that he does not dispute the most grievous fault of which Humfrey accused the musical establishment, namely that the King's Musick played out of tune, could not keep time and was possibly musically illiterate, or was at least inflexible. Although not excusable, such faults might have been understandable even several years after the interregnum, but to a gifted musician fresh from the French Court they must have been insupportable.

Humfrey, married to Henry Cooke's daughter Katherine, succeeded on Cooke's death on 13 July 1672 to his posts of composer in the Private Musick and of Master of the Children of the Chapel Royal. His composing career began early, for a small group of anthems can be dated to the years before 1664 – 'Have Mercy on me, O God', 'Almighty God, who mad'st thy blessed Son', and 'Haste thee, O God', as well as his contribution to 'The Club Anthem'. The bulk of his anthems date from the later 1660s, while his five devotional songs were probably written by 1672. The remainder of Humfrey's output consists of three Court codes from the 1670s, a group of lost anthems all com-

posed before 1664, twenty-two secular songs, and his contribution of two masques and a song to the music for *The Tempest*.
It is *The Tempest* which provides one of the few tangible links
with Purcell that can be identified. The production of *The Tempest* took place at the Dorset Garden theatre in March or April
1674, and under the King's instruction the men and boys of the
Chapel Royal and the members of the King's Musick took part.
Downes tells us that it was staged:

> having all New in it; as Scenes, Machines; particularly, one Scene
> Painted and *Myriads* of *Ariel* Spirits; and another flying away,
> with a Table Furnisht out with Fruits, Sweet meats and all sort of
> Viands; just as when Duke *Trinculo* and his Companions, were
> going to Dinner; all things perform'd in it so Admirably well, that
> not any succeeding Opera got more Money'.[20]

Purcell's voice had broken in 1673, but he cannot have been
unaware of the preparation of such a novel musical event, and
unless he was unwell or out of town, he would probably have
attended the performances. Purcell's own involvement with the
music from the *Tempest* shows an indebtedness to Humfrey,
illustrated in Example 1. There are other similarities, such as the
use of Humfrey's old-fashioned French style in 'Where does
the black fiend Ambition reside',[21] and although doubt has correctly been cast on the authorship of much of the music originally ascribed to Purcell, there can be no reason to suppose that
the other contenders for the authorship of these particular pieces
had an affinity with, or indeed memory of, Humfrey's setting.[22]

Perhaps the most intriguing aspect of Humfrey's output – and
an aspect of which Purcell, as a talented pupil, can hardly have
failed to be aware – is the use of distinctive, as yet unassimilated,
foreign styles. On the one hand there is 'O Give Thanks unto the
Lord', an anthem which is close to the Lullian *grand motet*;
while on the other 'Hear, O Heav'ns' is in a pure Italianate
style, which Dennison postulates may have been modelled on
Carissimi's motet 'Turbabuntur impii', a work certainly known
in England at this time.[23] 'O Give Thanks unto the Lord' is
Humfrey's largest anthem, representative of the festive texts to
which the composer was drawn, and its grandeur suggests that it

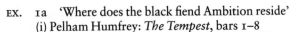

EX.   1a   'Where does the black fiend Ambition reside'
(i) Pelham Humfrey: *The Tempest*, bars 1–8

(ii) Henry Purcell?: *The Tempest*, (z 631/2a), bars 1–8

EX.   1b   'To your prisons below'
(i) Pelham Humfrey: *The Tempest*, bars 83–7

(ii) Henry Purcell?: *The Tempest* (z 631/14d), bars 1–9

may have been an occasional work, possibly for the Chapel Royal.[24] More cohesive in style and internal structure than many contemporary anthems, it is the large chorus and verse sections, setting the text 'This is the day which the Lord hath made', that is most redolent of the *grand motet*. The chorus sections have the opening text 'This is the day which the Lord hath made', while the verse, represented by an equivalent of the *petit choeur*, answers with 'we will rejoice and be glad of it', unaccompanied by the band. The impression of a crowd of somewhat vacuous believers being called upon by three of the faithful to rejoice is confirmed when the crowd and the orchestra finally join the soloists in the last four bars (Example 2). Dramatic devices such as these play a major role in the overall mood of the anthem, and it was the overall mood rather than the representation of single words and phrases that preoccupied Humfrey. As well as the use of the *petitchoeur* arrangement, other aspects of 'This is the day which the Lord hath made' which can be related to the French style include the extended key structure and the nine instrumental ritornellos which punctuate the anthem with dramatic effect. In a different league entirely is 'Hear, O Heav'ns'.

EX. 2   Pelham Humfrey: 'This is the day which the Lord hath
made', bars 195–209

Not only is it his shortest anthem, but it is also on a very small
scale, having just continuo accompaniment. Dennison's case for
the work's links with Carissimi's 'Turbabuntur impii', a case
which turns on the similarity of the declamatory, arpeggiated
opening phrases and the use of static harmony which accelerates
only towards a cadence, is particularly strong when it is remembered to how much Italian music Cooke, as Humfrey's master,
clearly had access.

It is Humfrey's journey to France that played such a formative

role in the style of the Restoration, as did that taken by John Banister (*c*1625–1679) about the same time.[25] There is more evidence to support Banister's journey 'to go into France on Special Service and return with expedition',[26] for it can be seen that on his return he established the Twelve Violins, along the lines of Louis XIV's *Petits Violons*, replacing an existing group directed by John Singleton and Matthew Locke.[27] His success in achieving this contributed to his downfall, for the Frenchman Grabu, brought to the Court first as master of the English

EX. 2 *(contd.)*

Chamber Music – 'here they talk also how the King's violin, Bannister, is mad that the King hath a Frenchman come to be chief of some part of the King's music, at which the Duke of York made great mirth'[28] – was appointed in Banister's place as leader of the Twelve Violins; a foreign, French-trained musician was now leader of a French-style ensemble.

Much of the discussion of Humfrey's music does not address the fact that the Italianate feel on the one hand, and the identification of French elements on the other, indicates a period of post-Restoration experimentation, and that the synthesis of these two styles can have only just been reached at the time of Humfrey's death, if indeed it can be said to have synthesized at all at this point. It is true to say that Humfrey's output is uneven, and rarely reaches the heights of which the reflective and grief-filled 'By the Waters of Babylon', with its dramatic layout and graphic harmonies, illustrated that he was capable (Example 3). However, it should be seen in context – Humfrey died at the age of 26, Purcell when he was 36, and Purcell's early works show as much unevenness – contrapuntally at least – as do Humfrey's. For the same reason, statements that, unlike Locke, Blow or Purcell, Humfrey 'confined himself to a small

EX.   3   Pelham Humfrey: 'By the Waters of Babylon', bars 74–84

EX. 3 (contd.)

number of fields, aware perhaps of his limitations' are comparatively meaningless, and it is clear that his death in 1674 while
the Court was at Windsor deprived England of a precocious
talent, whose owner could in time have enjoyed a career as
distinguished and as prolific as Purcell's.

The new French and Italian music, which Humfrey clearly
admired, appears to have had little attraction for Matthew
Locke (1622–77). The vigorous preface to his *Little Consort of
Three Parts* (h 132) attacks:

> ... *those* Mountebanks of wit, *who think it necessary to dis-
> parage all they meet with of their owne Countrey-mews, because
> there have been and are some excellent things done by Strangers, I
> shall make bold to tell them (and I hope my known experience in
> this* Science *will inforce them to confess me* a competent Judge)
> that I never yet saw any Forain Instrumental Composition (*a few*
> French Corants *excepted*) *worthy an* English *mans transcribing.*[29]

Locke's connection with the Purcell family can be traced
throughout Henry's early life. Indeed, when Henry was less than
a year old, Pepys records Locke in company with Thomas
Purcell, both Gentlemen of the Chapel Royal:

> Here I met with Mr Lock and Pursell, Maisters of the Musique;
> and with them to the Coffee-house into a room next the Water by
> ourselfs; where we spent an hour or two till Captain Taylor came
> to us, who told us that the House had voted the gates of the City to
> be made up again and the members of the City that are in prison
> to be let at liberty; and that Sir G. Booth's case be brought into the
> House tomorrow.
>
> Here we had a variety of brave Italian and Spainish songs and a
> Canon for 8 *Voc*; which Mr. Lock had newly made on these words:
> *Domine salvum fac Regem*, an admirable thing ... Here, out of
> the window it was a most pleasant sight to see the City from [one]
> end to the other with a glory about it, so high was the light of the
> Bonefires and so thick round the City, and the bells rang
> everywhere.[30]

Both Thomas Purcell and Locke became members of the
King's Musick, although the latter held a number of Court
appointments of considerable prestige, including private composer-in-ordinary to the King, composer in the wind music and a
new position of composer for the band of violins.

As well as these appointments, Locke, a practising Catholic, was organist to Charles's consort, Catherine of Braganza. The Queen's chapel was at St James's Palace from 1662 until 1671, and from that year at Somerset House. However, Locke's playing appears to have been considered old-fashioned by the Italians who were also employed there, for, while Giovanni Sebenico (at Court 1666–73) and Giovanni Battista Draghi (in London 1667, d 1708) successively played the 'great organ', he was relegated 'to a chamber organ [near]by'.[31]

Of Locke's relationship with Henry Purcell we have no record before about 1676, from which year the following now lost (and possibly forged) letter seems to date:[32]

> DEAR HARRY, – Some of the gentlemen of His Majestie's Musick will honor my poor lodgings with their company this evening, and I would have you come and join them. Bring with thee, Harry, thy last anthem, and also the canon we tried over together at our last meeting. Thine in all kindness,
>
> M. Locke
>
> *Savoy, March 16*

The transcription and authenticity of the letter cannot be confirmed, and its content is problematic since the picture it suggests is probably the one that we desire to find; nevertheless, there is other evidence to support the frequency of similar evenings of casual music-making and trying over of anthems, Pepys's diary being the most obvious source. Locke remained Henry Purcell's 'Worthy Friend' until the older composer's death in 1677, and was honoured by Purcell in the ode 'What hope for us remains now he is gone?' (z 472). Purcell's esteem may have been reciprocated, for Michael Tilmouth suggests that the major source for Locke's seven sets of consort music, his great scorebook, was left to his friend Purcell.[33] This bequest may have directly influenced Purcell's output, for the first fantasias (z 732–3) appear to have been written about the time of Locke's death, while most of the fantasias and the In nomines are known to have been composed during the summer of 1680. Further, Purcell divided his own manuscript in the same manner as did Locke – for compositions from two to eight parts – and used notational devices peculiar to, or at least typical of, Locke's score-book. If Tilmouth is correct, this burst of activity indicates a desire on the part of Purcell to emulate his friend and mentor; Holman suggests elsewhere in this volume that Purcell may have treated the composition of these pieces as an exercise, in which case the argument for an imitation of Locke's compositional organization is even stronger. As well as being influenced by the 'fam'd Italian Masters', these sonatas of Purcell's also provide a link to Lully. It has been shown that one of Purcell's *Ten Sonatas of Four Parts* (z 807; Example 4a), written in about 1680 but published posthumously in 1697, is constructed over 'Scocca pur', a ground which is attributed to the French composer by many, including André Danican Philidor, Lully's own copyist and arranger.[34] The ground first appears in an English source in 1679; it can be found frequently thereafter.[35] Purcell certainly knew it by 1689, for he 'carefully revised and corrected' the contents of John Playford's *Musick's Handmaid II*, in which it was included (Example 4b). As we shall see below, Lully was also to figure in Locke's career.

An essential part of Locke's public personality was his willingness to engage in pamphleteering. His preface to the *Little Consort of Three Parts*, upholding the superiority of English music over the efforts of foreigners, has already been mentioned; in 1666 he chose the polemical title *Modern Church-musick Preaccus'd, Censur'd, and Obstructed in its Performance before His Majesty, Aprill 1, 1666*, for the publication of his setting of *The Ten Commandments* (h 20). These two incidents were just skirmishes when compared to the battle which began after the publication of Thomas Salmon's *Essay to the Advancement of Musick* in early 1672. Salmon's tone, style and proposals attracted Locke's wrath; John Phillips and John Playford also entered the fray in support of Locke, while one 'N.E.' of Norwich came down on the side of Salmon.[36]

Salmon's propositions were for a new gamut of seven letters based on an octave cycle, for the use of the same lines and spaces to eliminate old clefs, and for the replacement of lute tablature with staff notation.[37] These were sensible attempts to deal with some of the practical problems of learning the notational

EX. 4a   Henry Purcell: Sonata of Four Parts no. 6 (z 807), bars 1–6

EX. 4b   'New Lessons for the Virginals' from John Playford's
          Musick's Handmaid II (1689), bars 1–11

system, but Locke, as a professional, failed to see the difficulties, and simply restated the current practice with selective examples. Locke's contradictory and extreme positions undermined his effectiveness as a pamphleteer, and we find him extolling the virtues of those members of the Chapel Royal whom he had roundly abused during the fiasco of the responses to *The Ten Commandments*. The essence of the debate – which in any case is not developed but is simply restated from pamphlet to pamphlet – is of less interest to us than the style in which it was conducted. Locke's initial reply was abusive of Salmon, and thereafter all four authors indulged themselves to the full, vigorously trading insults and finding *doubles entendres* in each other's writing with tortuous agility.[38]

Although the Purcell household would have followed the musical side of this debate, and both the older members and the young Henry would have sniggered over the *doubles entendres*, such pamphleteering was far from Purcell's own character; he was too practical to allow himself to be drawn into such profitless activity, and the little we know of him suggests that he possessed too much *sang-froid* to care a great deal. The only exception to this is the part he played in the writing of the introduction to *Dioclesian*, which certainly owes something to John Dryden.[39] As inspiration here Purcell could have taken Locke's polemical introduction to *The English Opera*, which espoused the cause of the genre. This volume was Locke's crowning achievement after he had fallen:

> into the theatrical way, and composed to the semioperas divers peices of vocall and instrumentall enterteinement, with very good sucess; and then gave way to the devine Purcell, and others, that were coming full saile into the superiority of the musicall faculty.[40]

That the involvement of Locke in the theatre influenced Purcell in this direction is probable; it is inconceivable that the younger composer did not at least attend any of the dramatic operas, or hear any of the music. It is always possible that he even performed in one of them. Theatrical music does not appear in Purcell's output until after Locke's death, when in 1680 he provided the songs, ensembles and choruses for

Nathaniel Lee's *Theodosius or The Force of Love* (z 606), 'being the first he e'er Compos'd for the Stage'. Locke's theatrical activities date at least from 1656, when he contributed the fourth entry to William Davenant's *The Siege of Rhodes* (h [63]); it is also possible that he contributed to the first version of the masque of *Cupid and Death* (h 59) in 1653. He went on to set songs for Charles II's coronation procession in 1661 (h [58]) and the recitatives, choruses and masques in Roger Staplyton's 1663 tragi-comedy *The Stepmother* (h [60]); he also wrote incidental music to a number of other plays, before the flurry of activity to which North refers.

One of Locke's most interesting achievements was *The Mask of Orpheus* (h 61/2) from Elkanah Settle's play *The Empress of Morocco*. The masque, a vehicle for a variety of music and dancing, and with a multiplicity of functions, here represented an 'Infernal Hell' to which Orpheus descended to retrieve Euridice from the clutches of Pluto. The work belongs to the magic and supernatural scenes found in some Restoration dramas, scenes which include Ismeron and croaking toad in *The Indian Queen* (z 630/13b). As a 'magic' scene – the masque opens with Orpheus taming the 'tortur'd spirits', disarming the threatening creatures who guard hell and banishing from their thoughts their 'Tyrant Kings' – it does not have the scoring that Plank has shown to be typical of the supernatural.[41] Locke resists all temptations to obvious text painting and vulgar effects, and relies on a consistent creation of atmosphere, exemplified by the subtle chromatic writing as Orpheus gently feels his way into Hades (Example 5).

Locke's theatrical activities culminated in the publication of his music for *The Tempest* (h 192/3), and the vocal numbers from *Psyche* (h 64) in the volume entitled *The English Opera*, mentioned above. The availability of such music by his mentor in printed form provides the context for parallels of structure and musical detail which can be drawn with Purcell's own stage works.[42] There are also similarities between individual numbers. For example, the chair dance in Purcell's *Dioclesian* resembles the dance of statues in *Psyche*,[43] while models for the Dance of Furies, and the hornpipe and dance for the Followers of Night in

EX. 5 Matthew Locke: *The Mask of Orpheus* (h 61), bars 1–10

The Fairy Queen, can be found in the storm music, and the lilk and canonic conclusion from Locke's *The Tempest*.[44] A further parallel has been drawn between the appearance of Locke's volume and Purcell's publication of his first dramatick opera, *Dioclesian*, but it is more likely that the latter's appearance relates to the printing in 1687 of Louis Grabu's music for the all-sung opera, *Albion and Albanius*.[45]

As Dennison points out, Locke's style in the 1660s and 1670s remained touched by pre-Restoration Italianate influences,[46] but in these last works for the stage the taint of the French style – so often abused by Locke – can be found in the dotted rhythms of the saraband and in the rhythmic construction of the courant.[47] This should not, however, be taken to indicate a deliberate departure on Locke's behalf, for it is one possible legacy of the curious circumstances surrounding the composition of *Psyche*.[48] Thomas Shadwell's version of the text was commissioned by

Thomas Betterton, the patentee of the Duke's Theatre, after a visit to Paris between 1671 and 1673. During this period, Lully's *tragédie-ballet* of *Psyché* by Molière, Quinault and Corneille was enjoying a successful run of some eighty performances; the work had had its première on 17 January 1671.[49] Locke might have had the opportunity to hear the instrumental music both to the Molière–Lully *comédie-ballet*, *Les Amants Magnifiques* of 1670, and to the 1671 *Psyché*, for it is possible that they were both performed at Court.[50] Further, he may also have consulted the score, since the manuscript which contains this music belonged at one time to Roger L'Estrange, the dedicatee of Locke's *Melothesia, or certain general rules for playing upon a continued-bass*, which was published in 1673.[51] In a final twist to this series of events, the generally accepted influence of foreign ideas on English music and opera is reversed. Lully, altering his work for a production in 1678, included two new scenes that are similar to those introduced into the original by Shadwell – the final drinking song to Bacchus and a scene for the Furies and Daemons in the Hades sequence – and have no antecedents in the French theatre.[52]

Locke's output after the Restoration, which includes eleven English verse anthems, was all probably heard and sung by Purcell. As with Humfrey, Locke had to grapple with the new instrumental anthem, attempting to give a series of contrasting musical episodes formal coherence.[53] His masterly control of the genre is demonstrated by the famous 1666 *A Song of Thanksgiving for His Majesty's Victory over the Dutch on St. James his Day* (h 15). This is an enormous work involving three choirs, viols and violins, organ and theorbos, and is laid out as Grand Chorus 'Be thou exalted, Lord'–Symphony I–'The King shall rejoice'–Symphony II–'He asked life of thee'–Symphony II (2)–'His honour is great in thy salvation'–Grand Chorus; it has rightly been referred to as an 'anthem within an anthem', the extended 'The King shall rejoice' forming a central section flanked by the full anthem-like grand choruses.[54] The number of choirs gives Locke the opportunity not only for their individual employment, but for the construction of antiphonal effects (Example 6).

EX. 6 Matthew Locke: 'Be thou exalted Lord in thyne own strength', *A Song of Thanksgiving for His Majesty's Victory over the Dutch . . .* (h 15), bars 53–5

Purcell's connection with Locke was revived again when in the 1690s he was employed revising the musical definitions for *The New World of Words* for Edward Phillips (1630–96), brother of John, one of the protagonists and supporters of Locke in the 'Advancement' debate. These definitions had been contributed by Locke to the earlier editions, while other entries had been provided on a range of subjects by such luminaries as Elias Ashmole, John Evelyn, Godfrey Kneller and Isaack Walton.[55] Also supporting Locke during the 'Advancement' incident was John Playford the elder (1623–86), the bookseller and music publisher who dominated the English music publishing trade for most of Purcell's life. His publications included *The English Dancing Master* and *Apollo's Banquet*, and in 1667 he produced what is possibly Purcell's first published composition, 'Sweet Tyraness', in *Catch that Catch Can*. In 1654 Playford produced *A Breefe Introduction to the Skill of Musick*, a volume which passed through many editions during the seventeenth century. It was this book that Playford's son, Henry (1657-c1707), asked Purcell to revise for its twelfth edition, published in 1694. As with Locke, Purcell's connection with Playford is encapsulated by his setting of Tate's 'A Pastoral Elegy on the death of Mr. John Playford' (z 464).[56]

It was in Purcell's 1694 revision of *A Breefe Introduction* that he acknowledged John Blow (1649–1708) as 'one of the Greatest Masters in the World'. As a fellow pupil, Henry Hall, wrote in his poem 'To his Esteemed Friend, Dr. Blow':

> The Art of Descant, late our Albion's boast
> With that if *staining* glass, we thought was lost;
> Till in this work we all with wonder view
> What ever art with order's notes can do,
> Corelli's heights, with great Bassani's too;
> And Britain's Orpheus learned his art from you.[57]

Blow was ten years Purcell's senior, and had left the Chapel Royal when his voice broke in 1664, some years before Purcell is presumed to have entered it. He was appointed organist of Westminster Abbey in 1668, to the King's Musick in 1669, and was sworn in as a Gentleman of the Chapel Royal in 1674. In that year he also succeeded Humfrey as Master of the Children, thus missing Purcell, whose voice had already broken. However, there can be little doubt that during Purcell's years as apprentice to John Hingeston, he was taught by Blow. Like Humfrey, Blow married a daughter of a Gentleman of the Chapel Royal, and, as

Hawkins suggests, appears to have been a vain, but generally decent, man:

> Dr. Blow was a very handsome man in his person, and remarkable for a gravity and decency in his deportment to his station, though he seems by some of his compositions to have been not altogether insensible to the delights of a convivial hour. He was a man of blameless morals, and of a benevolent temper; but was not so insensible of his own worth as to be totally free from the imputation of pride.[58]

It may well have been this same pride which encouraged Blow to publish *Amphion Anglicus*, an act which was viewed by his contemporaries such as Thomas Tudway as an extremely poor attempt to imitate Purcell's *Orpheus Britannicus*.[59] However, his influence on English musical life was immense, for as Master of the Children of the Chapel Royal for so many years his pupils were numerous, and included Tudway, Jeremiah Clarke, Daniel Purcell, William Croft and Bernard Gates; the last two were successively to follow Blow as Master of the Children.

The two most significant genres in Blow's output are the thirty-five odes and the large group of anthems. Of the odes, twenty-five were written for the Court, of which eighteen celebrated the New Year while the remainder were royal birthday odes – two each for Charles II, William III and Queen Anne, and one for the Duke of Gloucester. They span a large part of his career, beginning in 1678 with a New Year's Day ode, 'Dread Sir, the Prince of Light', and ending in 1700 with 'Come, Bring the Song', a birthday ode for Queen Anne. During the 1680s and 1690s Blow worked in conjunction with Purcell, Blow providing a New Year's Day ode for every year except 1689, and a birthday ode for Charles II, and Purcell providing birthday odes for Queen Mary and the music for other occasions such as the return of the King to Whitehall from Newmarket, from Scotland and after his Summer Progress, and on the wedding of Anne to Prince George.

The anthems span an even greater number of years, and consist of some twenty-eight orchestral anthems, and nearly one hundred verse and full anthems with organ. Blow's early works in these two genres are comparatively conservative, resembling the verse anthem of the early years of the Restoration. Both types of anthem have a bipartite overture, and both rely heavily on a dotted crotchet-quaver-crotchet rhythm. The spectacular word painting and other dramatic devices of the odes and grander anthems after the early 1680s can be seen clearly in the opening of the New Year's Day ode from 1684 (Example 7). Here, the setting features an intricate four-part texture, with extended melismas on Flatman's 'trembling' song, and a strident and insistent call to rise which can be heard prominently throughout the opening chorus. The growing floridity of both forms, but of the anthem in particular, has been attributed to the appearance on the scene of the famous bass John Gostling (c1650–1733).[60] It was at the coronation of James II in 1685 that Blow and the anthem had their finest moment. A glance at the list of music performed on that occasion shows that Blow provided three anthems to Purcell's two; Sandford lists 'Let Thy Hand be Strengthened', 'Behold, O God, our Defender' and 'God Spake Sometime in Visions', and 'I was Glad' and 'My Heart is Inditing', respectively. Also included were William Turner's 'Come Holy Ghost' and 'The King shall Rejoice', Child's *Te Deum*, and a setting of 'Zadok the Priest' by Henry Lawes (1596–1662), which was first sung at the coronation of Charles II. As a cross-section of the musical world in London at the time, this selection of composers could scarcely have been bettered. The coronation service was reorganized for James II, providing a compromise to satisfy his religious scruples, and at his request William Sancroft, Archbishop of Canterbury, omitted the communion service. As one would expect, those anthems written for the coronation contain some of Blow's grandest ideas. 'Behold, O God, our Defender' and 'Let Thy Hand be Strengthened' are both impressive full anthems with organ accompaniment, although the use of the form for whatever reason on such an occasion suggests a somewhat conservative approach. It does, however, throw into relief the new 'God Spake Sometimes in Visions', a verse anthem with strings. It is difficult to imagine a more impressive scene for an anthem, for:

EX. 7 John Blow: 'My Trembling Song, Awake, Arise', bars 1–6

... the *Gentlemen* of the *Chapel Royal*, with the *Instrumental Musick*, and the *Choir of Westminster*, sang and played together this *Verse-Anthem*, as a solemn *Conclusion* of the KINGS part of the CORONATION ... at the end of which *Anthem*, the *Trumpets*

> sounded, and all the *Drums* did beat, and all the *People* shouted, crying out, *GOD SAVE THE KING*.[61]

It is divided into eight parts – two trebles, two altos, tenor and three basses – and is articulated by five symphonies and ritornellos. By writing no solo vocal lines in the verses, Blow combines the straightforward full anthem with the newer, comparatively showy verse anthem, creating a large-scale work suitable for such an occasion. Blow's odes and anthems of the early 1690s are something of a disappointment after the achievement of the previous decade. The musical accompaniment and text setting are at times perfunctory, perhaps reflecting the difficulties mentioned above which were responsible for Purcell's intense activity in the theatre. Blow, however, had no such outlet, and his *oeuvre* shows a paucity of ideas during the early years of William and Mary's reign. After Purcell's death in 1695, Blow made great use of the antiphonal effects – such as those found in 'Hail, Thou Infant Year' – which he had largely eschewed during Purcell's lifetime, and both forms had a brief flowering in the last years of the century.[62]

The relationship of aspects of Blow's *Venus and Adonis*, 'A Masque for the Entertainment of the King', to Purcell's *Dido and Aeneas* has been the subject of much debate and will continue to be so, until the chronology of the two works is established. However, while nothing is known about the first performance of *Dido and Aeneas*, we do at least have a contemporary manuscript copy of Blow's masque, which suggests that the first performance was given at Court around 1683; *Venus and Adonis* was also given at Josias Priest's school in Chelsea, the venue of the only known seventeenth-century performance of Purcell's work.[63] The Court presentation had among its performers the actress Moll Davies, by this time a discarded mistress of Charles II, and their natural daughter, Lady Mary Tudor. This cast has given rise to the identification of possible topical allusions, for the little cupids are taught to spell the word 'mercenary', a probable reference to the King's latest mistress, Louise de Kéroualle, Duchess of Portsmouth, who had shown herself more adept at obtaining royal financial favours

EX. 8 John Blow: *Venus and Adonis*, Act II, bars 120–24

than had her predecessors.[64] Whatever the truth, Blow had created a bewitching drama, whose action is carried forward by a sophisticated flexible vocal line, which moves smoothly in and out of *arioso*-like passages, allowing for maximum expression (Example 8).

Apart from *Venus and Adonis*, Blow wrote very little theatre music, and that which survives is incidental music to plays. He provided songs for Nahum Tate's *The Loyal General* in 1680, Aphra Behn's *The Lucky Chance* in 1687, Nathaniel Lee's *The Princess of Cleeve* in 1689 and John Howe's *History of Adolphus* in 1691. It is probably only coincidental that both Blow and Purcell started their public theatrical careers in the same year; they met only briefly in the theatre, when they collaborated on the music for Robert Gould's tragedy *The Rival Sisters; or, The Violence of Love*, first performed at Drury Lane in 1695; the play was based on James Shirley's *The Maid's Revenge*. Blow set the Act II dialogue, 'To me you made a thousand vows', while Purcell provided the remaining songs, dances and instrumental music (z 609).

In addition to his other activities, Blow was one of the three organists of the Chapel Royal – the other two were Purcell and

82   THE PURCELL COMPANION

William Child. Further, both Blow and Purcell were associated
with the notorious competition between the organ builders
Bernard Smith and Renatus Harris for the installation of their
respective instruments in the Temple Church. Both instruments
were installed by the summer of 1684, and were demonstrated
for the Benchers, Blow and Purcell playing Smith's organ and
Draghi playing on the Harris instrument. Despite performances
on each organ on different days, and subsequently on both on
the same day, no decision was reached. The matter was not
resolved until 1688, when the infamous Judge Jeffreys selected
the Smith organ. Blow and Purcell are found again sitting in
judgment on organs, this time in 1686, at the church of St
Katherine Cree, where Purcell played Smith's new instrument
for Blow, Mr Mosses and Mr Fforcell; they declared that it had
been completed according to contract and was a satisfactory
instrument. Purcell then joined the rest of the panel to choose
the new organist.[65]

As can be seen, the careers of Purcell and Blow intertwined
throughout the younger man's life, an intertwining commemor-
ated by Henry Sacheverell in 'To Dr. John Blow and Mr Henry
Purcell':

> Hail mighty Pair! Of *Jubal's* Sacred Art,   *Dr.* John Blow
> The greatest Glory!——   *and Mr.* Henry
> Not skilful *Asaph* understood so well,   Purcell
> And *Heman* vainly labour'd to Excel.[66]

The great professional and, indeed, personal regret that Blow,
who had already been witness to Humfrey's will and untimely
demise, must have felt when writing his ode on the death of
Purcell, 'Mark how the Lark and Linnet Sing', can be imagined.

Blow had also been a contributor to what was, perhaps, one
of the most curious links between any of Purcell's contemporaries, *The Club Anthem* 'I will always give thanks', of about 1664.
What the 'club' was, one can only speculate, but its placing by
Dennison at the end of Humfrey's days as a chorister, days
which also saw Blow's voice break, suggests that it might have
been a personal pact, or an acknowledgment of the benefits of
the training and professional guidance offered by the Chapel

Royal at the point when two of the authors were about to leave it.

The third contributor to *The Club Anthem*, William Turner (1651–1740), the already mentioned composer of two of the anthems sung at the coronation of James II, provides a useful counter-example to those composers already mentioned in this chapter. He was more typical of the lesser Restoration composers than those figures of greater stature who taught and influenced Purcell. His career was one of reaction rather than action, for he produced with his serviceable talent works clearly modelled on those of others. The influence of Locke can be seen in the organization of the verses and the handling of the verses and choruses can be seen in his early anthems, while his service in D seems to have been modelled after Purcell's *Te Deum* and *Jubilate* (z 232). Further, he did not assimilate new ideas quickly, and it was not until the later 1670s that his anthems show a more modern organization of the verses and ritornellos, and the influence of the prevailing French style. Turner was an alto who became a chorister in the first years of the Restoration, had a brief career as Master of the Choristers of Lincoln Cathedral and who returned to sing as a Gentleman of the Chapel Royal for seventy-one years. As an accomplished alto, he sang the solos in a variety of Purcell's anthems and odes, including 'Hail! Bright Cecilia!' (z 328), the 1692 St Cecilia's Day ode; he also participated in theatrical performances, singing in Shadwell's *The Tempest* and in the 1675 *Calisto*, John Crowne's masque at Court. His contact with Purcell must have been on a regular basis both as a singer and as a composer; Purcell certainly heard, and probably played the organ accompaniment to, Turner's two now lost anthems for James II's coronation in 1685.

Similarly, another Chapel Royal alto, Michael Wise (c1648–1687), was the beneficiary of the developments of the age, but despite Boyce's placing of him among the 'geniuses of the Restoration', most of his anthems are worthy rather than interesting and really serve as a starting point for a discussion of what was not done rather than as significant achievements in their own right. Unlike Turner and, indeed, Blow, Humfrey and Purcell, Wise did not contribute to the French-style string anthem, but confined himself to writing verse anthems with organ accompaniment. Wise appears to have missed Purcell on several occasions; he left the Chapel Royal before Purcell had arrived, and was probably organist at Salisbury by that stage. He was not appointed back to the Chapel until after Purcell had left it, and was suspended at the time of the coronation of James II for an unspecified misdemeanour.[67] However, his appointment in 1676 to the Chapel as a countertenor to succeed Raphael Courteville (d 1675) was made at about the same time as Purcell was appointed Hingeston's assistant, and they were in professional contact thereafter. Wise died in mysterious circumstances, gossip suggesting that 'he was knock'd on the head and killed downright by the Night-watch at Salisbury for giving stubborne & refactory language to them on S. Bartholemew's at night'.[68]

Sadly, we have no record of Purcell's relationship with the singers who sang his anthems and performed his dramatick operas and theatre songs, singers whose voices may have shaped his settings and, indeed, have influenced the way in which the dramatick operas were written. Most prominent among these was the already mentioned bass, John Gostling, who succeeded William Tucker as a Gentleman of the Chapel Royal in February 1679. His voice was widely admired – Charles II, North and Evelyn are among those whose praises are recorded – and Purcell wrote numerous works for him, including the anthem 'They that Go Down to the Sea in Ships' (z 57).[69] He clearly had a great influence on the music that Purcell wrote, and it has been suggested that the increased flexibility of line apparent in the works of the early 1680s was due to his appearance on the scene.[70]

It was probably through Gostling's son William that Hawkins heard the story of the musical afternoon with Queen Mary:

> Having a mind one afternoon to be entertained with music, sent for Mr Gostling, then one of the chapel and afterwards subdean of St. Paul's, to Henry Purcell and Mrs Arabella Hunt, who had a very fine voice, and an admirable hand on the lute, with a request to attend her; they obeyed her commands; Mr Gostling and Mrs Hunt sang several compositions of Purcell, who accompanied

them on the harpsichord; at length the queen begining to grow tired, asked Mrs Hunt if she could not sing the old Scots ballad 'Cold and Raw', Mrs Hunt answered yes and sang it to her lute. Purcell was all the while sitting at the harpsichord unemployed, and not a little nettled at the queen's preference of a vulgar ballad to his music; but seeing her majesty delighted with this music, he determined that she should hear it upon another occasion; and accordingly in the next birthday song, *viz.*, that for the year 1692, he composed an air to the words 'May her bright example chace Vice in troops out of the land', the bass whereof is the tune 'Cold and Raw . . .'[71]

The soprano mentioned by Hawkins, Arabella Hunt (?1645/ 50–1705), was singing teacher to Princess Anne, and was greatly admired by the musical establishment; there are poems in praise of her voice by Congreve, and another set by John Blow. Although she guarded her virtue and reputation until the end and never appeared on the public stage, she performed in Crowne's masque *Calisto* in 1675, in which Turner had also appeared, opposite the notorious Charlotte Butler (*fl.* 1673–95) in the role of an African woman. Butler appears to have been a colourful personality, and she is one of the few singers of whom reports of a role in a Purcell opera survive:

> I remember in Purcell's excellent opera of *King Arthur*, when Mrs Butler, in the person of Cupid, was to call up Genius, she had the liberty to turne her face to the scean, and her back to the theater. She was in no concerne for her face, but sang a *recitativo* of calling towards the place where Genius was to rise, and performed it admirably, even beyond any thing I ever heard upon the English stage.[72]

Butler's importance to Purcell's music can be judged by the fact that she is the only soprano to be named in sources before *The Fairy Queen*.[73] Her defection to the Dublin stage after the 1692 performances of that opera, when she was refused a salary rise, suggests that a new song introduced into the opera in 1693 may have been written to accommodate the voice of Mrs Ayliff (*fl.* 1690–97), for whom Purcell had written a variety of theatre songs during the previous year.[74] Mrs Ayliff was not an actress-singer but, as Price points out, a professional musician.[75] Purcell obviously admired her voice, for she sang in two of Purcell's odes: the 1692 'Hail! Bright Cecilia!', and 'Celebrate this Festival', the 1693 ode for Queen Mary's birthday (z 321).

The early theatre songs and these first operas were performed by actors who could also sing; to this breed belonged singers such as Butler, Anne Bracegirdle (1671–1748) and William Mountfort (c1664–1692), but after the 1692 *Fairy-Queen* Purcell wrote no music for actor-singers. Not unnaturally, he appears to have preferred writing music for the professionals, but as Dryden implies, these performers were less successful in the characterization of their roles:

> ... his Second Act, was wonderfully diverting; where the scene was in Bedlam: & Mrs Bracegirdle and Solon were both mad: the Singing was wonderfully good. And the two whom I nam'd, sung better than Redding and Mrs Ayliff, whose trade it was: at least our partiality carryed it for them.[76]

This suggests that the partiality of the audience for Bracegirdle and Solon was based on their ability to carry their roles.

The theatrical shambles of the mid–1690s are documented elsewhere in this book.[77] The group of defecting actors who left the United Company for the cramped quarters of the converted tennis court in Lincoln's Inn Fields included most of the best actors and singers. The reasons why Purcell stayed with the parent company are unclear, although he may have felt partly responsible for the difficulties – as indeed he was, since it was the dramatick operas and their large casts which ate up the cash – or he may have wanted to see *The Indian Queen* produced in a house that was capable of spectacular staging. Whatever the reason, his 'Music supported a Company of young raw Actors against the best and most favour'd of that Time, and transported the Town for several years together',[78] and his death only months after the split deprived Rich of one of his greatest attractions.

Among the singers catapulted to fame by these events was Richard Leveridge (1670–1758). His first solo song was in Purcell's 'Take not a woman's anger ill' from Robert Gould's *The Rival Sisters* (z 609); later, he probably sang Bacchus in Purcell's masque in *Timon of Athens* (z 632), made his operatic début in Purcell's *The Indian Queen* (z 630), singing among other things the magician Ismeron, and appeared in *The Tempest* (z 631).[79] Leveridge appears to have sung Ismeron only in the first performances; thereafter, he sang Hymen, the High Priest and the bass part in the choruses. It may well have been this change in casting that was responsible for the curious partbook – 'Mr Leveridge: Indian Queen' – a unique survival whose creation cannot be fully accounted for.[80] Leveridge's repertoire continued to include Purcell's songs until his retirement from the stage in 1751; Burney recalled in his *General History* that he had heard him sing '. . . several of Purcell's base songs occasionally, in a style which forty years ago seemed antediluvian'. Antediluvian or not, it gave the eighteenth century a taste of Purcell's music learnt from the composer himself.

Among the others who sang in *The Indian Queen* were the young soprano Letitia Cross (*c*1677–1737), the treble Jemmy Bowen (*b c*1685) and John Freeman (*c*1666–1736), the last named being the only singer of first rank remaining at Dorset Garden. Freeman was also a veteran of *The Fairy Queen* and had made his name singing 'Sound fame' in *Dioclesian* in 1690. After a busy operatic career which included roles in dramatick operas such as *The Island Princess*, *Brutus of Alba* and *The Grove*, he became a Gentleman of the Chapel Royal in 1700, achieving a full post there on 23 December 1702. Although Cross and Bowen were still young, neither was an entirely inexperienced Purcell singer. Cross seems to have sung the composer's songs in both *The Conquest of Granada* (z 584) and *The Tempest* in the mid–1690s, while Bowen was singing Purcell's 'To arms, heroic Prince' (z 600) in *The Libertine* in the 1691–2 season; he can also be connected with the 1695 revival of *The Indian Queen* where he sang the role of the God of Dreams. It is about Bowen that one of the few comments attributed to Purcell was made, for when the singer:

> was practising a Song set by Mr PURCELL, some of the Music told him to grace and run a Division in such a Place. 'O *let him alone*, said *Mr. Purcell*; he will grace it more naturally than you, or I, can teach him'.[81]

These four theatre singers were those for whom Jeremiah Clarke (*c1673–1707*) wrote the ode on the death of Henry Purcell, 'Come, come along, for a dance and a song', given on stage at Drury Lane in December 1695. As both the trumpet voluntary and his music for *The Island Princess* show, Clarke's music is generally light and elegant, but with more than a touch of the ceremonial; his powerful music for 'Come, come along' is in another class altogether, for although the ceremonial remains, it is bizarre by comparison and includes 'Mr Purcell's Farewell' (Example 9), which is given its dirge-like quality by the bass and drum ostinato.

The British singers mentioned above were all rather robust when compared to one visiting singer whom Purcell probably

EX. 9   Jeremiah Clarke: Ode on the Death of Henry Purcell, 'Mr Purcell's Farewell', bars 1–14

heard, Giovanni Francesco Grossi, known as 'Siface' (1653–97).[82] An accomplished castrato soprano, his appearance in 1687 was not only a great novelty, but was a revelation as far as the standard and quality of his performance were concerned.[83] However, he appears to have been a hypochondriac, and did little singing during his visit; much of his time was spent complaining about being 'out of humour'. This being the case, it seems impossible to view Purcell's mournful harpsichord piece, *Siface's Farewell* (z 656; Example 10) in anything other than an ironical light.

It is appropriate, perhaps, that a singer and colleague of many years' standing was present at Purcell's interment. Stephen Crespion (c1649–1711) had been appointed Chanter of the Chapel Royal on 16 January 1684, and as such it fell to him to intone the funeral music over the composer's grave.

Perhaps a final question should be asked: who were Purcell's drinking pals? Purcell scholarship has never really recovered from the draconian action taken by the Purcell Society in the early twentieth century, when new texts were substituted for the bawdy ones in the collected edition. Writing in 1922, W. Barclay Squire refers to editions published after Purcell's death where editors, 'owing to the fact that in many cases the original words are so grossly indecent,' reprinted the music with new words. Squire implies that he made the best of a bad job, and that when the original texts could not be recovered he supplied texts of his own.[84] However, an examination of Squire's edition shows that the sources he cites have the original texts, and that the bawdier ones have been replaced with texts by J. A. Fuller-Maitland.[85] Example 11 shows the type of result that could be expected from their collaboration. Indecency is also the line taken by Westrup.[86] Even the new edition published by the Oxford University Press in 1987 replaces the word 'cunt' in the last phrase of the catch 'My Lady's coachman, John' with a chaste line, destroying not only the rhyme but the sense of the catch as well.[87] The embarrassment of scholars at the catches and glees has done little to assist in an assessment of their quality, their relationship to other catches and the occasions for which they were written.

EX.   10   Henry Purcell: *Siface's Farewell* (z 656)

EX. 11   Henry Purcell: 'Sir Walter Enjoying' (z 273), texted by J. A.
Fuller-Maitland; the original text is below

Sir Walter enjoying his damsel one night
He tickled and pleas'd her to so great a delight
That she cou'd not contain t'wards the end of the matter
But in rapture cry'd out: O dearest Sir Walter,
O dearest Sir Walter, O dearest Sir Walter,
O switter swatter, switter swatter, switter swatter, switter swatter.

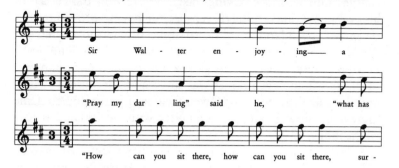

Purcell – like every other Restoration musician, or, indeed, seventeenth-century man of the world – appears to have been a sociable animal, both as a musician and as a drinker. There are the musical afternoons with Queen Mary referred to above, references to chamber music of a higher calibre with Roger North's family,[88] and to a tavern named after the composer. This time, eighteenth-century strictures can be found; Hawkins charges him with not having 'been very nice in the choice of his company', and to 'merit censure for having prostituted his invention, by adapting music to some of the most wretched ribaldry that was ever obtruded on the world for humour'.[89] Hawkins does, however, provide some concrete information – that a house in Wych Street was known as the Purcell's Head and that, like the house of Owen Swann in Bartholomew Lane known as Cobweb-hall, it was a tavern with musical and artistic connections.

A large number of Purcell's catches were included in such volumes as John Playford's *The Pleasant Musical Companion*, which started its long life in 1652 as *Catch that Catch Can*. By 1686 it had been enlarged, was in its seventh edition, and was known by its alternative title. It continued to be reprinted until about 1720. In the enlarged edition of 1686 Purcell is the most widely represented composer; by the 1707 edition his share of the one hundred and twenty-one catches had grown to fifty-two.

The type of bawdy texts complained of by Hawkins and Squire were not set only by Purcell, although this is the impression conveyed by their cursory treatment of the subject. A survey of the catches in the 1686 edition of *The Pleasant Musical Companion* reveals equally spicy texts set by Purcell's apparently staid contemporaries, including Blow's 'Galloping Joan' (Part I), Wilson's 'To see on fire a boiling pot', Smith's 'Have you not a chimney seen?', Lenton's 'Galloping Joan' (Part II) and Turner's 'Once did I see a maid'. There are also pieces by Locke, Tudway and Banister, as well as a group of minor composers including Thomas Farmer (*d* 1688), John Jackson (*d* 1688), John Reading (*c*1645–1692), John Moss (*fl.* 1662–84), William Isaack (*d* 1703) and Francis Farmelo (Farmeloe; *fl.* 1635–50); at least two of these figures were provincial cathedral organists. So ingrained was the assumption that these 'church composers' did not write such pieces that Myles Birket Foster included Michael Wise's bawdy catch 'When Judith had laid Holofernes' in his list of the composer's anthems.[90] Surprisingly, the catches by Richard Brown (*d* 1710), presumably the Brown most roundly condemned by Hawkins and others as having led Purcell into bad company, are mild.

The sociable nature of the performances of such music is illustrated clearly by the layout found in works such as *The Pleasant Musical Companion*, where the music is clearly arranged so that the book can be placed flat on a table and read from more than one direction.[91] This is borne out by the iconographical evidence of the title page of the first edition of the work published in 1652, which shows just such an arrangement.

That a convivial evening in the Purcell's Head Tavern (or elsewhere) may have been instrumental in hastening Purcell's death on 21 November 1695 remains a possibility, for despite attempts to dismiss the story by glamorizing Frances Purcell's devotion to her husband, it is quite conceivable that the poor woman, in an effort to keep her servants (and her sanity), gave orders that he should not be admitted to their house when appearing drunk after midnight. If this is so, she had time to repent at leisure, for she survived him by a decade, dying in 1706.

NOTES

1 'Ride a Cock Horse', *The World*, 21 February 1894 in Dan H. Lawrence, ed., *Shaw's Music* (London, 1981), III, 140.
2 John Blow, *Amphion Anglicus* (London, 1700), iii.
3 William Boyce, *Cathedral Music* (London, 1767), II, viii.
4 For example, comments can be found from 1689 – 'There shall be no musick in the Chapell, but the organ' (quoted in Donald Burrows, 'Handel and the English Chapel Royal' (Ph.D. diss., Open U., 1981), I, 22) – and 1691 – 'the King's Chappell shall be all the year through kept ... with solemn musick like a Collegiate church' (H. C. de Lafontaine, *The King's Musick* (London, 1909), 383).

5   See Donald Burrows, 'Theology, politics and instruments in church: musicians and monarchs in London, 1660–1760', *Göttinger Händel-Beiträge*, v (1993) 145–60; Burrows argues that the settings of Te Deum and *Jubilate* by Purcell, Blow and Turner were a deliberate attempt to re-establish instrumental music in the Chapel, at least for feast days.

6   'Dr. B——'s *answer* to Henry Purcel. [sic]', in Thomas Brown, *A Continuation or Second Part of the Letters from the Dead to the Living* (London, 1707), 164.

7   See Chapter 2, 22–3.

8   Quoted in Edmund H. Fellowes, *English Cathedral Music* (London, 1941; rev. J. A. Westrup, 1969), 131.

9   Thomas Tudway, *GB-Lbl* Harleian MS 7338, f. 3^r.

10   *Evelyn*, 28 October 1654; III, 144.

11   *Pepys*, 13 February 1667; VIII, 59.

12   Tudway, op. cit., f. 2^v; see also *Evelyn*, 21 December 1662; III, 347 and *Pepys*, 14 September 1662; III, 197. Tudway implies that Charles, 'a brisk & Airy Prince', was bored with the solemn and staid way of doing things.

13   Frederick Hudson and W. Roy Large, 'Child', *Grove VI*, IV, 230; see also Robert Shay, 'Purcell alla Palestrina', paper at the Baroque Conference, Durham 1992, who suggests that Purcell acquired this book around 1682 from an older colleague, and demonstrates that the music in Purcell's hand includes a large amount of older music by composers such as Tallis, Gibbons, Batten and Tomkins.

14   Tudway, op. cit., f.2^v says that Child 'proceeded in [his] Compositions according to ye old Style'.

15   *Pepys*, 26 February 1666; VII, 57–8.

16   Ibid., 21 December 1663; IV, 428.

17   Ibid., 14 December 1663; IV, 418–19.

18   The authorship of this anthem has been disputed for some time. Don Franklin (review, *Journal of the American Musicological Society*, xxviii (1975), 148) suggests that it is atypical of Humfrey, and, combined with some doubts about the sources themselves, suggests that Richard Hosier of Durham was the composer. Dennison (letter, *Journal of the American Musicological Society*, xxxi (1978), 541) rejects this primarily on stylistic grounds. Robert Ford (*Musical Times*, cxxxviii (1986), 459) proposes Richard Henman as the author, having also shown that the copytext (*GB-Lbl* Add. MS 30932) of the earlier anthem was in Henman's hand. Dennison (*Pelham Humfrey* (Oxford, 1986), 117) rejects this also – probably rightly – because Ford's theory does not fit the circumstantial evidence of Pepys's Diary.

19   *Pepys*, 15 November 1667; VIII, 530.

20   John Downes, *Roscius Anglicanus*, ed. Judith Milhous and Robert D. Hume (London, 1987), 73–4.

21   Peter Dennison, 'Humfrey', *Grove VI*, VIII, 779.

22   See Margaret Laurie, 'Did Purcell set the *Tempest*?', *Proceedings of the Royal Music Association*, xc (1963–4), 43–57; Laurie's carefully argued

case demonstrates that the only air that was ascribed to Purcell by his contemporaries was 'Dear pretty Youth'; the connection with Humfrey shown by Dennison suggests that more of the music included in the Harrison edition can perhaps be attributed to Purcell.

23 Peter Dennison, *Humfrey*, op. cit., 60; see *GB-Och* MS 53, 121.

24 Ibid., 64.

25 Such study abroad seems to have played a fairly regular part in musical education. In 1695, Nicholas Staggins recalled his 'Travels in France ... Italy, & other Forrin Parts, to capacitate & make my self fit for ye Service of His Late Ma^ty K^g Charles ye Second' (Petition of Nicholas Staggins to Sidney, Lord Godolphin, 5 June 1695, in Andrew Ashbee, ed., *Records of English Court Music* (Aldershot, 1991), V, 91). Such practicalities as clothes were thought of also, as the warrant to deliver to Cooke two suits and other clothing for Pelham Humfrey 'being for his Majesty's extraordinary service' shows. (Andrew Ashbee, ed., *Records of English Court Music* (Snodland, 1986), I, 64).

26 Quoted by Ian Spink, 'Banister', *Grove VI*, II, 117.

27 See Peter Holman, *Four and Twenty Fiddlers* (Oxford, 1993).

28 *Pepys*, 20 February 1667; VIII, 73.

29 Matthew Locke, *Little Consort of Three Parts* (London, 1656), 'To the Lovers and Practitioners of CONSORT-MUSICK'.

30 *Pepys*, 21 February 1660; I, 63.

31 John Wilson, ed., *Roger North on Music* (London, 1959), 348.

32 Communicated to William H. Cummings by E. F. Rimbault and printed by Cummings in *Purcell* (London, 1881), 27.

33 *GB-Lbl* Add. MS 17801; see Michael Tilmouth, 'Revisions in the Chamber Music of Matthew Locke', *Proceedings of the Royal Musical Association*, xcviii (1971–2), 100.

34 Robert Klakowich, '*Scocca pur*: the Genesis of an English Ground', *Journal of the Royal Musical Association*, cxvi (1991), 67; speculation has linked it to other Purcell works, including the ground bass of 'When I am laid in earth' from *Dido and Aeneas*; see also *Zimmerman I*, 395 (z 807).

35 Ibid., 66–7.

36 N. E. of Norwich, *To Mr. T. S.* (London, 1672), 17–18.

37 Lillian M. Ruff, 'Thomas Salmon's "Essay to the Advancement of Musick" ', *The Consort*, xxi (1964), 267–75, contains a clear discussion of Salmon's ideas.

38 See Olive Baldwin and Thelma Wilson, 'Music Advanced and Vindicated', *The Musical Times*, cxi (1970), 150 for examples of these.

39 Curtis A. Price, *Henry Purcell and the London Stage* (Cambridge, 1984), 264; see also Roswell G. Ham, 'Dryden's Dedication for *The Music of the Prophetesse*, 1691', *Publications of the Modern Language Association of America*, l (1935), 1065–75, who proposes John Dryden as the author of the preface.

40 *Roger North*, op. cit., 348.

41 Steven E. Plank, ' "And Now About the Caldron Sing": Music and the

Supernatural on the Restoration Stage', *Early Music*, xviii (1990), 392–407; see in particular 398ff.

42   See Rosamond Harding, *A Thematic Catalogue of the Works of Matthew Locke* (The Author [Oxford?], 1971), and Michael Tilmouth, ed., *Matthew Locke: Dramatic Music*, Musica Britannica, lx (London, 1986), xv, for listings of Locke's contributions to plays and other theatrical pieces.

43   Jennifer McDonald, 'Matthew Locke's *The English Opera* and the Theatre Music of Purcell', *Studies in Music* [W. Australia], xv (1981), 62–75.

44   *Locke: Dramatic Music*, op. cit., xxi.

45   McDonald, op. cit., 63. This is not to say that Purcell was using *Dioclesian* as an 'instrument of vindication' in an attempt to end French influence on the London stage. See Curtis A. Price, op. cit., 263–5 for a discussion of this issue.

46   Peter Dennison, ed., *Matthew Locke Incidental Music: The Tempest*, Musica da Camera, 41 (London, 1977), i.

47   Peter Dennison, 'The Sacred Music of Matthew Locke', *Music and Letters*, lx (1979), 66.

48   *Locke Incidental Music*, op. cit., Preface.

49   The original Lully-Molière-Corneille-Quinault *tragédie-ballet*, *Psyché*, was first performed in 1671; it had thirty-eight performances that year, thirty-four in 1672 and a further ten in 1673.

50   Murray Lefkowitz, 'Shadwell and Locke's *Psyche*: the French Connection', *Proceedings of the Royal Musical Association*, cvi (1979–80), 45.

51   John P. Cutts, 'Jacobean Masque and Stage Music', *Music and Letters*, xxxv (1954), 188.

52   In fact, as Lefkowitz, op. cit., points out, the music for the 1671 *Psyché* in this manuscript *GB-Lbl* Add. MS 10445 appears in the same order required by, and uses the same title contained in, the published libretto, and is therefore the only surviving manuscript relating to Lully's first production.

53   A detailed discussion of the Italianate influences in the instrumental anthem can be found in Dennison, 'Sacred Music', op. cit., 65ff.

54   Harding, op. cit., 16.

55   Michael Tilmouth, 'Henry Purcell, Assistant Lexicographer', *Musical Times*, c (1959), 326 lists some of the terms that Purcell must have revised and passed for publication.

56   It is unclear which John Playford is intended here. *Zimmerman I*, 211 uses Cummings's suggestion that it is John Playford Jr, the son of 'Honest John', the music publisher. There seem to be no grounds for this suggestion and Purcell's connection with John Playford senior was a long and intimate one.

57   John Blow, op. cit., iii.

58   John Hawkins, *A General History of the Science and Practice of Music* (London, 1776), IV, 494.

59   Hawkins, ibid., cites Tudway and others as having propounded this view.

60   Rosamond McGuinness, 'The Chronology of John Blow's Court Odes', *Music and Letters*, xlvi (1965), 106.

61 Francis Sandford, *The History of the Coronation of . . . James II* (London, 1687), 99–100.

62 Bruce Wood, ed., *John Blow: Anthems II*, Musica Britannica, l (London, 1984), xvi, makes the point that the smaller scale of the works of the early 1690s can be found even in Blow's coronation music for William and Mary.

63 See the libretto discovered by P. A. Hopkins in the Cambridge University Library and discussed in Richard Luckett, 'A New Source for "Venus and Adonis" ', *Musical Times*, cxxx (1989), 76–9.

64 John Buttrey, 'The Evolution of English Opera between 1656 and 1695: a Re-investigation' (Ph.D. diss., U. of Cambridge, 1967), 156–68.

65 A fuller account of this event can be found in Zimmermann II, 134–5.

66 John Blow, op. cit., ii.

67 E. F. Rimbault, ed., *The Old Cheque-Book. . .* (London, 1872), 129.

68 Anthony a Wood in *GB-Ob* Wood D. 19 (4), f. 136ᵛ; cited by Michael J. Smith, 'The Church Music of Michael Wise', *Musical Times*, cxiv (1973), 69.

69 According to Hawkins, op. cit., IV, 359–60, Charles II and the Duke of York had taken Gostling to entertain them while they tried out the King's new yacht the 'Fubbs'. They were caught in a storm, and providentially reached the coast, probably having all been violently sick.

70 McGuinness, op. cit., 106.

71 John Hawkins, op. cit., IV, 6–7, n*; see also Charles Burney, *A General History of Music* (London, 1776–89), III, 499–500.

72 *Roger North*, op. cit., 217.

73 Thelma Baldwin and Olive Wilson, 'Purcell's Sopranos', *Musical Times*, cxxiii (1982), 603.

74 Colley Cibber, *An Apology for the Life of Colley Cibber* (London, 1740), 94.

75 A discussion of the influence this appears to have had on the music of *The Fairy Queen* can be found in Curtis A. Price, op. cit., 344 ff.

76 Charles Ward, ed., *The Letters of John Dryden* (Duke, 1942), 53.

77 See Chapter 8.

78 Thomas Tudway, op. cit.

79 Thelma Baldwin and Olive Wilson, 'Richard Leveridge, 1670–1758; 1 Purcell and the Dramatick Operas', *Musical Times*, cxi (1970), 592; their claim that 'Purcell had not previously had a virtuoso bass singer available for stage music' and that we owe the elaborate music of *The Indian Queen* to his appearance is disputed by Curtis A. Price, op. cit., 130.

80 Charles Burney, op. cit., IV, 215.

81 Anthony Aston, *A Brief Supplement to Colley Cibber Esq; His Lives of the Late Famous Actors and Actresses* (The Author [London?], 1747), 18.

82 See Chapter 3, 43–4.

83 Michael Tilmouth, 'Grossi', *Grove VI*, VII, 744.

84 *Works I*, xxii.

85 Compare, for example, 'Young John the Gardener', 22 in *The Pleasant*

Musical Companion (London, 1686), a source cited by Squire, and 51 in *Works I*, xviii.

86 J. A. Westrup, 'Purcell', *Grove VI*, XV, 467.

87 See Paul Hillier, ed., *The Catch Book* (Oxford, 1987), 82.

88 In his biography of Francis North, Roger North recounts an afternoon of chamber music with Purcell, for when Francis was Keeper of the Great Seal, 'he caused the devine Purcell to bring his Itallian manner'd compositions; and with him on his harpsicord, my self and another violin, wee performed them more than once, of which Mr Purcell was not a little proud . . .'; see also John Hawkins, op. cit., IV, 507.

89 John Hawkins, op. cit., IV, 507.

90 Myles B. Foster, *Anthems and Anthem Composers* (London, 1901), 88: the catch, found in *GB-Lbl* Add. MS 29386, was published in *The Catch Club, or Merry Companions* (London, 1733), 30. This extraordinary circumstance was noticed by Michael J. Smith in 'The Church Music of Michael Wise', *Musical Times*, cxiv (1973), 73.

91 See, for example, 'The Third Part, containing Choice *Songs* for two Voices, Cantus & Bassus' in *The* SECOND BOOK *of the Pleasant Musical Companion* . . . (London, 1667, 2686).

III

'A COMPOSER FOR THE CHURCH AND CHAMBER'

5

Music for the Church

ERIC VAN TASSEL

The restoration of the monarchy in 1660 also meant the re-establishment of the Anglican Church, whose liturgy had been banned from public use for fifteen years. As a practical way to acquire a ready-made liturgical repertoire, the Chapel Royal and the principal cathedrals revived a substantial body of music from the pre-Civil War era. But they showed a decided preference for traditional full anthems and services over verse settings with solo voices – hoping, perhaps, by the very 'harmony and dignity of the Church style'[1] to support the established Church's claim to be the sole repository of England's 'primitive' religious tradition. One result was that constant exposure to the music of Tallis, Byrd and Gibbons gave young musicians – Henry Purcell among them – models of finely crafted, long-limbed polyphonic writing which would inform their own compositions.

But *gravitas* was not enough. To speak to laymen grown weary of the austerity and moralizing that had characterized much worship during the Commonwealth and Protectorate, liturgical music needed more drama and excitement, a more personal and outspoken mode, than classical polyphony could provide. And at a time when sectarian fervour had cost many lives, one may imagine the Church tolerating, even encouraging, in the choirstalls an emotional directness that would have been impolitic in the pulpit. As a consequence, the Chapel Royal anthem of this period wears its heart on its sleeve, acting out the extremes of penitential grief, righteous wrath and divine transport.

The texts of new anthems came almost exclusively from the psalter and collects of the Book of Common Prayer and from

the Authorized Version of the Bible. Perhaps composers, by general if tacit consent, thought thus to insure against stirring up controversy or falling, even inadvertently, into heterodoxy. Poetic anthem texts appear in the choirbooks only in early Stuart settings, while the ecstatic, almost erotic sort of devotional text set so effectively by Grandi or Carissimi would surely have been thought even more dangerous.

The Crown, too, took a close interest in anthem texts. For official fasts and thanksgivings, texts were specially chosen or assembled for their propaganda value – such as 'The Way of God Is an Undefiled Way' (z 56), 'King William then returned from Flanders'. And politics probably underlay, far more often than we can now prove, the selection or editing of anthem texts for ordinary or special Chapel Royal services, to support the official line on the issues of the day – implicitly identifying the much-plotted-against Charles II with the embattled King David of the Psalms, or even reading Isaiah's 'Suffering Servant' as an antetype of the martyred Charles I.[2]

But the King cared about more than just the words of anthems. He demanded that his Court, including his Chapel Royal, should equal in opulence and refinement the Bourbon Court at Paris and Versailles where he had spent his exile. He also required that when he went to pray he should not be bored; and since he 'never in his life could endure any [music] that he could not act by keeping the time',[3] he thought it quite reasonable that – when he was present for the service – the voices and the organ in his Chapel should be supported by a chamber group drawn from the royal violins, in the vivacious style that had become fashionable in France and Italy. When the composers of the Chapel Royal set about creating a repertoire of anthems featuring this violin consort, the results shocked some observers and delighted others, but could be ignored by none.[4]

A less conspicuous but ultimately more important innovation was the move away from polyphony and towards declamation over a basso continuo. The vocal line, liberated from its contrapuntal matrix, changed its phrasing and harmonic rhythm constantly, and personalized and dramatized the text with an explicit intensity of affect unknown to the Jacobeans.

Yet the new declamatory style, cross-bred with the violin band's stately *entrées* and lilting dance measures, was still tempered by its polyphonic inheritance and never crossed the line into outright recitative. In this respect, the near-total adherence to the language of the Bible and Prayer Book – embodying the Hebrew poets' technique of parallelism, and the pithy syntax and supple rhythms of sixteenth-century English – was of the greatest importance, and the language was a potent force in making Purcell's liturgical music quite unlike anything else he wrote.[5]

Purcell's anthems and services cover all the genres of his time, and as these genres are often differently defined by historians (using a variety of terminologies), it may be helpful to spell out the genre designations used in this chapter.[6]

In the **full anthem** and **full+verse anthem** the continuo is in effect a *basso seguente* following the lowest sounding voice part, and it could be omitted without serious harm to the musical logic (though *a cappella* performance was not envisaged in Purcell's time). The full+verse anthem (sometimes called 'full with

FIG. I   Liturgical genres, *c*1660–1700

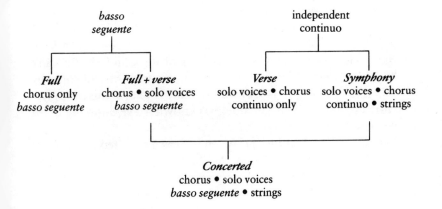

verses') differs from the full anthem in using, in alternation with the chorus, three or more soloists, who sing only as an ensemble and never as individuals. The continuo is theoretically optional in both verse and chorus sections (Ex. 25, 26).

The **verse anthem** and **symphony anthem** employ one or more solo voices and chorus, accompanied by a separate continuo part which is indispensable to the musical syntax (Ex. 4).[7] The symphony anthem is, in outline, a verse anthem to which a three- or four-part string ensemble has been added, to play an introductory 'symphony' and/or interludes ('ritornellos') and possibly to accompany the voices (Ex. 6, 8).[8]

The **concerted anthem** is a hybrid: its forces are those of a symphony anthem, but its musical fabric is approximately that of a full+verse anthem (i.e. there is no independent continuo, and the soloists sing only as an ensemble). The post-Restoration period saw only three genuine concerted anthems, those written by Blow and Purcell for the coronations of James II in 1685 and of William and Mary in 1689. As in the symphony anthem, the addition of the orchestral ensemble allows considerable formal elaboration; but in the absence of true solo verses these anthems retain the relatively impersonal mode of expression character-istic of full and full+verse anthems.

Henry Purcell, born less than a year before the restoration of Charles II, grew up immersed in the musical life of the Court and the Chapel Royal. Both his father and his uncle were Gentlemen of the Chapel and performers in the Private Musick; he began his musical career as a Child of the Chapel under Pelham Humfrey, and some time after he had left the choir (when his voice broke in 1673) he apparently studied with John Blow, Humfrey's successor as Master of the Children. By 1695 he had written at least seventy anthems – over fifty of them by 1685.[9] Although it is difficult to date some of his liturgical works with confidence,[10] enough is known to see this body of his work in four phases (see Fig. 2).

Up to c1679 (*see List 1*). When he was appointed Organist of Westminster Abbey about Michaelmas 1679, Purcell had already essayed every anthem genre at least once, including the symphony anthem (which could have found an outlet only at the Chapel Royal itself).[11] He gives the impression of having set out to master all the styles developed by Humfrey, Blow and Locke, testing the limits of each, with formal experiments such as 'Behold Now, Praise the Lord' (z 3), and a wide variety of expressive domains raging from the sensual beauty of 'My Beloved Spake' (z 28) to the intense drama of 'Turn Thou Us, O Good Lord' (z 62) and 'Blessed Be the Lord My Strength' (z 6) and the passionate gravity of 'Blow Up the Trumpet in Sion' (z 10).

c1680–82 (*see List 2*). Between the end of 1679 and the time of his appointment as one of the three Organists of the Chapel Royal in July 1682, along with a continuing stream of verse anthems, Purcell wrote most of his full and full+verse anthems and, at the end of this period, the full+verse Service in B flat and probably the Evening Service in G minor. To these years also belong four anthem-like works to Latin texts – probably intended for an ensemble of solo voices but no chorus, and best described as sacred madrigals with continuo – as well as a group of settings of contemporary metrical psalms and devotional texts probably composed for pious domestic entertainment.[12]

c1682–5 (*see List 3*). In a sudden shift of emphasis, from about 1682 to the early months of 1685 Purcell focused almost exclusively on symphony anthems. His appointment to the Chapel Royal – the only establishment where violins played a regular role in the service – obviously encouraged this change of direction; yet verse and full+verse anthems were always a regular part of the Chapel Royal repertoire, while a number of symphony anthems were copied for use at Westminster Abbey[13] (where presumably they were performed with the instrumental interludes reduced for the organ).[14] Two full anthems attributed to Purcell (z D4, z 59) may also date from this phase, which ends with his two anthems – one full, one concerted – for the coronation of James II.

In these years Purcell continued, if less avidly than in the past, to try out new formal and expressive approaches; this period saw the first anthems whose opening symphony uses an Italian-ate canzona (in 'Awake, Awake, Put On Thy Strength' (z 1) and 'I Was Glad' (z 19)) rather than a French-style 'tripla', and a

LIST 1   Anthems and related works c1676–80

	Z	date	genre	solos • chorus	strings	edition	text
My Beloved Spake	28	by c1677	Symphony	atbb • SATB	a4	Works II, xiii	Song of Sol. 2 +A
Turn Thou Us, O Good Lord	62	by c1678	Verse	atb • SATB		Works II, xxxii	BCP Collect
Lord, Who Can Tell How Oft He Offendeth	26	c1677	Verse	ttb • SATB		Works II, xxix	Psalm 19 +D
If the Lord Himself (fragment)	N66	c1677	Symphony	[-]b • [---]B	[a4]	Zimmerman I	Psalm 124 +A
Praise the Lord, Ye Servants (fragment)	N68	c1677	Symphony	[-]b • [---]B	[a4]	Zimmerman I	Psalm 113
Blow Up the Trumpet in Sion	10	by c1678	Full+verse	sssattb • SSAATTBB		Works II, xxviii	Joel 2
Behold Now, Praise the Lord	3	c1678	Symphony	atb • SATB	a4	Works II, xiii	Psalm 134 +D
O God, the King of Glory	34	by 2/1679	Full	• SATB		Works II, xxix	BCP Collect
I Will Sing unto the Lord	22	by 2/1679	Full+verse	ssa/atb[1] • SSATB		Works II, xxviii	Psalm 104
Blessed Be the Lord my Strength	6	by 2/1679	Verse	atb • SATB		Works II, xxviii	Psalm 144

Title	No.	Date	Type	Scoring	Source	Reference
Let God Arise	23	by 2/1679	Verse	tt • SATB	*Works II*, xxviii	Psalm 68
O Lord Our Governor	39	by 2/1679	Verse	sssbb • SATB	*Works II*, xxix	Psalm 8 +D
Blessed Is He Whose Unrighteousness . . .	8	late 1670s²	Verse	ssattb • SATB	*Works II*, xiii	Psalm 32 +A
Bow Down Thine Ear, O Lord	11	late 1670s²	Verse	satb • SATB	*Works II*, xiii	§ Psalm 86
O Consider My Adversity	32	[? by c1679]	Verse	atb • SATB	*Works II*, xxix	Psalm 119 (*Resh*) +D
Who Hath Believed Our Report?	64	c1679	Verse	attb • SATB	*Works II*, xiii	Isaiah 53
I Will Love Thee, O Lord	N67	[? c1679–80]	Verse	b • SATB	*Works II*, xxviii	Psalm 18
Save Me, O God	51	c1679–80²	Full+verse	ssa/atb¹ • SSATTB	*Works II*, xiii	Psalm 54
Out of the Deep Have I Called	45	? c1680	Verse	sab • SATB	*Works II*, xxxii	Psalm 130

Notes: ¹ ssa/atb = separate 3-part ensembles
² copied in autograph *GB-Cfm* 88: see List 2, n.1

§ discontinuous text verses (may indicate a topical anthem)
+A plus Alleluia
+D plus Doxology

LIST 2   Anthems and related works c1680–82

	Z	date	genre	solos • chorus	strings	edition	text
Gloria Patri et Filio	103	c1680	(Madrigal)	satb •		Works II, xxxii	Doxology
Jehova, Quam Multi Sunt Hostes Mei	135	c1680	(Madrigal)	ssatb		Works II, xxxii	Psalm 3
Beati Omnes Qui Timent Dominum	131	c1680	(Madrigal)	ssab		Works II, xxxii	Psalm 128 (Vulg. 127)
Domine, Non Est Exaltatum (torso)	102	c1680	(Madrigal)	[-]at[-] •		Works II, xxxii	Psalm 131 (Vulg. 130)
Hear Me, O Lord, and That Soon	13	c1679/ c1680–81¹	Verse	satb • SSATB		Works II, xiii	Psalm 143 +D
Give Sentence with Me, O God	12	by 11/1681	Verse	atb • SATB		8vo: Novello²	Psalm 43 +A
O Praise the Lord, All Ye Heathen	43	by 11/1681	Verse	tt • SATB		Works II, xxxii	Psalm 117 +D
Funeral Sentences (setting 1)	27	1670s/ c1680–82¹	Verse	satb • SATB		Works II, xiii	BCP Burial Service
Remember Not, Lord, Our Offences	50	c1680–82¹	Full	• SSATB		Works II, xxxii	BCP Litany
O God, Thou Hast Cast Us Out	36	c1680–82¹	Full+verse	ssaatb • SSAATB		Works II, xxix	Psalm 60
O Lord God of Hosts	37	c1680–82¹	Full+verse	ssaatb • SSAATTBB		Works II, xxix	Psalm 80

Title	z	Date	Type	Voicing	Source	Text
O God, Thou Art My God	35	c1680–82[1]	Full+verse	ssa/atb[3] • |:SATB:|[4]	*Works II*, xxix	Psalm 63 +A
Lord, How Long Wilt Thou Be Angry	25	c1680–82[1]	Full+verse	atb • SSATB	*Works II*, xxix	§ Psalm 79
O Lord, Thou Art My God	41	c1680–82[1]	Verse	atb • SATB	*Works II*, xxix	§ Isaiah 25 +A
Hear My Prayer, O Lord [part only?]	15	c1680–82[1]	[Full+verse]	• SSAATTBB	*Works II*, xxviii	Psalm 102
Let Mine Eyes Run Down with Tears	24	c1682	Verse	ssatb • SSATB	*Works II*, xxix	Jeremiah 14
Service (M/C/E) in B flat	230	by 10/1682	Full+verse	ssaatbb • |:SATB:|[4]	*Works I*, xxiii	BCP Liturgy
Hear My Prayer, O God	14	by 1683	Verse	atb • [s]ATB	*Works II*, xxviii	§ Psalm 55
Be Merciful unto Me	4	? by 1683	Verse	atb • SATB	*Works II*, xxviii	Psalm 56 +A
Magnificat and Nunc dimittis in G minor	231	[? by 1683]	Full+verse	ssaa/atb[3] • SATB	*Works I*, xxiii	BCP Liturgy

§   discontinuous text verses (may indicate a topical anthem)

+A plus Alleluia

+D plus Doxology

Notes:

[1] copied in autograph *GB-Cfm* 88 (the last 8 anthems, z 27–15, in this order)

[2] z 12 ed. E. Van Tassel & E. Higginbottom (Novello 1977)

[3] ssa/atb, ssa/atb = separate 3- and 4-part ensembles

[4] |:SATB:| = 4-part chorus with *decani/cantoris* exchanges

LIST 3   Anthems and related works c1682-5

	Z	date	genre	solos	• chorus	strings	edition	text
O God, They that Love Thy Name (inc.)	D4	[? c1682-5]	Full		• s[AT]B		Works II, xxxii	Psalm 5
Thy Righteousness, O God (inc.)	59	[? c1682-5]	Full		• s[AT]B		Works II, xxxii	Psalm 71
It Is a Good Thing to Give Thanks	18	c1682[1]	Symphony	atb	• SATB	a4	Works II, xiv	Psalm 92 +A
O Praise God in His Holiness	42	c1682-3[1]	Symphony	atbb	• SATB	a4	Works II, xiv	Psalm 150
Awake, Awake, Put On Thy Strength (inc.)	1	c1682-3[1]	Symphony	aab	• [SATB]	a4	Works II, xiv	Isaiah 51 +A
In Thee, O Lord, Do I Put My Trust	16	c1682-3[1]	Symphony	atb	• SATB	a4	Works II, xiv	§ Psalm 71 +A
The Lord Is My Light	55	c1683[1]	Symphony	atb	• SATB	a4	Works II, xiv	§ Psalm 27 +A
I Was Glad (setting 1)	19	c1683[1]	Symphony	atb	• SATB	a4	Works II, xiv	Psalm 122
My Heart Is Fixed, O God	29	c1683-5[1]	Symphony	atb	• SATB	a4	Works II, xiv	Psalm 57 +A
Praise the Lord, O My Soul, and All . . .	47	c1683-5[1]	Symphony	ssttbb	• SATB	a4	Works II, xiv	§ Psalm 103
Rejoice in the Lord Alway	49	c1683-5[1]	Symphony	atb	• s[AT]B	a4	Works II, xiv	Philippians 4
Why Do the Heathen . . .	65	c1684-5[1]	Symphony	atb	• SATB	a4	Works II, xvii	Psalm 2 +A

Title	Z	Date	Type		•	SATB	a	Source	Text
Unto Thee Will I Cry	63	*c*1684–5[1]	Symphony	atb	•	SATB	*a*4	*Works II*, xvii	Psalm 28 +A
I Will Give Thanks unto Thee, O Lord	20	early 1685[1]	Symphony	ssatb	•	SATB	*a*4	*Works II*, xvii	Psalm 138
They that Go Down to the Sea in Ships	57	early 1685[1]	Symphony	ab	•	SATB	*a*3	*Works II*, xxxii	Psalm 107
I Will Give Thanks unto the Lord	21	early 1685[2]	Symphony	tbb	•	SATB	*a*3	*Works II*, xxviii	Psalm 111
O Lord, Grant the King a Long Life	38	early 1685[2]	Symphony	atb	•	SATB	*a*3	*Works II*, xxix	§ Pss. 61/132
My Heart Is Inditing	30	for 4/1685[1]*	*Concerted*	ssaatbb	•	SSAATBBB	*a*4	*Works II*, xvii	§ Pss. 45/147, Is. 49 +A
I was Glad (*setting 2*)	—	for 4/1685	Full		•	SSATB		8vo: Novello[3]	Psalm 122 +D

Notes: [1] copied in this order (mostly autograph) in *GB-Lbl* RM 20.h.8
[2] these follow z 57 in RM 20.h.8 index only
[3] ed. B. Wood (Novello 1977)

* associated (by an early source) with a specific occasion

§ discontinuous text verses (may indicate a topical anthem)

+A plus Alleluia
+D plus Doxology

LIST 4   Anthems and related works c1686–95

	Z	date		genre	solos	• chorus	strings	edition	text
Thy Word Is a Lantern unto My Feet	61	? by c1686–7		Verse	atb	• SATB		*Works II,* xxxii	Psalm 119 (*Nun*) +A
Praise the Lord, O My Soul: O Lord . . .	48	1687†		Symphony	ab	• SATB	a3	*Works II,* xvii	§ Psalm 104
Thy Way, O God, Is Holy	60	1687†		Symphony[1]	ab	• SATB	a3	Gostling MS[2]	Psalm 77 +A
Sing unto God	52	1687†		Verse	b	• SATB		*Works II,* xxxii	Psalm 68 +A
Behold, I Bring You Glad Tidings	2	for 12/1687†		Symphony	atb	• SATB	a4	*Works II,* xxviii	Luke 2 +A
Blessed Are They that Fear the Lord	5	for 1/1688*		Symphony	ssab	• SATB	a4	*Works II,* xxviii	Psalm 128 +A
Blessed Is He that Considereth . . .	7	? c1688		Verse	atb	• SATB	a4	*Works II,* xxviii	Psalm 41 +D
O Sing unto the Lord	44	1688†		Symphony	sat/bb[3]	• SATB	a4	*Works II,* xvii	§ Psalm 96 +A
The Lord Is King, the Earth May Be Glad	54	1688†		Verse	b	• SATB		*Works II,* xxxii	Psalm 97 +A
Blessed Is the Man that Feareth . . .	9	for 12/1688*		Verse	ab[4]	• SATB		Gostling MS[2]	*Psalm 112* +A
Praise the Lord, O Jerusalem	46	for 4/1689		*Concerted*	ssatb	• SSATB	a4	*Works II,* xvii	§ Pss. 147/48/ 21, Is. 49 +A

The Lord Is King, and Hath Put On . . .	N69 [? c1689–90]	Verse	s	• SATB		*Works II*, xxxii	Psalm 93 +D
My Song Shall Be Alway	31 1690	Symphony	b	• SATB	a4	*Works II*, xxix	§ Psalm 89 +A
The Lord Is King, Be the People . . .	53 [? c1690–92]	Verse	ss	• SATB		*Works II*, xxxii	Psalm 99 +D +A
O Lord, Rebuke Me Not	40 c1692–3	Verse	ss	• SATB		*Works II*, xxix	Psalm 6
O Give Thanks unto the Lord	33 1693†	Verse[5]	satb	• SATB	[a3?]	*Works II*, xxix	§ Psalm 106
The Way of God Is an Undefiled Way	56 for 11/1694*	Verse	aab	• SAATB		*Works II*, xxxii	§ Psalm 18 +A
Te Deum and *Jubilate* in D	232 for 11/1694*	Symphony	ssaatb	• SSATB	a4+2Tr	*Works I*, xxiii	BCP Liturgy
Funeral Sentences (*setting 2*)	58C for 3/1695*	Full		• SATB		*Works II*, xxxii	BCP Burial Service

* associated (by an early source) with a specific occasion
† dated in a near-contemporary Ms
§ discontinuous text verses (may indicate a topical anthem)
+A plus Alleluia
+D plus Doxology

Notes:

[1] z 60 reworked (as verse anthem) *Works II*, xxxii

[2] *The Gostling Manuscript*, ed. F. B. Zimmerman (Austin and London, 1977)

[3] sat/bb = only 4 verse parts, variously satb and sabb

[4] z 9 reworked (for atb solos) *Works II*, xxviii

[5] z 33 printed as symphony anthem in *Works II*, but no source explicitly specifies strings

FIG. 2   Purcell's English anthems

Full	Full+verse	Verse	Symphony & Concerted
		c1676–80	
		c1680–2	
		c1682–5	
		c1686–95	

6 *full* anthems, counting z D4 and z 59 (here dated c168–2–5); z 58C (1695)

8 *full+verse* anthems, counting z 10 (c1678); z 51 (here dated c1679); z 15 (c1682)

29 *verse* anthems, counting z 27/17B/58B as one anthem (here dated c1680–82); z N69 (here dated c1689–90); z 33 (1693)

25 *symphony* anthems, counting z 60 (1687); 2 *concerted* anthems, viz. z 30 (1685) and z 46 (1689)

growing emphasis on the virtuosity of the Chapel Royal's singers.

c1686–95 (*see List 4*). Of the eighteen anthems scattered over the last ten years of Purcell's life, more than half are verse anthems; the remainder are symphony anthems, except for the concerted anthem 'Praise the Lord, O Jerusalem' (z 46) for the 1689 coronation and the full anthem 'Thou Knowest, Lord' (z 58C) sung at the burial of Queen Mary in March 1695. During these years, much of Purcell's time was claimed by theatre music and by odes and welcome songs (among which, stylistically, may be counted the *Te Deum* and *Jubilate* z 232, composed for St Cecilia's Day 1694). The proportion of symphony anthems in this period is very high, considering that the violins of the royal band were no longer in regular service at the Chapel Royal: if Purcell now got more than his fair share of their time, it may be because he seldom now wrote liturgical music except on commission for a special occasion.[15]

What makes the post-Restoration period 'the most picturesque in the history of English church music'[16] is its verse and symphony anthems. The verse-anthem genre already existed before 1600, but after 1600 it underwent a transformation: the musical language adopted a wide variety of new dialects, ranging from pure declamation to lyrical airs and dance measures; the spectrum of colours and textures was greatly enlarged, with voices in new relationships to one another and to the band of violins (now heard in English liturgical music for the first time); the mannered, word-centred style of the madrigal came into sharp confrontation with a musical rhetoric founded on the affect of an entire text, while both contended with the musicianly inclination to forgo affective detail for the sake of greater control of musical form.

An Elizabethan or Jacobean verse anthem usually has three or more verse sections, interleaved with choruses in what may be called an iambic sequence – v|F|v|F|v|F||. Although the verse sections may already be two or three times longer than the choruses, the alternation of chorus and verse punctuates the anthem and keeps soloists and chorus on an essentially equal footing.[17]

Purcell emulates this form in a few early anthems. The formal outline of the Funeral Sentences (z 27 – begun in the late 1670s and completed c1681–3)[18] is thoroughly Jacobean,[19] with three choruses, each a literal repeat of the preceding verse paragraph. The texture, a mix of homophony and imitation, looks on the page not unlike Gibbons or Tomkins; the use of an SATB ensemble throughout all the verses suppresses the soloist's overt self-dramatization. And Purcell builds his arch of affective tension with remarkably conservative means, yet reaches a climax at a level of intensity hardly encountered in the previous generation.

The part-writing, expressive but seldom naturalistic, produces unsettling harmonic transitions and tightens the screw of chromatic tension unrelentingly while using very little actual dissonance. The rising chromatic-scale fragment introduced just before Ex. 1 begins (d''-e^{b}''-$e^{\natural}''$-f'' in the treble on '*art justly dis*pleased') drives through all the parts, giving rise to a succession of augmented triads – a familiar enough harmony in the late seventeenth century, but one that in Purcell's music often carries special affective weight. There is a break in the clouds at bar 94, with the unlooked-for brightness of A major after C minor; but the shift from F minor to D major in bar 97 requires a wrenching linear progression in the exposed treble part[20] before the final ascent to a chord that combines d^{b}-g'-f'' in bar 99.

In terms of form, the Funeral Sentences was old-fashioned even before Purcell was born. The Jacobeans had already begun to vary the groupings of solo voices within an anthem, but they normally did so in discrete paragraphs separated by choruses: a solo verse (say) would not typically run into a four-part verse without an intervening chorus. The crucial change after 1660, the radical reduction of the role of the chorus, juxtaposes verse paragraphs – which might differ in texture, idiom, and even metre – without choral punctuation (e.g. Ex. 10, bars 32f). The verse anthem as Purcell received it from the hands of Humfrey and Blow was thus substantially vocal chamber music, to which the chorus adds an occasional glorious noise at strategic moments. A recurring theme in his anthems is his efforts to avert

EX. 1 Henry Purcell: Funeral Sentences (z 27), bars 79–102

EX. I *(contd.)*

the risk – a product of the very fecundity of the composer's imagination – that the anthem would degenerate into a string of unrelated events.[21]

Even if the division between verse paragraphs is normally marked by a discernible cadence, and the new verse almost always begins with new text, the ear nevertheless still asks for a clear indication of closure.[22] One of the most effective of such indicators is the echo-cadence – the immediate repetition of a final phrase, which may be a few notes or several bars in length. The repetition is most often literal (Ex. 2, verse; Ex. 3, chorus; Ex. 15, symphony), but it may involve some adaptation (Ex. 3, verse; Ex. 15, verse), or all may change except a melody line (Ex. 15, ritornello).

In large-scale formal terms, the most prominent landmark in the verse anthem is the chorus movement. In around three-quarters of Purcell's verse anthems, the chorus either appears only once, to end the anthem, or enters to mark a notional 'halfway' point and then returns (perhaps with identical music)

EX.   2   Henry Purcell: 'O Give Thanks' (z 33), bars 125–36

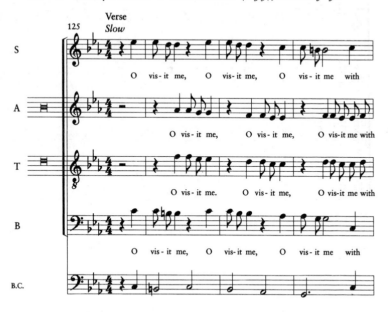

to end the work. In two-thirds of his surviving symphony anthems, the chorus remains silent until the final paragraph.[23]

There are only a handful of exceptions to these stereotyped uses of the chorus. 'I Was Glad' (setting 1, z 19), 'Unto Thee Will I Cry' (z 63), and 'Behold, I Bring You Glad Tidings' (z 2) modify – sometimes profoundly – the balance and proportions of the two-chorus form for programmatic reasons. 'O Lord, Grant the King a Long Life' (z 38), hastily assembled during the King's illness in 1685, has no chorus save for a few Amens.[24] 'O Sing unto the Lord' (z 44, 1688) and 'O Give Thanks unto the Lord' (z 33, 1693) leave the post-Restoration verse-anthem tradition behind, not only casting the chorus in the role of the congregation of all believers, in a form of play-acting,[25] but, more important, exploring quite new formal approaches in which soloists and chorus interact more freely.

In pursuit of formal unity, a chorus may be linked thematically to a preceding verse paragraph through literal repetition (Ex. 1), more or less direct rescoring (Ex. 3), or substantial revision or recomposition (Ex. 4). The ear is also offered a recognizable connection when the chorus uses new thematic material, but set to the same text as the verse, perhaps with a thematic allusion to the verse material. In Ex. 5 (in a tactic perhaps suggested by the echo-cadence), the chorus becomes more like the verse as it proceeds (bars 50f/55f). The penultimate chorus of 'O Sing unto the Lord' ('O worship the Lord') begins with a rescoring of the verse but continues with new text, set to new thematic material that is distinctively choral in conception.

When Charles II gave orders that a contingent of violins

EX. 3   Henry Purcell: 'I Will Give Thanks unto the Lord' (z 21), bars 257–86

should serve in the Chapel Royal, the composers there had no pattern for what music the violins should play; both viols and wind instruments had been used in English church music before the Interregnum, but the violin consort came from a different and hitherto wholly secular culture. The solution they devised was to borrow forms and idioms that the same violinists played for the King's secular entertainment.[26] So the anthem usually opens with a stately introduction in slow duple metre, whose associations with a royal procession or *entrée* could be explained as invoking the presence of the monarch of heaven. The dancelike 'tripla' that normally follows, giving the King something to keep time to, could be interpreted as a dance of joy before the Lord or a grave and graceful meditation.

Purcell seems to have adopted the premiss without much questioning it. Of his twenty-three surviving symphony

EX. 4 Henry Purcell: 'Blessed Be the Lord My Strength' (z 6), bars 31–44

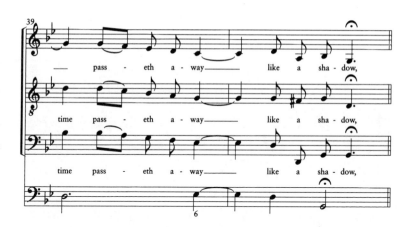

EX. 4 (contd.)

anthems, fourteen have two-movement symphonies of the
duple+triple type, and four have a tripla movement only.[27] Of
these anthems, twelve mark the 'halfway' point with a literal
repeat of all or part of the opening symphony;[28] one other
anthem repeats instead the ritornello that follows the first
verse.[29]

The verses in a symphony anthem naturally tend to build
thematic links with the ritornellos even more than with
choruses, but through much the same means: straight rescoring
of a verse, thematic derivation from verse material (Ex. 9), or –
less often – anticipation of an *ensuing* verse, either by rescoring
or by thematic derivation (Ex. 15).[30] 'O Sing unto the Lord'
shows a later stage of formal evolution in several respects, one
of which is illustrated in Ex. 6. The opening motif of the symphony (*a*) forms the outline of the fugue subject in the canzona
that follows (*b*) and returns in inversion during the fugue (*c*),
before reappearing as the start of the first verse, where the continuo line enters into an enthusiastic imitative exchange with the
voice (*d*).

Following Humfrey's example, Purcell sometimes repeats not

EX. 5 Henry Purcell: 'Blessed Is He Whose Unrighteousness Is Forgiven' (z 8), bars 45–56

EX.   5   (*contd.*)

a single verse, ritornello, or chorus but a larger sequence of paragraphs – e.g. a verse-ritornello pair, or a verse-chorus pair – as in Fig. 3.[31] From there it is a short step to the repetition, or thematic development, of a motif or phrase as a refrain. One of Purcell's most engaging examples is in 'Blessed Are They that Fear the Lord' (z 5). As the blessings of patriarchy are enumerated in a series of declamatory solos, each is endorsed by a pair of trebles – the voices of children or of angels – on the refrain 'O well is thee!' When the bass embarks on an accompanied *arioso* on a broader scale, we perforce assume that the 'Well is thee' refrain has served its purpose; so its return at bar 135 is a surprise. After another (still longer) lyrical interlude for the alto in triple metre, the refrain returns yet again and seizes the reins altogether: only now, with all four solo voices (in antiphonal pairs) taking up the refrain theme for the first time, are the words 'O well is thee' allowed to reach their conclusion 'and happy shalt thou be'.[32]

EX. 6 Henry Purcell: 'O sing unto the Lord' (z 44):
(*a*) bars 1–7, (*b*) bars 19–22, (*c*) bar 26, (*d*) bars 45–51

EX. 6 *(contd.)*

(c)

(d)

The primary force that propels a Purcell anthem forward, however, is not its architectural form but the expressive setting of the
text. The most radical innovation in the post-Restoration verse-
anthem idiom was the transformation of musical speech by the
introduction of two new elements. First, with the violin band
came a bluff, dancelike melodic and rhythmic phraseology from
across the English Channel; secondly, the independent continuo
liberated the vocal parts and challenged them to dramatize the
text. And that challenge awoke Purcell's deep enthusiasm for
the madrigalian tradition of word-painting or pictorialism – the
use of distinctive musical gestures to illustrate words or phrases.

Purcell's word-painting, ranging from the most direct ono-
matopoeia to the most subtle intellectual symbolism, is in-
separable from expressiveness. The dotted-quaver–semiquaver
melismas that mimic 'the singing of birds' also express delight at

FIG. 3   'Thy Way, O God, Is Holy' (z 60), 1687

		no. of bars*	text	musical links	
¶1	symphony	16		anticipates ¶2a	A^1
¶2a	verse	26	'Thy way, O God'		A^2
¶2b	ritornello	8		evolves from ¶2a	A^3
¶3a^1	verse	8	'Thou art the God'		B
¶3a^2	|	20	'Thou art the God'		
¶3c	|	26	'Thy way, O God'	identical to ¶2a	A^2
¶4	symphony	16		identical to ¶1	A^1
¶5a	verse	24	'The voice'		
¶5b	ritornello	8		identical to ¶2b	A^3
¶6a	verse	8	'Thou art the God'	identical to ¶3a^1	B
¶6b	|	26	'Thy way, O God'	identical to ¶2a	A^2
¶7	chorus	7	'Alleluia'		
total		193			

*Not counting probable but undocumented repeats

the coming of spring ('My Beloved Spake'); those that depict stylized laughter on such words as 'felicity' or 'rejoice' also embody the exhilaration of faith (e.g. 'the felicity of thy chosen' in 'O Give Thanks unto the Lord', z 33; 'glad' in Ex. 15).[33] The same word is visualized in '*round* about thy table' ('Blessed Are They that Fear the Lord', z 5)[34] and in 'the *round* world' (Ex. 8); but the one plays lightly on the subtext of family merriment, while the other opens out to embrace a universe. A descending scale in steady crotchets not only mimes the movement of those who 'fear the Lord and walk in his ways' ('Blessed Are They') but also (supported by a rich euphony of parallel thirds and sixths) makes their inner faith visible. In 'I Was Glad', setting 1 (z 19), as 'the tribes go up' on a rising point of imitation, the voices gradually converge rhythmically, but they do not actually meet until the last quaver of the common-time section, on '(Isra)el'. At that cadence they sound as if standing on tiptoe with eagerness 'to testify unto Israel', and their pent-up joy breaks out in the tripla on 'to give thanks' and whirls into a dance of exultation.

The pictorial merges almost imperceptibly into the metaphorical in the falling fourths of 'they die' (Praise the Lord, O My Soul: O Lord My God', z 48) or the agitated scotch snaps of 'pluck me not away' and 'break them down' ('Unto Thee Will I Cry', z 63). The dulcet harmonies of 'the voice of the turtle' ('My Beloved Spake') are not a world away from the reposeful consonances of 'the peace of God that passeth all understanding' ('Rejoice in the Lord Alway', z 49).

Some of Purcell's most vivid pictorialisms exploit the qualities of the voice itself. The treble who begins 'Out of the Deep' (z 45) at the bottom of his range sounds faltering and discouraged, but his voice gains strength – and hope – as he rises through an octave to call hopefully upon God. Depending on the context, a fall to a low tessitura – where the voices of necessity grow muffled and faint – may be acting out furtiveness ('they lay wait for my soul' in 'Be Merciful unto Me', z 4) or 'reverence' ('Why Do the Heathen So Furiously Rage', z 65); a similar descent accompanies 'the sheep before his shearers is dumb' and 'openeth he not his mouth' in 'Who Hath Believed Our Report' (z 64). Such effects can also be metaphorical, as when prayer begins 'secretly among the faithful' but the chord-spacing grows clearer and brighter 'in the congregation' (see Ex. 7).

In a lighter vein, pictorialism can include a kind of role-playing or vocal dressing-up. It is tempting to imagine Purcell, in a mischievous mood, scoring 'O Lord Our Governor' (z 39) for the unusual verse group of SSSBB just so that he could give the 'babes and sucklings' verse to three trebles. Several instances of acted-out dialogue convey just that faintly Gilbertian air:

> (soloist expresses the wish) 'O that men would . . .';
>   (chorus complies) 'O praise the Lord' ('They that Go
>   Down to the Sea in Ships', z 57)
> (soloist) 'O Lord, grant the King . . .', (chorus of loyal
>   subjects) 'Amen' ('O Lord, Grant the King a Long Life',
>   z 38)

EX. 7 Henry Purcell: 'I Will Give Thanks unto the Lord' (z 21),
bars 51–7

(*angel*) 'Behold . . .', (*angelic choir*) 'Glad tidings'
  ('Behold, I Bring You Glad Tidings', z 2)
(*soloist*) 'let all the people say' (*chorus*) 'Amen' ('O Give
  Thanks unto the Lord', z 33)

When the soloist in 'O Sing unto the Lord' demands 'a *new*
song', the choir offers a new metre;[35] when he addresses his
second request to 'all the whole earth', the response changes
from imitation to the more massive – universal? – homophony.

EX. 8   Henry Purcell: 'O Sing unto the Lord' (z 44), bars 267–76

273

made the round___ world so sure_ that it can - not be mov - ed.

round___ world so sure___ that it can - not be mov - ed.

round___ world so sure that it can - not be mov - ed.

Verse

made the round___ world_ so_ sure_ that it can - not be mov-ed.

In Ex. 8³⁶ (as elsewhere), acting-out is not only a harmless conceit but a subliminal way of involving the hearer in the community's declaration of faith.

Yet in an utterly different kind of role-playing, in 'Who Hath Believed Our Report', a repeated fragment of text acquires a peculiar rhetorical force, as if the prophet were unable to contain his grief or his outrage: 'he was taken from prison to judgment – [*higher pitch*: just think of it!] from *prison* to *judgment*!'

In the late-Renaissance madrigal, word-painting sometimes asked the hearer to make a rarefied intellectual connection – say, between open semibreves and 'eyes', or black notation and 'night' – and the ability to perceive such recondite allusions may have been one mark of a true connoisseur. Some of Purcell's imagery seems to ask an analogous intellectual leap. There is 'the laborious effort to push what "cannot be moved" '[37] in Ex. 8 (cf. the similar circling motion on 'yet do I not swerve' in 'O Consider My Adversity', z 32). Fanfare-like figures in dotted rhythms are vivid images of war (e.g. the reveille that begins 'Awake, Awake, Put On Thy Strength', z 1, not only in the opening verse but in both movements of the symphony): from there it is but a short step to imagery of kingship, and thence to the grave processional measures of a royal *entrée* – and who but God is entitled to royal music?[38] So when the soloist in 'O Sing unto the Lord' offers to 'declare his honour', he does so in the proud rhythm of a royal procession.

Long-held notes, unchanging harmonies and/or prolonged melismas or sequences constantly recur for *topoi* ranging from 'a long life' ('O Lord, Grant the King a Long Life', z 38), 'stand fast for ever' ('I Will Give Thanks unto the Lord', z 21), through 'set me up upon a rock' ('The Lord Is My Light', z 55) and 'I do not forget' ('O Consider My Adversity'), to 'everlasting' and 'world without end' ('O Give Thanks', z 33, one instance among many). But when in 'O Give Thanks' a comparably florid skein of notes unwinds on 'all his praise' and even on 'the noble acts of the Lord', another kind of symbolism may be at work, which might be called the ornamentation of nobility. The wealth of embellishment in Ex. 9[39] may be an aural analogue of the fine and costly stuffs worn only by the nobility, or of the rich and subtle carvings that adorn only the dwellings of the high and mighty. By the same token, the appreciation of such craftsmanship (whether Grinling Gibbons's or Purcell's or Gostling's) is a cultural refinement denied to the low-born. This interpretation, though it may seem far-fetched, would explain not only the motivation but also the intuitive aptness of the roulades and sequences that proliferate around references to the deity (e.g. 'how excellent is thy name' in 'O Lord Our Governor'); and noble ornament merges with gestures of strife and triumph in the bravura style of the 1680s, as the psalmist speaks of the majesty of the King of Glory as well as the wrath of the God of Battles.

EX. 9   Henry Purcell: 'O Give Thanks' (z 33), bars 89–111

EX. 9 *(contd.)*

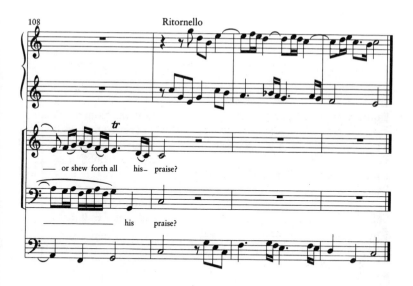

Another kind of intellectual or conceptual image-making appeals to the hearer's awareness of musical concepts themselves. When Purcell begins 'In Thee, O Lord, Do I Put My Trust' (z 16) with a ground bass – one of only seven or eight in his whole anthem corpus – the ten unvarying statements of a five-bar bass figure noteworthy for its directness, which then supplies the motivic material for the upper parts, prepare us for the anthem's theme of unwavering trust in God. Pictorialism of this kind reaches an apogee in 'Rejoice in the Lord Alway', whose very form is one overarching metaphor. The text 'Rejoice . . . alway, and again I say rejoice' leads Purcell straight to this strategy: to act out the words 'again I say' he recalls the main tripla section for verse and chorus[40] repeatedly, almost obsessively (Fig. 4): there are contrasting passages of great beauty, but none can prevail over the tripla, and the last words of the verse trio are still '. . . and again'.

Most satisfying of all, however, is when individual images converge to work in concert. The second verse of 'Hear My Prayer, O God' (z 14 – see Ex. 10) is such a concentration of images. A chromatic tremor of the voice on 'disquieted'

FIG. 4   'Rejoice in the Lord Alway' (z 49), c1682–5

		no. of bars*	text	musical links	
¶1	prelude	31			
¶2	verse	12	'Rejoice'		A^1
¶3a	ritornello	24		evolved from ¶2	A^2
¶3b	|	24		related to ¶3a	B
¶4	verse	12	'Rejoice'	identical to ¶2	A^1
¶4b	ritornello	2		cadence from ¶3a	
¶4c	verse	11	'Let your'		
¶5	chorus	21	'Rejoice'	derived from ¶2	A^3
¶6a	ritornello	24		identical to ¶3a	A^2
¶6b	|	24		identical to ¶3b	B
¶7a	verse	22	'Be careful'		
¶7b	|	16	'And the peace'		Z
¶7c	ritornello	16		evolved from ¶7b	Z
¶8	verse	12	'Rejoice'	identical to ¶2	A^1
¶9	ritornello	12		identical to ¶3a	A^2
¶10	chorus	21	'Rejoice'	identical to ¶5	A^3
¶1–5		137			
¶6–10		147			
total		284			

*Counting repeats

(intensified by voice-pairing on the restatement) is immediately followed by a coda with more affective themes, a quaking melisma (incorporating a diminished fourth) for 'trembling', a falling major seventh for 'horrible dread', and a tumbling, headlong fall on 'overwhelmed'.[41] In Ex. 20 the bass's figure in bar 89, too 'heavy' to rise, and his 'disquieted' line in bar 91 are answered by the balm of diatonic thirds in the upper voices.

In 'Let God Arise' (z 23), Purcell's essay in the duet style of Monteverdi or Grandi, the two voices vie to outdo one another in word-painting. On 'Let God arise' a vaulting rise of an octave becomes a ninth; on 'enemies be scattered' a plunging fall in semiquavers is elongated on repetition. The ungodly 'flee'

EX. 10 Henry Purcell: 'Hear My Prayer, O God' (z 14), bars 22–37

EX. 10 (contd.)

(scotch snap); 'as the smoke vanisheth' (a drop of an octave; and
the last word is muttered to 'vanishing' semiquavers) they are
'driven' (the voices 'drive' one another through a chain of
suspensions); 'as wax melteth at the fire' (viscous syncopations
in a slow melisma) so 'the ungodly perish' (by being hurled to
the bottom of each tenor's range). After all that turmoil in just
thirty-five bars, the chorus is entitled to 'let the righteous be
glad' in a dancing tripla. In the second verse movement, it is the
faithful who witness the power of the Lord, beginning with a
pair of canonic phrases at the unison: one voice 'leads' the other
up the scale on 'thou wentest forth . . .' and down again on
'thou wentest through the wilderness'. 'The earth shook' is
depicted not just with a tremor of semiquavers but also with a
seismic fault line – an unmediated shift from A major to C
minor.

Some of Purcell's finest inventions, marrying naturalism and
expressiveness, are in the Funeral Sentences. There is affective
power in the sudden drop in pitch at 'full of *misery*' or in the
way that 'secrets of our hearts', shifting abruptly to a low tessitura, forces each singer to find a quieter, more confiding quality
of voice. The rising and falling line of 'He cometh up and is cut
down' is almost too graceful for its subject matter; but Purcell
reminds us of that matter by drawing the falling line further

down each time – at first an octave, but finally as much as an eleventh in the bass – and when the phrase concludes with '. . . is cut down like a flower' he adds a wan little ornament in the alto.

Mirroring the arch of 'cometh up . . . cut down' on a more probing level of meaning, an aspiring rise on 'In the midst of life' is cut off sharply, and the line plunges precipitously on 'we are in death'. The imitation on 'ne'er continueth in one stay' sends an unsettled, disjunct line wandering through the voices (half of the entries falsify the natural word-stresses by entering a crotchet 'late'), and Purcell underlines the idea of restlessness with a plethora of false relations.

The constant movement from one affect or image to the next enlivens and energizes the anthem, but it also challenges the composer to maintain coherence and consistency: to write declamatory movements that are neither shapeless recitative nor an aimless, anecdotal stroll from one dazzling gesture to the next.

The survival of classical polyphony (thanks to the extensive revival of older church music) offered Chapel Royal composers a living model of a shapely line and a sense of tonal planning. The language of the Prayer Book and the Bible, imbued with the parallelism that is the heartbeat of Hebrew poetry, fostered the moulding of 'musical prose' into balanced periods – in effect, antecedent and consequent.

In Ex. 11 the psalmist, by building the first and third phrases upon parallel metaphors of distance, invites Purcell to draw matching wide arcs: rising and falling in bars 233ff, falling and rising in bars 238f. Thus the nine bars form a single bipartite clause, with each of these two extreme gestures forming an antecedent that is answered by a more contained melodic consequent over a slightly more mobile bass.

The propensity of Elizabethan English to fall into something approaching a free metrical gait contributes to an early example of the stylizing of Purcell's declamation in Ex. 12. The twining melisma on 'green' makes an audible allusion to fecundity that is wonderfully apposite to the words, but it must have been motivated as much by the impulse towards songlike stylization, for

EX. 11   Henry Purcell: 'Praise the Lord, O My Soul, and All that Is
Within Me' (z 47), bars 233–53

the melisma which prolongs 'green' transforms a line of biblical prose into the balanced rhythm of a poetic couplet.[42]

The ordering of through-composed antecedent and consequent into well-rounded declamatory periods relies constantly on artful repetition, of a few syllables or of an entire phrase; inexact repetition opens the door to variety and tonal movement. Verbal parallelism, as in Ex. 11, suggests an equally fruitful musical parallelism; the declamatory composer falls into the habit of saying everything twice. When the things he says are as outlandish as Ex. 13, the repetition convinces us that they really did happen and lets us savour them twice; lengthening the clause by repeating each half allows greater tonal variety; and sometimes the second statement actually trumps the first – in Ex. 13, by rising higher and sinking deeper.

Even more promising than saying the same thing twice is saying almost the same thing twice. In Ex. 14, the second 'who teacheth . . . to fight' is (as it were) the cousin of the first, repeating its rhythm but imposing a quite new melodic line. Thus the antecedent generates its own consequent, unlocking new expressive potential in the same text: the first statement, taking a cue from the phrase before, focuses on pitch-accenting key

EX. 12　Henry Purcell: 'My Beloved Spake' (z 28), bars 174–94

words – *strength, war, fight* – but the restatement, a rhythmic cousin, forsakes that approach in favour of warlike imagery, with common-chord notes that suggest a bugle-call.

Ex. 14 also shows how Purcell's vocal lines evolve from freer declamation to more organized shaping, even within a single declamatory phrase, which becomes more formal or more song-like as it proceeds: here it is only at 'my strength' (as in Ex. 18, at 'and to whom') that the ear begins to believe it can trust the barlines.

Notwithstanding this impulse towards greater lyricism, the declamatory style remains at heart anti-metrical and anti-periodic; but it plays off against the other new element in post-Restoration style, the 'tripla' – instrumental in origin, and infused with springy dance rhythms in stereotyped patterns (♩♩. ♪│♩. ♪♪) and simple hemiolas (♩. ♪♪│♩ ♩. ♪) from Versailles. The language of the tripla – utterly new to English church music in the 1660s, and virtually obsolete by the end of the century – becomes the genre's most distinctive sound and its strongest

EX.   13   Henry Purcell: 'I Will Give Thanks unto Thee, O Lord'
(z 20), bars 235–46

secularizing influence. Indeed, 'My beloved is mine' in 'My Beloved Spake', 'Therefore will I praise thee' in 'I Was Glad' (setting 1) and 'As long as I live' in the full+verse anthem 'O God, Thou Art My God' (z 35) are all dances – if perhaps dances before the altar.

An excess of strictly regular triplas for Alleluias and instrumental movements is, as many critics have suggested, one of the weakest features of post–1660 anthem style. Like his contemporaries, Purcell does seem to resort to a tripla when he can't

EX. 14 Henry Purcell: 'Blessed Be the Lord My Strength' (z 6), bars I–II

think of anything more distinctive. But sometimes the setting of words to music is just that: 'setting', as a jeweller sets a fine stone, providing the words with a background and showcase: thus in 'Give Sentence with Me' (z 12), 'and defend my cause . . . O deliver me from the deceitful and wicked man' is all set to the same relentlessly genial quick tripla.

But it will not do to think of triple metre only as an ebullient dance measure. The tripla sometimes resolves the tension of a declamatory episode: the bass solo in 'In Thee, O Lord, Do I Put My Trust' (z 16) to the words 'O what great troubles and adversities . . .' becomes a mere prelude to the tripla on 'Yet didst thou turn and refresh me'. In 'Behold, I Bring You Glad Tidings' (z 2), the response to the principal angel's solemn 'Behold . . .' is a joyous tripla from a celestial trio. The tripla is also an apt idiom for many of the lyrical airs, with rounded songlike shape and a strong sense of formal closure, that are the Purcell anthem's nearest approach to the genuinely discrete movements of the Continental cantata (Ex. 15).

Some of these set-pieces frankly set aside the ideal of speech-rhythm in favour of more shapely melodic form; but some lesser airs succeed in drawing the natural 'feet' of biblical prose into equally natural metrical periods. In Ex. 16 the words (as edited by Purcell, to be sure) fall so naturally into anapaests or dactyls that they cry out for a tripla, and the steadily climbing crotchets are aimed like an arrow at the goal of the ascent – the altar.[43] But Purcell, taking care to avoid the obvious, lengthens the first phrase from four bars to five on its repeat (bars 65–9); and the final 'O Lord my God' (bars 78ff) at first resists the expected four-bar shape, to enhance the impact of the restatement, which does grant the fulfilment of a four-bar conclusion (bars 85–8).

Purcell normally assigns such *arioso* passages to alto or tenor soloists; a rare exception for bass is the late anthem 'My Song Shall Be Alway' (z 31), where both the opening paragraph and the final Alleluia are in a more lyrical vein than the usual bravura bass solos. Such music is not for just any singer; many of Purcell's anthems clearly require soloists of exceptional gifts, for along with lyrical airs and sprightly dance pieces go vivid examples of word-painting that demand both unusual agility and an exceptional range.

Unlike the Caccinian style, which had a brief vogue in Caroline England with Porter and others,[44] Purcell's broken-chord figures and hurtling runs, daredevil leaps, sharply dotted rhythms and rapid-fire declamation all move within an active and purposeful harmonic space. Even in an early work like 'O Lord Our Governor' (z 39, by 1679), the line starts to form

EX. 15 Henry Purcell: 'I Was Glad', setting 1 (z 19), bars 7–80

EX. 15 (contd.)

EX. 15 (*contd.*)

EX. 16 Henry Purcell: 'Give Sentence with Me' (z 12), bars 61–88
(ed. E. Van Tassel and E. Higginbottom)

embryonic sequences and ordered periods that look forward to the later Baroque. In the course of the 1680s, sequence (an idea that is, of course, inherent in European art music) becomes a distinct characteristic of Purcell's bravura writing, as an outgrowth of the habit of phrase-repetition: see e.g. Ex. 20, bar 89, or the bracketed figures in Ex. 9 and 10.

While pictorialism continues to play a significant role in virtuoso passages in the anthems of Purcell's last decade, he seems less than ever satisfied with imagery or virtuosity alone; increasingly, melismatic or florid figures also obey a formalizing impulse to group themselves into pairs or small sequences in such works as 'Blessed Is the Man' (z 9), 'Blessed Are They that Fear the Lord' (z 5), 'Blessed Is He that Considereth the Poor' (z 7), 'The Lord Is King, Be the People Never So Impatient' (z 53), and 'The Way of God Is an Undefiled Way' (z 56). And in these years the sequence becomes more important (even if embellishment is not involved) as a force for order and coherence, in, for example, 'O Sing unto the Lord' (z 44, 1688); Ex. 6 (symphony and first verse); and 'O Give Thanks' (1693), Ex. 9. The solo anthems 'The Lord Is King, the Earth May Be Glad' (z 54, 1688) and 'My Song Shall Be Alway' (z 31, 1690) are still more thoroughly saturated with sequences.

Purcell included such bravura showpieces in some anthems almost from the start of his career; but virtuosity as such began to loom larger in his work when the 'stupendious base'[45] John Gostling joined the Chapel Royal in 1679. Even then, his talents were featured somewhat cautiously at first, and it seems that only after 1682 – when Purcell himself became one of the Organists of the Chapel Royal and presumably could be surer of getting the right singer for a particularly challenging assignment – did he make a point of including a set-piece for bass in almost every anthem (Ex. 11, 13).

The virtuoso bass solos of 'It Is a Good Thing to Give Thanks' (z 18) and 'O Praise God in His Holiness' (z 42 – both c1682) are still integrated with the ATB trio, whose other members also get their moment in the sun; but it is a straw in the wind when, a year or two later, 'Why Do the Heathen' (z 65) and 'Unto Thee Will I Cry' (z 63) both give the opening verse to the bass alone.

Here Purcell is testing the limits of the soloist's unusual range (in some cases with the safety-valve of an *ossia* line); but after the two-and-a-half-octave climax of 'I Will Give Thanks unto Thee' (z 20), including unmediated leaps of a tenth and a twelfth (Ex. 13 – probably dated early in 1685), Purcell does not hesitate to ask the singer for what he wants.

'They that Go Down to the Sea in Ships' (z 57, apparently dating from early in 1685) represents a breakthrough: as if accepting that even Gostling might be nearing the limits of sheer acrobatics, Purcell now offers him instead a vehicle that is musically more mature and stylistically better integrated. The piece holds together exceptionally well, starting with a symphony tripla that anticipates both main themes of the following verse. Every bar of that verse is alive with exceptionally vivid imagery: dazzling contrasts of height and depth, climaxing on 'carried up to heaven and down again to the deep', on which (as in Ex. 13) the restatement climbs higher and plunges deeper; uniquely colourful figures for 'their soul melteth', 'they reel to and fro', and 'stagger'; and finally a hint of punch-drunk fuddlement on 'at their wit's end'. All these startling images are linked by the unceasing rocking of the waves in triple time, by a constant imitative interplay between voice and continuo, and by the exceptional use of the violins to accompany the verse throughout. After that uproarious verse, however, we might overlook the strength and unity of the rest of the anthem, which is entirely shared by bass and alto: the chromatic 'cry unto the Lord', the deft picturing of the storm's end by recalling earlier figuration but with gradually relaxing intensity, the dual acting-out of 'the waves . . . are still' (Ex. 17: first a generous use of the dramatic power of silence, then a dynamic marking rare if not unique for its time).

The virtuoso alto soloist shares the spotlight with the bass in this way throughout the years 1682–5 and beyond (cf. Ex. 9). The Chapel Royal at this time boasted several very fine high and low countertenors (Turner, Boucher, Howell, Damascene), but the high countertenor John Abell was apparently regarded as exceptional, and it seems that a number of virtuoso anthems were written specifically to show off the team of Gostling and

Abell.[46] In several of these anthems ('I Will Give Thanks unto the Lord', z 21; 'Sing unto God', z 52; 'The Lord Is King, the Earth May Be Glad'; 'My Song Shall Be Alway') Purcell introduces a new vein of declamatory *arioso*, a driving vocal line over a 'motoric' bass; and few of these anthems are without at least

EX.   17   Henry Purcell: 'They that Go Down to the Sea in Ships'
(z 57), bars 133–53

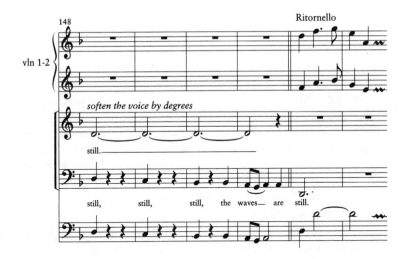

one verse paragraph that is more reflective and allows the soloist(s) to display another kind of prowess. But at times Purcell seems to be taking the easy way out – as when he recycles the 'still waves' of 'They that Go Down to the Sea' for 'Praise the Lord, O My Soul: O Lord My God' (z 48) without recapturing the expressive commitment or, especially, the strongly motivated tonal structure of the original.[47]

To Humfrey and those he influenced, who set such a high value on expressive, speech-like word-setting, the disciplined interplay of parts in ensemble writing must have seemed cool and impersonal; and classical imitation, in particular, would always threaten both to dull the declamatory edge and to obscure the words. Yet the pull of polyphony was also strong, for it offered a wider palette of timbres and textures and the potential for greater harmonic interest and formal organization on a larger scale.

One solution to this dilemma was the subject-answer dialogue[48] – a technique that might also be called 'imitation at a distance', as if stretching the time-interval of classical imitation so far that entries overlap barely, if at all. Thus the text and any distinctive word-setting gestures begin by being clearly audible;

and because each restatement can be just a rhythmic cousin of those before it, the subject-answer dialogue frees the answering phrase to explore new gestural or tonal paths.

Ex. 18 begins with a solo statement in two phrases[49] (bars 1ff, 3ff); the bass (bars 5–9) answers the first phrase tonally, but for the second strikes out in a new direction, as a rhythmic cousin of the tenor original. Bars 9–13 introduce a texture that we may call 'broken homophony', three voices moving together while the fourth takes its own rhythm. While the first phrase here is only a distant cousin, the second (bars 11ff), especially in the alto, does recall the melodic contours of an earlier statement – but what it recalls is not the original tenor line but its reshaped version from bars 7ff.

Like the subject-answer dialogue, broken homophony keeps the words audible while extending a clause for more diverse musical substance and harmonic interest. The same ends are served by treating a pair of voices as a single polyphonic entrant – as in the free imitative fabric of Ex. 18–20 and 23, where alliances constantly break up and re-form, and the texture may evolve at any moment into true homophony or true imitation. Voice-pairing can also intensify the affective harmonies of a declamatory passage, as in Ex. 10; and, like many other aspects of the declamatory idiom, it seems a natural setting for acting-out or role-playing – hence Ex. 19, where the heavy-hearted sinner is solitary, but his two comforters speak together.[50]

Ex. 10, bars 22–6, with a single bipartite clause shared out between two voices, stands on the threshold of a kind of stichomythic exchange among several solo voices that seems to go back to Humfrey.[51] The intensely felt 'Let Mine Eyes Run Down with Tears' (z 24) extends this idea: in its second verse paragraph, clauses as long as four bars or as short as four notes are tossed from hand to hand; the dialogue is interrupted first by five-part homophony and then by close imitation interweaving three distinct motifs. Later in the anthem ('Do not abhor us'), two contrasting clauses in passionately expressive declamation migrate from one voice to another, pursued by a short refrain-like figure.[52] In 'Who Hath Believed Our Report', the exchange of text phrases (from 'He hath no form') in clauses of 6, 9, 6½

EX. 18 Henry Purcell: 'Who Hath Believed Our Report' (z 64),
bars 1–17

EX. 18 (*contd.*)

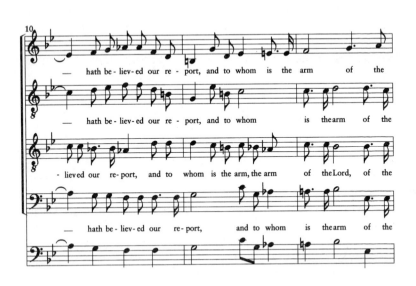

and 10½ bars seems to be dramaturgical in conception: as the whole nation of Israel has sinned against Isaiah's Suffering Servant, so the words of repentance must come from many speakers and not one (an interpretation supported by the sudden change to four-part homophony at 'All we like sheep'). Such exchanges often give rise to a refrain effect: thus, in 'Blessed Is the Man that Feareth the Lord' (z 9) 'a good man' is heard first as part of a longer line but then recurs, with its musical motif, as an anchor to which ensuing clauses of text are secured.

Purcell delights in imitation – the bedrock of classical polyphony – that reveals its Renaissance ancestry even in the presence of an obligatory continuo,[53] yet it is striking how little his imitative subjects compromise 'pure' speech-rhythms. However, while in writing for chorus he tends to begin a point of imitation in classical fashion, in verse ensembles he often prefaces the imitation with a preliminary statement in the style of a subject-answer dialogue,[54] as if in deference to the Humfreyan principle of allowing an expressive subject and its text to be heard clearly at least once.

Purcell shows an endless fascination with the classical polyphonists' techniques of double counterpoint and the inversion of a subject – or, if possible, both at once. Ex. 19 offers paired-

EX.   19   Henry Purcell: 'In Thee, O Lord' (z 16), bars 77–92

EX. 20 Henry Purcell: 'Give Sentence with Me' (z 12), bars 88–94
(ed. E. Van Tassel and E. Higginbottom)

EX. 21 Henry Purcell: 'Let Mine Eyes Run Down with Tears'
(z 24), bars 1–10

EX.   21   (*contd.*)

voice imitation (or broken homophony) with shifting alliances among the voices, on a simple figure *rectus* and *inversus*, leading to three-part imitation combining both forms of the theme. The parallelism of biblical prose lends itself naturally to antecedent and consequent, subject and countersubject, as in Ex. 21. The main subject in Ex. 20 comprises both antecedent and consequent (bass, bars 88f and 90ff), in addition to which an independent countersubject enters almost at once (alto and tenor, bars 90f).[55]

Purcell's imitative writing is seldom divorced from pictorial and affective gestures. Ex. 21 uses double counterpoint to convey two forms of imagery at once: the initial subject (bar 1) pictorializes 'run down', while in the countersubject (S2, bar 3) the 'unceasing' repeated notes are a madrigalian rendering of the words in audible form.[56] In a lighter vein, in the first chorus of 'O Lord Our Governor' (z 39), after four bars of solid homophony for 'sheep and oxen', the fowls and fishes flit across the music in playful imitation.

The sound of imitation itself is a favourite metaphor. In 'Save Me, O God' (z 51) 'strangers rise up' as an ascending motif bustles upwards through the voice parts (Ex. 22); in 'Who Hath Believed Our Report' imitation depicts the ungodly crowding round, 'oppressing' and 'afflicting' with taunts and blows (Ex. 23). In Ex. 25, as dotted rhythms act out the word 'laugh' in a familiar trope, the jostling of imitative entries suggests the boorish jeering of the 'enemies'. A change of texture from homophony to imitation reinforces a metaphor in Ex. 24, where the unanimous cry of the faithful ('Voce mea . . .') is answered by five-part imitation because Jehovah ('respondit mihi . . .') is, after all, everywhere.

The declamatory style gives such prominence to the personalized drama of the individual vocal line – whether alone or intertwined in imitation – that homophonic declamation can astonish merely by contrast.[57] It can also focus attention on a harmonic effect, as in the famous 'voice of the turtle' passage in 'My Beloved Spake', or in Ex. 24: here the mimetic effect of massed voices lends additional force to the cry to God, but the sudden shift from C major to C minor adds a kind of harmonic question-mark (answered in the major-key solidity and certitude of the imitative reply).[58]

The homophonic chorus can rejoice and dance with obvious delight but can also convey a wider range of affects, from unchallengeable divine authority ('he hath commanded' in 'I Will Give Thanks unto the Lord', z 21) and the unanimity of the faithful ('all we like sheep' in 'Who Hath Believed Our Report'; or Ex. 24, bars 39f) to the implacability of the ungodly ('Where is their God' in 'Blow Up the Trumpet in Sion', z 10).[59] Perhaps most powerful of all is the almost mesmerized and mesmerizing effect of utter simplicity in Ex. 3 and 4.

It is the ability to transcend imagery, lyricism and polyphonic technique by merging them in a persuasive new musical language that vindicates the hectic, self-conscious tone of some of Purcell's verse anthems. There seems so much to say, so little time or room in which to say it: the hearer is exhorted and seduced and swept along on a racing current of musical events more varied, and perhaps more energetic and colourful, than in

EX.   22   Henry Purcell: 'Save Me, O God' (z 51), bars 13–27

21
me, and ty- rants which have not God be - fore their
me, and ty- rants which have not God be - fore their
me, and ty- rants which have not God be - fore their eyes
23
eyes seek, seek aft - er my
eyes seek aft - er my
seek, seek aft - er my
25
soul, seek, seek aft - er my soul.
soul, seek aft - er my soul.
soul, seek aft - er my soul.

EX. 23 Henry Purcell: 'Who Hath Believed Our Report' (z 64),
bars 79–85

EX. 24 Henry Purcell: 'Jehova, Quam Multi Sunt Hostes Mei'
(z 135), bars 39–46

EX.   24   (*contd.*)

the church music of any other era. Even when – as sometimes happens in the symphony anthems of 1682–5 – the music seems to lack any loftier cohesive force, that energy and that colour may still carry the day; and when Purcell adds a wider and deeper emotional undercurrent and a finer sense of balance and proportion between paragraphs, the result is arguably as affecting as anything he ever wrote, and as musical as anything ever composed for the English Church.

Although the post-Restoration full anthem could not have evolved without Elizabethan and Jacobean precedents, it quickly became something quite other; its inheritance of the sinewy line of classical polyphony, under the influence of the verse anthem, placed a greater emphasis on homophony and took on stronger flavours in melody and harmony, and even borrowed the dance rhythms of the symphony anthem. The full+verse genre, which emerged only in the 1670s, was perhaps primarily a response to an appetite whetted by the high drama of the verse anthem, an

appetite for greater textural variety, more obvious formal struc-
turing, and more generous histrionic gestures.[60]

Purcell's full anthems (without verses) are simple but not
unsubtle. The early 'O God, the King of Glory' (z 34) may look
very Jacobean on the page, with its alternation of homophony
and imitation and its rising points of imitation at beginning and
end on the word 'exalt'. But the celestial tessitura at 'into
heaven' and the sudden brightness of D major come from a
newer source, and the 'comfort' of the Holy Ghost takes the
surprising form of a short burst of tripla. The more traditional
'Remember Not, Lord, Our Offences' (z 50) is remarkable for
its formal lucidity. It begins and ends homophonically; repeating
the first phrase but not the second at the beginning (*aab*, bars
1–13) and vice versa at the end (*abb*, bars 30–43) is a nice
economy that yet leaves some room for tonal movement. The
central section in double counterpoint (bars 13–30) draws a
precise emotional curve by letting the diatonic first motif
('neither take thou vengeance . . .') be gradually swallowed up
by the chromatic second motif ('but spare us . . .'), whose dis-
sonances and false relations raise the tension to a climax.

The recently rediscovered full anthem 'I Was Glad' (setting
2),[61] for the coronation of James II, is more sectional in form,
partly because of its striking use of pictorialisms. The dotted
flourish on 'glad' and the steady climbing motif on 'We will go'
match the figures on these words given to the alto solo in
Purcell's earlier symphony setting, though the full anthem does
not try to re-create the 'gathering' imagery and the luminous
tessitura of 'to testify unto Israel' in z 19, or the lambent colouring of 'O pray for the peace . . .'

Purcell's last anthem, 'Thou Knowest, Lord',[62] stands at the
opposite expressive pole from 'I Was Glad'. It is as if the
emotions stirred by the death of the Queen – who was, by all
accounts, genuinely beloved both at Court and in the country –
were too deep for so explicit an outpouring of musical lamen-
tation as the earlier Funeral Sentences. Purcell's writing here,
almost purely homophonic and with a minimum of dissonance,
is so understated that the most modest of gestures – the fragmentary repetitions of 'Shut not', 'O God', 'suffer us not', and

'for any pains of death'; and the motivic diminished fourth b^b-$f^\#$ in the last clause – seem to cry aloud.

With one exception ('Blow Up the Trumpet'), all of Purcell's full+verse anthems date from $c1680$–82; all are similar in form, beginning and ending with a chorus and using one or two short verse paragraphs – thus either F|v|F or F|v|F|v|F.[63] They are also, as a group, quite similar in tone. The texture (of verses and choruses alike) moves easily between imitation and a flexible homophony; the verses are laced with expressive (if often rather obvious) harmonic effects, ranging (in 'O God, Thou Art My God') from plangent, rather gentle dissonances at 'My soul thirsteth' to the trebles' sweet chains of thirds at 'thy loving kindness'. Two of these anthems also use a larger verse ensemble. In the one verse paragraph of 'O God, Thou Hast Cast Us Out' (z 36) the ATB and SSA trios exchange statements and then unite for a five- and six-part climax on the same material. 'O Lord God of Hosts' (z 37) has two verse movements. The first, an exchange of trios (Ex. 25), shows how the stereotyped habit of phrase-repetition can open the way to tonal movement. Similarly, in the second verse (Ex. 26) each of the two phrases ('Turn us ...' and 'shew the light ...') seems to have explored the affective possibilities of its material the first time, only to reveal new ones when Purcell holds much the same matter up to a different light. But the self-dramatization of the verse-anthem soloist is absent, even in the form of subject-answer dialogues: it is of the essence of the full anthem that the community of faith expresses itself communally.

The texts for these full+verse anthems, which all focus on the personal relationship of the believer to his God, give rise to a musical language that looks somewhat formulaic on the page but is in fact richly expressive – and not without some vivid pictorialisms. At the beginning of 'O God, Thou Art My God', homophony pictures the never-failing certitude of God's presence – 'thou art my God' – in contrast to imitation on a disjunct motif to depict 'seeking'. The second chorus paragraph comprises two imitative clauses: the first, on another disjunct 'seeking' figure, ends in a solid cadence on 'holiness'; the second opposes disjunct and conjunct motifs ('that I might behold') in a

EX. 25 Henry Purcell: 'O Lord God of Hosts' (z 37), bars 29–58

EX.   25   (*contd.*)

EX. 25 (*contd.*)

dual point of imitation that evolves into an interplay between the conjunct motif and its own inversion as the psalmist beholds God's 'power and glory'.

The SSA verse section of 'O God, Thou Art My God' and the ensuing chorus are oddly secular in effect, with an exceedingly tidy and four-square *decani/cantoris/tutti* phrase structure well matched by thematic material of an almost rococo regularity. A similarly elegant, if less worldly, impression is created by the rhythms of a stately dance that ends 'Lord, How Long Wilt Thou Be Angry' (z 25) – underlined by a change to a very

EX. 26 Henry Purcell: 'O Lord God of Hosts' (z 37), bars 64–94

EX. 26 (*contd.*)

Turn us, turn us a-gain, O God, O God of

Turn us, turn us a-gain, O God, O God of

Turn us, turn us a-gain, O God, O God of

Turn us, turn us a-gain, O God, O God of

Turn us, turn us a-gain, O God, O God of

hosts: shew the light, the light of thy coun-ten-ance,

hosts: shew the

hosts: shew the light of thy coun-ten-ance,

hosts: shew the light, the

hosts: shew the light of thy coun-ten-ance, and we shall, we

EX.   26   (*contd.*)

'modern'-sounding C major. These triplas, lacking any very great concentration of dissonance, gain harmonic interest from such minimal gestures as the final tripla of 'Lord, How Long' where the intensification of false relations[64] and diminished intervals serves notice of an approaching cadence.

When the mood is less jubilant than meditative, the tripla imparts an effect of confiding intimacy. Perhaps the finest such tripla is the penultimate section of 'O Lord God of Hosts' (Ex. 26). In the first of two contrasting phrases, movement in the upper voices cannot overcome the static inertia of the lower ones (from bar 66) – perhaps a metaphor for the soul's reluctance to be 'turned'. The suspensions in the second clause (from bar 69) again present moving parts pulling against static ones, but now in linear terms. There is little harmonic originality here in any analytical sense; but nothing shows more clearly how Purcell rose to the characteristically Baroque challenge to use commonplaces as a test of, and a stimulus to, the imagination. The crowning achievement of this movement is the relation between statement and repetition: the return of the wistful little rising figure e'-f'-g' (A2, bar 66) in a quite different context (A1, bar 81); the increased harmonic variety in the homophonic phrase (compare e.g. bar 68 with bars 84f); above all, the skill with which Purcell erects a single arch of tension and resolution spanning an apparently binary thematic scheme.[65]

Purcell's full+verse anthems contain some of his finest imitative writing. Some subjects, of course, are based on word-painting – notably the 'laughing' subject in Ex. 25, which gains in affective power from the aural effect of a host of voices heard from all directions. This encircling effect is shared by several subjects that use vividly jagged figures as a metaphor for 'seeking' ('O God, Thou Art My God') or 'scattering' ('O God, Thou Hast Cast Us Out'). At the opposite pole are scalar subjects that draw an implacable strength from their clear directionality, evoking the unswerving march of righteousness (not least the righteousness of Charles II): 'tread down our enemies' in 'O God, Thou Hast Cast Us Out'; 'will we not go back' in 'O Lord God of Hosts'.[66]

But when the matter in hand is not hope but damnation, the polyphonic fabric can take on a dark, even frightening texture – as in 'O God, Thou Hast Cast Us Out', when the homophonic 'Thou hast moved the land' (SAB) is pierced by the treble cry 'heal the sores thereof' entering more than an octave higher; thereafter the first motif is repeatedly attacked by the second, in increasingly dissonant unprepared entries.

The fanfares that open 'Blow Up the Trumpet in Sion' (z 10) suggest a grand festival anthem. But the enharmonic solemnity of 'sanctify a fast' seems a bit odd, and the augmented triads at 'sanctify the congregation' reveal that this is not the trumpet 'in the new moon' of Psalm 81, but the harsh trumpet that 'sounds an alarm'. It is for no token fast of ritual penance that it summons elders (TTB) and infants (SSSA), commands bridegroom and bride to abandon the joys of their wedding-night – all these with 'role-playing' voice-groupings. The priests are to weep even within the Temple itself (chromatic-scale phrases in pungent contrary motion), for nothing less than utter disaster has befallen Israel. All the pictorialisms are revealed as mere prologue to the pleas of the faithful for mercy (augmented triads again, and twisting, anguished suspensions); but the anthem ends in desolate, devastated stillness, with the scoffing heathen having the last word: 'Where is their God?'

This bleak ending makes one suspect that this is no ordinary anthem, even for a penitential season. The text is not a proper lesson for any holy day in the seventeenth-century Prayer Book, but it is possible to guess that the most apt occasion in the post-Restoration calendar for so extreme an expression of penitence is 30 January, the commemoration of Charles I's execution.[67] Whatever the specific occasion, we may imagine the shock – of surprise or even of dismay – as the music began, and the congregation in the Chapel Royal or, more likely, the Abbey looked about them and wondered if Purcell had utterly mistaken the day; and we may imagine the delight of composer and cognoscenti as the truth unfolded.

As in the verse anthems, many of Purcell's full and full+verse points of imitation – e.g. 'O God, Thou Hast Cast Us Out', bars 1ff; 'I Was Glad', bars 13ff – are built up from an antecedent and consequent so sharply contrasted that each appears auton-omous; but true double counterpoint is also abundant – good examples are in 'O God, Thou Hast Cast Us Out', bars 23ff and bars 38ff; 'Lord, How Long Wilt Thou Be Angry', bars 54ff; 'Remember Not, Lord, Our Offences', bars 13ff; 'O Lord God of Hosts', bars 109ff. Many of Purcell's most triumphant double points of imitation come from a single motif and its own inver-sion: 'Lord, How Long Wilt Thou Be Angry', bars 84ff; 'O Lord God of Hosts', bars 1ff and 15ff.

'I Was Glad' ends in a rather spectacular *tour de force* of imitation: in addition to the subject both *rectus* and *inversus*, its augmentation joins in, both *rectus* and *inversus*; and the whole is crowned in *double* augmentation. But the magnificent torso 'Hear My Prayer, O Lord' is perhaps the greater achievement, sustaining a single imitative clause over an immense span (thirty-four bars) using two radically different subjects and the inversions of both. What makes it not just a technical but an artistic triumph is the subjects themselves – powerful aural images of pain and supplication, whose struggle and resolution are rich in meaning as well as in craft.

The two coronation anthems 'My Heart Is Inditing' (z 30) and 'Praise the Lord, O Jerusalem'[68] are usually grouped with the symphony anthems; and 'My Heart Is Inditing' does begin with a symphony like (though on a far larger scale than) those of late-1680s symphony anthems – first, a spacious and harmonically restless common-time movement; then, an imitative canzona in triple metre, rich in sequences and alluding briefly to the first motif of the vocal movement to follow. But these anthems were composed not for the Chapel Royal but for the joint vocal forces of the Chapel and Westminster Abbey (in 1685, some twenty boys and forty-eight men) with the full Twenty-four Violins (not the one-to-a-part contingent that had played in the Chapel ever since the Restoration), and those relatively massive forces have left an indelible mark on the build of the music. The strings, rather than punctuating the verses (their primary role in the typical symphony anthem), are largely used to support and enrich the vocal movements; and the character of those movements, both verse and full, is close to that of a full+verse anthem.

'My Heart Is Inditing' brought the 1685 ceremony to an end with the crowning of the Queen, Mary of Modena. Even (or especially) in a work conceived on such a monumental scale, Purcell always pursues an openness and clarity of texture. The six- and seven-part verse paragraphs make much use of the subdivision familiar from full+verse anthems – one verse starts with SST/AAB, another with SSAB/ATBB etc. Several chorus passages begin in imitation; after the first full-chorus cadence the continuation ('I speak of the things') begins with SSA, ATBB, then SAATB, SSABB – as if to keep the texture lucid and open as long as possible. So when the full chorus does make a homophonic entry ('With joy and gladness'; later, 'Praise the Lord, O Jerusalem') the effect is overwhelming.

Naked histrionics or pictorialism of the Chapel Royal variety would be out of place here, but the drama of the situation is not lost on Purcell. The Queen was not unpopular, but she was after all a Catholic (and foreign into the bargain), and her husband's Catholicism made many of his subjects uneasy about the future. It is likely that the text of the anthem[69] was deliberately edited to emphasize a wife's duty to forsake her homeland and devote herself to her husband's dynasty; and the music takes a similar line. There is a peculiarly light-footed, as it were feminine, delicacy in the imitation at 'At his right hand shall stand the Queen', picturing her as demurely submissive; and the scoring of the 'ornamentation of nobility' on 'glorious' creates breadth and richness without heaviness.[70] The 'virgins' who escort the Queen have a grave purity; when the music swings into 'joy and gladness' it gradually takes on weight as they approach the King, and by the time the chorus reaches 'and shall enter . . .' it is clear that this palace is a massive and masculine affair.

The most touching moment comes at 'Hearken O daughter'. When the verse begins, in duple metre, its message is a grave, almost sorrowful admonition to 'forget also thine own people'; but with the tripla the bride's loss is turned to eagerness, as the same 'hearken' motif is imbued with forward momentum, alive with an electrifying promise: 'Instead of thy fathers thou shalt have children'.

'Praise the Lord, O Jerusalem' is smaller in scale and less highly structured than 'My Heart Is Inditing'. Its apparently hesitant use of the strings – e.g. dropping them out at 'God upholdeth . . .' – may reflect haste in composition, or may even be taking account of having less rehearsal time or less-seasoned performers than four years earlier. Nevertheless, the balance of strings and voices in the first verse section is both judicious and subtle. The voices begin alone;[71] then the strings play alone; only then do they unite. Dropping out the violins for the imitative section 'For kings . . .' may have simplified rehearsal, but it also strengthens the contrast at the return of 'Praise the Lord', with its sidewise leap from D major to B♭.

This time the anthem was to be sung at the joint crowning of both King and Queen, who were to be nominally equal and 'co-regnant' (a novel and controversial arrangement); but the King this time was Dutch William, regarded by many as an opportunist if not a usurper, and Purcell's anthem was not the place to dwell on the scriptural subservience of a bride to her husband and his domain. So 'Praise the Lord', with none of the drama of 'My Heart Is Inditing', may be feeling its way rather cautiously, but it has a sombre majesty uniquely its own; and the spinning-out of 'for ever' shows a glint of the pictorial showmanship familiar in the Chapel Royal.

From 1552 onwards, the Anglican liturgy permitted alternative canticles for Mattins and Evensong in an effort to mollify extremes of theological opinion; certain texts, venerated by some for their ties with the Church's history, were decried by others as crypto-papist. While the post-Restoration Church (to judge from surviving manuscripts) found a use for both old and new settings of a variety of canticles, few composers wrote a single service setting that included every possible alternative. We may guess that the impulse which drove Purcell to do so in the early 1680s was of a piece with the careful collecting of his works in fair-copy albums like *GB-Lbl* RM 20.h.8.

The revival of older liturgical music at the Restoration virtually ignored the more adventurous verse services of Byrd, Gibbons, Tomkins et al. in favour of full services – in fact, some of the plainest full services of their era. This emphasis owed something to expediency – these so-called 'short services' would be easier for choirs to learn than more elaborate ones – but it is also likely that their age and their austere simplicity together were a political metaphor about the antiquity and continuity of the old hierarchy and the old liturgy.

The structural mainspring of the typical pre-Commonwealth short service is the simple repetition of short phrases in alternation by the two sides of the choir (*decani* and *cantoris*), which can build up to an almost obsessive patterning. In a variation on this idea, prophetic of post-Restoration developments, answering phrases are not identical but are recognizably cut from the same musical cloth; or in a *decani/cantoris* exchange the two outer parts may remain the same while the inner parts are varied – a foretaste of the characteristically Baroque polarization of treble and bass.

Though Purcell uses the *decani/cantoris* exchange in only one anthem (z 35), it is a central feature of several of the longer canticles in his B♭ Service (z 230); but he makes far more use of the full+verse principle, often in clauses longer than the single phrases typical of the *decani/cantoris* mosaic in Byrd or Tomkins. In this service, as in his full+verse anthems, Purcell uses two or more three- and four-part verse groups separately, in alternation, or together. The 'standard' SSA and ATB trios predominate but are varied with SABB, AATB, SST and SSATB, and may unite (as in the anthems 'O God, Thou hast Cast Us Out' and 'O Lord God of Hosts') in a six- or seven-part ensemble.

This service relies heavily on homophony and 'broken homophony', but Purcell also gives free rein to his love of canon. Following a substantial tradition (which, again, may arise in part because canon conveys an air of antiquity), he includes at least one canon in every movement of the service (except the *Kyrie*): in six of the seven Doxologies, and also in other passages in the *Te Deum, Benedictus, Jubilate* and *Creed* (twice). Purcell introduces more different textures, more variously deployed, than are found in most pre-1645 services; and he varies the 'sectional rhythm' noticeably between the various canticles.

The B♭ Service is utilitarian music, designed to cover a lot of text with dispatch; yet Purcell manages to maintain a pleasing consistency of musical vocabulary and formal unity. It is possible that he intended to link many of the canticles by the use of a unifying 'head-motif' of a rising sequence of fourths and thirds or fourths and seconds.[72] But this may be to read deliberate intent into what is no more than common musical coin – especially considering the importance of embryonic sequences in shaping both ordinary themes and canonic subjects.

On such a modest stage, any histrionic gesture makes a considerable impact. In the *Te Deum*, antiphonal treatment of 'The glorious company . . . /The goodly fellowship . . . /The noble army . . . /The holy Church . . .' suggests a mild form of acting-out: *cantoris/decani/cantoris* appear as apostles, prophets and martyrs, then unite as the whole Church. A comparable exchange on 'To thee all angels . . . /To thee Cherubin . . .' invites similar casting, for verse ATB/SSA; the united host's cry of 'Holy, holy, holy' brings in the full choir. A classic madrigalism acts out the 'Filioque' doctrine of the Trinity in the *Creed*, by uniting two verse trios on the crucial word: 'And I believe in the Holy Ghost . . .' (SSA) 'who proceedeth from the Father and the Son' (ATB), 'who with the Father and the Son' (SSA) '*together, together* is worshipped and glorified' (SSAATB). And in the mode of 'intellectual' pictorialism, this passage on the Trinity is the only appearance of triple metre in the *Creed*.

Purcell seldom shares Blow's delight in rather outré points of imitation.[73] Rather, what seem to attract him most are touches of colour and movement: the sweetness of 'green things', a remarkable shiver at 'frost and cold' (both in *Benedicite*); the chance to fuse, in a single phrase in the *Magnificat*, madrigalian images for 'put down' (falling fifths), 'the mighty' (triadic fanfare line) and 'exalted' (sustained high tessitura). Other pictorial gestures in the service range from obvious mimicry to the most indirect association: 'lift them up', rising figures (*Te Deum*); 'raise up', a rising tessitura (*Benedictus*); 'came down', falling fifths (*Creed*); 'with trumpets', fanfares (*Cantate*); 'tender mercy', sweet harmonies (*Benedictus*); 'rejoice and give thanks', dotted melismas (*Cantate*); 'round world', curving melismas (*Cantate*); 'confounded', a wandering subject and its inversion (*Te Deum*); 'all generations', breaking into polyphony to symbolize profusion (*Magnificat*); 'the sharpness of death', numerous sharps in notation (*Creed*).

Though shot through with such pictorialisms, the B♭ Service is very sparing in its use of affective harmonies, as in the *Creed* at 'for us [sinful] men', 'incarnate', 'crucified'. Likewise, at 'We therefore pray thee...' in the *Te Deum*, the mildest of false relations suffice to express supplication, with pedal notes to depict confidence in redemption. This kind of expressive restraint – especially in the light of such harmonically searing anthems as 'Blow Up the Trumpet in Sion' or 'Hear My Prayer, O Lord' – may indicate that liturgical convention expected greater detachment and *gravitas* in canticle settings than in anthems,[74] but a more pressing consideration was surely the premium placed on brevity.

Long passages in triple metre – something that would have surprised Purcell's grandfathers in a service setting – play a large part in z 230: more than one-third of the bars in the entire service, and well over half in some canticles (*Benedicite, Cantate domino, Creed*). Purcell's other full+verse service, the G minor

Magnificat and *Nunc dimittis* (z 231), is wholly in triple metre except for the Doxology in the *Nunc dimittis* – which may well not be by Purcell.[75] In consequence this service tends to sound rather 'modern' and, with its excess of parallel thirds, at times sails close to glibness. Yet beneath a veneer of secularity this even-tempered little work, though it affects little of the high-flown gesture, is intriguingly responsive to the text. The tessitura rising to a high point on the first syllable of 'magnify'; the dotted melismas on 'rejoice'; the energetically disjunct point of imitation on 'scattered'; the rising figure on 'exalted', with a lower cadence on 'meek' – all these can be matched in the apparently more serious-minded B♭ Service. But the G minor Service also has its own brand of pictorialism, which might have seemed too delicate in the larger work: the sudden fall in tessitura on 'lowliness', the hushed phrasing on 'holy', perhaps even the strained harmonies on 'sent empty away'. Many of Purcell's contemporaries took the convention associating certain figures with martial pride (or arrogance) as their cue for dotted rhythms or fanfares at 'shewed strength', 'glory of thy people', and 'the imagination of their hearts'. Here, however, Purcell replaces the expected trumpet-calls (which in this music would be like entering a boudoir in boots and spurs) with engaging little dotted-rhythm melismas in parallel thirds.

The orchestrally accompanied D major *Te Deum* and *Jubilate* (z 232), composed for the St Cecilia's Day festivities of 1694, is an essentially new kind of church music, public and rather impersonal in scale. It has little in common with Purcell's symphony anthems, still less with z 230; the orchestra is no longer the Chapel Royal chamber group but a much more substantial affair assembled *ad hoc* for an event unconnected with the liturgy in any usual sense.

The work can hardly be called an unqualified success. Where the two full+verse services have at their best a kind of breathless urgency – the exchange of short antiphonal phrases, even if it is perfunctoriness well disguised, certainly sustains musical momentum – here musical substance and performing forces are out of proportion, and in places the work seems fragmentary and unco-ordinated. The resulting impression of bittiness might have seemed like fluency and versatility in a less magniloquent context (as, precisely, it does in many anthems).

Some pictorial touches, especially in chorus movements, rank with those in the best of Purcell's anthems – the *tutti* angelic chorus on 'Holy', the symbolism of an unending diurnal round in the stubborn alternation of tonic and dominant at 'Day by day . . .', or the boldly marching point of imitation on 'O go your way'. The tripla with chains of dotted figures at 'O be joyful . . . gladness . . . with a song' has a long ancestry in symphony anthems (though the festive sound-picture of alto and trumpet duet is new). The big choruses include some allusive imagery – particularly the metaphor of endlessness in the melismas on 'father everlasting', 'world without end' (in both canticles), 'let me *never* be confounded', and 'generation to generation' – and foreshadow the high-Baroque oratorio style. The style but not the scale, for such chorus movements are hamstrung not only by thematic short-windedness but also by the trumpets' tonal limitations. The consequence is too often a *forte* assault upon material too frail to sustain it.

But there are moments of beauty and insight, such as the paradox of martial innocence, depicted in the treble fanfares on 'glory'. And a special grace, perhaps bearing the mark of Purcell's years in the theatre, flows through the meditative solos and duos: the alto's reflective and visionary 'Vouchsafe . . .', and the AB duo 'For the Lord is gracious', with a limpid sweetness rarely found in the heroic Gostling–Abell anthems. Such glimpses of the beauty of holiness, unparalleled in English church music, give yet further cause – if it were needed – to mourn Purcell's death only a year after this work was first heard.

NOTES

My views on the subject of this chapter have been more pervasively guided by previous writers' work than I can acknowledge on specific points, so I apologize if I have inadvertently plagiarized Christopher Dearnley, *English Church Music 1650–1750* (London, 1970); Peter Dennison, 'Two Studies of Purcell's Sacred Music: (*a*) The Stylistic Origins of the Early Church Music', in F. W. Sternfeld,

Nigel Fortune and Edward Olleson, eds., *Essays on Opera and English Music in Honour of Sir Jack Westrup* (Oxford, 1975), 44–61; Anthony Lewis, 'English Church Music', in Anthony Lewis and Nigel Fortune, eds, *Opera and Church Music 1630–1750*, New Oxford History of Music (Oxford, 1975), V, 493–556; C. H. H. Parry, *The Music of the Seventeenth Century*, Oxford History of Music (Oxford, 1902), III, 259–84; Watkins Shaw, 'Church Music in England from the Reformation to the Present Day', in F. Blume, ed., *Protestant Church Music: A History* (London, 1974), 691–732. I have also profited from reading two unpublished dissertations, whose authors I gladly thank: Robert Manning, 'Purcell's Anthems: an Analytical Study of the Music and Its Context' (Ph.D. diss., U. of Birmingham, 1979); Katherine T. Rohre, ' "The Energy of English Words": a Linguistic Approach to Henry Purcell's Methods of Setting Texts' (Ph.D. diss., Princeton U., 1980). And I have tired the sun with talking with wiser Purcellian heads than mine, among them Clifford Bartlett, Ian Cheverton, Roger Evans, Ellen Harris, Edward Higginbottom, the late Peter le Huray, Richard Luckett, Andrew Parrott, Robert Shay, Peter Williams and Bruce Wood.

For reasons of space, this chapter says far too little about performance practice. An excellent summary is Bruce Wood's introduction to *John Blow: Anthems II: Anthems with Orchestra*, Musica Britannica, l (London, 1984), xx–xxiii. Indispensable data and interpretation appear in Jeremy Noble, 'Purcell and the Chapel Royal', in Imogen Holst, ed., *Henry Purcell 1659–1695: Essays on His Music* (Oxford, 1959), 52–66. Peter Holman, *Four and Twenty Fiddlers* (Oxford, 1993), shows that the violin band in the Chapel Royal was virtually always one to a part, with continuo support from lutes or theorbos and bass viols; that the Chapel placed soloists, choir and violins some little (but perceptible) distance from one another; and that the pitch standard in the Chapel was higher than elsewhere at Court, or than in the theatres.

As for my own views, I have little to add to what I have written elsewhere – 'English Church Music c.1660–1700', *Early Music*, vi (1978), 572–8; and vii (1979), 85–8 – except to assert the importance of theorbos in the Chapel Royal continuo, and to reiterate my conviction that, notwithstanding the importance in the Chapel of high countertenors (i.e. falsettists) such as Howell and Abell, the low countertenor was the voice that Purcell expected for the majority of his verse alto parts. (In some of the music examples I have used the octave-transposing 'tenor' clef for an alto part merely to avoid excessive ledger lines. This should not obscure the important distinction between high and low countertenor – in Ex. 15, for instance, which I think was very likely intended for a high countertenor.)

1   Thomas Tudway, introduction to *GB-Lbl* MS Harl. 7342, cited by Christopher Hogwood, 'Thomas Tudway's History of Music', in C. Hogwood and R. Luckett, eds., *Music in Eighteenth-century England* (Cambridge, 1983), 42.

2   *Zimmerman II*, ch. 5, rightly stresses the importance of anthem texts as propaganda, but many of Zimmerman's ascriptions of undated Purcell anthems to specific events must be read with caution; and I know of no

evidence to support the implication that anthem texts were chosen by consulting the Lectionary.

3 John Wilson, ed., *Roger North on Music* (London, 1959), 299.

4 E.g. *Pepys*, 14 September 1662; III, 196–8; *Evelyn*, 21 December 1662; III, 347–8.

5 Of Purcell's seventy surviving anthem texts (counting the Funeral Sentences but not the Latin settings), fifty-five come from the Psalms (Prayer Book version), five from other parts of the Prayer Book, six from the Old Testament and two from the New. Two anthems, for the coronations of 1685 and 1689, combine psalm texts and verses from Isaiah.

6 For convenience, I speak here of anthems; service settings could in principle appear in all these genres. In fact Purcell, like most of his contemporaries, wrote only full+verse services (z 230 and z 231) apart from the orchestrally accompanied *Te Deum* and *Jubilate* (z 232).

7 As it is in pre-Commonwealth verse anthems and services, which however usually have a written-out organ part rather than a continuo part. Cf. the Jacobean-style organ introduction in Ex. 14.

8 It is moot whether the violins routinely played *colla parte* with the chorus.

9 Neither Blow (whose working life was nearly twice as long as Purcell's) nor Humfrey wrote as many anthems *per annum* as Purcell.

10 See Eric Van Tassel, 'Two Purcell Discoveries – 1: "Give Sentence" ', *Musical Times*, cxviii (1977), 381. From 1685 on, the dating can often be fairly explicit.

11 Purcell's appointment in 1677 as Composer in Ordinary for the Violins in succession to Matthew Locke (Peter Holman, op. cit., 327) may have been a practical stimulus for the composition of his early symphony anthems.

   The fragmentary survival of z N66 and z N68 (see *Zimmerman I*, 63–8; note that z N66 is also in Zimmerman's MS '20') is a hint that other symphony anthems by Purcell may have existed and are wholly lost.

12 z 130–44, 181–200; published in *Works II*, xxx, and discussed in some detail by Nigel Fortune in 'Two Studies of Purcell's Sacred Music: (*b*) The Domestic Sacred Music', in *Essays . . . in Honour of Sir Jack Westrup*, 62–78. They are not included in this chapter: they appear in no liturgical MSS of the time, and their texts would have been strikingly out of place among the anthems then in use.

13 Eric Van Tassel, 'Two Purcell Discoveries', op. cit., especially n. 7.

14 Such adaptations of symphony anthems were frequently made for use in provincial cathedrals, and they became commonplace in the Chapel Royal itself after the budget cuts under James II and especially after the exclusion of the royal band from Chapel Royal duties in 1690 (see Peter Holman, op. cit., especially 413f, 431f).

15 An inference borne out by the high proportion of anthems to which Gostling and other copyists assign precise dates. See F. B. Zimmerman, ed., *The Gostling Manuscript* (Austin and London, 1977). I am indebted to Joanna Hitchcock, the Director of the University of Texas Press, for making a copy of this important facsimile available to me.

16 E. H. Fellowes, *English Cathedral Music* (London, rev. 5/1969), 129.

17   Peter le Huray, *Music and the Reformation in England 1549–1660* (London, 1967, repr. Cambridge, 1978), shows how much the verse-anthem form could vary in the work of Byrd (Table 23), Morley (Table 24), Giles (Table 26), Tomkins (Table 29) and Gibbons (Table 31).

18   Perhaps modelled on Blow's 'O Lord I have Sinned', composed for the state funeral of General Monck (Lord Albemarle) in 1670; this anthem, like z 27, combines an archaic musical form with the intensely expressive harmonic idiom of the 1670s.

19   Indeed, the continuo which defines a verse anthem is only intermittently indispensable here.

20   This gave copyists some trouble: the second crotchet – $a^{\flat}$ in the autograph *GB-Cfm* 88 – is $a^{\natural}$ in Blow's organ-book *GB-Mp* f.370, and d'' in Isaack's *GB-Cfm* 117.

21   This risk may be a primary reason why Purcell makes very few key changes (if any) within an anthem, and why he almost never goes further afield than the relative or parallel major or minor.

22   Especially since the anthem lacks the formal clues of metre and rhyme offered by a poetic text.

23   *One chorus*: verse anthems z 26, 12, 14, 7, 9; symphony anthems z 3*, 18, 42*, 1, 16, 55, 29*, 47, 65, 57, 60, 5. *Two choruses*: verse anthems z 62, 6, 23, 11, 32, 64, N67, 45, 13, 43, 41, 24, 4, 61, 54*, N69, 53, 40, 56*; symphony anthems z 28*, 49*, 20*, 21, 48, 31. (*Italic* = the two chorus movements are identical; an asterisk indicates a section for soloists and chorus antiphonally or together.) The fragmentary z N66 and z N68 probably fell into one of these categories.

24   'Blessed Are They that Fear the Lord' (z 5) is another occasional anthem, composed in January 1688 for official thanksgiving services for the politically momentous pregnancy of James II's Catholic Queen; again, haste in composition and rehearsal may explain why it settles for a single chorus all of three bars long.

25   See pp. 132–5, 169, 185, 190 below.

26   Peter Dennison (*Pelham Humfrey* (Oxford, 1986), 24–9) shows that Lully, the English composers' principal role model, made little stylistic distinction between sacred and secular.

27   z 2 (1687) and z 44 (1688) have a duple-time canzona instead of the tripla; z 16 (*c*1682–5) begins with a triple-metre ground; z 29 (*c*1682–5) begins with a verse section; z 49 (*c*1682–5) begins with a common-time 'prelude', and its first verse is, in effect, the missing symphony tripla (see n.40, below).

28   Often shown in contemporary MSS merely by a rubric such as 'tripla Symph. as before'.

29   As do z 29 and z 49, two of the five anthems cited as exceptions in n. 27 above. Both the symphony tripla and the first ritornello of z 19 are inextricably related to the intervening alto verse (cf. Ex. 15), so Purcell creates instead a new tripla for the 'halfway' interlude. In each of these cases – as in those that have no strong instrumental interlude halfway through the anthem: z 16 and 57 (both *c*1682–5); z 2 (1687); z 5 and 44

(both 1688) – there is a clear thematic or dramaturgical reason for the structural anomaly.

30 In the same anthem ('I Was Glad'), another *arioso* (the more stylized 'For there is the seat', for tenor) is preceded by a complete statement in the strings, in a manner resembling theatrical practice.

31 In the right-hand column of Fig. 3, capital letters indicate identical musical material. The figure is based on the symphony-anthem version found in the Gostling MS (*Au*, no shelf-mark), 119–23, but the verse-anthem version in *Works II*, xxxii, 91–100, probably a later working after the violins were withdrawn from the Chapel Royal, presents the same formal picture.

32 For a more pervasive refrain, see Fig. 4 below.

33 Purcell's laughter can sound very different when the dotted rhythm is reversed to a 'scotch snap' and the image is the Almighty's scorn for the ungodly: 'Why Do the Heathen So Furiously Rage' (z 65).

34 Cf. the Latin counterpart in 'Beati Omnes' (z 131).

35 Underlining the idea of newness, the unconventional form of the introductory symphony makes this chorus the first appearance of triple metre in the anthem.

36 The syntax of '*that* it is he' is explained by the foregoing command to 'Tell it out among the heathen *that* the Lord is King . . .'

37 E. H. Fellowes, op. cit., 170.

38 We may suppose that a Chapel Royal composer was not reluctant to liken the attributes of the deity to those of his own employer.

39 For that matter, the extravagant language of Ex. 15 may be celebrating the sumptuous beauty of the Temple as much as the believer's delight in the Law.

40 He makes this verse, on its first appearance, serve in place of a symphony tripla, by reducing the introductory symphony to a sonorous common-time prelude (which has earned the anthem its nickname of 'Bell Anthem').

41 The bass is so overwrought that the descending figure, aiming for the dominant *d*, stumbles past it to $B^\flat$ and must climb – a little shamefacedly – back up to *d* for the cadence.

42 The *arioso* that follows, on the other hand, moulds the irregular prose of its text into such a songlike shape only by scanning it isochronously and restorting liberally to repetition.

43 Just as the second phrase in Ex. 15 (bars 42–6) is aimed at 'house'.

44 See e.g. Peter le Huray, ed., *The Treasury of English Church Music*, II, (London, 1965, repr. Cambridge, 1982), 232ff.

45 *Evelyn*, 28 January 1685; IV, 404.

46 After the Revolution of 1688–9 Abell, who did not conceal his Catholic sympathies, was apparently dismissed from the royal service; Gostling soldiered on without him in a few anthems such as 'My Song Shall Be Alway' (z 31) and 'The Way of God' (z 56).

47 As in 'The Way of God' at 'Thou hast made mine enemies', where the harmony freezes as if mesmerized by the soloist's virtuosity.

48 As the technique is defined by Peter Dennison, a subject announced in one solo voice 'is answered by a second solo voice with a phrase that can bear

only a slight resemblance to the subject, but which becomes its consequent'. Dennison, *Pelham Humfrey*, 49.

49 This bipartite division is of course another product of biblical parallelism.

50 But this is an early and perhaps half-hearted example: the voices abandon
their 'roles' almost immediately, to share the thematic material equally.

51 Cf. 'Wash you/Make you clean . . .' in Humfrey's 'Hear, O Heavens'
(Musica Britannica, xxxiv, 85).

52 Purcell's revision of this passage, as well as sharpening the harmonic focus,
adds two highly dramatic features: the desperate, breathless urgency of the
involuntary-seeming text-repetition 'Do not, oh do not . . .' (the 'oh'
utterly unsanctioned by scripture), and the transformation of the admoni-
tory 'remember' – a prominent recurring motif in the first version, in the
reworking it is almost subliminal until its sudden emergence in homophony, to devastating effect: cf. *Works II*, xxix, 10–13 and 17f.

53 In this as in other ways, Purcell shows the influence of Locke (e.g. Musica
Britannica, xxxviii, 122f) as against that of Humfrey.

54 See e.g. Ex. 4 and 21, and even Ex. 22, bar 16, compared with the chorus
entry in Ex. 25, bar 52.

55 See p. 186 below for the spectacular climax of 'I Was Glad' (setting 2).

56 The notes themselves (in seventeenth-century handwriting) would look
like teardrops to a hardened pictorialist.

57 As in 'Let Mine Eyes Run Down with Tears' (z 24) at the appalled question
'Hast thou utterly rejected Judah?'

58 Indeed, the declamatory style exerts a powerful, if slightly unexpected,
influence on Purcell's chorus writing. Although the chorus paragraph in
Ex. 5 is recomposed from the foregoing solo clause, its homophonic
rhythm takes its cue directly from the solo verse.

59 Cf. the mocking 'Sing us one of the songs' in Humfrey's 'By the Waters of
Babylon' and the ghastly climax of the same anthem (Musica Britannica,
xxxiv, 11 and 21).

60 Not one full anthem by Cooke or Humfrey is known. We may imagine
them too much caught up in the challenge of forging the new verse-
anthem style to pay attention to composing in what must have seemed
an outmoded language. (To be sure, Humfrey's compact and ingenious
full+verse *service* is a model of its kind.)

61 Bruce Wood, 'Two Purcell Discoveries – 2: A Coronation Anthem Lost
and Found', *Musical Times*, cxviii (1977), 466–8. The anthem has no
catalogue number in *Zimmerman I*.

62 A full-anthem setting (z 58C) of a text which Purcell had set much earlier
as the last part of the Funeral Sentences (z 58B).

63 Although it is the independent continuo that defines the distinction
between verse anthem and full+verse anthem, borderline cases (like 'Save
Me, O God', z 51) may be more helpfully classified in terms of form. In a
verse anthem the chorus functions essentially as punctuation, while in
a full+verse anthem it is the verse that is there for variety or relief. The
characteristic full+verse setting begins with a full section; no normal verse
or symphony anthem does so. While an *a cappella* performance of (say)

the Funeral Sentences would be musically bearable – if dreadfully thin – the v|F|v|F|v|F structure of that work is so clearly in the verse-anthem mould that it seems merely eccentric to classify it as full+verse.

64 A progression like the $e^{\natural}$-d'-$e^{b'}$ of bar 91 testifies to Purcell's loyalty to horizontal part-writing, even in these proto-Baroque surroundings.

65 Compare the bass line in the two clauses: the narrow ambit and C major plainness of bars 67ff lack the tension of the octave leap and the linear diminished fourth of bars 83ff; correspondingly, the diminished triad and the abrupt fall of a major sixth at bars 77ff lack the finality of the scale line and the fall of a fifth at bars 89–93.

66 Cf. the marching subjects noted earlier for such *topoi* as 'walking'; but the reference here is less mimetic and more metaphorical.

67 Two faint traces of evidence support this idea. First, the liturgy for 30 January does include Joel 2, albeit a different passage. Secondly, in one of Purcell's rare self-borrowings from the church music, 'Blow Up the Trumpet' shares a passage ('Spare thy people') with 'Turn Thou Us, O Good Lord' (z 62: because the passage is slightly less elaborate – and, I think, less effective – in z 62, I suggest that is the earlier of the two). No occasion is documented for z 62 either, but its text *is* specified for 30 January.

68 It has not always been accepted that 'Praise the Lord' was indeed composed for the 1689 coronation; but see Anselm Hughes, 'Music of the Coronation over a Thousand Years', *Proceedings of the Royal Musical Association*, lxxix (1952–3), 81–100 (especially 94); and correspondence in *Musical Times*, cxix (1978), 938, and cxx (1979), 1, 22, 114.

69 The two concerted anthems are extreme examples of the editing of anthem texts for state occasions; they are the only anthems by Purcell that mix texts from both Prayer Book and Bible.

70 Purcell's vocal orchestration is scrupulously judged: the copyist uses all seven clefs from G2 to F3 to differentiate the vocal parts, and the two lowest chorus parts converge at the unison or octave to strengthen a few crucial cadences.

71 On a motif established in the common-time movement of the symphony, creating a quasi-*da capo* effect also heard in some symphony anthems of the period, like 'Awake, Awake' (z 1, c1682–3), 'Behold, I Bring You Glad Tidings' (z 2, 1687), or 'O Sing unto the Lord' (z 44, 1688).

72 E.g. *Te Deum*, 'When thou took'st'; *Benedictus*, 'Blessed be the Lord'; *Creed*, 'And ascended', 'And I look'; *Nunc dimittis*, 'Lord, now lettest thou'. A related figure has the intervals filled in diatonically: *Benedictus*, 'And thou, Child'; *Magnificat*, 'And hath exalted'.

73 E.g. 'Abraham . . .' in Blow's *Magnificat* in A, 8vo ed. Watkins Shaw (Stainer & Bell, 1941).

74 It may also reflect a respectful reluctance to appear to outdo the ancients, since the grave simplicity of Byrd's or Farrant's services was constantly on display at the Chapel Royal and Westminster Abbey.

75 See *Zimmerman I*, 231; and a letter by Brian Crosby in *Musical Times*, cxxiv (1983), 746.

6

Purcell's Odes: A Reappraisal

BRUCE WOOD

Purcell's odes have suffered long neglect. Only two of them, 'Hail! Bright Cecilia!' and 'Come Ye Sons of Art Away', are regularly performed, and until the late 1980s few had ever been commercially recorded, while the others remained, for most music lovers, mere titles in a work list. Yet of all the genres in which Purcell composed, the odes offer us by far the fullest picture of his musical development. Most of his church music was written by 1688, and all his major stage works (with the possible exception of *Dido and Aeneas*[1]) after that date, while his instrumental chamber music nearly all belongs to the late 1670s and early 1680s. In contrast, only one year between 1680 and 1695 – revolutionary 1688 – cannot claim an ode (or at any rate a complete and authenticated one[2]), while in several years Purcell produced two, and in one year three. And whereas much of his music is impossible to date precisely, all but one of his odes can be assigned not merely to the relevant year but to particular occasions.

Most of them were written for the same group of performers: the choir of the Chapel Royal;[3] soloists drawn from among their number, from the Private Musick, and during the 1690s from the theatre also; and the royal string band,[4] supplemented in a few works by woodwind and brass. By their excellence, both collective and individual, these musicians gave Purcell plenty of stimulus. The same cannot, alas, be said of the poets who turned out the texts of the odes. Even Purcell could manage only fustian stuff to garb some of these flatulent encomia; but he contrived to clothe most of them in new robes of glory that can, at least in performance, hide their naked literary poverty. Nevertheless, the task of setting royal odes to music was one that court composers probably regarded not as a chore but rather as a welcome opportunity. After all, whatever aesthetic shortcomings might mar its text, the finished work doubtless had more rehearsal time devoted to it than did the average anthem with strings, while the actual performance was the centrepiece of an occasion far more important than a mere Sunday service in Chapel. The care which Purcell lavished on his royal odes suggests that he approached their composition not with resignation but with an enthusiasm that the passing years did nothing to dim.

Throughout the 1660s and 1670s, only two regular occasions in the Court calendar – the New Year and the King's birthday – had been celebrated with odes, whose composition was the preserve of a very small circle of musicians. The three settings that survive from the late 1670s are all by Blow,[5] and it seems likely that he had dutifully turned out two such works every year since the death of Pelham Humfrey in 1674. The advent of Purcell as a Court composer might have been expected to result in a division of this labour. In fact, however, his early royal odes had a new function, as welcome songs marking the end of various royal absences from London. Blow, meanwhile, continued to be responsible for composing odes for the New Year and, along with William Turner, for the King's birthday.

The provision of odes specific to the latter occasion ceased under James II, whose birthday (14 October) followed closely on the Court's autumn return to London – an event which continued to be celebrated, as it had been in the previous reign, with a welcome song set by Purcell. In at least one year, 1686, the ode seems to have been performed on the birthday despite being couched in the terms of a welcome song.[6] After the Revolution the pattern changed again. No more welcome songs were composed,[7] but a birthday ode was required for each of the joint monarchs; Purcell had the more grateful task of composing for Queen Mary, and the short straw – providing ode settings for the gruff William III – was drawn jointly by Staggins and Blow. The latter also maintained, for a further decade, his long series of New Year odes.

Purcell's earliest odes, then, constituted a new element in a well established and carefully regulated pattern. Their acceptance of the most obvious model, the odes of Blow, is therefore hardly surprising: but Purcell was quick to stamp his individuality upon the genre, and his first ode, 'Welcome, Vicegerent' (z 340), represents an auspicious start despite its obvious weaknesses. These have been attributed to youth and inexperience,[8] but such indulgence disregards Purcell's precocity (the wonderfully assured and exuberant symphony anthem 'My Beloved Spake' (z 28), for example, had been composed some three years earlier[9]). A likelier explanation lies in the poverty of the text – scarcely congenial, one imagines, to a composer accustomed to setting the majestic English of Coverdale, Cranmer and the King James Bible.

Whatever the reason, the music of 'Welcome, Vicegerent' is, for Purcell, exceptionally variable in quality. Its unevenness is apparent from the start. The common-time opening movement of the symphony consists largely of clichés spun out through sequential repetition; but the fugal triple-time section is lively, neatly crafted and full of surprises – not least the rhetorical syncopated chords at its centre. A bigger surprise, however, is that this second movement is promptly repeated in full as an accompaniment to the opening chorus. There is a precedent for this ingenious procedure in the second verse of Blow's symphony anthem 'The Lord is my Shepherd', composed three or four years earlier,[10] and a parallel to it in the first verse of Purcell's own anthem 'O Praise God in His Holiness' (z 42), composed around the same time as the ode. But it outshines both, for in Blow's anthem the four instrumental lines of the symphony are reduced to three for the accompaniment, and anyway soon turn aside from direct repetition, while in that of Purcell the restatement is confined to the outer parts.

The remainder of the work is of less interest. Its central ritornello is indeed almost tedious – based on a five-note melodic idea which was to serve Purcell well in a subsequent ode, 'From Hardy Climes' (z 325), and in the Second Music of *The Fairy Queen* (z 629/2a), but which here, doggedly worked at for 112 bars including repeats, outstays its welcome. The general layout of the ode is unadventurous: not least the tonal plan, with excursions only to the tonic minor and the dominant major and minor, though one oddity occurs in the penultimate movement. This tenor solo with chorus repeats, 'Music, the food of love', is restated in full by the strings, not in the same key but a fourth higher, producing a curiously lop-sided effect which Purcell wisely avoided in subsequent works.

A more striking feature of the ode is its high proportion of writing for the full choir, which takes three of the eight vocal movements in their entirety and participates in three more. There was a recent precedent for this: Blow's 1679 New Year ode 'Great Janus, though the Festival be Thine', which actually opens with a chorus – a bold innovation – and ends with an imposing example in six parts (five vocal and one instrumental), resembling choruses in previous odes only in its stolidly homophonic texture. Purcell was more inventive: the final chorus of 'Welcome, Vicegerent' is also in six parts (this time with two independent lines for the violins), but offers a deft display of double counterpoint, complete with inversions of one of the subjects – all packed into a dozen bars.

In other respects, however, 'Welcome, Vicegerent' sets a pattern for Purcell's odes over the next three or four years. It lacks only one ingredient that was to become familiar: the ground bass. This, however, was first introduced, not by Purcell but by Blow, whose 1681 New Year ode 'Great Sir, the Joy of All our Hearts' contains an extended movement built on a ground of stepwise running quavers – one of several kinds of bass that have come to be thought of as typically Purcellian. This is by no means the earliest ground of known date in the output of either composer; but it supplied Purcell with a model, soundly crafted if not particularly imaginative, for what came to be one of his favourite types of ground-bass composition – the solo air, rounded off with a ritornello which either repeats or develops its material – though Blow's air is instead punctuated with two related ritornellos, so as to form a neat ternary structure (Example 1).

Purcell took up the device in his very next ode, 'Swifter, Isis, Swifter Flow' (z 366), composed in the autumn of the same year;

EX. 1   John Blow, 'Great Sir, the Joy of all our Hearts' (*GB-Bu* MS
5001, pp. 86–8)

avoiding the obvious riposte of using a similar bass, he produced instead one of the most idiosyncratic of all his grounds.[11] He was probably driven to seek an extraneous technical challenge by the dismal standard of the (happily anonymous) text:

> Hark, Hark! just now my listening ears
>   Are struck with the repeated sound
> Of lab'ring oars, and it appears
>   By growing strong, they're this way bound.
> See, see, it is the royal barge:
>   O how she does my eyes delight;
> Let bells ring, and great guns discharge,
>   Whilst num'rous bonfires banish night.

The bass line, imitated by the upper parts in the two ritornellos which frame the air, employs a curiously ponderous crotchet arpeggio, hinting at a trumpet fanfare, but possibly suggested rather by the 'lab'ring oars' of the text. The air is not one of Purcell's happiest efforts: besides inelegant leaps, it contains some untidy word-repetition ('See, see, it is the royal barge, See, see, it is: O, O, O, O, O . . .'). He was more at ease in the fluent Italianate duet for trebles, singing mostly in parallel sixths, 'The king whose absence like the sun'. Though not strictly a ground – the bass of running quavers develops freely after the first few statements – the movement conveys an impression of tight discipline, to which the neat symmetry of its vocal phrases also contributes. Its close cousins can be found in more than one of Purcell's subsequent odes.

'Swifter, Isis' is also of interest as being Purcell's earliest work to include woodwind parts. These are decidedly limited in scope (though the players may also have doubled the violin parts with oboes elsewhere in the work): one bass solo is accompanied by recorders, and one brief instrumental movement – the ritornello that follows the ground-bass air already described – has an independent part for oboe. The intended performers were probably the French woodwind players who had been supernumerary Court musicians since 1678;[12] Purcell wrote for them again in his next welcome song, 'What Shall be Done in Behalf of the Man?' (z 341; composed in the late spring, on the return of

EX.   2a   John Blow, 'Sing Unto the Lord, O Ye Saints', bars 130–42

the Duke of York from Scotland). Here he again confined the woodwind parts to two movements – the opening solo and one recurring ritornello. The latter, with its deftly turned antiphonal structure, is reminiscent of Lully; but it has a closer and home-lier relative (Example 2) in one of Blow's anthems, 'Sing Unto the Lord, O Ye Saints', though that work, composed about the same time, cannot be dated precisely enough to identify it as precursor or derivative.[13] This ritornello apart, Purcell's treat-ment of the woodwind, while more assured than in 'Swifter, Isis', is no match for that of Blow, who fully exploited the

EX.   2b   Henry Purcell, 'What Shall be Done in Behalf of the Man'
(z 341/3e), bars 171–83

unusual combination called for in his anthem – two recorders,
doubling on tenor oboes – both in instrumental and in vocal
movements. He showed himself to be equally resourceful in a
second anthem, 'Lord, Who shall Dwell in Thy Tabernacle?',
employing the recorders and strings not only antiphonally but
also in rich five-part polyphony.[14] In these early years Blow was
still the bolder pioneer.

EX. 3 Henry Purcell, 'The Summer's Absence Unconcerned we Bear' (z 337/10a), bars 337–40

In his autumn 1682 welcome song, 'The Summer's Absence Unconcerned we Bear' (z 377), Purcell was content to re-use several formulae from 'Swifter, Isis', though they are subtly modified or combined. A lyrical duet for trebles, 'All hearts should smile', exploits parallel thirds instead of sixths; a sizeable movement – not a duet, as in the earlier ode, but an air, 'These had by their ill-usage drove', repeated as a ritornello – is constructed over a ground-like running bass obviously indebted to Blow (Example 3; cf. Example 1, above); and a genuine ground-bass movement, 'And when late from your throne', is built not on arpeggio patterns but on that familiar cliché, the descending tetrachord. The work also contains what was, for Purcell, an important novelty: a declamatory bass solo taking full advantage of the vocal range of John Gostling. In this he followed the lead of Blow, who had some nine months earlier, in the New Year ode 'Arise, Great Monarch', created his first solo for 'that stupendious Base'[15] (Example 4). But whereas Blow wastes the first of the sensational bottom Ds on a weak and unimportant final syllable, Purcell tellingly reserves all of them for important words; he also gives this magisterial piece of writing pride of place at the beginning of his ode, whereas Blow buries his effort in the middle. Both solos were surprisingly long delayed, for Gostling's prowess in these nether vocal regions had been recognised even before he became a Gentleman of the Chapel Royal, in February 1679.[16]

To 1683 belong three of Purcell's odes. 'From Hardy Climes', celebrating Princess Anne's wedding on 28 July to Prince George of Denmark, has many engaging features. The vivacious second section of its French overture, in 6/8 – Purcell's first such movement in compound time – is a flattering imitation, albeit more disciplined in its phrase structure and its pattern of entries, of that in Blow's ode 'Dread Sir, Father Janus', for New Year 1683

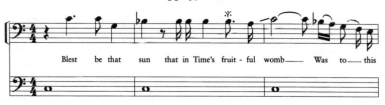

EX. 4a John Blow, 'Arise, Great Monarch' (*GB-Bu* MS 5001,
pp. 59–60)

(Example 5). The first vocal movement takes its cue from the same source (Example 6): the pairing of a rhetorical declamatory opening and a triple-time dance-song – a form Italian in origin, but long established in England – might seem an obvious opening gambit for royal odes, but was in fact almost untried in such a context.[17] The example by Blow, delivered with customary panache by Gostling, must have been suitably arresting, but that by Purcell proves to be an altogether grander affair: the air modulates freely, while the declamatory section contains some telling details (the unexpected C natural on 'dangerous', the vividly pictorial moment of stasis on 'gaze'). The only other solo movement in the ode, the tenor solo 'The sparrow and the gentle dove', has an elegant melodic line underpinned by confidently

EX. 4b Henry Purcell, 'The Summer's Absence Unconcerned we Bear' (z 337/2), bars 52–9

striding quavers that not only form the bass line but also sketch some of the harmony – a ground-bass air for the first time fully characteristic of the mature Purcell; here too an exemplar is to be found in Blow's 'Dread Sir, Father Janus' (Example 7), but again it was the younger composer who developed his material more resourcefully and at greater length. The remaining movements of the ode, however, show him to less advantage: though deftly turned, much of its music is stubbornly unmemorable.

The autumn welcome song for the King, in contrast, is memorable indeed. The anonymous text of 'Fly, Bold Rebellion' (z 324) is a limping undistinguished affair, but the spectacle it celebrates – a monarch triumphant, routing his enemies – fired the composer's imagination and elicited one of his finest works thus far, sacred or secular. From the start the music has a swaggering confidence, strikingly akin to that of Purcell's contemporaneous anthem 'The Lord is my Light and my Salvation' (z 55) – probably a sacred counterpart to the ode.[18] The fleet-footed second movement of the overture to the ode is followed by

EX.   5a   John Blow, 'Dread Sir, Father Janus' (*GB-Bu* MS 5001, pp. 31–2)

EX. 5b   Henry Purcell, 'From Hardy Climes' (z 337/1b), bars
12–28

EX. 5b (*contd.*)

Purcell's earliest verse ensemble in as many as five parts –
unusual also in employing double counterpoint for dramatic
rather than purely musical effect, as phrase and counter-phrase
pronouncing sentence of banishment upon 'bold Rebellion'
pass from voice to voice like shouts from a loyal crowd. This
elaborate opening is balanced by a richly sonorous closing

ensemble and chorus in no fewer than seven and six parts respectively.

In between come equal delights. A pithy bass air in which Justice throws down the Rye House plotters to Avernus (conjured up, predictably, by a bottom D from Gostling) gives another respectful nod in the direction of Blow's 1683 New Year ode[19] (Example 8). Three airs for the higher voices are all binary and square-phrased, but each is distinctive in character and memorably beautiful in detail (especially the twist of line and harmony depicting 'rivers from their channels turned'), and each associated ritornello has unusually rich inner part-writing. The two imaginatively contrasted trios in the middle of the work – high voices in the first, low in the second – maintain the same high quality of invention. Even where the text is at its most unpromising the music does not falter:

> Come then, change your notes, disloyal crowd,
> You that already have been too loud
>   With importunate follies and clamours;
> 'Tis no business of yours
> To dispute the high powers
>   As if you were the government framers.

This passage stands out in bold relief, thanks to its forceful rhythms in duple metre, its close vocal spacing, and its tonal isolation (in F minor, still a most unusual key[20]). Another noteworthy feature of the work is the succession of dignified choruses which buttress its structure. Though scarcely longer than its immediate predecessor, it is far grander in conception, avoiding any change of metre for long stretches, and securing balance as well as variety by the judicious disposition of such few shifts as it does admit.

Purcell may already have been at work on his next ode when 'Fly, Bold Rebellion' was in rehearsal, for the two performances were only eight weeks apart.[21] 'Welcome to All the Pleasures' (z 339), though unconnected with the Court – it was composed in celebration of St Cecilia's Day – is very similar in layout to Purcell's royal odes and, like its immediate predecessor, a masterpiece. Yet it has few specific points of contact with that

EX.   6a   John Blow, 'Dread Sir, Father Janus' (*GB-Bu* MS 5001,
pp. 33–4)

work, save its inclusion of a fine ground-bass air and ritornello
('Here the deities approve') and its use of a key even more
unusual than F minor (E major, the tonic major, in which it
ends). It does not rival the grandeur of 'Fly, Bold Rebellion',
having no ensemble with more than three parts and no chorus
with more than four, though it does have two fully independent
violin parts in the final chorus (a texture hitherto avoided, curiously, in both Purcell's and Blow's odes despite being occasionally found in their anthems).[22] Besides its melodic grace, and its

EX. 6b Henry Purcell, 'From Hardy Climes' (z 325/2, 3a), bars
41–53, 72–9

EX.   7a   John Blow, 'Dread Sir, Father Janus' (*GB-Bu* MS 5001,
p. 43)

EX.   7b   Henry Purcell, 'From Hardy Climes' (z 325/8a), bars
245–8

greater intricacy of texture (including an unusual opening in
sustained double counterpoint) than Purcell permitted himself
in royal odes, perhaps the most remarkable feature of the work
is its highly original ending: the final tonic chord lasts for six
bars, descending through all the instrumental and vocal parts
and finally dwindling into silence.

Composed the same year as 'Welcome to All the Pleasures',
'Laudate Ceciliam' (z 329) has long been regarded as a companion work. But it bears scant resemblance to any of Purcell's
odes. He himself termed it a 'Latine Song',[23] and may well have
written it for private performance by musical friends at Oxford
– a context which would explain its abstruse notation in white
notes only, its Latin text, its ingenious cyclic construction and its
economical scoring (two violins and continuo, with only three
solo voices and no chorus).[24] One further work is traditionally
classed as a Cecilian ode, and assigned by some authorities to
1683. 'Raise, Raise the Voice' (z 334), however, unlike any
known Cecilian ode of the period, includes no mention of
music's patroness, instead invoking Apollo,[25] though it does also
mention 'sacred Musick's holy day'. It is not connected with the
'official' Cecilian festivities founded in 1683, but even before
that date there were less formal celebrations, which evidently
continued for many years.[26] 'Raise, Raise the Voice' accords well
with an intimate context. It is laid out on a modest scale, and
requires only small forces – three soloists, three-part chorus
and three-part strings. Its construction, despite the inclusion of a

EX. 8a John Blow, 'Dread Sir, Father Janus' (*GB-Bu* MS 5001, pp. 49–50)

The sons of the earth, The post-hu-mous birth Of the foul Drag-on's teeth spit their ven-om in vain; The ser-pen-tine elves___ Will ru-in___ them-selves: Great Charles in his right___ for___ ev-er shall reign,

resourcefully contrived air, chorus and ritornello on a ground, is simple – especially the tonal design, with every movement centred on the tonic, minor or major. Its closest kin are not Purcell's odes but his symphony songs, such as 'If ever I more Riches did Desire' (z 544) – a work with which it probably also shares a date in the mid-1680s.

Purcell's last welcome song for Charles II, 'From those Serene and Rapturous Joys' (z 326), falls well below the level of 'Fly, Bold Rebellion'. It opens impressively enough: the symphony is vigorously propelled by robust harmony, and the first verse, initially resembling a routine *arioso* movement, soon reveals itself as something new – a declamatory air with an active bass

EX.   8b   Henry Purcell, 'Fly, Bold Rebellion' (z 325/2c), bars
81–101

line and neat symmetries of phrase structure – and gives rise to a substantial, generously detailed ritornello. But the final section, though unusually economical in construction – a related air and chorus, introduced and separated by a recurring ritornello – is vapid. Also unconventional in structure, but much stronger in musical ideas, is the chorus 'Welcome home', first stated in the tonic major, and later repeated (with adjustments) in the subdominant. Its string accompaniment in running parallel thirds suggests direct Italian influence, but something very similar is to be found in an intriguing fragment (Example 9), all that survives of the final chorus in Blow's symphony anthem 'Sing Unto the Lord, O Ye Saints', dating from about 1682. Before the repetition of Purcell's chorus comes a bass solo – another tribute to the artistry of Gostling – summed up by Westrup as being 'of small interest except as a reminder of the exaggerated attention paid to vocal ornament at the time'.[27] Even this scathing verdict is not as harsh as the progression from an augmented to a perfect unison that occurs when the vocal line, preoccupied with depicting 'drooping flowers', grates against the instrumental bass (Example 10) – a rare instance of a solecism on Purcell's part. As so often, the best number in the ode is a ground-bass air, with a ritornello full of harmonic piquancy. The text likens the return of the King to the raising of Lazarus: a bizarre piece of hyperbole, but set to music of haunting eloquence.

The first of Purcell's odes for James II makes a fresh start in a quite literal sense: instead of opening with a symphony, it plunges straight into a solo number – a gesture prompted by the imagery of the text:

> Why are all the Muses mute?
> Why sleeps the viol and the lute?
> Why hangs untuned the idle lyre?
> Awake! 'tis Caesar does inspire
> And animate the vocal choir.

This *coup de théâtre* no doubt seized the attention of its royal hearers (and of the composer's brother Daniel who, after a decent interval, appropriated it in response to a similar verbal

EX.   9a   John Blow, 'Sing Unto the Lord, O Ye Saints', bars 363–6

EX.   9b   Henry Purcell, 'From those Serene and Rapturous Joys'
(z 326/4), bars 144–50

EX. 10   Henry Purcell, 'From those Serene and Rapturous Joys'
(z 326/7), bars 254–6

the sick - ly heads of— droop - ing flowers,

cue[28]). But it was not a new idea: Purcell's own anthem 'My Heart is Fixed' (z 29),[29] composed in about 1683, opens with a verse ensemble, as does Humfrey's 'Rejoice in the Lord',[30] written some ten years earlier still. Neither anthem, in fact, has a symphony as such[31] – a sizeable ritornello serving instead – whereas in the ode a conventional bipartite symphony is placed second. This softening of a hitherto inflexible structural formula did not continue, either in Purcell's anthems (unlike those of Blow, which eventually dispensed with an autonomous symphony[32]) or in his odes. The opening symphony remained prominent, and it was the ritornellos which, in the later odes, sometimes cut loose from their thematic context and subsequently all but disappeared. The process is already under way in 'Why are All the Muses Mute?' (z 343), where the ritornello following the treble duet 'So Jove scarce settled in his sky' is a free-standing rondo, unconnected with either of the flanking vocal movements.

The symphony, when it arrives, discloses a clear link with Blow's anthem 'The Lord is King', though who borrowed from whom is uncertain (Example 11). Then follows a bipartite tenor solo whose declamatory opening, instead of being conventionally rhapsodic, is in repeated binary form, while the first strain of its triple-time air is not repeated – another blurring of a stereotype, and again one which, in the event, led nowhere. The ensuing chorus is unremarkable, save for an extraordinary instance of line favoured above euphony (Example 12). The by now inevitable air on a ground, 'Britain, now thou art great', is

EX. 11a   John Blow, 'The Lord is King' (version in A minor), bars
1–5

not one of Purcell's best, sitting on the tonic chord for a whole
bar and relying overmuch on the same chain of suspensions, and
the ensemble and chorus which follow are dull. But the bass
solo 'Accurs'd Rebellion rear'd his head', yet another vehicle for
Gostling, is tightly packed with musical images, stirring even
though familiar, for the infernal monster and the avenging thunder which do battle in its text. The music is cunningly intensified
by close imitation – a device apparent also in the following duet
for trebles, where it spices parallel writing more usually left
bland. Purcell's skill in extending material is twice displayed in
the remainder of the ode. First, a routine choral repeat of a
neatly crafted binary air, 'The many-headed beast is quelled', is
quite transformed by its curiously detailed cadences. Then, after
a rather contrived duet for basses, another binary air, 'O how
blest is the Isle', is first richly harmonized as a ritornello, and
then reworked as an expressive closing chorus, culminating in a
beautifully controlled chromatic descent of a tenth. This fine
movement lingers in the memory, masking what might other-

EX. 11b   Henry Purcell, 'Why are All the Muses Mute?' (z 343/2a),
bars 37–44

wise be the piecemeal impression left by a distinctly uneven ode
with six different key centres and no fewer than sixteen changes
of metre.

'Ye Tuneful Muses' (z 344), composed in 1686, is Purcell's
best ode since 'Fly, Bold Rebellion'. Its overture exudes nobility
and gravitas, heightened by the double counterpoint in its
second section, and by the perfectly timed rhetoric of the bass
entries. The opening duet for basses, vastly superior to the similarly scored number in the previous year's ode, is an eloquent
fusion of declamation and melody, memorably intensified by
languishing chromaticism. It includes a brazenly direct crib from
Blow's 1686 New Year ode 'Hail, Monarch, Sprung of Race
Divine' (Example 13): evidently Purcell, though now approaching the height of his powers, was still not above picking his old
teacher's brains when occasion offered. A brief but dignified

EX. 12 Henry Purcell, 'Why are All the Muses Mute?' (z 343/3b),
bars 126–8

chorus rounds off the first section of the ode. The next is the celebrated succession of air, chorus and ritornello employing the ballad tune 'Hey then, up go we', by turns as a bass line and as an instrumental obbligato – an ingenious contrapuntal feat but not particularly convincing otherwise: only the ritornello manages to sound thoroughly Purcellian, unconstrained by the presence of the interloper in the bass.

Next comes the customary showpiece for Gostling, 'In his just praise', anodyne in its musical imagery (descending chromaticism for 'dangers', a long-held note for 'co-lasting like the sun'), but tightly constructed, with neat imitations between voice and strings. The following chorus is nondescript, apart from its famously naïve open-note scrubbing on the violin at the words 'Tune all your strings' (the forerunner of analogous effects, albeit scored for full orchestra, in *The Yorkshire Feast Song* (z 333), *Dioclesian* (z 627) and 'Arise, my Muse' (z 320)). A square-phrased and banal depiction of 'the rattling of drums and the trumpet's loud sound', spun out interminably with episodes and changes of scoring, presumably reflects the fact that earlier on the day of performance the King had inspected his

EX. 13a   John Blow, 'Hail, Monarch, Sprung of Race Divine'
(*GB-Lcm* MS 1098, ff. 145–145ᵛ)

EX. 13b   Henry Purcell, 'Ye Tuneful Muses' (z 344/2), bars 113–17

household troops.[33] There follows, unexpectedly, a meltingly beautiful trio, with antiphonal phrases for recorders, in praise not of the King but of the powers of music. The sentiment is not incongruous – these lines of text complete the syntax and sense of the preceding ones, evoking drums and trumpets – but Purcell's setting, one of the most intense passages in any of his royal odes, creates a startling contrast. A delicate ground-bass air follows, whose exquisitely detailed ritornello is centred – uniquely among those in Purcell's grounds – in the dominant of the air, and tries vainly to restart in other keys. The remaining movements are rescued from ordinariness by attractive asymmetries of phrase structure.

Purcell's last authenticated ode for James II, 'Sound the Trumpet, Beat the Drum' (z 335), was also to prove his most popular: so much so that its central movement, 'Let Caesar and Urania live' – a purposefully contrapuntal ground-bass duet for countertenors, the earliest of several such in his output – was still repeatedly being borrowed intact by composers of royal odes more than half a century after his death.[34] The ode as a whole, however, is uneven. Much of the writing for full choir has more dignity than substance, and the final chorus outstays its welcome, with a flurry of quavers springing from each seemingly conclusive cadence. More impressive is the orchestral accompaniment in the last two choruses, the string parts being wholly independent instead of mostly doubling the voices. The best of the vocal movements are solos. The lyrical ground-bass air, 'Crown the year', exemplifies a technique Purcell was increasingly to favour, the bass line patterned with rests – here daringly placed on strong beats so as to intensify the drooping chromaticisms. The penultimate movement, another offering to Gostling, is a bipartite solo in the grand manner.

The two biggest instrumental movements are also very impressive. In the triple section of the opening symphony each instrument in turn has a pedal – dominant, tonic, subdominant: a neat scheme, and a refreshing change from the usual climactic dominant pedal in the bass. More arresting is the mighty chaconne, interpolated (there is no other word for it) towards the end: it is unconnected with the movements that flank it and, at 128 bars, grossly out of scale with them. The suggestion that it may have served as a choreographic interlude[35] is not supported by any external evidence. Whatever the reason for its inclusion, it employs one of the baldest of bass-line clichés – long familiar to both Purcell and Blow[36] – with supple resourcefulness.

Thus ended Purcell's series of odes for the Stuart Court. By now he had completed all but two of his symphony anthems – works in the genre which had, twenty-five years earlier, given rise to the ode. How far had the two types diverged?

It is evident that Purcell himself regarded them as quite distinct. For all his professionalism he treated the texts of his odes less seriously (as well he might) than those of his anthems. In the final movement of 'From Hardy Climes', for instance, he blithely repeats the first two lines before beginning the third, in defiance of sense as well as syntax:

> Hence without scheme or figure to descry,
> Events to come from your nativity
> Do we foretell . . .

Where the doggerel is at its feeblest, as in the concluding chorus in 'Swifter, Isis',

> No trumpet be heard in this place, or drum-beat
> But in compliment, or to invite you to eat . . .

Purcell usually despatches it with all decent speed. But occasionally it seems as if he cannot resist poking fun at some hapless poetaster. In 'What Shall be Done in Behalf of the Man', for instance, his setting of one passage parcels out the sycophantic sentiments among the soloists as if they were a gaggle of Court flatterers (Example 14).

Such details apart, the most marked difference is that the odes are musically simpler. They include more solos and duets than larger ensembles, and the latter tend to be largely or entirely homophonic – indeed, most of the odes contain very little contrapuntal writing at all, except in their overtures. Simple dance-song movements, unknown in the anthems, occur quite

EX.   14   Henry Purcell, 'What Shall be Done in Behalf of the Man?'
(z 341/7), bars 312–19

frequently in the odes, usually as solos (for instance, 'Music, the food of love' in 'Welcome, Vicegerent' or the very similar 'Beauty, thou scene of love' in 'Welcome to All the Pleasures'), but occasionally scored for verse ensemble or chorus ('Welcome, dread Sir, to town' in 'Swifter, Isis').

Extension of material is also managed somewhat differently. In Purcell's anthems, material from a vocal passage is nearly always carefully reworked if it recurs in a ritornello; in his odes, however, he was frequently content with mere repetition – sometimes on an extended scale. In 'What Shall be Done in Behalf of the Man?' a duet in repeated binary form, 'May all factious troubles cease', is first restated in its entirety, with each strain given to the chorus and the strings in turn, and then sung yet again, complete with internal repeats, by the chorus. In 'Ye Tuneful Muses', likewise, a ritornello in rondo form is twice repeated entire by the voices to produce a movement totalling 128 bars.

In tonal planning, conversely, the odes are much more complex than the anthems, even though many of the latter are comparable in scale. The earliest of the Court odes, 'Welcome, Vicegerent', is conservative, its first few movements being in C minor and its last few in C major, with a central group in G major. But Purcell quickly grew more adventurous. Only a year later, in 'Swifter, Isis', an opening in G major leads to sections in G minor, C major, A minor, F major, D minor, and finally G minor again. The 1684 ode 'From those Serene and Rapturous Joys' likewise moves from D minor through D major, B minor, G major, E minor, and A minor back to D major; while 'Why are All the Muses Mute?' (1865), which is in D minor, even includes one section in the Neapolitan E flat major – whence the music moves, with a bump, straight to C major. Perhaps the boldest, or oddest, plan is that of 'Sound the Trumpet, Beat the Drum', which at the end of the overture plunges into the subdominant major, and never returns to the home tonic until near the end, though it includes movements in five other keys. In contrast, none of Purcell's symphony anthems composed before 1685 goes beyond a shift from tonic minor to major or vice versa, while the most adventurous in his entire output – 'My Heart is Inditing' (z 30; 1685) and 'O Sing unto the Lord' (z 44; 1688) – are content with the further addition of the relative minor.

Though generally relying on simple techniques for extension of material, Purcell's odes contain numerous examples of an art that conceals art. Almost every one of them has at least one ground-bass movement – nearly always a solo air and ritornello, both in repeated binary form – and several include more than one. In his thirty instrumental anthems, by contrast, only four grounds are to be found – two of them occurring in an instrumental prelude or symphony, one unifying a lengthy antiphonal exchange between verse and chorus, and only one (a duet and ritornello in 'O Sing unto the Lord') resembling the ground-bass airs in the odes.

There are marked differences in vocal scoring between Purcell's odes and anthems. Very few of the numerous verse ensembles in his symphony anthems include treble parts; yet most of his early odes include a treble duet, or a larger ensemble containing two treble parts. (The fact that Purcell – and Blow too, for that matter – largely avoided the use of solo boys in symphony anthems is puzzling, for there are plenty of treble verse parts in their anthems with organ.) And from the mid–1680s onwards almost every one of Purcell's odes included a duet for basses or countertenors – vocal combinations never encountered in his symphony anthems.

Finally, there was an important difference in performance practice, often overlooked nowadays, between odes and anthems. In chapel the instrumentalists, drawn from the Twenty-four Violins, served on a rota, playing one to a part: symphony anthems must have approached the intimacy of chamber music, except in their brief passages for full choir. But there is some evidence that a substantial body of instrumentalists took part in performances of the odes, lending these works greater weight and richer sonority than their sacred counterparts.[37]

Purcell's first birthday ode for Queen Mary opens not, as usual, with a French overture but with an Italian sinfonia. In adopting this innovation he may well have been influenced by G. B. Draghi's setting of the ode for St Cecilia's Day 1687, Dryden's 'From Harmony';[38] Purcell had already followed suit in the last four of his symphony anthems,[39] and for the rest of his life he preferred the Italian model to the French, except in his music for the stage. Draghi's setting also includes independent trumpet parts – their earliest appearance in the English orchestra;[40] they are handled tentatively, entering only in one solo number and one chorus, and soon merging with the violin parts, but Purcell evidently took note. In 1689, it seems, they were not yet available for a royal ode, and he had to content himself with using fanfare-like ideas, notably in the overture. He borrowed instead a different feature of Draghi's scoring: the division of the strings into five parts (not the three-viola French scoring but its Italian cousin, with two violins and two violas[41]). Blow, in his 1690 New Year ode 'With Cheerful Hearts Let All Appear', promptly did the same.[42] But whereas Draghi had confined the five-part scoring to the overture, two short ritornellos and one solo verse in his ode – the remainder being laid out conventionally – both English composers employed it throughout, the cumulative effect being far more telling.

Thanks to this exotic scoring, the orchestral movements of

Purcell's ode abound in moments of gorgeous opulence. Equally striking, however, is the vigorous counterpoint of its opening chorus, repeated after a duet and a solo air so as to form a large musical unit – a graceful reciprocal acknowledgment, this, of the structural planning in Blow's 1688 New Year ode 'Ye Sons of Phoebus'.[43] There is eloquence, as well as ingenuity, in two ground-bass airs, which are placed close together – a piece of bravado only Purcell could have carried off, for all their contrast: 'This does our fertile Isle' is constructed over his shortest ground (just two crotchets, dominant and tonic), and 'By beauteous softness' over one of his longest (twenty-four quavers). A fine declamatory solo for Gostling, 'It was a work of full as great a weight', combines lofty rhetoric with poise and symmetry; and the final chorus, with its compact phrases and exuberant roulades, has an Italianate brilliance that outshines anything in Purcell's output hitherto.

The other ode he composed in 1689, 'Celestial Music' (z 322), is in comparison unremarkable, save in the flourish with which he again places two ground-bass movements side by side. Otherwise it is a modest piece of work – suitably so, considering that the text was by a pupil in a local school. Why the busy and eminent Purcell should have set such a text is unknown: one can only speculate that he was friendly with Maidwell, the schoolmaster in whose house the ode was performed. It must have been intended for professional performers, to judge by the technical demands of the solo numbers, which contain the work's few features of interest: moments of poignant angularity relieve the conventional roulades in 'When Orpheus sang' (the only movement not in the home tonic), while several turns of phrase in 'Thus Virgil's genius' recall those of another air, 'No more shall we the great Eliza boast', in the ode composed for the Queen's birthday less than four months previously. A more substantial borrowing is the overture of 'Celestial Music', taken from the 1685 coronation anthem 'My Heart is Inditing' and forming the most imposing movement in the ode.

Purcell's next ode was vastly more ambitious. It was written for the annual London dinner, at the end of March 1690, of the Yorkshire Society, an association of North Country worthies.

Thomas Durfey, who wrote the text, described *The Yorkshire Feast Song* ('Of old, when heroes thought it bold') as one of Purcell's finest works; but in our own century it has had a mixed reception, Arundell and Holland sharing Durfey's enthusiasm for it, Westrup dismissing it as stodgy and unadventurous.[44] Certainly the tonal scheme is very limited, with only two sections in minor keys amid a great deal of extrovert writing in D major. But it is precisely to this celebratory aspect that the work owes its seminal importance, as the first English score for full Baroque orchestra; what later generations might disparage as an excess of pomp must have thrilled the first audience. Purcell marshals his forces with astonishing assurance, his orchestral technique far outstripping that of Draghi in the Cecilian ode already mentioned; in particular the colour is heightened by the inclusion of oboes as well as recorders, while the trumpets – which are actually employed more sparingly, and hence more tellingly, than detractors of the work have implied – are always given fully independent parts. Why Purcell produced so elaborate a work for this particular commission, eclipsing the most lavish productions even of the Cecilian festival hitherto, remains a mystery: perhaps the explanation is simply that the Yorkshiremen could afford plenty of brass!

Quite apart from its orchestral panoply, the ode is notable for some first-rate music – especially in its solo movements. The best of these are 'The pale and the purple rose', a celebration of the Wars of the Roses, with a rattling orchestral ostinato for opposing groups of strings and oboes, vividly evoking the clash of arms, and 'So when the glittering Queen of Night', a hauntingly beautiful air on a ground, with accompanying strings that circle as hypnotically as the bass. Two other numbers, the solo air 'The bashful Thames' and the duet 'And in each track of glory', are reworked with rich inner-part detail – contrapuntal as well as harmonic – to form memorably expressive choruses. And *The Yorkshire Feast Song* is of interest for more than purely musical reasons. Its text, ostensibly a celebration of 'the City and County of York', is also a transparent and virulently anti-Catholic allegory on the Glorious Revolution. Purcell's acceptance of a private (and therefore quite unofficial) commission to set such a text surely disposes of the 'trace of a question', which has exercised more than one authority,[45] as to whether he was a covert Catholic.

A month or so after this noteworthy première came the Queen's birthday, for which Purcell composed another ambitious ode, 'Arise, my Muse'. This work not only emulates *The Yorkshire Feast Song* in employing trumpets and oboes – their first appearance in a royal ode – but also retains the five-part string scoring of the 1689 birthday ode 'Now does the Glorious Day Appear' (z 332), giving it a richness of orchestral effect that is unique in Purcell's output. Its most specific points of contact are not, however, with either of these other odes, but with *Dioclesian*, and they form the earliest of several such links between his odes and his major stage works of the 1690s. He was probably at work on 'Arise, my Muse' at the same time as on *Dioclesian*, whose première was only a few weeks after the Queen's birthday, and something of his striving after orchestral effect in this, the first of his dramatick operas, is reflected in the ode. The most conspicuous of the similarities between the two scores are the inclusion in each of a ritornello scored for woodwind, brass and continuo without strings; and of a flourish for full orchestra in response to the words 'Sound [all] your instruments' – a gesture also elicited by a similar verbal cue in *The Yorkshire Feast Song*. (The fully notated examples in the two odes perhaps offer useful models for performance of the impromptu one in the opera.) The greatest intrinsic musical interest among the orchestral movements of 'Arise, my Muse', however, lies in the overture, an Italian sinfonia in which Purcell for the first time employs bold antiphonal exchanges between strings and brass: their rising triadic pattern anticipates that in the first few bars of 'Hail! Bright Cecilia!' (z 328). The germ of this idea can be detected at the very opening of Blow's 1690 New Year ode 'With Cheerful Hearts', though there, scored for strings alone, it is much less effective, and Blow quickly abandons it after a few bars. Purcell, in contrast, resourcefully expands it – even, in 'Hail! Bright Cecilia!', by calmly inverting his material (Example 15).

Just as with *The Yorkshire Feast Song*, however, it is not the

resplendent orchestral garb of 'Arise, my Muse' that leaves
the deepest impression, but its solos: the bold declamatory opening number; the exquisite air 'See how the glitt'ring Ruler of the
day', steadily unfolding its lyrical phrases over a hesitant ground
bass; the sombre bipartite song 'And since the time's distress' –
surely written with Gostling in mind, but tactfully avoiding the
low notes which he seems to have lost suddenly around this
time;[46] and the melting lament of the final section, 'But ah! I see
Eusebia drown'd in tears'. Most of these solo numbers have
elaborately wrought instrumental accompaniment, as do all the
choral movements, but of purely orchestral writing there is little:
besides the opening symphony, only the one ritornello already
mentioned. Over the decade since Purcell had composed his first
ode, the orchestral function had changed beyond recognition.

For all its wealth of invention, 'Arise, my Muse' is a less
carefully finished piece of work than its predecessor. It may even
be literally unfinished, for the last seventeen lines of Durfey's
poem as published, including a 'Chorus of All' temptingly full of
musical imagery, are not included in Purcell's setting – which is,
moreover, the shortest of all his odes for Queen Mary, both
in number of bars and in duration. The work ends abruptly,
dismissing the entreaties of poor abandoned Eusebia, with

EX.   15a   John Blow, 'With Cheerful Hearts' (*GB-Lcm* MS 1079,
f. 179)

EX. 15b   Henry Purcell, 'Arise, my Muse' (z 320/1), bars 1–10

EX. 15C   Henry Purcell, 'Hail! Bright Cecilia!' (z 328/1), bars 1–10

cheerful insensitivity, in only twenty bars. The effect has been criticised as comic,[47] but more curious is that the concluding section is so perfunctory: it merely reworks a preceding bass solo to form a chorus that, though decidedly martial in character, does not even utilize the available trumpets: an unthinkable omission, without parallel elsewhere in Purcell's music. Perhaps he was obliged by the pressure of work on *Dioclesian* to round off the ode in a hurry, choosing a point in the text which, though not ideal, at least made a possible ending.

Speed would certainly have been essential when he came to write his next ode for the Queen's birthday if, as some authorities believe, he spent the three or four months immediately beforehand with King William's entourage in Holland.[48] But 'Welcome, Welcome, Glorious Morn' (z 338) betrays no obvious sign of haste: on the contrary, it is much the grandest and most elaborately wrought of all the royal odes thus far. After the overture, with its brilliant display of independent oboe as well as trumpet writing – something hitherto found only in the ostentatious score of *Dioclesian* – the music explores almost every available vocal and instrumental combination: movements for one, two and three voices with continuo; solos with single obbligato parts or full-scale accompaniments for oboes, strings, or trumpets; and choruses variously accompanied by strings (with or without oboes)[49] and by the full band. Even the one *tutti* ritornello differs from the overture, in having no independent parts for the oboes, which are left by implication to double either the strings or the trumpets.

Beneath its fine feathers, however, the music is not of the highest quality. Too many of the movements rely on florid and conventional roulades, both on suitable words ('glorious', 'prolongs', 'joys', 'fly', and so forth) and on quite inappropriate ones ('only', 'thou'). Of greater interest is the structural aspect. One noteworthy innovation is that the opening ground-bass air is ternary, not binary; another, that the work is organized into four large sections, by means variously of tonality, scoring, and repetition of material. The first section, in the tonic, consists of a solo reworked by the chorus, another movement for solo voices, and (as in the 1689 ode) a repeat of the chorus; the second, in the subdominant minor and the tonic, is a succession of duet, solo, and verse repeated as chorus. The first section is balanced by the third, which is in the tonic minor and formed of a solo partially repeated by the chorus, followed by another solo and another chorus; the second section in its turn is balanced by the fourth, in the relative minor and the tonic, which comprises a duet, a solo, and an air reworked to form a concluding chorus (strongly resembling that of the contemporaneous *King Arthur*). Purcell was to return to this kind of large-scale organization in two further odes, to even more telling effect.

The 1692 Queen Mary ode, 'Love's Goddess Sure was Blind' (z 331), marks in some respects a reversion to older methods: it is laid out on a modest scale and scored for strings alone.[50] Yet the tonal planning of the music compensates for any want of variety in its scoring: no two consecutive numbers, except the overture and the opening air, are in the same key, instead alternating between the home tonic and related keys in a manner analogous to the thematic structure of a rondo. In view of the competing claims of other work – the première of *The Fairy Queen* was given only a week or so after the Queen's birthday[51] – the suitability of Sedley's unusually reflective text for an intimate setting must have seemed providential to Purcell, and he created for it some of the loveliest music to be found among his Court compositions.

An unusually high proportion of the solo and ensemble writing it contains is given to the upper voices, resulting in an overall effect of great delicacy. Lyrical simplicity abounds: three of the four solo numbers are unpretentious binary airs, whose ritornellos merely flesh them out with inner parts. One of them is for treble – a voice hitherto given scarcely any solo work, as distinct from ensemble parts, in Purcell's odes. 'Long may she reign' has the limpid directness of the popular airs in his stage works, suggesting that it may have been written not for a Chapel chorister but for a singer from the theatre[52] (a connection which, as we shall see, became explicit in the following year's birthday ode). Another high-voice air, 'May her blest example' (composed for countertenor, though long familiar as a soprano number thanks to an error in the old Purcell Society edition[53]), famously employs as its bass the folksong 'Cold and raw', reputedly a favourite of the Queen's.[54] The melody is pointedly played *tasto solo* the first time it enters: perhaps Purcell was anxious that she might otherwise miss it! The closing chorus, with its anticipation of mourning for her eventual death – a curious and all too prophetic literary fancy – attains an intensity rare in royal command works, even those of Purcell.

Six months after 'Love's Goddess Sure was Blind' came an ode that could hardly be more different. 'Hail! Bright Cecilia!' – the grandest of seventeenth-century English odes, and the finest – is too familiar, and too much written about elsewhere, to need any description here. What is worth nothing, however, is how logically it fits both into the sequence of Purcell's other odes and into the Cecilian series. As in his 1683 Cecilian ode, 'Welcome to All the Pleasures', Purcell was able to draw on models already well tried in his Court odes for every one of its movements; but this time there was a difference – one of sheer scale. 'Hail! Bright Cecilia!' is one of his most spacious pieces of musical architecture – not least in tonal terms, its thirteen movements being disposed among no fewer than nine different keys and yielding nearly as much variety as the whole of *The Fairy Queen*. The grandeur of the work represents an obvious (and entirely successful) attempt to outdo the previous year's Cecilian offering, by Blow ('The Glorious Day is Come'[55]), which had in turn matched the orchestral palette of Purcell's most ambitious ode hitherto ('Welcome, Welcome, Glorious Morn'), and run to double its length: evidently Blow too had taken note of Draghi's 1687 ode. Purcell proceeded to outbid them both, not merely in scale and lavishness but also in sheer vitality. The orchestra is the largest he ever called for, and includes kettle-drums, whose first explicitly notated orchestral use in England had occurred only the previous year, in Blow's Cecilian ode, with Purcell following suit six months afterwards in *The Fairy Queen*. Vocal colour was also plentiful at the first performance of 'Hail! Bright Cecilia!': the autograph score names no fewer than thirteen soloists.[56] Even more variety is afforded by a semi-chorus, with the number of voices specified in the score – another device borrowed from Draghi – accompanied by a similarly reduced orchestra.

The performing score of the 1693 birthday ode, 'Celebrate this Festival' (z 321), also survives.[57] It is in the handwriting of two copyists, neither of them a member of the royal musical establishment but both long associated with it: John Walter, organist of Eton College, and his colleague William Isaack.[58] They worked on the score by turns, in short stints of a few pages – an indication that speed was essential. Presumably the autograph was, most uncharacteristically, too roughly written to be usable for copying parts or taking rehearsals: another sign of haste, as is Purcell's re-use of two movements from the overture of 'Hail! Bright Cecilia!' (shorn of its parts for kettle-drums and for second trumpet, the latter perhaps simply for economy's sake but more probably because a particular trumpeter was unavailable – for instance through being abroad in the royal service).[59]

If he was indeed pressed for time – as he may have been because of theatrical commitments, though it was otherwise a slack period for him[60] – Purcell proceeded to make a rod for his own back. The poem of 'Celebrate this Festival', the first such offering of Nahum Tate's laureateship, is shorter than average, but the setting is the longest and most elaborate of all the royal odes of the 1690s. Its orchestral splendour, with two superb trumpet airs, other solos accompanied by strings or recorders, and two attractive ritornellos for oboes alone, rivals that of 'Welcome, Welcome, Glorious Morn'. It eschews large-scale structural symmetries, save for a repetition of the opening duet and chorus framing a contrasting number, but makes liberal use of ternary form: most significantly, perhaps, in place of Purcell's customary binary pattern, in a ground-bass air, 'Crown the altar', and a duet with ostinato bass figures, 'Britain, now thy cares beguile', but more conspicuously in 'Thus for a righteous cause', a full-scale *da capo* aria which, with its alternating common and triple time, is clearly modelled on another recent trumpet air, 'Thus the gloomy world' in *The Fairy Queen*. There is also a lengthy ensemble, 'Happy realm beyond expressing', in rondo form, a structure which Purcell had not used in such a context since 1686.

More striking than structural innovation or orchestral opulence, however, is the sheer abundance of musical ideas in the ode. The work has been described in detail elsewhere,[61] but one feature of it will bear remark: the inclusion, as in 'Love's Goddess Sure was Blind', of a direct and tuneful solo number of the kind that had made Purcell pre-eminent as a theatre composer. 'Kindly treat Maria's day' (which was almost certainly the first vocal number from any of his odes to appear in print[62] – a clear indication of its tuneful appeal) could easily have been written for one of the singing actresses of the United Company, but the name which appears in the performing score at this point is that of one of the Company's professional singers, Mrs Ayliff. She also had to negotiate the long and tricky roulades of 'Let sullen Discord smile'; the equally taxing triplets of ''Tis sacred', however, were entrusted to 'the Boy' – perhaps an early appearance by Jemmy Bowen. Both these airs, taking their cue from showpiece solos in *The Fairy Queen* and 'Hail! Bright Cecilia!' are notably more technically demanding than any in Purcell's previous royal odes. The same is true of the florid duet passages for trebles in the opening ensemble – in which, as also in 'Britain, now thy cares beguile', the two joined forces, Mrs Ayliff taking the first treble part in both numbers.

Another conspicuous newcomer among the soloists was the high countertenor John Howell,[63] who had sung the upper part of one duet in 'Hail! Bright Cecilia!'. Purcell now exploited his distinctive voice to full effect in 'Crown the altar', the only solo air he ever notated in the mezzo-soprano clef: it lies entirely above middle C and soars repeatedly, above the deliberate tread of its ground bass, up to top D. A more conventional countertenor voice (that of Anthony Robert, of the Private Musick, in the first performance) is required for the air 'Return, fond Muse'. This haunting movement in solemn C minor and stately triple metre, punctuated by gossamer phrases for a trio of recorders alone, recalls the magical sound-world of 'See, even Night herself is here' in *The Fairy Queen*. Even more affecting is the mellifluous air 'I envy not the pride of May', written for the tenor Alexander Damascene (himself a prolific composer of songs). It gains an especial magic from its tonal remoteness in the far-flung mediant major – in this instance E major, an exotic key not visited by Purcell in any work since 'Welcome to All the Pleasures', a decade earlier; another echo of that work is the lingering *diminuendo* ending, on a tonic chord held for six bars.

Between this and Purcell's last birthday ode for Queen Mary comes a work for a less exalted context. 'Great Parent, Hail' (z 327) was composed for the centennial celebrations of Trinity College, Dublin. The quaint theory that this commission identifies Purcell as an Irishman[64] is needlessly far-fetched, for there is an obvious explanation – namely that he was involved thanks to his previous collaborations with the author of the text, Nahum Tate, who was a Trinity graduate. Neither of them exerted himself. Tate's poem is a wretched piece of hack-work; Purcell responded with choruses more pompous than substantial, and solo numbers more florid than expressive. In places the musical rhetoric teeters on the brink of self-parody, as with the endless reiterations of the word 'repeated' in the duet 'After war's alarms'. The work is episodic and in large part perfunctory; even the expected ground-bass number is lacking. The orchestra consists only of recorders and strings, with the latter kept so busy playing fanfare figures that the lack of trumpets, unfortunate in a celebratory work, is not glossed over but perversely emphasized.

The next ode stands at the opposite extreme. Purcell's last for Queen Mary, it is also his finest. 'Come Ye Sons of Art Away' (z 323) is not on quite such a grand scale as its immediate predecessor, 'Celebrate this Festival', but it is more lucidly planned as a whole, falling into four big blocks defined by both structure and tonality: an opening sequence in the tonic, framed (after the overture) by statements of the opening air and chorus; a pair of solos in the tonic minor, one with its associated ritornello and the other reworked as a chorus; a pair of solos in the dominant, major and minor; and a concluding rondo-form duet and chorus in the tonic. The orchestra is used quite sparingly – four of the seven solo numbers are accompanied by continuo alone – but the choruses are brilliantly orchestrated, especially in the ceaselessly shifting unison and octave doubling of the voices. The work has an exhilarating range of style: open-hearted popular melodies in the opening and closing numbers; no fewer than three masterly ground-bass movements; and an exquisite declamatory air, 'Bid the graces', whose obbligato oboe part recalls that of the celebrated Plaint in *The Fairy Queen*.[65] One expected ingredient, the trumpet obbligato, is conspicuous by its absence – intentionally. The poet (almost certainly Tate,[66] who as Laureate knew the Court circle intimately) had slipped in a small joke for the initiated:

> Sound the trumpet, while around
> You make the list'ning shores rebound.

Purcell, of course, took the cue, leaving the Shores – Matthew and William, expert trumpeters in the royal band – to sit through this movement, instruments on laps.[67] Both of them were fully occupied in the opening and closing choruses of the ode, but curiously enough there is only a single trumpet part in the overture, a dignified Italian sinfonia in four movements. Possibly Purcell wrote this number first, simply repeating the instrumentation of 'Celebrate this Festival', before learning that a second player could be spared from military duties for some real music-making.

A conspicuous trumpet part was *de rigueur* in his last Court ode, 'Who can from Joy Refrain' (z 342), composed for the birthday of the Duke of Gloucester. This sickly and deformed six-year-old, heir apparent to the throne and repository of hopes for a Stuart succession, delighted in trumpet music, though this was merely a facet of his enthusiasm for all things military – something pathetically ill-assorted with his physical frailty. The feebleness of the poor little fellow is equalled by that of the text of the ode, cruelly inapposite in its obsequious bombast:

> Sound the trumpet, beat the warlike drums:
>   The Prince will be with laurels crown'd
> Before his manhood comes . . .
>
> If now he burns with noble flame,
>   When grown, what will he do?
> From pole to pole he'll stretch his fame
>   And all the world subdue.

This sort of thing may well have stuck in the gullet of Purcell, several of whose own children had died young; he was, moreover, hard pressed with other projects while working on the ode.[68] At all events he made only a limited effort. The piece starts well, with a spirited trumpet overture (shared with *Timon of Athens*, for which it was probably composed[69]); but the setting itself lacks distinction, even in its one trumpet air, and is marred in places by short-windedness – notably in the bass air 'The father's brave', and also in the oboe introduction to the soprano solo 'The graces in his mother shine', whose loss of impetus is a particular disappointment following an opening phrase of almost Bach-like amplitude and nobility. And though Purcell was moved to create one movement of tender beauty, the ground-bass air 'A Prince of glorious race', he managed only a very plain harmonization of it for a ritornello. The concluding chaconne, while undeniably colourful, is rather mechanical in detail and, at nearly 250 bars including repeats, disproportionately long.

'Who can from Joy Refrain?' forms a depressing codicil to Purcell's legacy of Court odes. But the six others he had composed since the revolution, together with the one Cecilian offering, had enriched the genre far more even than his earlier odes. To the listener their most obviously innovative feature is probably their sumptuous orchestral writing: their variety both of tone-colour as such and also of the endlessly inventive instrumental doubling of choral parts. Other features, however, also undergo transformation in the late odes. Their structural and tonal planning becomes more and more resourceful; and their breadth of style increases, to encompass simple lyrical tunes at one extreme and intricate contrapuntal choruses at the other.

Extended choral counterpoint was something Purcell had largely avoided in his odes for Charles II and James II, yet the first of his odes for Mary has an opening chorus worthy of Handel in its sturdy self-assurance; the third of them ends with a vigorous display including an entry in augmentation; and the 1693 ode includes an eight-part chorus that crams nearly thirty entries into six bars of smooth and effortless double counterpoint. In 'Hail! Bright Cecilia!', even more remarkably, Purcell employs counterpoint not only for its own sake but also as a highly specific means of illuminating ideas in the text: the universe, 'made up of various parts' which engage in a masterly contrapuntal display (including inversions) before gloriously coalescing into 'one perfect harmony'; and the celestial improvement of Cecilia's 'former skill', symbolized in a passage of double counterpoint for six voices instead of the prevailing four.

Purcell's odes naturally invite comparison with his contribution to their parent genre, the symphony anthem. Since this became virtually extinct in 1688, his late odes have no sacred counterparts. But the best among the earlier ones, such as 'Fly, Bold Rebellion', are equal in musical quality to the finest of his contemporaneous anthems, and even the somewhat inferior odes for James II are eclipsed by only one sacred masterpiece of their period, 'O Sing unto the Lord' (z 44). All in all, Purcell displayed greater creative vitality in his odes than in his anthems – not least in that they are less dependent on formulae, as witness the cluster of three odes composed in 1683, all sharply distinct in character and structure. He may well have placed a higher value (as Blow certainly did)[70] on his sacred compositions, but some of his odes reach equally great heights, and even the weakest of them are rarely perfunctory.

Some of the blame for their past neglect must be borne by the dismal effusions which Purcell was obliged to set, and which over the years have been roundly execrated by several writers.[71] But purely literary fastidiousness has not prevented acceptance of his stage works,[72] and we should not continue allowing it to obstruct performance of his odes. If we do, we are the losers by at least a third of his output of sizeable works – several of them among his finest.

NOTES

1 See Bruce Wood and Andrew Pinnock, ' "Unscarr'd by turning times"?: the Dating of Purcell's *Dido and Aeneas*', *Early Music*, xx (1992), 373–90.

2 A fragment beginning 'The noise of foreign wars' seems highly likely to

belong to an autumn 1688 welcome song for the King. It is preserved among a collection devoted almost exclusively to music by Purcell; its musical style accords well with that of Purcell in the late 1680s; and its text is highly apposite to the unsettled political climate of the months immediately before the Glorious Revolution. See Nigel Fortune, 'A New Purcell Source', *Music Review*, xxv (1964), 109–13, and *Works II*, xviii (Novello, scheduled for publication during 1995).

3   Although there is no evidence as to whether the Chapel choir was normally turned out in full, we may safely presume that the chorus at least decently outnumbered the soloists (who may, of course, have been part of it). The only performing score of a royal ode apparently associated with its first performance (that of 'Celebrate this Festival', in *GB-Ob* MS Mus.c.28, ff. 78v–99) names no fewer than twelve solo singers, including five countertenors and four basses. By way of comparison, the autograph score of 'Hail! Bright Cecilia!' (*GB-Ob* MS Mus.c.26, ff. 23–69v) names thirteen soloists, again apparently for the première.

4   Here again the evidence as to numbers is scanty; but see p. 233.

5   For evidence as to the dating of Blow's Court odes, see Rosamond McGuinness, *English Court Odes* (Oxford, 1971), 15–23.

6   Ralph Vaughan Williams, the first modern editor of these works, suggested that all three of Purcell's welcome songs for James II were probably performed on the King's birthday: see *Works I*, xviii (London, 1909), ii–iv. In 1685 this was apparently not so: on 10 October Samuel Pepys wrote to Sir Robert Southwell that 'To night wee have had a mighty Musique-Entertainment at Court for the welcomeing home the King and Queene' (R. G. Howard, ed., *Letters and the Second Diary of Samuel Pepys* (London, 1932), 171); though John Evelyn recorded on 15 October that 'Being the Kings birth-day, was a solemn Ball at Court; And Musique of Instruments & Voices before the Ball' (*Evelyn*, 15 October 1685; IV, 480). In 1686 and 1687 there is no evidence of a musical performance on either date, but the King's birthday was 'observed with great solemnity' (1686), and 'observed by ringing of bells &c' (1687), according to Narcissus Luttrell, *A Brief Historical Relation of State Affairs from September 1678 to April 1714* (Oxford, 1857), I, 386. The military references in the text of the 1686 ode are explicable only in the light of the troop review carried out by the King on his birthday morning that year: ibid., 386.

7   This may well have been because, owing to the demands of affairs of state, the custom of removing the Court to Windsor for the summer months was no longer regularly observed.

8   See for instance J. A. Westrup, *Purcell* (London, 1937), 172.

9   It survives in *GB-Lbl* Add. MS 50860 and *J-Tn* MS N-5/10 – Chapel Royal bass partbooks – in the handwriting of William Tucker and preceding works attributed to 'Mr' Blow. Tucker died in February 1679; Blow was granted his doctorate in December 1677.

10 Attributed to 'Mr' Blow in *GB-Lbl* Add. MS 50860 and *J-Tn* MS N-5/10: see note 9, above.

11 For an extended discussion of this topic, see Rosamond McGuinness, 'The

Ground-Bass in the English Court Ode', *Music and Letters*, li (1970), 118–40, 265–78.

12 Andrew Ashbee, *Records of English Court Music* (Snodland, 1986), I, 179.

13 Musica Britannica, l, xix.

14 Ibid., 49–68.

15 *Evelyn*, 28 January 1685; IV, 404.

16 J. A. Westrup, op. cit., 303–4.

17 The first vocal movement of Cooke's 'Good Morrow to the Year' (1666) (*GB-Bu* Barber MS 5001, 1–9) is an exiguous declamatory passage for bass, followed by an equally tiny triple-time air for treble; that of Humfrey's 'See, Mighty Sir' (1670?) (*GB-Lbl* Add. MS 33287, ff. 69*v*–71*v*) is a tenor solo, with a declamatory opening successively in quadruple and duple time, followed by a triple-time air. There is no other English example before 1683 of a bipartite solo serving as the opening vocal number in an ode, or for that matter in a symphony anthem. (Locke's 'I will hear what the Lord God will say'), printed in Musica Britannica, xxxviii, 82–8, which begins with such a movement, is not a complete anthem but forms the concluding portion of 'Lord, Thou hast been Gracious', which survives – severed from it, and misattributed to Blow – only in *GB-Lbl* Add. MS 31444, ff. 184–8*v*: see Bruce Wood, 'John Blow's Anthems with Orchestra' (Ph.D. diss, U. of Cambridge, 1976), iv: 242–56, 273, and v: 432–3.)

18 A special thanksgiving for the frustration of the Rye House Plot was held on 9 September (Narcissus Luttrell, op. cit., 279). 'The Lord is my Light and my Salvation' is a setting of Psalm 27, vv. 1, 3, 5, 6, 7 – strikingly apposite for such a purpose. The exact date of its composition is unknown, but in Purcell's fair-copy album (*GB-Lbl* MS RM 20.h.8) it is the fifth of fourteen of his anthems copied between the autumn of 1681, when he appears to have acquired the volume, and the end of 1684: see Imogen Holst, ed., *Henry Purcell 1659–1695: Essays on his Music* (London, 1959), 112–15.

19 Noted in Rosamond McGuinness, *English Court Odes*, 103–4.

20 It was not, however, a key whose use was confined to music of sombre or penitential mood. Among the handful of works in this key by Purcell's immediate predecessors are not only Humfrey's 'O Lord my God' but also Blow's 'Sing we Merrily', or rather its recurring principal instrumental symphony – the vocal sections being in the tonic major.

21 The Court had returned to London on 25 September (Narcissus Luttrell, op. cit., 281).

22 See for example Purcell's 'O Praise God in his Holiness', composed c1681 (*Works I*, xiv), and Blow's 'I Beheld, and Lo, a Great Multitude', composed by 1677 (Musica Britannica, XVI, forthcoming).

23 It is thus designated in the autograph score, *GB-Lbl* MS RM 20.h.8, f. 188*v*.

24 See Martin Adams, 'Purcell's *Laudate Ceciliam*', in *Irish Musical Studies* (Dublin, 1990), 227–47.

25 There is likewise no mention of St Cecilia in the anonymous text of Blow's

'Welcome, Welcome, Every Guest', hitherto regarded as a Cecilian ode: see William Henry Husk, *Musical Celebrations on St Cecilia's Day* (London, 1857), 37, 173.

26 *Zimmerman II*, 71. See also Blow's *Amphion Anglicus* (London, 1700), 205–16: 'A SONG . . . *at an Entertainment of* MUSICK *in* York Buildings'. This is the concluding chorus of the ode 'Welcome, Welcome, Every Guest', two other excerpts of which are included elsewhere in the collection (pp. 1–5). The complete work is extant in *GB-Lbl* Add. MS 31457, ff. 1–10v (autograph). Its text celebrates music, but makes no mention of St Cecilia; the setting, with an accompaniment elaborately scored for full orchestra including trumpets, clearly dates from the 1690s.

27 J. A. Westrup, op. cit., 177.

28 See his Cecilian ode 'Begin, and Strike th'Harmonious Lyre' (1693), in *GB-Lbl* Add. MS 30934, ff. 59v–78v.

29 *Works I*, xiv, 112–30.

30 *Musica Britannica*, xxxv, 47–53.

31 *Works I*, xiv, 112–30. The opening symphony of this anthem might have been supposed lost, but the work survives in not one but two autograph scores – the rough draft (*GB-Bu* MS 5001, 308–18) and the composer's fair-copy album (*GB-Lbl* MS RM 20.h.8, ff. 28v–32).

32 Bruce Wood, op. cit., v, 142–5.

33 See note 3, above.

34 *Grove's Dictionary* (1st edn, London, 1879–89), 'Purcell, Henry' (article by William Henry Husk).

35 Ibid., 103–4.

36 Cf. the concluding section of Purcell's early motet 'Beati omnes qui timent dominum' (*Works I*, xxxii, 143–6), which employs a minor-key version of the ground in common time; also that of Blow's anthem 'Blessed is the Man that hath not Walked' (*Musica Britannica*, l, 13–17), where it is in common time and in the major.

37 Peter Holman, *Four and Twenty Fiddlers* (Oxford, 1993), 423.

38 *GB-Lcm* MS 1097, ff. 85–112.

39 'Behold, I Bring you Glad Tidings' (Christmas 1687), 'O Sing unto the Lord' (1688), 'Praise the Lord, O Jerusalem' (1689) and 'My Song shall be Alway' (1690).

40 Trumpets had been used in the orchestra as early as 1675, in Locke's *Psyche*, but they have no independent parts, and the score is not even specific as to which movements should include them. See *Musica Britannica*, li. Among the music composed for the coronation of James II, in 1685, was a work in six-part score for trumpets, oboes and strings, which was performed by an orchestra numbering forty players: see Andrew Ashbee, *Records of English Court Music*, (Snodland, 1987), II, 12.

41 Purcell's Overture in G minor (*Works II*, xxxi, 85–90), also in the Italianate five-part scoring, has hitherto been regarded as an early work – an assumption now challenged by Peter Holman (op. cit., 427), who suggests that it belongs to the period around 1690 and is the overture to a lost ode. However, all the odes Purcell is known to have composed around this date

are extant. It is interesting to note that Purcell never employed the French scoring, though it was long known in London. Its use in Grabu's *Albion and Albanius* (1685) did however draw an eventual response from him: the sumptuous scoring of *Dioclesian* for full orchestra.

42 *GB-Lcm* MS 1079, ff. 179–84v.

43 *GB-Lcm* MS 1079, ff. 159–78v.

44 J. A. Westrup, op. cit., 66, 194; Dennis Arundell, *Henry Purcell* (London, 1927), 104–5; Arthur Keith Holland, *Henry Purcell* (London, 1932), 160–62.

45 *Zimmerman II*, 164–5; Curtis A. Price, *Henry Purcell and the London Stage* (Cambridge, 1984), 316–17.

46 The writing in this solo gives no hint of any impairment to Gostling's compass, but nothing similar is to be found in any of Purcell's subsequent works. Gostling seems, indeed, to have disappeared from the limelight altogether in the early 1690s. Neither of the only two Purcell works that survive in their original performing score, complete with the names of solo singers – 'Hail! Bright Cecilia!' (1692), in *GB-Ob* MS Mus.c.26, and 'Celebrate this Festival' (1693), in *GB-Ob* MS Mus.c.28 – even contains a solo allocated to Gostling, let alone obviously written for him.

47 *Zimmerman II*, 185.

48 Ibid., 192–5; see also John Buttrey, 'Did Purcell go to Holland?', *Musical Times*, cx (1969), 929–31.

49 The only primary source of the ode (*GB-Lbl* Add. MS 31447, ff. 112–21) contains few specific directions as to oboe doubling.

50 *Works I*, xxiv, edited by Geoffrey Shaw (Novello, 1924), designates the obbligato parts in the duet 'Many such days may she behold' for recorders, but there is not a shred of evidence for this. See the new edition (Novello, 1994).

51 The première of this work was given during the first week in May.

52 The only previous example of a treble solo in any of Purcell's royal odes is 'My prayers are heard', in 'Welcome, Welcome, Glorious Morn'; since this sets words purporting to be uttered by a goddess (and does so in phrases long enough to tax even adult lungs), it too may well have been composed for a soprano from the theatre rather than a Chapel chorister.

53 See note 50, above.

54 John Hawkins, *A General History of the Science and Practice of Music*, (London, 1776, R 1853/1963), II, 564.

55 Edition Eulenburg no. 1078.

56 *GB-Ob* MS Mus.c.26, ff. 23–69v.

57 *GB-Ob* MS Mus.c.28, ff. 78v–99.

58 See Bruce Wood, 'A Note on Two Cambridge Manuscripts and their Copyists', *Music and Letters*, lvi (1975), 308–12, and Peter Holman, 'Bartholomew Isaack and "Mr Isaack" of Eton: a Confusing Tale of Restoration Musicians', *Musical Times*, cxxviii (1978), 381–5.

59 Cuts had been made in the royal musical establishment in the spring of 1690, on the orders of William III (Peter Holman, op. cit., 431), but this had not prevented Purcell from scoring his birthday odes for the Queen in

that and the following year for a full Baroque orchestra, including two trumpets.

60 Zimmerman II, 223.

61 J. A. Westrup, op. cit., 187–8.

62 In The Gentleman's Journal, April 1693; it was also included in Comes amoris ... The Fifth Book ... (London, 1694). It was several months before a second vocal number from any of Purcell's royal odes appeared in print: the countertenor solo 'May her blest example', from 'Love's Goddess Sure was Blind', was included in the fourth book of Comes amoris, advertised in the London Gazette on 14 December 1693. Two vocal numbers from Purcell odes not composed for the Court also appeared in print very early. The duet 'And in each tract of glory', from The Yorkshire Feast Song, was included in the first book of Thesaurus Musicus, dated 1693 (the month of publication being unknown); and the celebrated countertenor solo ''Tis Nature's Voice', from 'Hail! Bright Cecilia!', was issued by Thomas Cross in two distinct single-sheet folios – presumably during 1693, though neither is dated.

63 Howell had been a supernumerary member of the Chapel Royal since 1691, but this was his first known appearance as a soloist in a royal ode.

64 W. H. Grattan Flood, 'Irish Ancestry of Garland, Dowland, Campion and Purcell', Music and Letters, iii (1922), 59–65.

65 In Orpheus Britannicus the obbligato part in the Plaint is designated for violin – a scoring found nowhere else in Purcell's theatre music. It seems far more convincing as a piece of oboe writing, and was actually marked 'Hoboy' in one manuscript, according to the original Purcell Society Edition of The Fairy-Queen (London, 1901). The editor, John Shedlock, referred (p. ii) to this source as one of three volumes at GB-Lcm; but it is no longer traceable there.

66 The poem contains couplets strongly reminiscent of earlier ones by Tate: for example, 'Call the jolly swains away / To celebrate Cecilia's day', and 'Tune the viol, touch the lute, / Wake the harp, inspire the flute', both from his 1685 Cecilian ode (printed in full in William Henry Husk, op. cit., 147–8), and 'Jolly Shepherds, come away / To celebrate this genial day', from the Prologue to Dido and Aeneas. It seems highly improbable that any other poet would plagiarize the work of the Poet Laureate for use in a royal ode.

67 Don Smithers, 'Shore', Grove VI, xvii, 262.

68 Zimmerman II, 259.

69 The version belonging to the ode includes a few small embellishments of melodic and inner-part detail, more likely added here than removed in the version belonging to Timon of Athens. Other differences, in the bass line, are probably the result of transposition a tone down, to the C major of the ode, rather than up, to the D major of Timon: in particular the low B flat in bar 73 of the overture to the ode is a note rarely found in Purcell's music, though it was available on the bass violin. On the other hand the overture to Timon is the only movement in that work to include a part for the trumpet, which is prominent throughout the ode.

70 In the preface to *Amphion Anglicus*, his published volume of secular vocal music, Blow promises a second collection, this time of 'Church-Services, *and* Divine Compositions. *To those, in truth, I have ever more especially consecrated the Thoughts of my whole Life. All the rest I consider but as the Blossoms, or rather the Leaves; those I only esteem as the Fruits of all my Labours in this kind.*'

71 Dennis Arundell, op. cit., 94; Arthur Keith Holland, op. cit., 154–60; J. A. Westrup, op. cit., 78, 172.

72 It has, however, grievously distorted our view of them by discouraging revival in their intended context.

7

Consort Music

PETER HOLMAN

The music discussed in this chapter can hardly be said to be little known. The Chacony in G minor (z 730), for instance, is one of the most frequently performed and recorded pieces of Purcell; yet it belongs to a genre beset by problems, ambiguities and misunderstandings. The problems begin with terminology. Should the Chacony be classified as chamber music or orchestral music? Or does it belong to a third category, theatre music? For that matter, do the terms 'chamber music' and 'orchestral music' as they are understood today have much bearing on the performing situations Purcell would have known? And if we place the Chacony under the heading 'Music for Strings', can we be sure that it was not performed with the participation of wind instruments? Thus, I have preferred the term 'consort music', for it allows us avoid the preconceptions that are associated with our modern classifications. And it enables me to deal with Purcell's theatre suites, which usually receive short shrift in surveys that also have to deal with *Dido and Aeneas* and *The Fairy Queen*. In any case, like the rest of the music discussed here, the theatre suites are best understood in the context of the history of English consort music.

When Purcell wrote his first consort music in his late teens he was contributing to a tradition that was about a century old. The arts of making and playing sets of instruments – and writing polyphonic music for them – had been established in England during the reigns of Henry VII and Henry VIII, but it was not until Elizabeth's reign that a coherent and sizeable repertoire of contrapuntal music emerged for them. At first it was written mainly by Court composers, and was intended largely for professionals; they used shawms and other loud wind instruments outdoors or in large halls, while viols were more suitable in small rooms; violins, with their sprightly articulation, were ideal for dance music. The consort repertoire became focused on the viol in the reign of James I, when the instrument began to be played by amateurs; hitherto, amateurs had tended to learn solo instruments such as the cittern, lute and virginals. The viol consort repertoire consisted mainly of fantasias in three, four, five and six parts, intended for various combinations of treble, tenor and bass viols. But the graver sort of dance music was also considered suitable, and motets and madrigals were often played in instrumental versions.

In the reign of James I a group of Court composers under the patronage of Prince Charles developed a new type of consort music; it was similar to, but not necessarily derived from, the innovations of the early Baroque in Italy. A crucial change was the introduction of the chamber organ, which freed composers from the necessity of maintaining continuous full-voiced harmony, and enabled them to develop combinations analogous to the Italian duo and trio sonata, though after about 1620 the organ was also generally added to viol consorts. It was either played from score, or from specially written parts; figured bass was not generally used by English organists until after 1660.

Another important change was the introduction of the violin into contrapuntal consort music. The instrument had hitherto been associated almost exclusively with dance music, so Orlando Gibbons and Thomas Lupo wrote fantasias for it in a dance-like idiom, and John Coprario developed the fantasia suite, a fixed sequence of fantasia–alman–galliard, scored for one or two violins, bass viol and organ. In Charles I's reign William Lawes added to the fantasia suite repertoire, and he and other Court composers wrote dance suites for such combinations as violin, bass viol, harp and theorbo, and two violins, two bass viols and two theorboes. The Civil War disrupted the settled pattern of musical life, forcing Court musicians to fend for themselves. But consort music flourished: 'many chose rather to fidle at home, then to goe out, and be knockt on the head abroad', as Roger North put it.[1] The upheaval also created the conditions for the dissemination of the violin and its Court repertoire into the wider musical community; by the end of the Commonwealth, amateurs such as Anthony à Wood and Samuel Pepys were playing the instrument, and the viol consort was in decline.

When Charles II was restored to the throne in the spring of 1660 the royal music was reformed virtually as it had stood in 1642. The instrumentalists were still divided into the many, who performed in the public areas of the Court, and a select few, collectively called the Private Musick, who had access to the King's private apartments. The violin band (enlarged in 1660 as the Twenty-four Violins) belonged to the former, while two of its violinists also served in the Private Musick, playing contrapuntal consort music in a group called the Broken Consort. But Charles II had, in North's words, 'an utter detestation of Fancys', and preferred the violin-band dance music he had grown accustomed to during his years of exile on the Continent.[2] He gave the Twenty-four Violins an enhanced role in Court life: groups from it began to play in the Chapel Royal, when the King went to the theatre, and even in the private apartments – which eventually put an end to the great tradition of Court consort music.

Purcell's early consort music must be considered in the light of these developments, for he was essentially a Court composer in his youth; indeed, he was virtually born into the royal music: his father and uncle were members of the Chapel Royal; he was a Chapel Royal choirboy himself; he received a Court post as a tuner and repairer of instruments when his voice broke at the age of 14; and he succeeded Matthew Locke as one of the composers for the Twenty-Four Violins in 1677. We know virtually nothing for sure about when and why he wrote his early consort music, but it is a reasonable assumption that the bulk of it was written as part of his Court activities, and we shall see that particular pieces do conform to the styles, forms and scorings established for the Broken Consort and the Twenty-four Violins.

Identifying the Court consort repertoire is not easy, for no performing material associated with the Twenty-four Violins or

1 Henry Purcell 1659–5, from the chalk drawing attributed to John
Closterman. Probably drawn from life about 1694.

2   The City of Westminster, from engravings by William Hollar, showing the seat of Parliament; St Margaret's Church, Purcell's parish church throughout his life; the Abbey Church of St Peter; and the Palace of Whitehall with the Chapel of St James, in which the choir of the Chapel Royal sang for much of the Restoration.

3 One of Purcell's Italian connections. Autograph transcription for
viols of Monteverdi's *Cruda Amarilli*

Purcell's monarchs:

(a) Charles II (1660–85)

(b) James II (1685–8)

(c) William III (1689–1702)

(d) Mary II (1689–94)

5   The coronation procession of James II, 23 April 1685. Among the
'Gentlemen of the Chapel Royal in number 32', were Purcell, John
Blow, William Child, Nicholas Staggins and Michael Wise.

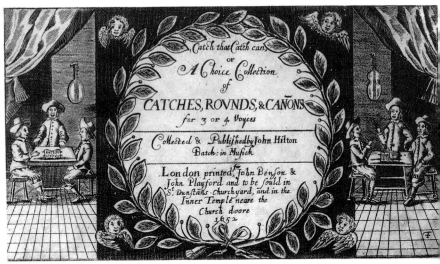

6   Performing Catches. The title page from Henry Playford's *Catch
that Catch Can* of 1652. The 1667 edition contains what is considered
to be Purcell's earliest composition, 'Sweet Tyraness'.

7 'I, Henry Purcell, of the City of Westminster, gentleman, being dangerously ill as to the constitution of my body, but in good and perfect mind and memory . . .'. Purcell's will, 21 November 1695.

8   The interior of Westminster Abbey as ordered for the Coronation
of James II. In the lower-left gallery stood 'the Quire of Westminster',
while in the gallery behind the pulpit were 'the Master and the King's
Choir of Instrumental Musick'. Purcell's anthems 'I was glad' and 'My
heart is inditing' were performed on this occasion.

9 The Cabal. Thought to be a group portrait of members of the early Restoration Private Musick, from left to right possibly Humphrey Madge (*d* 1679), Thomas Baltzar (*c* 1630–1663), ?John Singleton (*d*. 1686), Davis Mell (1604–62) and Charles Evans (*fl*. 1660–84).

10   The Dorset Garden Theatre, where most of Purcell's dramatick
operas were performed.
(a) The river front of the theatre, finished in 1671.

(b) A conjectural cross-section of the auditorium.

11   Thomas Betterton (1635–1710),
the actor, manager and opera
producer, and co-manager of the
Duke's Company when it moved into
the new Dorset Garden Theatre in
1671. A specialist in the multi-media
spectacular, he was the chief
proponent of Purcell's dramatick
operas.

12 Restoration stagings.
(a) Witches in *Macbeth*.

(b) The meeting of Titania and Oberon in *A Midsummer Night's Dream*.

13 *The Fairy-Queen* at Covent Garden in 1946, conducted by
Constant Lambert and designed by Michael Aryton, with choreography
by Frederick Ashton. Margaret Rawlings as Titania, Robert Helpmann
as Oberon, Richard Ellis as Hymen and David Davenport as Phoebus.

15 *Right Dido and Aeneas* in Jack Edwards's 1985 production for
Opera Restor'd. Act III, 'With drooping wings ye Cupids come'.
Bronwen Mills as Dido and Susan Bisatt as Belinda.

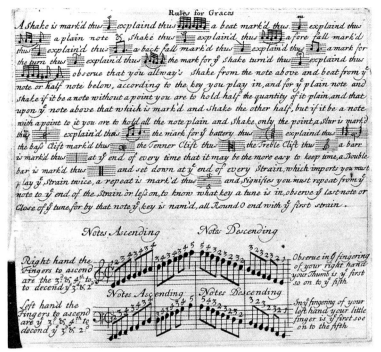

14 'Rules for Graces' with Purcell's *A Choice Collection of Lessons for the Harpsichord or Spinet*, published by Frances Purcell in 1697.

16　Gorges House, the home of Josias Priest's school for young ladies and the venue for the 1689 performance of *Dido and Aeneas*.

the Broken Consort seems to have survived; it was probably kept at Court, and would have been destroyed in the fire that consumed Whitehall Palace in 1698.[3] What remains of their repertoires has come down to us either in the form of scores, copied by the composers and their associates to preserve them for posterity, or in sets of parts copied for the use of professional or amateur groups outside the Court. Thus, four of the five main manuscripts that preserve Purcell's early consort music are scores. One (British Library, Add. MS 30930) is autograph, dated 1680, and the other three (British Library, Add. MS 33236 and RM 20.h.9, and New York Public Library, Drexel MS 5061) also seem to come from the Court milieu: Add. MS 33236 and Drexel MS 5061 contain pieces that were probably copied directly from Add. MS 30930, and I have tentatively identified the copyist of Drexel MS 5061 as a member of the Isaack family of organists and choirmen, two of whom were choirboys in the Restoration Chapel Royal.[4] The one manuscript intended for performance, the recently discovered bass partbook Yale University Library, Osborn MS 515, contains some early Purcell autographs.[5]

Nevertheless, the Twenty-four Violins and the Broken Consort belonged to different traditions of consort music, which developed their own genres and types of scoring. The repertoire of the Twenty-four Violins is most easily recognized by its scoring. It was essentially a late survival of a Renaissance violin band: it played dance music in four parts – violin, two violas and bass – until the mid–1670s, and the modern 'string quartet' layout thereafter.[6] Violin bands traditionally played without continuo, for their full-voiced music did not require any additional harmonic support, though continuo instruments would have been required to accompany the voices in concerted vocal works.[7] English violin bands probably continued to play without continuo in some circumstances throughout Purcell's lifetime; his theatre suites were published in 1697 without a continuo part or any figures in the bass, and the same is true of the theatre suites subsequently published by Walsh and Hare. By contrast, continuo instruments were an essential part of chamber ensembles such as the Broken Consort that usually had no inner parts to fill the gap between the trebles and the bass. Indeed, the name 'Broken Consort' implies a mixed ensemble, consisting of at least three instrumental families: violins, bass viol, keyboard and/or theorbo(es). It is neither here nor there that Locke and Purcell wrote music of this sort without any specific indication of continuo instruments: they would have accompanied it from score, and probably wrote their autograph scores partly for that purpose.

The two repertoires are more difficult to disentangle by genre, for the fashionable dances of the day tend to occur in both. But some genres are associated more with one than the other: pavans and fantasias belong to the contrapuntal tradition, while overtures and chaconnes are essentially orchestral forms, though they are sometimes found in cut-down form in domestic manuscripts. A case in point is Osborn MS 515, which contains three overtures among eight unique pieces in Purcell's autograph.[8] Seven of them are now fragments, but the eighth, the Staircase Overture (not in *Zimmerman I*) was scored up in the late eighteenth century by Philip Hayes from, it seems, the partbooks of which Osborn MS 515 is the sole survivor; the set was still complete in 1848, when it appeared in the sale of the Reverend Samuel Picart's library. Hayes copied parts for two violins, bass (the one in Osborn MS 515) and a separate, simplified continuo. An inner part must be missing, since the harmonies are often incomplete, and even a number of the first and last chords of sections have no third. The continuo part may be a later addition, devised to compensate for the missing viola; it certainly contributes nothing to the work in its four-part form, and it could be the work of Hayes himself.

The Staircase Overture is probably Purcell's earliest surviving consort piece. It is an example of a type of overture that was common in England between the early 1660s, when the genre arrived from France, and the late 1670s, when Lully's mature examples began to circulate. The first section is more like an alman than the opening of a true overture, and the second section is a jig-like dance in two strains, not a fugue; Lully is said to have started the fashion for fugues in overtures with his ballet *Alcidiane* of 1658, but it was a while before they ousted the non-

EX. 1 Matthew Locke: Alman, from 'The Rare Theatrical'
(h 251), bars 4–7

contrapuntal type of second strain. The rushing scales of the opening (which presumably gave it the title 'Staircase Overture') inevitably call to mind the famous storm passage in the 'Curtain Tune' or Overture of Locke's *Tempest* music, though Locke also used the idea in several other works, including a four-part alman in 'The Rare Theatrical', a large manuscript collection of his music for the Twenty-four Violins (Example 1).[9] Locke's influence can also be heard in the rapid modulations of the second section, though the duple-time coda, which dives unexpectedly into B flat minor, may derive from the Prelude to Robert Smith's suite 'New Year's Day' (New York Public Library, Drexel MS 3849, pp. 47–50), which uses the same trick in the same key. Smith probably wrote it for New Year celebrations at Court shortly before his untimely death in 1675; a date around the same time also makes sense for the Staircase Overture, though we have no means of knowing whether it was actually performed by the Twenty-four Violins.

Not much more need be said about Purcell's overtures, for the genre was essentially a preface to vocal music (there are nearly fifty examples scattered through his works at the head of verse anthems, Court odes, 'symphony songs' and theatrical scores), and it began to have a life of its own only in the 1690s when his later examples, detached from their parent works, began to be performed in concerts. Of the three overtures in RM 20.h.9, one, printed as an independent work in *Works II*, xxxi, 82–4, actually comes from the 1681 Court ode 'Swifter, Isis, Swifter Flow' (z 336), and the Overtures in D minor and G minor (z 771 and z 772) also probably come from lost odes, though z 772 seems not to be an early work, as is usually said. The scoring of this fine piece, two violins, two violas and bass, was common in late seventeenth-century Italy – it was used by such composers as Giovanni Legrenzi, Giovanni Battista Vitali, Giovanni Bononcini and Antonio Caldara – and there was a brief vogue for it in England following its use in Giovanni Battista Draghi's influential St Cecilia ode of 1687, the original setting of Dryden's 'From Harmony, from Heavenly Harmony'.[10] Purcell used it in 1689 and 1690 for his Queen Mary birthday odes 'Now Does the Glorious Day Appear' (z 332) and 'Arise, my Muse' (z 320), while Blow used it for his 1690 New Year ode 'With Cheerful Hearts Let All Appear'. Thus z 772 probably dates from 1687–90.

The early history of the chaconne is a confused and confusing subject, mainly because the word was used at various times to describe a number of different but related things. In early seventeenth-century Italy *ciacona* meant a dance step as well as the music to accompany that dance, which tended to consist of variations over a short triple-time major-key chord sequence, most familiar to us today from Monteverdi's duet 'Zefiro torna'.

During the seventeenth century it gradually became confused with the *passacaglia*, a separate triple-time dance usually accompanied by minor-key variations on four notes descending by step from tonic to dominant. Most early chaconnes and passacaglias are for guitar, lute and keyboard, but Lully wrote orchestral chaconnes as early as 1658 for his ballet *Alcidiane*, and most English examples are found in the violin-band repertoire. The chaconne probably arrived in England in the mid–1670s. There are none by John Banister and Matthew Locke, who wrote most of the Court dance music in the 1660s and early 1670s, and the earliest dateable example seems to be a three-part 'Chacone' by Robert Smith (*d* 1675) in Oxford, Christ Church Library (Mus. MS 1183, f. 9) and published in *Tripla concordia* (London, 1677), p. 30; the pieces labelled 'Chiconae' by Locke in the second set of 'The Broken Consort' and in *Tripla concordia* do not use ground basses.[11]

Most of Purcell's chaconnes, like his overtures, occur in the context of large-scale vocal works, and several have sections for solo voices and chorus, like many chaconnes in French operas; an obvious model would have been the 'Chacon' that takes up much of Act II of Louis Grabu's opera *Albion and Albanius*, performed in London in 1685. Some of Purcell's chaconnes, such as the 'Dance for the Chinese Man and Woman' in *The Fairy Queen* (z 629/51) or 'Triumph, victorious Love' in *Dioclesian* (z 627/38) (Purcell did not label it a chaconne, but it uses the *ciacona* more or less in its traditional form) would have been danced, but others, such as the chaconne in *The Gordian Knot Unty'd* (z 597/6) or the one in *King Arthur* (z 628/1), belong to suites of incidental music, and were played in a concert-like situation before the play; they presumably illustrate the genre in transition from functional dance to abstract concert piece. Neither piece was new when it was used in the theatre: z 597/6 appears as a separate piece in Osborn MS 515, while z 628/1 is also found in the 1687 Court ode 'Sound the Trumpet, Beat the Drum' (z 335/7).

We have no means of knowing whether the Chacony in G minor (z 730) was written for dancing or as abstract music. The Chacony (the word is just an English variant of 'chaconne') is undoubtedly early, for it appears in Add. MS 30930 in a group of miscellaneous pieces appended to the four-part fantasias. It was this context that perhaps led Zimmerman to catalogue it under the heading 'Fantasias and Related Forms', and it is often performed with more of the solemnity of a fantasia than the vigour of a dance. Yet it certainly conforms to the style and scoring of the chaconne genre, and is more suitable for dancing to than, say, Blow's Chaconne in G, written about the same time, which has elaborate fugal passages and complex rhythmic patterns.[12] Blow's work also has a separate continuo part, which is needed at times to complete the harmonies – a sign, as we have seen, of domestic consort music. The Chacony, by contrast, has no continuo part (despite the impression given in *Works II*, xxxi, 61–7), and never needs one.

Indeed, the Chacony is all the more effective because, as in the best of Locke's orchestral dance music, there is a tension between the conventions of the dance genre and an astonishingly rich and adventurous musical language. The eight-bar ground is similar to the one in z 628/1, and consists of the descending fourth of the passacaglia balanced by a cadence. But it is cunningly inflected – the second bar is unexpectedly F *sharp* and the fifth B *natural* – and it is harmonized with the greatest richness and freedom. The effect is all the more powerful because the writing is nobly restrained and the structure is so clearly articulated by pairs of events, like symmetrical columns: the ground remains in G minor throughout the eighteen variations, except for nos 6 and 14, when it is extended by means of a series of transitory modulations; there are two variations with the bass silent, nos 8 and 11, when the ground migrates respectively to the first violin and the viola; a passage of running quavers in a descending pattern in no. 9 is matched by ascending quavers in no. 14, and so on.

The musical language of the Chacony is less French than is often thought. It uses the characteristic | |. ⸢ rhythm of much French triple-time dance music, and there is a good deal of writing in patterns of dotted notes. But the rhythms are too complex for the French system of *notes inégales* to be used with much success, and the richly dissonant inner parts are far removed from the bland inner parts of most French orchestral music – the *parties de remplissage* that were often farmed out by Lully and his contemporaries to assistants. There is some evidence that the *parties de remplissage* system was also used in England, but Locke and Purcell clearly wrote their own inner parts, and were too steeped in the English consort tradition to allow them to be less interesting than the outer parts.

It is instructive to compare the Chacony with a ground bass written about the same time in the domestic consort tradition. z 731 is usually called a fantasia today, though it is just headed '3 parts upon a Ground' in the only complete source, RM 20.h.9, and it belongs to the genre known at the time as 'divisions on a ground', or just 'grounds'. In RM 20.h.9 it is written out in D major for three violins and continuo, but it has the rubric 'playd 2 notes higher for F[lutes]', and there is an autograph fragment in British Library, Add. MS 30932 with the opening of the second treble in F major and in the French violin clef. This led Thurston Dart to suggest that the piece was originally written for recorders, pointing out that in D major the bass goes down to *BB*, below the range of the cello and the ordinary bass viol.[13] There is some force in this argument, particularly since three French wind players are known to have worked at Court from about 1675 to 1682, which is probably why Blow and Purcell included oboes and recorders in the Court odes and other vocal music they wrote at that time. Nevertheless, the bass could have been played as it stood in D on a bass violin, or on a 'double bass' viol with an *AA* string, an instrument used in consort music at Court before the Civil War, and by Blow in his anthem 'Lord, Who Shall Dwell in Thy Tabernacle?'.[14] The D major version certainly exploits the open strings of the violins in a highly effective way. It is possible that Purcell had both instruments in mind, much as Continental composers sometimes published instrumental music with double clefs and key signatures, expecting players to read the music in the treble clef on the oboe, flute and violin, but in the French violin clef a third higher on the recorder.

z 731 is a fascinating synthesis of the diverse idioms of consort music current in the late 1670s. The work starts with the

EX.   2   Henry Purcell: Three parts upon a Ground (z 731) F major
version, bars 17–21

stately dotted rhythms of the chaconne, but it soon ventures far
beyond the idiom of orchestral dance music. A passage of canon
appears, the first of four, slipped in so casually that it is easy to
miss the fact that the row of notes in the first treble is simultaneously inverted in the second, and played backwards in the
third (Example 2). Such contrapuntal virtuosity was unpre-
cedented in English divisions on a ground, which are mostly for
a single violin or bass viol, though in his *Compendium of Practical Music* (London, 2/1667) Christopher Simpson showed how
three-part canons might be made over the same six-note ground;
Purcell himself wrote in the 1694 edition of Playford's *An Intro-*

duction to the Skill of Musick that 'Composing upon a *Ground*'
was 'a very easie thing to do, and requires but little Judgement',
but that 'to maintain *Fuges* upon it' would be difficult, being
confined like a *Canon* to a *Plain Song*'.[15] Much of the fast pas-
sage-work in z 731 is fugal or semi-canonic, and is probably
derived from the canonic division writing favoured by John Jenkins in many of his fantasia suites. The last few bars are marked
'drag', as in many fantasia suites, but nothing in that repertoire
prepares us for its breathtaking side-slipping harmonies
(Example 3).

The three-treble scoring of z 731, also used in the Pavan in G
minor z 752, is worthy of comment. The striking sonority of
three violins and continuo was popular on the Continent from
early in the century, but the earliest piece in the English repertoire seems to be the ten-movement Suite in C by the German
virtuoso violinist Thomas Baltzar.[16] (The expatriate composer
William Young published some three-violin sonatas at
Innsbruck in 1653, but there is no sign that they were known in
England; he died there in 1662, so the William Young who
served at the Restoration Court was a different man.[17]) Baltzar
arrived in London from Sweden in the winter of 1655–6, and
received a place in the Private Musick (not the Twenty-four
Violins, as is often said) in the summer of 1661, which brought
the number of violinists in the group up to three. Baltzar died
suddenly in July 1663, but his influence remained. There is an
excellent set of fantasia suites for three violins, bass viol and
continuo by John Jenkins, who was a colleague of Baltzar in the
Private Musick, and the tradition was continued later by, among
others, the Neapolitan violinist Nicola Matteis, whose D minor
divisions for three violins and continuo in the Bodleian Library
(MSS Mus. Sch. E. 400–3) must have been known to Purcell, for
the bass part is also in Osborn MS 515.

Purcell was evidently attracted to the archaic form of the
pavan in his youth. In addition to z 752, which is next to
the Chacony in Add. MS 30930, there are four for two violins
and continuo in Add. MS 33236, in G minor (z 751), A minor
(z 749), A major (z 748) and B flat major (z 750) – an orderly
rising sequence that suggests that Purcell intended a complete set

EX.   3   Henry Purcell: Three parts upon a Ground (z 731) F major
version, bars 137–44

with one in every common key. In addition, there are two more, both in F minor, among the autograph fragments in Osborn MS 515. Not much can be said about them – except that the second strain of one is in triple time, so it must have been more like an overture than a conventional pavan. But z 748–51 clearly belong to a rather different tradition than z 752, and a comparison between them and it can tell us a good deal about the sources of Purcell's consort style.

Briefly stated, z 752 is modelled on the type of pavan common in the form's heyday around 1600. It is a large-scale work, with three sections or strains of ten and a half, nine and a half and twelve breves. The strains are sharply contrasted, and each is based on a different 'topic'. The second, for instance, is largely taken up with rising and falling chromatic lines in the manner of a Jacobean chromatic pavan, while the third consists of a single point of counterpoint (Example 4). Jenkins is the obvious model here. He was fond of fugal passages in which the subject and its inversion are worked simultaneously, undergoing a series of subtle melodic and rhythmic changes in the process. More generally, Purcell uses a harmonic idiom in z 752 closer to the plain but purposeful style of Jenkins than the more coloured idiom of Locke. Jenkins was certainly the last English composer apart from Purcell to write large-scale pavans of the older type – there are some fine examples in his Lyra Consorts, written probably in the 1650s – though it was still current in Germany, and Baltzar started each of his four consort suites with one. Thurston Dart's suggestion that z 752 was written in 1677 as a memorial to Locke is surely wide of the mark.[18] It would have been a more fitting tribute to Jenkins, who died in the next year, though there is no actual evidence that it is an elegy for anyone.

Locke's influence is felt much more strongly in the four three-part pavans. They are typical examples of the form in its last phase, and seem to be modelled on the ones that open a number of Locke's two-violin suites, including those in the second set of 'The Broken Consort'. They still have three strains, but they are based on the more modern crotchet beat, with bars in 4/4; indeed z 751 is dominated by a dotted quaver-semiquaver figure, and sounds more like a solemn alman than a true pavan. A single mood tends to prevail, and interest is created less by the counterpoint than by the Locke-like melodic and harmonic idiom: angular melodic writing goes hand-in-hand with intense passing dissonance and rapid, unexpected modulations. If these pieces are less interesting than most of Purcell's consort music, it is not because they are badly written in any way – even in the Staircase Overture Purcell's part-writing is assured – but because they are written in an idiom that is limited in scope; z 752 is a more memorable piece because its more expansive idiom allowed Purcell's imagination to flower.

A puzzling aspect of Purcell's pavans is that they survive as isolated pieces – apart from one of the fragmentary F minor pavans, which is paired with a minuet-like movement. All of those by Locke and his contemporaries are placed at the head of suites, and we have to go back to the reign of Charles I – to the pavans in William Lawes's harp consorts or in Jenkins's five- and six-part viol consorts – before finding a number of independent examples. We have no means of knowing whether Purcell intended to write the rest of the suites, whether they were written and are lost, or whether he was just indulging in a bout of archaism.

Much the same could be said of Purcell's fantasias. It is often said that they are indebted to Locke's four-part viol fantasias, and so they are in some respects. But Locke, and virtually every other consort composer after about 1640, wrote fantasias in company with dance movements, be they single airs, as in Jenkins's fantasy-air pairs, two dances, as in the fantasia suite proper, or three, as in many of Locke's suites. Purcell's fantasias appear as single items in Add. MS 30930, grouped according to the number of parts: three fantasias in three parts (z 732–4), nine in four parts (z 735–43), dated between 10 June and 31 August 1680, the opening section of a tenth (z 744), dated 24 February 1682/3, the five-part Fantasia upon One Note (z 745), and two In nomines, in six parts (z 746) and seven parts (z 747). Purcell's plan, similar to that used by Locke in his autograph score (British Library, Add. MS 17801), was evidently to build up a large collection of fantasias organized in an orderly sequence from the smallest combinations to the largest. But to

EX. 4 Henry Purcell: Pavan in G minor (z 752), bars 22–33

judge from the number of pages left blank, and the headings 'Here Begineth ye 5 Part: Fantazies' and 'Here Begineth ye 6, 7 and 8 part Fantazia's', the scheme was never completed.

Why did Purcell write his fantasias? It can hardly have been for performance on viols, for the viol consort was passing into history even when Purcell was a child. In Oxford the change came in the late 1650s: Anthony à Wood wrote that 'before the restoration of K. Charles 2, and especially after, viols began to be out of fashion and only violins used, as treble, tenor and bass-violin'.[19] Roger North thought that it was Baltzar's example that precipitated the change: 'One Baltazar a Swede, about the time of the Restauration came over, and shewed so much mastery upon that instrument, that gentlemen, following also the humour of the Court, fell in *pesle mesle*, and soon thrust out the treble viol.'[20]

It also seems that Purcell's fantasias were not known at the time as viol music. North, who knew the composer and played with him on several occasions, thought that the viol consort repertoire had ended with Jenkins and Locke: 'after Mr Jenkens I know but one poderose consort of that kind composed, which was Mr M. Lock's 4 parts, worthy to bring up the 'rere, after which wee are to expect no more of that style'.[21] It used to be thought that Purcell wrote his fantasias for consorts of violins, or for mixed ensembles of violins and viols. But the dance-like idiom used in those English fantasias and fantasia suites that were written for violins is conspicuous by its absence – there are no passages of triple time, for instance – and Purcell nearly always conforms to the part ranges and types of figuration traditionally used in the viol consort repertoire. It is true that the treble part of z 740 goes up to *d'''*, but this note has as little precedent in violin music as in viol music; *c'''*, the fourth-finger extension in first position on the *e''* string, was the normal upper limit of violin parts in consort music, in England as on the Continent.

The simplest explanation is that Purcell wrote his fantasias within the English viol consort tradition, but as composition exercises rather than as performance material. Indeed, all the completed four-part fantasias were composed in a few weeks in

June and August 1680, the fruit, clearly, of a period devoted to the intensive study of contrapuntal techniques. 'The best way to be acquainted with 'em,' Purcell wrote in *An Introduction to the Skill of Musick*, 'is to score much, and chuse the best Authors.'[22] He was thinking of ground basses, but his studies must have ranged over much of the consort repertoire. In some cases the objects of his study are known: part of Monteverdi's madrigal 'Cruda Amarilli' exists in Purcell's hand, copied in score without words; madrigals by Monteverdi, Marenzio and other Italian composers occur in instrumental versions in Jacobean manuscripts, and some have been identified as the models for fantasias by Ferrabosco, Coprario and others.[23] Another manuscript contains a copy in Purcell's hand of an eight-part canon by John Bull on the Miserere plainsong, organ parts for fantasias by Orlando Gibbons and fantasia-suites by Coprario, as well as several Monteverdi madrigals – including 'Cruda Amarilli'.[24]

Purcell's studies seem to have gone right back to the beginning of the consort tradition. The two In nomines, in six and seven parts, belong to a genre that had its origin in John Taverner's mass 'Gloria tibi Trinitas', written probably in the 1520s.[25] A passage in the Benedictus at the words 'In nomine Domini' was detached from the mass, and became the model for more than 150 instrumental pieces written between the 1550s and the 1640s using the 'Gloria tibi Trinitas' plainsong as a *cantus firmus*. Purcell was almost certainly the only composer to write In nomines after then: the six-part examples by Jenkins were probably written in the 1630s, while the five-part 'In nomine fantasia' by 'J. B.' in the Bodleian Library (MSS Mus. Sch. 473–8), ascribed by Dart and others to John Banister, seems to be by the parliamentary official John Browne (1608–91), and was written in imitation of one of Lawes's six-part In nomines, probably in the 1640s.[26]

In many respects, z 747 is closer in style to sixteenth- rather than seventeenth-century In nomines. The only other examples of seven-part writing in the English consort repertoire are two In nomines by Robert Parsons (*d* 1570), and a fragmentary one by Robert White (*d* 1574) in the British Library (Add. MS 32377).[27]

Purcell followed tradition by placing the *cantus firmus* in even breves in the alto part, and surrounded it with smooth polyphony, rising and falling in minims and crotchets; the edifice is articulated, with a sure sense of architecture, by two bars of rich seven-part harmony placed exactly at the mid-way point. We are a long way here from the busy writing in quavers and semiquavers of In nomines by Ferrabosco, Gibbons and Jenkins, or the sharp fantasy-like contrasts of those by Lawes; indeed, only a delicious slide into B flat minor towards the end suddenly makes the listener aware that this is music from around 1680, not 1580. z 746 sounds even more archaic, and uses a technique found in early sixteenth-century motets; the *cantus firmus* provides the material for all the counterpoint, and is speeded up so that it can be heard as a tune (Example 5).

The rest of Purcell's fantasias are more modern in style, not because they are necessarily later than the undated z 746 and z 747, but because the models were more recent. The three-part fantasias are relatively small in scale, with a rapid succession of ideas, busy counterpoint and lively syncopation; they owe much to Orlando Gibbons's published set (*c*1620), a cornerstone of the three-part repertoire that was still circulating in Purcell's lifetime.[28] Purcell's four-part fantasias are on a larger scale, and have more sharply defined and contrasted sections; their main models are Locke's fantasias, particularly those in the Consort of Four Parts.[29] z 736 and z 740 begin with 'slow introductions' marked off with a double bar (which may or may not indicate a repeat), as in a number of Locke works, including Fantasias nos 1, 3 and 5 of the Consort of Four Parts. All the four-part fantasias except z 742 have brief chordal passages in the middle, some marked 'Slow' or 'Drag', that act as interludes between the sections of busy counterpoint, and z 737 and z 739 also end with a passage marked 'Slow'. The resulting patterns, effectively Fast-Slow-Fast, Slow-Fast-Slow-Fast, or Fast-Slow-Fast-Slow, are the ones most commonly found in Locke, though it must be said that most of the tempo changes in the modern editions of Locke are the work of his editors. Purcell's tempo marks nearly always accompany changes to faster or slower note values, so it may be that they should be thought of as descriptive rather than prescriptive, and that the fantasias of both composers should be played with more or less a consistent pulse.[30]

Locke's influence on Purcell's fantasias can be heard most clearly in the details of the harmonic writing, such as the highly coloured cadences with unprepared dominant sevenths and false

EX.   5   Henry Purcell: In nomine a6 (z 746), bars 14–23

relations. False relations seem to have been developed originally as a simple means of avoiding consecutives in cadences made in more than four parts, and they became less common after 1600 because most composers had by then mastered the techniques of five- and six-part writing; Locke and his followers revived the device for expressive purposes, and used it as often in three- and four-part writing as in music in larger numbers of parts. Purcell's fantasias also contain some examples of medium-range harmonic patterns characteristic of Locke: compare, for instance, the beautiful coda of z 733, which juxtaposes an F major cadence with an E major chord, returning to F by chromatic degrees, with a passage at the end of Locke's Fantasia no. 2 in D minor from the Consort of Four Parts (Example 6).

On the larger scale, however, his harmonic style is as close to Jenkins as to Locke. Jenkins was more interested in smooth, wide-ranging modulations than in sudden wild transitions; in fact, several of his four-part fantasias range right round the key cycle, involving enharmonic transitions.[31] Purcell does not go that far, but in some of the four-part fantasias cadences are made or approached in virtually all the common keys: the 'Brisk' section of z 739, for instance, touches on D minor, A minor, G major, C minor, B flat major, E flat major, F minor, A flat major,

EX.   6a   Matthew Locke: Fantasia from Consort of Four Parts no. 2
(h 136/2), bars 73–83

EX.   6b   Henry Purcell: Fantasia a3 (z 733), bars 47–67

EX.   6b   *(contd.)*

B flat major, G major, E minor, A minor and C major in twelve
bars (Example 7). This passage neatly illustrates the synthesis
Purcell achieved between the styles of his two great predecessors: the harmonic planning is reminiscent of Jenkins, but the
speed with which it is executed makes the music sound like
Locke. Indeed, Locke's music tends to be uniquely unsettling in
its effect, in part because relatively conventional harmonic
events are presented at a frenetic pace.

But when all is said and done there are several aspects of
Purcell's fantasias that cannot be accounted for in the music
of his immediate predecessors. Nothing could have prepared his
contemporaries for the playful five-part Fantasia upon One
Note z 745, in which a *cantus firmus* is reduced *ad absurdum* to
a single middle C – the object being, evidently, to demonstrate
that even the severest limitation need not restrict the imagination. One has to go back to the reign of James I, to John Bull
and Elway Bevin (whose canons were praised by Purcell in *An
Introduction to the Skill of Musick*[32]), before encountering a
body of English music so taken up with formal contrapuntal
devices. Triple invertible counterpoint (modestly labelled by
Purcell 'Another sort of Fugeing') is effortlessly demonstrated in
the 'Brisk' section of z 734. Inversion ('per Arsin & Thesin') is
found in most of the fantasias, but it is combined with augmentation and double augmentation in the opening section of z 738,
and with single, double and triple augmentation in an astonishing passage towards the end of z 743. Yet Purcell's interest in
formal counterpoint was not just a by-product of his studies of
the English consort repertoire, nor did it cease when he stopped

EX. 7 Henry Purcell: Fantasia a4 (z 739), bars 33–45

EX. 7 (*contd.*)

writing fantasias. It also seems to have been one of the reasons – perhaps the main reason – why he began to study and imitate Italian trio sonatas; in the sonata, he wrote in *An Introduction to the Skill of Musick*, 'you will find *Double* and *Treble Fuges* also reverted and augmented in their *Canzona's*, with a great deal of Art mixed with good Air, which is the Perfection of a Master'.[33]

Most if not all of Purcell's trio sonatas probably come from the early 1680s. Twelve (z 790–801) were published by the author in a finely engraved edition, *Sonnata's of III Parts* (London, 1683).[34] The rest, z 802–11, appeared in *Ten Sonata's in Four Parts* (London, 1697), though eight of them are in Add. MS 30930 in whole or part, and there is no reason to think that the other two, nos 6 and 7, are any later. Their scoring has caused much confusion. Despite their titles, both sets consist of four partbooks and use the same instruments: two violins, bass viol and organ or harpsichord. In describing the 1683 set as 'of three parts' Purcell was following Italian practice, which did not count the continuo as a separate part; in the same way, Corelli's trio sonatas were said to be '*à tre*' though they were printed in four partbooks. It also seems that Purcell did not intend originally to publish a separate continuo part; according to the preface the publication 'had been abroad in the world much sooner, but that he has now seen fit to cause the whole Thorough Bass to be Engraven, which was a thing quite besides his first Resolutions'. His original plan may have been to combine the continuo and bass on one stave in a single part; if so, it would have proved impractical, so often do they diverge. The 1697 set was presumably said to be 'of four parts' because there were four partbooks. This was the rule in eighteenth-century England: Handel's op. 6 concertos, for instance, were published as 'Twelve Grand Concertos in Seven Parts' because there were seven partbooks; the music is almost never in seven real parts.

Purcell's sonatas do not seem to be products of the Court milieu. Roger North wrote that when he first lived in London, in the early 1670s, he was one of 'that company which introduc't the Itallian composed enterteinements of musick which they call *Sonnata's*'.[35] At the time the fashion at Court was only for 'the theatricall musick and French air in song', but the Norths and their friends preferred Italian composers, 'for their measures were just and quick, set off with wonderful solemne *Grave's*, and full of variety'. Purcell himself certainly moved in such circles, for North remembered that his brother Francis, the Lord Chief Justice, 'caused the devine Purcell to bring his Itallian manner'd compositions; and with him on his harpsicord, my self and another violin, wee performed them more than once, of which Mr Purcell was not a little proud, nor was it a common thing for one of his dignity to be so enterteined'.[36] Incidentally, it is unlikely that Purcell's sonatas were performed in the Chapel Royal, as has been suggested. Sonatas were used in the liturgy in Italy and parts of Catholic Europe north of the Alps, but there is no evidence that the same was true in Anglican churches and chapels, even at Court. The string players who served in the Chapel Royal in the 1670s and 1680s were there, it seems, to play the string parts of verse anthems, not sonatas.

According to the preface of the 1683 set Purcell 'faithfully endeavour'd a just imitation of the most fam'd Italian Masters' in his sonatas, and much ink has been spilt trying to identify them. Roger North wrote that 'severall little printed consorts came over from Italy, as Cazzati, Vitali, and other lesser scrapps which were made use of in corners', and English manuscript copies do exist of many Italian printed sonatas; a good example is British Library, Add. MS 31436, probably copied by someone in the North circle, which combines items from Vitali's op. 9 (Venice, 1684) and the trio sonata anthology *Scielta della suonate* (Bologna, 1680).[37] The problem is that most of the manuscripts cannot be dated exactly, so we do not know, for instance, whether Corelli's op. 1 (Rome, 1681) arrived in time for Purcell to take note of it; an exception is British Library, Add. MS 31431, dated 1680 and owned by Sir Gabriel Roberts (c1630–1715), which includes sonatas from Legrenzi's op. 2 (Venice, 1655), Cazzati's op. 18 (Venice, 1656) and Vitali's op. 2 (Bologna, 1667) and op. 5 (Bologna, 1669).[38] To judge from the number of surviving copies, the Italian instrumental music most admired in Restoration England was a group of unpublished works known as sonatas by the Roman lutenist Lelio

Colista; they exist in at least seven English manuscripts, and Purcell printed a passage of one of them in *An Introduction to the Skill of Musick* as an example of 'double descant'.[39] In fact, they are labelled 'simfonia' rather than 'sonata' in the main Italian source, and about half of them – including the one quoted by Purcell – are actually by the Milanese violinist Carlo Ambrogio Lonati, who worked in Rome from about 1668 to 1677.

The relationship between Purcell's sonatas and those by the 'fam'd Italian Masters' is complex, and is not yet fully understood. By and large, though, Purcell seems to have looked to the works of the older generation of Italians for his models, such as Cazzati (*b c*1620), Legrenzi (*b* 1626) and Colista (*b* 1629), rather than those of his near contemporaries, such as Corelli (*b* 1653) and Bassani (*b c*1657). His sonatas are '*à tre*' rather than '*à due*', which means that the bass viol contributes to the musical argument on more or less equal terms with the violins, often parting company with the continuo. The sonata '*à tre*' was a conservative contrapuntal form, descended from the early seventeenth-century canzona, while the more forward-looking sonata '*à due*', with its purely harmonic continuo (normally played in Italy without the support of a melody instrument), was closer in style to secular vocal music and dance music.[40] There is certainly no sign in Purcell of the slightly later distinction, formalized in Corelli's trio sonatas, between the *da chiesa* and *da camera* types: dances are mixed freely with 'abstract' movements, as in mid-century sonatas.

Purcell mostly uses formal patterns established long before Corelli. His sonatas tend to consist of five or more short, linked sections rather than the more modern sequence of four discrete movements, the type that predominates in Corelli's op. 1. There are a few thematic relationships between movements, a common device earlier in the century, and in several cases they are used to give the effect of a recapitulation: the fugal opening themes of the sonatas in A minor and G major (1683, nos 5 and 8, z 794 and z 797) both return before the end combined with new material, a device found in a number of the sonatas in Legrenzi's op. 2.[41] The slow movements often use the common Italian pattern in which a short opening phrase is followed after a pause by a repetition in the dominant, which is then extended by modulations through a number of keys. The fast movements tend either to be essays in the canzona style – whether or not they are actually labelled 'canzona' – or to be cast as triple-time dances. There is only one example, the Vivace of the Sonata in G minor (1697, no. 8, z 803) of the type of running bass movement familiar to us from Corelli, and none of the driving non-fugal Allegro we think of as the epitome of the later Italian Baroque style. This sort of movement was originally associated with the sonata 'à due', but crept into the sonata 'à tre' in the 1680s; there are early examples in Corelli's op. 1 and Bassani's op. 5 (Bologna, 1683).

The canzona movements of Purcell's sonatas are closely modelled on those in the Colista–Lonati repertoire. A common type presents two themes at the outset in invertible counterpoint ('double fugeing' in *An Introduction to the Skill of Musick*), one striding in minims and crotchets, the other running in quavers and semiquavers; they are present in some form throughout the movement, so the object of the exercise is to keep up the interest by constantly combining them in new ways, using inversion, augmentation and stretto (Example 8). In another type the themes are presented successively, the second arriving just as the ear is beginning to tire of the first. In some cases, as in the Canzona of the Sonata in A minor (1697, no. 3, z 804) they are combined, while in others, such as the jig-like movement that succeeds it, the second supplants the first. In a related type, also found in the sonatas 'à tre' of Legrenzi's op. 2, the canzona emerges out of, and is effectively the second section of, a galliard-like movement in 3/2, as in the Sonata in G (1683, no. 8, z 797) or a minuet-like movement in 3/4, as in the Sonata in D (1697, no. 10, z 811). Purcell always marks the first section Largo or Poco Largo and the second Allegro, but it is unlikely that he intended much of a change of pace, given that Largo was 'a middle movement' in tempo, according to the preface of the 1683 sonatas. Indeed, these double-barrelled movements are most effective when their contrasted elements – simple dance and elaborate counterpoint – are united in a single tempo.

EX. 8   Henry Purcell: Sonata in B flat (z 791/1)
(a) bars 1–6

(b) bars 11–13

(c) bars 17–20

(d) bars 24–6

The rarest type of canzona in Purcell's sonatas is the one where a single theme predominates, but gives way at regular intervals to freer episodes. This, of course, was to be the standard pattern of the eighteenth-century fugue, and it is significant that the best example is in z 811, Purcell's most consistently modern trio sonata. The triadic theme, in the fashionable D major fanfare style of Italian trumpet music, is matched by unusually simple harmonies, see-sawing regularly between tonic and dominant before being swept into the dominant proper by an episode of rising and falling sequences (Example 9). It is easy to be beguiled by the noble simplicity of this music into missing

EX. 9 Henry Purcell: Sonata in D (z 811/1b), bars 39–47

* The figures above the stave come from the autograph, the ones below from the printed parts.

its subtleties: how naturally a fragment of the countersubject provides, in inversion where necessary, all the material for the episode; and how easily and casually the subject itself is inverted on its return.

Purcell's sonatas do not seem to have been very successful in their day. They certainly circulated more widely than the rest of his early consort music by virtue of their appearance in print. But they do not seem to have sold very well: Frances Purcell extended the time-limit for subscriptions to the second set in the hope of 'greater encouragement', and reduced the price in 1699; there were still unsold copies left at her death in 1706.[42] The problem was partly the familiar one that the public saw no reason to prefer an imitation to the genuine article. Corelli's trio sonatas circulated in England in manuscript in the 1680s, and were all readily available in Antwerp reprints of the Italian editions by the early 1690s. 'Then came over Corelly's first consort,' Roger North wrote, 'that cleared the ground of all other sorts of musick whatsoever. By degrees the rest of his consorts, and at last the conciertos came, all which are to the musicians like the bread of life.'[43] North admired Purcell's 'noble set of sonnatas' which he thought 'very artificiall and good musick', but admitted that they were 'clog'd with somewhat of an English vein, for which they are unworthily despised'.[44] Today taste has come full circle: we tend to like music 'clog'd' with the 'English vein', such as the Sonata in C minor (1683, no. 9, z 798). But Purcell and his contemporaries had good reason to welcome the clarity, order and logic of the Corelli style; they were tired of the perpetual surprise of earlier English music as well as the lack of seriousness of the French style – 'the levity, and balladry of our neighbours', as the preface to the 1683 sonatas put it. In particular, Corelli's sequential patterns and logical modulation schemes were obvious models for a generation of English composers who were trying to clarify and expand the horizons of their own harmonic thinking.

It is likely, too, that Purcell's sonatas suffered because they were serious contrapuntal works, clearly intended to appeal to the player rather than the listener. During the 1690s the English gentry and upper middle class gradually became accustomed to listening to music in public concerts and in the theatre rather than playing it at home. An increasing number of publications of consort music were appearing in London, but they tended to be recycled concert and theatre works rather than genuine chamber music: the fashion was for theatre suites, or for sonatas that combined virtuosity and tunefulness with novel combinations of recorders, oboes, strings and even trumpet, as in those published by the Moravian composer Gottfried Finger and the German Gottfried Keller, who were partners in a London concert series in the 1690s.

To judge from the number of copies surviving in British and American libraries, *A Collection of Ayres, Compos'd for the Theatre, and upon other Occasions* (London, 1697) was a more successful proposition for Frances Purcell than the 1697 trio sonatas. *Ayres for the Theatre*, as it was known for short in newspaper advertisements, contains the thirteen suites Purcell wrote for plays given in the London theatres between June 1690 (Betterton's adaptation of *The Prophetess; or, The History of Dioclesian* by Massinger and Fletcher) and September 1695 (George Powell's adaptation of *Bonduca* by Beaumont and Fletcher). As far as is known, it includes all of Purcell's theatre suites; it does not contain anything but theatre music, despite the 'other occasions' mentioned on the title page. It omits z 593, the incomplete suite for *The Double Marriage* by Fletcher and Massinger, which appears complete in Yale University Library (Filmer MS 9) with a more convincing attribution to Louis Grabu, and z 632/1–9, the suite for Shadwell's version of Shakespeare's *Timon of Athens*, which seems to be by James Paisible apart from the overture, also found in Purcell's ode 'Who Can from Joy Refrain?' (z 342/1). z 609/1–9, the suite for Robert Gould's *The Rival Sisters*, is a similar case: the overture is by Purcell, borrowed from the ode 'Love's Goddess Sure was Blind' (z 331/1), but the rest (which only survives in two parts) is more doubtful, and may be by the violinist John Ridgley.[45]

Ayres for the Theatre marks a crucial stage in the dissemination of English theatre suites. The practice of composing suites of incidental music for plays goes back to the early 1660s – the first identifiable one is by John Banister for *The Indian*

Queen of 1664 – but the surviving repertoire is small before the 1680s. Even then suites tend to survive in manuscripts connected with the theatres, and they are often found in the form that they would have been played there, with the overture in the middle of the work, preceded by the three or four movements that served as preliminary 'first music' and 'second music' (used to warn the audience that the play was about to begin), and followed by four 'act tunes' (used as interval music). *Ayres for the Theatre* was not the first publication of theatre suites. Locke included his for Shadwell's version of *The Tempest* in the score of *Psyche* (London, 1675), Grabu included one in *Albion and Albanius* (London, 1687), as did Purcell in *Dioclesian* (London, 1691), and there is certainly some theatre music in the collections of consort music of the 1680s and 1690s, such as Thomas Farmer's *A Consort of Musick in Four Parts* (London, 1686), and John Lenton and Thomas Tollett's *A Consort of Musick of Three Parts* (London, 1692). However, *Ayres for the Theatre* was the first publication devoted entirely to theatre suites, and it became the model for Walsh and Hare's series of more than fifty theatre suites, published in the first decade of the eighteenth century under the title *Harmonia anglicana*.

In *Ayres for the Theatre* the movements of the suites were shuffled to make satisfactory sequences for use in concerts, often ordered by key. The one for *The Indian Queen* (z 630), for instance, starts in C minor with the overture (no. 3), and proceeds by way of C major (nos 4*a* and 6*a*), F major (nos 1*a*, 2*d*, 1*b*, 2*a*), D minor (no. 22), A minor (no. 17*b*) to A major (no. 18). Two movements, nos. 6*a* and 17*b*, are instrumental versions of vocal numbers, the solo and chorus 'I come to sing great Zempoalla's story' and the duet and chorus 'We, the spirits of the air', and were probably included as 'hit songs' from the show. *Ayres for the Theatre* is the primary source for most of the suites for ordinary spoken plays, so in most cases we do not know what the original theatre order was. There are secondary manuscripts of *Abdelazer* (z 570), *Amphitryon* (z 572), *Distressed Innocence* (z 577), *The Gordian Knot Unty'd* (z 597) and *The Virtuous Wife* (z 611) that give the movements in theatre order, but it is not clear in all cases what authority they have.[46]

Ayres for the Theatre has been much maligned as a source of Purcell's theatre music on the grounds that it is inaccurate, and that it wantonly omits essential wind and brass parts. In fact, the suites for conventional plays were clearly written just for strings and are not incomplete (though they might well have been performed at the time with the strings doubled by oboes and bassoon), and the collection is no more inaccurate than most contemporary publications of consort music. True, the suites from the semi-operas do have movements with missing parts – the worst case is the overture to *The Fairy Queen* (z 629/3), printed without trumpets. But in general the selections were made with skill and discrimination, and the resulting suites make excellent concert material, as the anonymous editor of the 1697 volume (Daniel Purcell?) clearly intended.

Writing theatre suites evidently satisfied any need Purcell might have had in the last five years of his life to add to the consort repertoire, for the only pieces in *Works II*, xxxi that clearly date from after 1690 are the Sonata in D for trumpet and strings (z 850), which was probably written as the overture to a lost ode, and the March and Canzona z 860 for 'flat trumpets', played at Queen Mary's funeral in 1695 as well as in a revival of Shadwell's play *The Libertine*.[47] Purcell evidently took the writing of his theatre suites seriously, and Curtis Price has rightly remarked that 'one can hardly find a single lacklustre piece' in *Ayres for the Theatre*.[48] Yet there are surprisingly few signs that Purcell tried to convey the mood of the play in his suites, beyond a tendency to preface tragedies such as *Abdelazer*, *Bonduca* (z 574) and *Distressed Innocence* with overtures wholly or partly in the minor. In *Bonduca*, Price has argued, he went further: the overture, scored for trumpet and strings (the trumpet part is not in *Ayres for the Theatre* or *Works I*, xvi, and is still unpublished), prefigures the dénouement of Fletcher's bloodthirsty tragedy by turning at the end of the fugue from C major to a wild chromatic close in C minor (Example 10).[49]

The overtures to Purcell's theatre suites are often characterized as 'French', but the first sections of many of them lack the

EX. 10 Henry Purcell: Overture from *Bonduca* (z 574/1), bars
104–15

characteristic dotted rhythm of the mature French type, being cast either in patterns of interlocking semiquavers, as in *Abdela-zer* or *The Virtuous Wife* (z 611/1), or as a flowing allemande-like passage, as in *Amphitryon* and *Distressed Innocence*; nei-ther type requires overdotting, and they are best played as writ-ten. The fugue in the *Amphitryon* overture is a rare example in Purcell of a common type in Lully: it is in triple time, with a subject in flowing quavers that enters in sequence from first violin to bass (note, however, that the second violin comes in a bar too late in *Works I*, xvi, 22). Some of the fugues in Purcell's overtures are actually more Italian than French: the duple-time one in *Abdelazer* with its striding chromatic theme would not be out of place in an Italian-style sonata, and the same can be said of the closely argued fugue in *The Virtuous Wife*. These fine pieces are virtually monothematic, but Purcell also favoured the type in which the first theme is replaced halfway through by a second, as in *The Double Dealer* (z 592/1) or *The Married Beau* (z 603/1), a device that enabled him to expand the dimensions of his fugues without diluting their contrapuntal energy in episodes.

The rest of the theatre suites are, if anything, less French than the overtures. There is no shortage of elegant minuets and minuet-like airs, some of which – such as the heartfelt piece in *The Gordian Knot Unty'd* (z 597/3) – are cast in the French *rondeau* pattern. But the most common dance is the hornpipe (fifteen examples in the nine suites for ordinary spoken plays), and throughout there is a preponderance of breezy, tuneful airs, some of which achieved the status of popular tunes: successive editions of *The Dancing Master* until the 1720s contain the hornpipe from *Abdelazer* (z 570/8; not to be confused with the *rondeau* in hornpipe rhythm, z 570/2, made famous by Britten), one of the hornpipes from *Bonduca* (z 574/7), and the hornpipe from *Dioclesian* (z 627/4) under the titles 'The hole in the wall', 'Westminster Hall' and 'The siege of Limerick'; z 627/4 also circulated as the song 'O how happy's he that from busi-ness free' (z 403), the words added to the tune by the actor William Mountfort.[50] Posthumous fame of this sort is telling evidence that the English musical world took *Ayres for the*

Theatre and its delightful suites to its collective heart, and did not easily relinquish it.

NOTES

1 John Wilson, ed., *Roger North on Music* (London, 1959), 294.

2 Ibid., 350.

3 H. Watkins Shaw, 'A Collection of Musical Manuscripts in the Autograph of Henry Purcell and other English Composers *c.* 1665–85', *The Library*, xiv (1959), 126–31.

4 Peter Holman, 'Bartholomew Isaack and "Mr Isaack" of Eton: A Confusing Tale of Restoration Musicians', *Musical Times*, cxxviii (1987), 381–5; Peter Holman, ed., *Matthew Locke, The Rare Theatrical, New York Public Library, Drexel* MS 3976, Music in London Entertainment 1660–1800, A4 (London, 1989), xi–xii.

5 Alan Browning, 'Purcell's "Stairre Case Overture"', *Musical Times*, cxxi (1980), 768–9; Robert Ford, 'Osborn MS 515, a Guardbook of Restoration Instrumental Music', *Fontes artis musicae*, xxx (1983), 174–84; see also the 1990 revision of *Works II*, xxxi, xiv–xvi.

6 See Peter Holman, ed., *Matthew Locke: The Rare Theatrical*, op. cit., xvii–xix; the point is discussed further in Peter Holman, *Four and Twenty Fiddlers: The Violin at the English Court 1540–1690* (Oxford, 1993), 316, 318.

7 The point is discussed further in Peter Holman, *Four and Twenty Fiddlers*, 384–5; for contemporary French practice, see Graham Sadler, 'The Role of the Keyboard Continuo in French Opera 1673–1776', *Early Music*, viii (1980), 148–57.

8 Edited in *Works II*, xxxi, 76–8, 106–9.

9 Peter Holman, ed., *Matthew Locke: The Rare Theatrical*, op. cit., 85; there is a modern edition in Sydney Beck, ed., *Matthew Locke: Eight Suites in Four Parts from 'Consort Music'* (New York, 1942), 10.

10 The point is discussed further in Peter Holman, *Four and Twenty Fiddlers*, 425–30; see also Ernest Brennecke, 'Dryden's Odes and Draghi's Music', *Publications of the Modern Language Association of America*, xlix (1934), 1–36.

11 Michael Tilmouth, ed., *Matthew Locke: Chamber Music II*, Musica Britannica, xxxii (London, 1972), 48–9; Peter Holman, ed., *Suite in G from Tripla Concordia* (London, 1980), 7.

12 H. Watkins Shaw, ed., *John Blow: Chaconne for String Orchestra* (London, 1958).

13 The F major version is in *Works II*, xxxi, 52–60, the D major in Denis Stevens and Thurston Dart, ed., *Henry Purcell: Fantasia Three Parts upon a Ground* (London, 1953).

14 Bruce Wood, ed., *John Blow: Anthems II: Anthems with Orchestra*,

Musica Britannica, l (London, 1984) no. 3; the 'double bass' viol is discussed further in Peter Holman, *Four and Twenty Fiddlers*, 216–17, 410.

15 Phillip J. Lord, ed., *Christopher Simpson: A Compendium of Practical Music* (Oxford, 1970), 87–8; W. Barclay Squire, 'Purcell as Theorist', *Sammelbände der Internationalen Musik-Gesellschaft*, vi (1904–5), 567.

16 Peter Holman, 'Thomas Baltzar (?1631–1663), the "Incomperable Lubicer on the Violin" ', *Chelys*, xiii (1984), 3–38.

17 Helene Wessely and Othmar Wessely, ed., *William Young (d 1662): Sonate A 3. 4. E 5. (1653)*, Denkmäler der Tonkunst in österreich, cxxxv (Graz, 1983).

18 Thurston Dart, 'Purcell's Chamber Music', *Proceedings of the Royal Musical Association*, lxxxv (1958–9), 89.

19 Derek Shute, 'Anthony à Wood and his Manuscript Wood D19 (4) at the Bodleian Library, Oxford: An Annotated Transcription' (Ph.D. diss., International Institute for Advanced Studies, Clayton, Mo., 1979), II, 99.

20 *Roger North*, op. cit., 300–301.

21 Ibid., 301.

22 Barclay Squire, op. cit., 567.

23 Franklin Zimmerman, 'Purcell and Monteverdi', *Musical Times*, xcix (1958), 368–9; see also Craig Monson, *Voices and Viols in England, 1600–1650: The Sources and the Music* (Ann Arbor, 1982); Joan Wess, 'Musica Transalpina, Parody and the Emerging Jacobean Viol Fantasia', *Chelys*, xv (1986), 25.

24 Thurston Dart, 'Purcell and Bull', *Musical Times*, civ (1963), 30–31.

25 Colin Hand, *John Taverner, his Life and Music* (London, 1978), 46–52.

26 David Pinto, 'William Lawes's Music for Viol Consort', *Early Music*, vi (1978), 14–15.

27 Paul Doe, ed., *Elizabethan Consort Music I*, Musica Britannica, xliv (London, 1979), nos 74, 75.

28 John Harper, ed., *Orlando Gibbons: Consort Music*, Musica Britannica, xlviii (London, 1982), nos 7–15.

29 Michael Tilmouth, ed., *Matthew Locke: Chamber Music II*, op. cit., 57–97.

30 On this point, see Ellen TeSelle Boal, 'Purcell's Clock Tempos and the Fantasias', *Journal of the Viola da Gamba Society of America*, xx (1983), 24–39.

31 See, for instance, Andrew Ashbee, ed., *John Jenkins: Consort Music of Four Parts*, Musica Britannica, xxvi (London, 1969), nos 41, 44.

32 Barclay Squire, op. cit., 552.

33 Ibid., 557–8.

34 There is a facsimile edition of the 1683 print, edited by Richard Luckett (Cambridge, 1975).

35 *Roger North*, op. cit., 25.

36 Ibid., 47.

37 Peter Holman, 'Suites by Jenkins Rediscovered', *Early Music*, vi (1978),

26; Robert Perry Thompson, 'English Music Manuscripts and the Fine Paper Trade, 1648–1688' (Ph.D. diss. U. of London, 1988), 436–7.

38   Ibid., 436–43.

39   Barclay Squire, op. cit., 557; see Peter Allsop, 'Problems of Ascription in the Roman *Simfonia* of the Late Seventeenth Century: Colista and Lonati', *The Music Review*, l (1989), 34–44; Robert Perry Thompson, op. cit., 450–53.

40   Peter Allsop, 'Secular Influences in the Bolognese Sonata da Chiesa', *Proceedings of the Royal Musical Association*, civ (1977–8), 89–100; Peter Allsop, 'The Role of the Stringed Bass as a Continuo Instrument in Italian Seventeenth-Century Instrumental Music', *Chelys*, viii (1978–9), 31–7.

41   Stephen Bonta, ed., *The Instrumental Music of Giovanni Legrenzi: Sonate a Due e Tre Opus 2 1655*, Harvard Publications in Music, xiv (Cambridge, Mass., 1984), nos 1, 3, 5, 10–15.

42   Michael Tilmouth, 'The Technique and Forms of Purcell's Sonatas', *Music and Letters*, xl (1959), 121.

43   *Roger North*, op. cit., 311.

44   Ibid., 310.

45   *Zimmerman I*, 288.

46   *Zimmerman I*, 240–41, 252–3, 271–3, 289–90; Curtis A. Price, *Henry Purcell and the London Stage* (Cambridge, 1984), 150–2.

47   For the date of z 760, see *Zimmerman I*, 275 and Curtis A. Price, op. cit., 116–17; for the flat trumpet, see Andrew Pinnock, 'A Wider Role for the Flat Trumpet', *The Galpin Society Journal*, xlii (1989), 105–11; Crispian Steele-Perkins, 'Practical Observations on Natural, Slide and Flat Trumpets', ibid., 122–7; David Rycroft, 'Flat Trumpets Facts and Figures', ibid., 134–42.

48   Curtis A. Price, op. cit., 66.

49   Ibid., 118–19.

50   Jeremy Barlow, ed., *The Complete Country Dance Tunes from Playford's Dancing Master* (London, 1985), nos 343, 377, 392; Cyrus Lawrence Day and Eleanore Boswell Murrie, *English Song Books 1651–1702, a Bibliography* (London, 1940), no. 2474.

IV

PURCELL AND THE THEATRE

8

The Theatrical Background

EDWARD A. LANGHANS

Merlin *waves his Wand; the Scene changes, and discovers the British Ocean in a Storm,* AEolus *in a Cloud above: Four Winds hanging,* &c. . . . AEolus *ascends, and the four Winds fly off. The Scene opens, and discovers a calm Sea, to the end of the House* [i.e. stage]. *An* Island *arises, to a soft Tune;* Britannia *seated in the Island, with Fishermen at her Feet,* &c. *The Tune changes; the Fishermen come ashore, and Dance a while; After which,* Pan *and a* Nereide *come on the Stage, and sing* . . . The Scene opens above, and discovers the Order of the Garter.

King Arthur: or, The British Worthy: A Dramatick Opera
(London, 1691; 45–50); music by Henry Purcell,
text by John Dryden

What can we make of stage directions like these? How were they carried out – if, indeed, they were? What sort of theatres did they have in Purcell's time that invited authors and composers to request theatrical effects of this nature? Were the playhouses equipped to present such spectacles because people like Purcell and Dryden demanded them, or were the effects called for with the hope that technicians could devise ways to produce them?

Questions raised by a study of Restoration theatre cannot always be answered, for reliable primary source materials are scanty. We have opera and play texts, several promptbooks (but not for musical theatre works), pictures of performers (but usually not performing), a few contemporary descriptions from diaries and letters, maps showing theatre locations and sometimes the exteriors of the buildings, a handful of illustrations of stages set with scenery, one section view of a theatre, and incomplete theatre accounts.[1] Consequently, conjectural reconstructions of Restoration theatres do not abound, especially for the 1680s and 1690s. Yet to appreciate Henry Purcell's dramatic pieces we need to gather what materials there are and try to understand the theatrical conditions under which he laboured, especially the physical features of the playhouses for which he composed and the audiences he sought to please.

London had two official public theatres when Purcell began his association with them in 1680: Dorset Garden, the Duke's Company playhouse, built in 1671 by the troupe created by Sir William Davenant; and Drury Lane, built in 1674 and operated by Thomas Killigrew and the King's Company of performers. Hard times forced the groups to merge in 1682, becoming the United Company, and for that organization Purcell did most of his theatrical work.[2] One would have supposed that a city the size of London, about 600,000, could have supported more than one company and two playhouses and provided playwrights and composers with more opportunities to ply their trades. But it could not.

With the restoration of the monarchy in 1660 England had seen a revival not of the popular public theatre of Shakespeare's time – open-air, scenery-less, economical, catering to all classes – but of the more elegant and spectacular indoor Court theatre of the designer Inigo Jones. There was a brief flirtation in 1660 with the idea of reviving the public theatre Shakespeare knew, however. In the summer of 1660 Charles II granted patents to Killigrew and Davenant, both playwrights and courtiers. Killigrew moved quickly and had a troupe in operation by November 1660, using a converted tennis court in Vere Street that had (apparently) a scenery-less stage; boys played female roles at first, as in the pre-war public theatres. Davenant, in his rival playhouse in Lincoln's Inn Fields, took longer to begin performing, but he followed the old Court theatre model and won London's favour by using scenery and actresses. The profound effect these had on the subsequent history of the English-speaking theatre cannot be overestimated. Imagine what entertainment might be like today if the Shakespearian public theatre – its architectural features, staging methods, and the kinds of plays written for it – had become the standard in 1660 and had been followed to this day. The Court tradition probably would have been revived sooner or later by commercial managers, but the old public playhouse customs might have survived and flourished side by side with it.

But that is not what happened and, for better or for worse, theatre in the English-speaking world today probably owes a greater debt to Renaissance Court entertainments than to Shakespeare's public theatre. One consequence in the Restoration period was an audience that was not as elite as has often been pictured but which was certainly dominated for many years by members of the upper class.[3] Their taste – and the taste of Charles II and his courtiers, many of whom came regularly to see shows – helped determine the theatrical fare. As Dr Johnson later wrote, 'The drama's laws, the drama's patrons give, / For we that live to please, must please to live.'[4]

When King Charles died in 1685 the era of absolute monarchy was coming to an end, the tastes of the dilettantes of the 1660s and 1670s were fading, audiences were becoming relatively more varied, and drama that had catered strongly to the aristocracy was changing. Purcell became active in the theatre when it was undergoing a difficult and important transition.

During his period the audience grew to enjoy visual spectacle, semi-operas that joined (but did not necessarily blend) music and drama, lofty characters and patriotic gestures. Did artists like Purcell, Dryden and their producer Thomas Betterton help change the taste of the theatre-going public by guiding drama away from the amoral, witty sex comedies that marked the earlier age? Or did they simply perceive the social trends and cater to the new tastes? We cannot know for certain.

Though audiences were changing in the 1680s, playhouses were not. No new theatres were built between 1674 and 1705, and there were no essential alterations to the existing ones until after Purcell's death. The decisions made by Davenant and followed by Killigrew in the 1660s – the way Restoration theatres were laid out and operated – remained constant, and their architectural features and equipment invited composers and playwrights to create the kinds of entertainments they did.

Two theatres were operated by the United Company from 1682 to 1694–5: Drury Lane (usually) for straight plays, and

Dorset Garden (usually) for spectacle productions. The buildings were probably quite similar in their main features, though Dorset Garden was larger, more highly decorated and – consequently? – perhaps acoustically better for musical works. When Purcell walked into either one he would have seen, from the rear of the auditorium, something similar to opera houses of today: seating on the auditorium floor (the 'pit'), tiers of boxes forming a rough U partly enclosing that pit, galleries above the boxes, along the sides and at the back of the auditorium, and a proscenium arch creating a picture frame for the stage behind the curtain.[5]

The capacity was probably no more than 1000, and the crucial dimensions – of Drury Lane, for which we have the most evidence – suggest the intimacy that was then common: approximately 28 feet from auditorium floor to ceiling, 55 feet from the furthest seat in the house to the curtain line, and 52 feet from the inside wall on one side of the auditorium to the inside wall on the other. This was a remarkably small space in which to entertain an audience of even 500 or 600; maximum capacity was managed in what we would now consider uncomfortable ways. Most of the seating was on backless, armless benches and, probably in the Restoration and certainly in the eighteenth century, aisles were formed by lifting hinged portions of the benches, thus providing extra seating when these 'flaps' were down. Increased capacity was also achieved by spacing the rows of benches very close together, with only about 12 inches between the front of one bench and the back of the one in front of it; the benches were roughly 21 inches high instead of the 18 inches we are accustomed to. Thus people partly sat and partly leaned back on benches, occupying a space, per spectator, approximately 18 inches wide by 24 inches deep rather than our 18 by 36.[6] Occupants of the boxes presumably had more comfortable seating. But spectators had grown accustomed to what they found in theatres and seem not to have complained.[7]

The placement of the musicians varied from theatre to theatre and time to time. The only picture we have of a music room, at Dorset Garden, shows it above the proscenium arch, but at some houses it may have been at one side or in front of the stage.

Acoustically, the Restoration theatres were probably satisfactory. Contemporary comments on sound are scarce and early. On 8 May 1663 the diarist Samuel Pepys visited the new theatre in Bridges Street and noted that 'the Musique being below, and most of it sounding under the very stage, there is no hearing of the bases at all, nor very well of the trebles, which sure must be mended'.[8] Years later, on 26 February 1669, Pepys went to the same playhouse and noticed that 'the music is the better, by how much the House the emptier'.[9] By Purcell's day new theatres had been built, and we do not know their acoustical qualities. One might guess, however, that the composer would not have continued working for Drury Lane and Dorset Garden for fifteen years had the sound of his music been unacceptable.

Auditoria in Restoration times were illuminated by chandeliers suspended from the ceiling, sconces along the sides and back, and windows which caught the afternoon sun. In some continental theatres the chandeliers could be pulled up into ceiling alcoves to control the amount of light, and a degree of dimming was also achieved by lowering canisters over the candles.[10] But there was no way of plunging spectators into darkness during performances, and had blackouts been possible audiences might have bristled; they were accustomed to seeing themselves during the show. This, indeed, is one of the most important differences between theatre-going experiences then and now.

Until the advent of electricity in the late nineteenth century, people witnessed performances in auditoria that were illuminated, more or less, from start to finish. This made spectators very aware of themselves as part of the theatrical event, and they went to the theatre as much for the social occasion as for the performance. The French visitor Henry Misson described Drury Lane in 1698:

> The Pit is an Amphitheater, fill'd with Benches without Backboards, and adorn'd and cover'd with green Cloth. Men of Quality, particularly the younger Sort, some Ladies of Reputation and Vertue, and abundance of Damsels that haunt for Prey, sit all together in this Place, Higgledy-piggledy, chatter, toy, play, hear, hear not. Farther up, against the Wall, under the first Gallery, and

just opposite to the Stage, rises another Amphitheater, which is taken up by Persons of the best Quality, among whom are generally very few Men. The Galleries, whereof there are only two rows [i.e. tiers], are fill'd with none but ordinary People, particularly the Upper one.[11]

The unruly audience behaviour is confirmed in such other sources as Act IV of Thomas Shadwell's *A True Widow*, which satirizes disruptive playgoers. How naughty audiences really were, and how often, is difficult to ascertain, but remarkably few complaints about audience behaviour have been discovered. Good performances could apparently galvanize customers into attention.

A feature of English theatres which must have pleased Henry Purcell was the forestage. It is variously called the apron, proscenium (i.e. in front of the scene), or proscenium stage: a performing area forward of the curtain line, perhaps 30 feet wide by 15 feet deep – virtually a full stage in itself – usually unencumbered by scenery and properties and, architecturally, embraced by the audience. Performers, according to the actor Colley Cibber, remembering from 1740, loved it: 'the Voice was then more in the Centre of the House, so that the most distant Ear had scarce the least Doubt, or Difficulty in hearing what fell from the weakest Utterance . . .'[12] The use of the forestage is not fully known, but logic suggests that when scenery served as an environment for the characters, the apron was very likely left unused. Instinctively, however, performers gravitate toward their audience, and when the scenery in a Purcellian production was merely a decorative background, the forestage probably became the main playing area. Most of the solo singing was presumably done there. It was like the Shakespearian platform stage, from which the Restoration apron descended.[13]

It was flanked by proscenium doors – another feature typical of British Baroque theatres and also inherited from the early public playhouses. The architect Christopher Wren drew a section view of a Restoration playhouse about 1672 and showed two doors opening on to the forestage from each side.[14] The doors were a constant reminder that, no matter how realistic the scenery might be, this was still a place of make-believe. Even in forest scenes, there stood the proscenium doors; the audience accepted that convention as easily as it accepted the stage chandeliers, visible changes of scenery, characters in seventeenth-century fashions regardless of a play's period, and the auditorium remaining illuminated throughout the performance.

The forestage floor, like that of the scenic area behind the curtain line, was raked (sloped; hence, upstage and downstage), as was the fashion in virtually all theatres using scenery painted in perspective. The Wren section drawing shows that the rake was gentle enough to be used by performers without danger. It enhanced the painted vistas stretching as far as the eye could see when, in reality, the back of the scenic area was only about 30 feet from the curtain line.[15] Upstage of the proscenium doors was the arch – an opening in the structural wall separating the auditorium from the stage and framing the scenic area. It may have been shaped like an arch or squared off, square or rectangular, taller than wide, or wider than tall.[16] The shape doesn't really matter; what is important is that a theatre then had a sizeable forestage, side doors opening on to it, and a picture frame through which spectators viewed the scenery.

The depth of the scenic area varied with the theatre. Dorset Garden's must have been generous, for the exterior was, according to Morgan and Ogilby's 1677 map, about 147 feet deep. Drury Lane was shallower, measuring about 110 feet. This difference may have been one of the reasons why the United Company usually chose Dorset Garden for operatic productions.

If Purcell had stood at the curtain line and looked upstage he would have seen a series of wings on each side of the performing area, probably a pair at each wing position, though Wren seems to show only one, with sufficient space between each position to permit entrances 'within the scene'. Wren's section has four wing positions, with hanging borders above each. The borders and wings created, in effect, a series of inner proscenia – picture frames, with each successive frame a bit smaller, enhancing the perspective effect and masking the off- and above-stage areas from the view of most spectators. On the wings and borders might have been painted – in perspective – the walls and ceiling of a room or rows of trees with overhanging branches or steep cliffs with the sky above or, indeed, whatever an author might request – or something as close to it as the scenekeeper could manage. It became standard for even provincial theatres to stock a street, forest, seashore, fancy and simple interiors, and so on.

King Arthur requires a pavilion scene with tents, a prospect of winter (perhaps especially painted for the show), a deep wood, a wood with a bridge (a slightly different setting from the deep wood but one which economically may have used some of the same scenic elements), a view of the ocean in a storm, a view of the ocean calm (the same setting with some elements changed to suggest fair weather?), and a few unspecified locales that could have been created by using stock palace interiors. We know from promptbooks and a contemporary French source, Mahelot's *Memoirs*, that clever mixing of units from one setting with those from another could simplify the staging of elaborate shows. But from such sources we also know that authors did not necessarily get what they asked for scenically, and audiences were probably none the wiser – until the printed text came out.[17]

The series of side wings with their borders made for remarkably swift and simple changes of scenery, though careful co-ordination was required. The wings stood in grooves running offstage left and right; steadying the wings at their tops were suspended grooves matching those on the floor. At the sound of the prompter's whistle, stage crews simultaneously pulled off the no. 1 wings at each position, revealing, already standing in place, the no. 2 wings. Overhead, the borders were pulled up to reveal a second set at each position. An infinite number of scene changes could be managed, since a setting not in view could be completely withdrawn and replaced with new wings and borders. In Italy and France in the 1640s Giacomo Torelli had introduced a mechanical system for changing scenery, and though there is evidence that the English tried it out, they usually preferred manual shifting, for reasons (economical? chauvinistic?) they kept to themselves. The scenery was normally changed in view of the audience – *a vista*. A few surviving theatres from the eighteenth century (the court theatre at Drottningholm, Sweden, being the most famous example) have period scenery still in use, and the magical transformations, especially in near-candlelight, are a delight.

The scenic area in a Restoration theatre could be closed off part-way upstage by pairs of sliding shutters, painted in perspective, with hanging borders of their own. Wren depicts three shutters (two would have sufficed), close together, upstage of the fourth wings. The shutters were wide enough to slide all the way to the centre of the stage from each side, forming a 'prospect'. Stagehands could draw off the no. 1 shutters to reveal the no. 2 shutters as workers overhead pulled up the first borders to reveal the second.[18]

Many plays from the period call for 'discoveries', as in *King Arthur*: '*The Scene opens, and discovers a calm sea*'. The no. 1 shutters simply drew off to reveal a pre-set tableau in the area upstage of the shutters.[19] Also: 'The Scene opens above, and discovers the Order of the Garter.'[20] The upper grooves that steadied the tops of the lower shutters were constructed to serve also as the bottom grooves for an upper set. This allowed technicians to open the lower shutters to show, as in *King Arthur*, a vista of a calm sea, with the sky overhead, painted on the upper shutters and borders. The 'sky' shutters then drew off to show a vision of the Order of the Garter painted on the no. 2 upper shutters.[21]

Because they had to be light for easy handling, the wings and shutters (and borders?) were usually made of cloth attached to wood frames, even as flats are made in the theatre today and as they have been made since at least the Renaissance. They could be straight-edged or profiled, solid or 'cut' (see-through). The wing-shutter-border system was so flexible, so simple, and so inexpensive – except for all those stagehands or the elaborate machinery needed for mechanical shifting – that it was used until late in the nineteenth century.

As the stage directions in *King Arthur* make clear, a theatre needed other technical features to cope with such special effects as people and/or scenery hanging in mid-air or rising from below. By Baroque times machinery for all these effects was common, though, typically, the English did not reveal the workings of these stage secrets as readily as did their continental counterparts. Theatres then, as now, had space above the stage (the 'flies'), and in the attic pulleys could be placed to drop ropes to the stage; at one side of the flies were workmen to manipulate the other ends of the ropes. By using tracks running under the roof and across the width of the stage, the pulleys could be movable; this allowed an object to be flown across the stage and up and down. A French refinement, pictured in a sketch by the French designer Bérain in 1698, allowed flying 'machines' – clouds, winged horses, chariots – to cross the stage, move up and down, and rotate.[22] So it was possible to fly almost anything, large or small, over any portion of the scenic area. Dryden and Purcell did not ask for anything new in *King Arthur*; indeed, the experienced Dryden seemed so certain that the Dorset Garden machinist would know what to do that he simply tacked '&c' on to some of his stage directions.

A sophisticated stage might have a half-dozen large and small trapdoors. Modern stages are usually designed so that virtually any portion of the floor can be opened, but Baroque stages with their grooves and/or slots in the floor could allow traps only where they would not interfere with the scenery. Units such as an 'island' might appear to audiences to have real depth, but, like the wings and shutters, most were probably flat – no more than an inch thick but painted to look solid. That being the case, some traps were simply narrow slots in the stage floor through which a 'mountain' might rise. Anything three-dimensional would require the use of a regular trap.

Simulating the sea was sometimes done simply by sliding profiled low scenic units – cut and painted to look like waves – back and forth across the stage. More sophisticated and remarkably believable from the audience was a wave-machine, described along with numerous other devices in an early Baroque primer of scenes and machines, Nicola Sabbattini's *Pratica* of 1638.[23] The waves looked like columns placed on their sides just above the stage floor, painted to simulate sea water and foam, and revolved by workers from offstage – vigorously for a stormy sea and slowly for a calm one. The wave machine at Drottningholm is made up of half a dozen such rotating units, each looking like large drill bits.

The Drottningholm theatre still has its Baroque equipment, and a colour film was made to show it off: mechanized wings, drops, ladders of clouds, a goddess coming down in a cloud machine (and hanging on to her narrow perch for dear life), a trapdoor in action, wave machinery, and miraculous changes from one setting to another. The substage and attic survive with their clutter of old (mostly wood) machinery, and the whole provides ample proof that the perspective painting did, indeed, make wings appear to be solid side walls, and borders the actual beams of a ceiling. Baroque theatres all over Europe specialized in such make-believe.

Roger North said Restoration audiences were not worth Purcell's talent: 'There was so much of admirable musick in that opera [*King Arthur*], that it's no wonder it's lost; for the English have no care of what's good, and therefore deserve it not.'[24] But that was one of the paradoxes of the period: people paid to come to the theatre and then sometimes paid little attention to the performance. Other paradoxes included elite patrons in cramped seating, spectacular productions in tiny playhouses, realism in scenic effects with stage chandeliers in full view, licentious spectators attending moralistic shows, and people with little musical interest going to operas. Purcell might have appreciated today's more polite theatre-goers, but modern spectators may not realize what they are missing by not having experienced a Baroque performance, rich with scenic splendour and elaborate machines, presented by singers who were experienced actors and probably pretty good vocalists, and greeted by an audience who might not have had the taste North wished but who went to the theatre with enthusiasm, eager to enjoy themselves and to relish the music and spectacle.

NOTES

1   The most interesting sources are first editions of plays with detailed stage directions, among them Charles Davenant's *Circe*, John Dryden's *Amphitryon* and *The Indian Emperour*, Thomas Shadwell's *The Tempest*, and

Elkanah Settle's (?) *The Fairy Queen*, for all of which Purcell supplied music – but we can never be sure directions were carried out.

   One discovered Restoration promptbook contains some MS music warnings and cues: a copy of Dryden's *Tyrannick Love* (1672) at the Folger Shakespeare Library; see Edward A. Langhans, *Restoration Promptbooks* (Carbondale, Ill., 1981), 31–4.

2 London had a third theatre, a converted tennis court in Lincoln's Inn Fields, which had ceased serving as a playhouse in 1674 when Drury Lane opened but would see theatrical life again just before Purcell's death in 1695, when London again had rival producing companies. Another tennis-court theatre, in Vere Street, Clare Market, had been abandoned in 1663, and a 'nursery' for the training of young performers had a brief existence in the late 1660s and early 1670s but seems not to have operated in Purcell's time. See Leslie Hotson, *The Commonwealth and Restoration Stage* (Cambridge, Mass., 1928), and William van Lennep, ed., *The London Stage: Part I 1660–1700* (Carbondale, Ill., 1965).

3 Recent studies include Harold Love, 'Who were the Restoration Audience?', and Arthur H. Scouten and Robert D. Hume, ' "Restoration Comedy" and its Audiences, 1660–1776', *Yearbook of English Studies*, x (1980), 21–44 and 45–69. See also David Roberts, *The Ladies: Female Patronage of Restoration Drama 1660–1700* (Oxford, 1989).

4 From his Prologue for the season opening of Drury Lane Theatre on 15 September 1747, spoken by David Garrick. E. L. McAdam, Jr., ed., *The Works of Samuel Johnson* (New Haven, 1964), VI, 89.

5 On the theatres, see Edward A. Langhans, 'Wren's Restoration Playhouse', *Theatre Notebook*, xviii (1964), 91–100, and 'A Conjectural Reconstruction of the Dorset Garden Theatre', *Theatre Survey*, xiii (1972), 74–93; the latter generated responses by John R. Spring and Robert D. Hume in *Theatre Notebook*, xxxi, xxxiii, xxxiv, and xxxvi. Mark A. Radice, 'Theater Architecture at the Time of Purcell and its Influence on his "Dramatick Operas" ', *Musical Quarterly*, lxxiv (1990), 98–130, is useful but occasionally misleading, as when he mistakes the Sheldonian 'Theatre at Oxford' for a playhouse (120) and confuses one London theatre with another (123, 126). See also Donald C. Mullin and Bruce Koenig, 'Christopher Wren's Theatre Royal', *Theatre Notebook*, xxi (1967), 180–87; Colin Visser, 'French Opera and the Making of the Dorset Garden Theatre', *Theatre Research International*, vi (1981), 163–71; and Jocelyn Powell, *Restoration Theatre Production* (London, 1984).

6 The architect George Saunders still complained about cramped seating in the eighteenth century: 'the public should not submit to be crowded into such narrow seats: 1 foot 9 inches is the whole space here [Covent Garden Theatre] allowed for seat and void . . .' *A Treatise on Theatres* (London, 1790; rev. New York, 1968), 83–4.

7 In the 1690s Christopher Rich, the lawyer-manager of Drury Lane, increased the capacity by cutting back the popular forestage and adding more pit benches and two stage boxes, according to B. R. S. Fone, ed., *An Apology for the Life of Colley Cibber* [1740] (Ann Arbor, 1968), 225.

Rich probably realized only an additional £10 when the house was full. Ironically, the theatres did not need extra capacity except on occasion, but theatre planners think in terms of maximum, not minimum, capacity.

8 *Pepys*, 8 May 1663; IV, 128.

9 Ibid., 26 February 1669; IX, 459.

10 See Donald C. Mullin, *The Development of the Playhouse* (Berkeley, 1970), 30; Barnard Hewitt, ed., *The Renaissance Stage: Documents of Serlio, Sabbattini and Furttenbach* (Coral Gables, 1958), 111–12; and Gösta Bergman, *Lighting in the Theatre* (Totowa, 1977). The acting areas of theatres were similarly lighted by chandeliers hanging above the stage and candles positioned behind the side wings.

11 Alois M. Nagler, ed., *Sources of Theatrical History* (New York, 1952), 208.

12 Colley Cibber, op. cit., 225. Cibber knew Purcell; he was married to one of Henry's singing students, Katherine, the daughter of Sergeant Trumpeter Matthias Shore.

13 The Bristol Old Vic, even after modern renovations, is today something like a Restoration theatre. The capacity is only 647. Built in 1766, it was about the same size as the intimate Drury Lane that Purcell knew.

14 The original drawing is in All Souls College Library, Oxford. Some playhouses may have had only one door on each side of the forestage, and John Lacy's *The Old Troop* (1672) seems to call for three. But passageways between the wings in the scenic area could be used for entrances and seem sometimes to have been referred to as doors. Above Restoration proscenium entrances were balconies, usable as performing areas or for audience seating. The British clung to the tradition of the doors into the nineteenth century, even when they were no longer used in many productions.

15 Richard Leacroft's reconstruction of Drury Lane as Purcell would have known it shows not only a raked stage floor but auditorium side walls canted inward to match the gently sloping ceiling; both helped the perspective effect created by the scenery on stage. See *Architectural Review*, cx (1951), 44, and Richard and Helen Leacroft, *Theatre and Playhouse* (London, 1984), 73.

16 The shape may sometimes have been determined by the land on which a theatre was built: a slender plot may have dictated a narrow and high proscenium opening. Similarly, the shape of a printed page may have affected how an engraver pictured a stage. Drawings of Dorset Garden show a high opening, but an illustration of the Drury Lane proscenium in Perrin's *Ariane* (1674) depicts a rectangle on its side. The Dorset Garden engraver had a standard quarto page to work with, but the Drury Lane artist was given a fold-out page and a drawing space wider than it was high.

17 Henry Carrington Lancaster, ed., *Le mémoire de Mahelot* (Paris, 1920), and Edward A. Langhans, *Eighteenth-Century British and Irish Prompt-books* (New York, 1987), 32, 176.

18 Wren shows no scenic units further upstage, where the floor flattens out,

but his drawing seems to have been abandoned, incomplete. It was torn up and either not used at all or used as a basis for revised, perhaps final, drawings of (we think) the 1674 Drury Lane Theatre.

19   A few Restoration plays call for two discoveries in succession. For this, a second shutter position was created upstage of the first, with sufficient space between – a kind of 'inner stage' – to set up whatever required revelation. After the first discovered scene was played, the second shutters could be opened to show the deepest reaches of the stage. Alternatively, if stage depth and multiple shutter positions were lacking, after a discovered scene was performed, the shutters could close over it, a new discovery could be set up behind the closed scenic units, and the shutters could re-open.

20   Upper shutters were used by Inigo Jones in 1640 in *Salmacida Spolia*, the last great Caroline masque. See Richard Southern, *Changeable Scenery* (London, 1952), 78–9.

21   It is conceivable that the upper shutters opened to show a raised stage with performers in action, but that would have required heavy platforms in an area of the stage that needed to be kept uncluttered to accommodate wave- and flying-machines.

22   See Margarete Baur-Heinhold, *The Baroque Theatre*, trans. Mary Whittall (New York, 1967), 135.

23   Trans. in Barnard Hewitt, op. cit., 43–177.

24   John Wilson, ed., *Roger North on Music* (London, 1959), 218.

9

The Theatre Music

ROGER SAVAGE

i   A Career at the Playhouse

Vera Effigies HENRICI PURCELL, *Aetat: Suae 24.* The words on
the plinth under the 1683 portrait-engraving invite us to believe
that what we see is a true likeness of Purcell in his early 20s:
fashionably wigged, stylishly dressed, big-eyed, strong-featured
and serious. The portrait – it is the frontispiece to the substantial
Sonnatas of III Parts[1] – shows a confident and capable young
maestro who has very definitely arrived. And arrived Purcell
had. By the end of 1683 he could point to a remarkable body of
achievement that included trio sonatas and fantasias, pavans
and *In nomines*, Latin psalms and English anthems, a comprehensive 'service' for the Anglican rite, several full-dress musical
odes for the House of Stuart and at least two for the cult of St
Cecilia. In addition he was quite securely entrenched – or so it
must have seemed – at two linked centres of power and patronage, the Abbey of St Peter at Westminster and the Court of
Charles II (with its Chapel Royal) based at the Palace of Whitehall. And he served both institutions not only as composer but
as organist and keeper of instruments too. A formidable musical
all-rounder operating on the inside of things high Tory and high
Anglican was HENRICUS PURCELL in 1683. Indeed, he seems to
have been such a busy and earnest man about Whitehall and
Westminster that year, and for several years after it, that we
might be forgiven for wondering on the evidence of his professional life there whether he would have had the time, or
indeed the inclination, even to take ship down the Thames to
visit the playhouses described in the previous chapter, let alone

write music for them. What would the composer of '*Jehovah, quam multi sunt hostes mei*' and '3 Parts upon a Ground' go to Drury Lane or Dorset Garden *for*? The question is asked more generally of all serious Londoners by Purcell's contemporary James Wright in *The Humours and Conversations of the Town*:

> What wou'd you go to the Play for? To see a Whore that has Lain with all the Beaux of the Pit; nay, perhaps with ev'ry Player on the Stage, act a Virgin, or a Vertuous Wife? Or to be dun'd all round with the impertinent Discourse of Beardless Fops to the Orange-Wenches . . . : of the Rake-Hells, talking loud to one another; or the perpetual Chat of the Noisy Coquets, that come there to get Cullies, and to disturb, not mind the Play. Or what Effect has all the Plays upon you? Are not your Fops in the Pit and Boxes incorrigible to all the Endeavours of your Writers, in their Pro-logues and Epilogues, or the variety of Characters that have been made to reform them? Tho a Play be a generous Diversion, yet 'tis better to read than see, unless one cou'd see it without these Inconveniences.[2]

Yet those inconveniences, if indeed he saw them as such, did not keep Purcell away from the theatre, or from writing a very great deal of theatre music. Admittedly there was not a lot of it before 1683, the year of that earnest *vera effigies*, though the small amount there was did include a set of songs (z 606/5–9) sung 'betwixt the acts' of *Theodosius* (a sober tragedy by the un-sober Nathaniel Lee) that were thought notable enough to be published in score along with the script of the play in 1680: quite an honour for any composer at the time, let alone a mere 20-year-old. But in the dozen years between 1683 and Purcell's death in 1695 the case was altered: then he was involved with well over forty shows mounted at Drury Lane and Dorset Garden, supplying things for them on any scale that was required, from a single 90-second song to an elaborate score of close on two hours and a quarter. His music seems to have become quite a selling point for those houses:

> The theatre his worth well knew,
> Saw how by him its greatness grew . . .

wrote an unknown 'lover of music' in an elegy on his death.

'How was the Scene forlorn, and how despis'd', wrote George Granville (later Lord Lansdowne) around 1700, thinking of the pulling power of Purcell's setting of a masque of lovers and drinkers which had been added to a Restoration version of Shakespeare's *Timon of Athens* (z 632/10–19),

> When *Tymon*, without Musick, moraliz'd?
> *Shakespears* sublime in vain entic'd the Throng,
> Without the Charm of *Purcel's* Syren Song.[3]

Some of his theatre songs even became famous enough for turn-of-the-century playwrights to slip glancing allusions to them into their city comedies. For instance, the boorish Sir John Brute, disguised as a bold virago in Vanburgh's 1726 revision of his *Provoked Wife*, tries in Act IV to terrorize the Covent Garden watch with cries of:

> Sirrah, I am Bonduca, queen of the Welshmen, and with a leek as long as my pedigree I will destroy your Roman legion in an instant. Britons, strike home.

('Britons, strike home!' [z 574/16] was the warlike song of the Druids composed by Purcell for a 1695 revision of John Fletcher's Jacobean Boadicea play *Bonduca*; it served as something of a 'Rule, Britannia!' until 'Rule, Britannia!' itself got written about half a century later.)

Indeed, so fertile and famous did Purcell become as a theatre composer that on the next occasion after the 1683 *Sonnatas* that a portrait of him appeared as the frontispiece to a volume of his music – in the posthumous and significantly titled *Orpheus Britannicus* of 1698 – fully half the eighty items which made up that 'Collection of All the Choicest Songs for One, Two, and Three Voices Compos'd By Mr. Henry Purcell' are pieces which originated in the playhouse.

How could this be? Was Purcell schizophrenic between Whitehall-Westminster and theatreland? Was he moonlighting at Dorset Garden and Drury Lane when the princes of Church and State were not looking?

Not really. For one thing, it was accepted practice by the time Purcell came of age that musicians at the Abbey should find additional outlets for their talents (and input for their purses) elsewhere, and the theatre was a better place than most to do this. Some stern Westminster theologians might disapprove, but, as Purcell's teacher and fellow organist John Blow is made to remind him jauntily in a spoof exchange of letters between the two of them invented by their contemporary Tom Brown, 'men of our profession hang between the church and the play-house, as Mahomet's tomb does between two load-stones, and must equally incline to both because by both we are equally supported'.[4] As for any disapproval from Court, Purcell's first royal employer, Charles II, was unlikely to object to a composer-in-ordinary of his writing music for the theatre. After all, the restoration of fully functioning public playhouses for spoken drama to London in 1660 after the theatre-starved years of the Commonwealth had been closely bound up with the restoration of the monarchy after its continental exile at the same time; and the two companies running Dorset Garden and Drury Lane in Purcell's early 20s did so under patents from the King. Charles himself went to the public playhouses often and sometimes ordered royal command performances for the Hall Theatre at Court. He was even prepared to provide instrumentalists from his household and singers from his Chapel Royal when the play-house patentees down-river needed them, thus cavalierly over-riding a pious order in his father's reign that

> none of the said Choristers or Children of the Chapell . . . shall be used or imployed as Comedians, or Stage Players, or to exercise or acte any Stage plaies, Interludes, Comedies, or Tragedies; for that it is not fitt or desent that such as should sing the praises of God Almighty should be trained or imployed in lascivious and prophane exercises.[5]

So a Court composer of Charles's might be publicly 'profane' without great scruple if he had a mind to. And Purcell, it seems, had such a mind. Theatre music, after all, could sometimes be as earnest-sounding as the 1683 *vera effigies* of Purcell is earnest-looking, and when it was not – well, perhaps one can catch a hint of amused irony even in that sober official gaze.

Purcell had been a Chapel Royal boy himself, and possibly

came by some direct stage experience that way. Indeed, if his voice had not broken just a few months beforehand, he would probably have been up there on stage with his Chapel-fellows on loan from the King, singing and acting benign sea-sprites and vindictive devils in a pair of brief 'masques' that were worked into a spectacular version of Shakespeare's 65-year-old *Tempest* given at Dorset Garden in the spring of 1674: a version which involved many of the best composers and two of the liveliest dramatists then active in London. The music for the masques was provided by Pelham Humfrey, who was young Purcell's composition teacher at or near that time; so, if not actually on stage, the 14-year-old may well have been in the thick of back-stage preparations for a show which was something of an epoch-maker, and which, with its preliminary 'musics' and 'cur-tain tune', its 'act-tunes', inset-songs and elaborate masquing set-pieces, could be seen as providing the agenda for most of his own later theatre work. Yet if Purcell was indeed on hand for *The Tempest*, it was simply as the culmination of a boyhood in which he had either glimpsed from his cradle, broken bread with or sat at the feet of several notable musicians with strong theatrical connections: among them Henry Lawes and Chris-topher Gibbons, who had written music for lengthy and elabor-ate masques under Charles I and the Commonwealth, and who were close neighbours of the Purcell family when Henry was very young; Henry's own father, who died when the boy was around 5 but who had earlier acted and sung in a pioneer-ing 'operatic' piece, Sir William Davenant's *The Siege of Rhodes* (its music by a consortium of five composers); Matthew Locke, writer of some of the most striking theatre music of the 1660s and 1670s, whom Purcell was able to describe as 'his worthy friend' in a precocious elegy on the older man's death in 1677; and Pelham Humfrey himself, who taught Purcell for a few months at the end of a career which had included a two-year visit to continental Europe at the King's behest to soak up the latest foreign modes, theatrical modes *à la* Lully and Molière doubtless included.[6]

Given all this, and given the dramatic flair Purcell displays in so much of his early non-theatrical work (for instance, the

characteristic instant fixing of a strong mood at the start of
'*Jehovah, quam multi*' and the fine shape-making out of vivid
contrasting elements in pieces as various as the 'Fantasia upon
One Note', the anthem 'My Beloved Spake' and the mad-song
'Bess of Bedlam'), there is nothing very surprising about his
getting involved with the playhouse managements of Drury
Lane and Dorset Garden: managements which, conveniently for
him perhaps, coalesced in 1682 with the setting up of a United
Company which was to have a monopoly of the London stage
until a few months before the composer's death in November
1695. Indeed, if anything, it is rather more surprising that, after
the fairly substantial score for *Theodosius* (involving those interact numbers and quite a big sung initiation-scene as well), the
stream of his music for the public theatres through the 1680s
should apparently be such a thin one: quite possibly not much
more than a dozen songs. However, in 1690 the skies suddenly
opened and the trickle became a flood. In the last five years of
his life Purcell seems to have been responsible in all for close on
twelve hours' worth of theatre music.

Only twelve songs in the 1680s (post-*Theodosius*) but twelve
hours in the early 1690s? The contrast in fact may not be quite
that extreme. Perhaps there was theatre music for Drury Lane
and Dorset Garden in the 1680s which has been lost; and of
course at a different venue in that decade there was the remarkable *Dido and Aeneas* (z 626), a weighty if not lengthy piece for
private performance which has largely survived. Perhaps, too,
some of the extant scores Purcell wrote for United Company
revivals of plays which had been originally given in the 1660s
and 1670s were composed for restagings in the 1680s and not,
as scholars tend to think, in the 1690s. (A particular question
mark hangs over an impressive invocation scene for Charles
Davenant's *Circe* [z 575].) Yet even at a very sceptical, conservative estimate, the years 1690–95 produced over ten hours of
playhouse music, which beats by at least an hour the combined
length of the twenty-four odes for sundry occasions Purcell
wrote throughout the whole of his composing life!

Why then did the relative trickle become an absolute flood? If
there was one definite and determining reason, it is lost to us.

Still, there are several speculative possibilities, and the truth may well lie among them. For a start, Purcell under Charles II in the early 1680s may simply have been too busy with anthems, odes, canticles, catches, songs, sonatas and so forth for Westminster and Whitehall (to say nothing of *Dido and Aeneas*) to allow much time for public-theatre work, however attractive the idea of it might have been: a state of affairs which began to change under James II between 1685 and 1688 – James's taste was for Italian music and musicians – and changed very much more after the Glorious Revolution with the arrival of Dutch William. (William was a bellicose Calvinist whose interest in music seems not to have extended beyond what Dryden's 'Song for St Cecilia's Day' calls 'the trumpet's loud clangour' and 'the double double double beat / Of the thund'ring drum'.) So perhaps it was simply that, when not busy with the superb series of six birthday odes which he wrote for William's more congenial consort Mary, Purcell post-1688 found that he had composing time on his hands for other things, including a lot of things for Drury Lane and Dorset Garden. And who knows? He may have had outstanding bills on his hands too. Court and Abbey payments to musicians were often in arrears, and matters cannot have improved financially in the late 1680s and early 1690s, when there was probably less for an English composer of Purcell's cast to do at the royal and holy end of town. So financial worlds needed to be – and were – found elsewhere. Pupils were taken. Worthy institutions other than the courtly and ecclesiastical were tangled with: Trinity College, Dublin; the academies of Mr Maidwell and Mr Priest; the London committee of the stewards of the feasting Nobility and Gentry of the City and County of York; the high-minded Musical Society (a *re*-tangling this, a return after nearly a decade to the setting of Cecilian odes). And if the actors at Drury Lane and Dorset Garden were coming up with offer after offer for Purcell's services – and if (as they may have done) they actually paid on the nail – who was he to turn the offers down?

Then, beyond matters of time and cash-flow, there may have been ideological and aesthetic reasons for trickle becoming flood in the 1690s. Again it is speculation, but reasonable speculation, that the Purcell of the 1680s felt himself very much to be a Charles II's man. On an artistic level this would mean that, however strong his English roots and however great his assimilative interest in the achievements of Italian contemporaries like Carissimi and Corelli, he would take French culture, the culture of most of Charles's years of exile, especially seriously. (Having had the francophile Pelham Humfrey as a composition teacher could only have intensified this.) In the 1680s, theatre music *à la mode de France* meant the new-fangled French opera: the *tragédies lyriques* of Lully, through-sung, mythological, often balletic and with a strong allegiance to an absolutist Court. There were attempts at the time to set up French opera, or something like it, in England; a French-trained composer (the Spaniard Louis, or Luis, Grabu) was even brought over to provide the music for the only full-length, through-sung, English-texted opera of the Restoration period to be given in public, *Albion and Albanius*. It is into this context that Purcell's *Dido* most comfortably fits, as a small-scale native *tragédie lyrique*, eclectically yet brilliantly written by Charles's composer-in-ordinary for professional private performance – at Court, quite possibly, which is where persuasive recent scholarship has suggested it very likely had its première (*most* likely in 1684).[7] Purcell perhaps hoped at that time that his theatrical energies would henceforth be spent on becoming the English Lully, purveyor-in-ordinary of Anglo-French lyric tragedies to the Stuarts. But Charles's death in 1685 and the Glorious Revolution three years later put paid to all that in one way and another. The result? As every schoolboy knows, *Dido* remained Purcell's one and only opera, as we would usually define 'opera'; and, apart from a fine set of Dorset Garden mad-songs for Tom Durfey's *A Fool's Preferment* (z 571), his theatrical skills seem not to have got much more exercise until 1690. Then, however, he found a good genius in the shape of Thomas Betterton, who was as much an all-rounder in theatre as Purcell was in music: actor, administrator, writer, adapter, deviser of décors and general ideologue of the United Company; a man with ways of his own of marrying traditional English culture with progressive notions from France (a country he had visited several times as Charles

II's scout for new theatrical ideas).[8] Betterton managed to get Purcell busily involved at Dorset Garden in an elaborate adaptation of Massinger and Fletcher's 70-year-old play of ancient Roman magic *The Prophetess* (or, as it came to be known, *Dioclesian*), in many ways a successor to that spectacular *Tempest* of 1674 which had quite probably had the 14-year-old Henry running about backstage. And after *Dioclesian* (z 627), the deluge: the five-year flood of theatre scores of all shapes and sizes for Drury Lane and Dorset Garden which virtually gave Purcell a career independent of Abbey and Court.

In the early 1690s he must have become very familiar with Betterton and the apartment he kept over the portico at Dorset Garden (close to Dorset Stairs, whence it was about a mile upstream by river-boat to Westminster Stairs and Purcell's properties nearby at Bowling Alley and Marsham Street). Indeed, if the composer's double-career activities struck anyone as dangerous moonlighting, it might very well have been Betterton who was piqued when Purcell had occasionally to stay upriver composing a Divine Hymn for Playford's *Harmonia Sacra*, an ode for Her Majesty's birthday or a festal *Te Deum* and *Jubilate* for St Cecilia's Day. Perhaps Purcell came to know Betterton's most celebrated house dramatist John Dryden particularly well at this time too. Dryden was certainly to be an important presence in his last years. The poet, almost three decades the composer's senior, seems not to have paid him much attention until the success of *Dioclesian*, though they *had* had a collaborator in common in the 1680s: Nahum Tate, librettist of *Dido and Aeneas* for Purcell and co-author with Dryden of the second part of the great Tory-loyalist epic satire *Absalom and Achitophel*. But things changed in the 1690s. It is striking how many of the 1690s stagings by Betterton's company which had music by Purcell were connected somehow with Dryden and his circle: either new plays entirely Dryden's own, or new collaborations, or revivals of old solo plays and collaborations, or plays by close friends and special protégés like Thomas Southerne and William Congreve. In all, a good twenty of the forty theatre scores Purcell certainly or most likely wrote in the 1690s are Dryden-linked in one or other of these ways. In return, so to speak, Dryden now becomes quite a Purcell fan. He praises the composer in two of his urbane dedicatory epistles (the ones to *Amphitryon* and *King Arthur*); he ghosts the weighty dedication which appears over Purcell's name in the published score of *Dioclesian*; and all too soon he is writing 'Mark how the lark and linnet sing . . .', his elegy on the composer's death. It would be interesting to know whether personal circumstances gave the two men a special closeness. Dryden, who converted to Catholicism in the mid-1680s, disdained to be a Vicar of Bray at the Glorious Revolution. As a result he soon lost his Poet Laureateship and turned (or rather *re*-turned) to play-writing, partly because it gave him an independent creative platform and partly because he needed the cash. 'Age has overtaken me,' he wrote in the summer of 1692 in his 'Discourse on Satire'; 'and want, a more insufferable evil, through the changes of the times has wholly disenabled me.' Granted Purcell had not lost all *his* establishment appointments and was a youngish man still; but beyond that, how many special affinities did he feel with the Grand Old Man through the changes of the times, in matters financial, artistic, political – religious even?[9]

Not that such feelings, in so far as they existed, led the composer to polarize his theatrical and Church/State work in matters stylistic. He speaks the same language up-river and down, showing the same attachments to particular forms and the same idiosyncrasies of word-setting regardless of address. His musical evolution is even-footed too. When his style broadens somewhat with the *Dioclesian* music in 1690, allowing among other things a more extensive use of big effects for chorus and strong instrumental colours, that broadening – adumbrated to an extent in the 'Yorkshire Feast Song' (z 333) earlier the same year – can also soon be felt in the non-theatrical work. For instance, the slow-turning kaleidoscope of trumpets, oboes and violins that interrupts the imposing vocal chaconne 'Triumph, victorious love' in *Dioclesian* turns again (to different music) at the start of the final chorus of the 1692 ode 'Hail! Bright Cecilia!' (z 328/13), just as the grandiose overture to that ode has a structure and rhetoric very close to the orchestral 'Sonata while the Sun Rises' in Act IV of the Dorset Garden adaptation of Shakespeare's *A Midsummer*

Night's Dream as *The Fairy Queen* (z 629). Again, musical jokes are shared between addresses theatrical and non-theatrical. Does one of the airs in the Court ode 'Love's Goddess Sure was Blind this Day' have the rough 'Scotch' tune 'Stingo' ('Cold and raw the north did blow') as its bass line (z 331/6)? Then 'Lilliburlero', the great pop-song of the Glorious Revolution, serves the same function – and more wittily because better hidden – in a jig for the mysterious public-theatre comedy *The Gordian Knot Unty'd* (z 597/5).[10] Court odes sometimes even lend whole instrumental numbers to the playhouse. Thus the chaconne in 'Sound the Trumpet' for King James in 1687 and the overture to 'Arise, my Muse' for Queen Mary in 1690 both reappear in the pre-musics for the Purcell-Dryden patriotic spectacular *King Arthur* at Dorset Garden in 1691 (z 628/1 and 4): a subtle gesture of political reconciliation, perhaps, or perhaps simply a dipping into a convenient bottom drawer.

This lending was a two-way business. When Mary died in 1695, Purcell provided an awesome march for her obsequies, but did not write it especially for the occasion. He took it from the 'flat-trumpet' prelude he had written a few years before to a scene of infernal spirits poised to claim the soul of Don John (aka Don Juan) in Thomas Shadwell's play *The Libertine* (z 600/ 2 and 860/1). Clearly no treasonable slur was intended. Her late Majesty was not by implication frivolously showbizzy, notoriously licentious or – God forbid – hell-bent. Only the awesomeness, the sense of momentous Last Things, was a constant: the fitness to function of the notes and instruments. This held both up-river and down.

ii Ayres and Songs for the Theatre

Fitness to function is an important characteristic of Purcell's public-playhouse music as a whole; doubtless he would not have been invited back so often if it had not been. But the concern to be properly functional is especially worth stressing where he is writing fairly brief vocal or instrumental numbers to be set into or placed around large structures of predominantly spoken drama. Not that 'functional' with Purcell means drably utilitarian. There is a great deal of very fine music in the inset-songs which are dotted about these spoken plays – a use of song at least a century old by Purcell's time – and also in the pieces written to give the drama a frame, so to speak: to divert the audience while it is waiting for the play to begin, to herald the drawing of the curtain, and to fill some or all of the space between the acts.

With his framing music as with his inset-songs, Purcell is writing in quite a long tradition. Such preluding and interluding went back beyond the Commonwealth at least as far as the 1630s; but it firmed up in the 1660s with the convention that a single composer – in that decade Matthew Locke, for instance, or John Banister – would undertake to supply on his own the complete set of framing pieces needed for a new play or the revival after a longish gap of an old one.[11] Such a set, in the case of its *inter*-act music anyway, might on rare occasions include vocal numbers. (The tradition of sung *intermedi* can be traced back at least as far as *c*1500 in northern Italy.) Those solo songs of Purcell's that were placed 'betwixt the acts' of Lee's *Theodosius* in 1680 and subsequently printed with the script are a case in point. Still, with Purcell as with his elders (and also with such gifted contemporaries and juniors as Paisible, Finger, Eccles, Clarke and Croft), the framing music was most often purely instrumental, scored in the main for a four-part ensemble of strings. From Purcell himself we have thirteen sets of such music, each associated with a particular show. Between them they form a remarkable horde of overtures, airs, minuets, bour-rées, marches, rondeaux, chaconnes, hornpipes, jigs and 'trum-pet-tunes': over 100 pieces in all, with one or two sarabands and fashionable 'Scotch' tunes thrown in for variety. 'What wou'd you go to the Play for?' asks James Wright, stressing the squalor and inconvenience and suggesting you should stay at home and read a good script. Well, in part at least you would go to hear instrumental pieces of this sort, from a framing set by Purcell himself perhaps, or by one of his talented colleagues; pieces like the wittily ingenious 'Hornpipe on a Ground' (z 603/9) – quintessentially Purcellian title – which he wrote for John Crowne's comedy *The Married Beau* and which casts a benign shadow forward over the 'Ostinato' movement of the *St Paul's Suite* for strings by the eager Purcell revivalist Gustav Holst 220 years later, or the weighty Rondeau (z 570/2) for Aphra Behn's tragedy *Abdelazer*, which became the basis for *The Young Person's Guide to the Orchestra*, a work from the middle of Benjamin Britten's most Purcellian decade, the 1940s.[12]

The scale of the great majority of Purcell's framing pieces is pretty small: an average of less than two minutes (repeats included) for all types except the overtures, and for them an average of barely a minute more. If laid end to end and played one after another, the movements of a complete set of framing music would normally weigh in at under a quarter of an hour. *Multum in parvo*, however; the leanness is not a symptom of musical undernourishment. True, there was not space in this context for the cumulative intensity of a big brooding structure like the fine (and probably early) Chacony for strings in G minor (z 730) – a concert piece most like; but to hear the full set of framing numbers for, say, *Abdelazer* or *The Married Beau* or *The Gordian Knot* performed as a continuous sequence is to cover a wide emotional terrain, yet in music that is consistently Purcellian in its seemingly effortless melodic shapeliness, in the richness of its part-writing (the inner parts especially), in its characteristic counterpointing of the wittily elegant with the introspectively poignant, and in its fondness for wrong-footing the listener by setting up innocent musical expectations and then adventurously thwarting them. However, sets of Restoration framing music from Locke's to Croft's via Purcell's were not in the first instance meant to be heard laid out end to end as a sequence. It was only after their playhouse premières that some of them might earn a second life of this sort outside the theatre, brought together and reordered to form continuous and shapely suites for private music-making or the newish public 'music meetings'. (This is the form in which the thirteen Purcell sets were published by John Heptinstall for the composer's widow and executrix in 1697 as *A Collection of Ayres, Compos'd for the Theatre*.) But in that very first instance, in the playhouse itself, the numbers making up a set were strung out like lanterns across the whole theatrical event.

The event began well before the curtain was drawn, as Restoration theatre audiences – by modern standards anyway – arrived early. There was no other foolproof way of ensuring oneself a seat; and besides, the playhouses described for us in the previous chapter were vivid, lively, fashionable places to be; the play was by no means the only thing they had to offer. Music lovers particularly could not afford to cut things too fine if they wanted to catch the first numbers of the set of framing music. 'Before the Comedy begins,' writes Lorenzo Magalotti of a visit to London in Purcell's tenth year (though it might equally well be in his twentieth or thirtieth), 'that the audience may not be tired with waiting, the most delightful symphonies are played; on which account many persons come early to enjoy this agreeable amusement.'[13] Londoners knew these pre-show 'symphonies' as 'musics'. There were traditionally three of them, perhaps reflecting the three 'soundings' before a pre-Commonwealth play. They were presumably performed with considerable gaps in between, so that the audience should have some opportunity to give quite undivided attention to the things its more satiric observers describe it enjoying most of all: gossiping, flirting, ogling, flaunting, caballing, orange-buying and (where the young gallants and roarers at.least were concerned) whore-hunting. In Purcell's case, the First and Second Musics each comprised one or a couple of the pieces included in the framing set for that particular play, while the Third Music, close to curtain-time, was the set's 'overture'.

There was a splendid custom in the Restoration that, if you undertook to leave the playhouse by the end of the show's first act, you were not charged for admission. This could be convenient, charitable even, if you were a gallant in search of one of the masked playhouse prostitutes. ('I gallop round the Pit,' boasts one such young dog, Frank Wildblood, in Elkanah Settle's comedy-spectacular of 1697, *The World in the Moon*, 'hear the last Musick, pick up a Mask, and carry her off before the Play; and so save the poor Whore her Half Crown.') It could also be a blessing if you more chastely wanted a free sample of the latest playhouse score by Purcell, Eccles, Finger or whomever. Theophilus Cibber, son of one of the comedians in Betterton's United Company, and someone who liked to see a full house all through the show, testily describes the sort of person who, because

> he loved music (or pretended a taste for it), would take a place in the pit, to hear the First and Second Music (which latter used to be some select piece), but prudently retired, taking his money again at the door before the Third Music.[14]

Were the First and Second Musics Purcell wrote always especially 'delightful', 'agreeable' and 'select', more arresting and consequential than other parts of his sets of framing music? Sadly it is not possible to say for certain, since his thirteen surviving sets divide fairly evenly into those where we definitely know the order of playing in the theatre, those where we have some clues but little certainty and those where we don't know the order at all. However, our certain knowledge that the First Music to *King Arthur* comprised the impressively Apollonian chaconne borrowed from 'Sound the Trumpet', and the near certainty – the evidence is in a manuscript of around 1700 – that the equally strong but more plangent chaconne in the framing set for *The Gordian Knot Unty'd* was that show's First Music, do suggest that First Musics at least could be especially ear-catching.

Further, when a pre-music was in two sections, the sections could be cunningly balanced; and a two-section First Music could also balance effectively with a two-section Second Music. Witness what we definitely know to have been the First and Second Musics to *The Fairy Queen* and *The Indian Queen*, two 1690s shows adapted from earlier plays: the former a thorough-going reworking of *A Midsummer Night's Dream*, the latter a far less radical revision (with name unchanged) of a 'heroic' drama of life among the Aztecs and Incas written in 1663 by Dryden and his brother-in-law Sir Robert Howard. Further still, the fitness to function of the First and Second Musics in these particular scores is a matter not simply of a lively but rather generalized playhouse aptness – the equivalent in sound of the stylish pilasters and arcades of the building's auditorium – but also of an aptness to the mood of the drama soon to begin on stage. The mercuriality and tenderness of the *Fairy Queen* Musics (z 629/1 and 2) are as proper to the play they precede as the trenchant, assured, feet-on-the-ground *Indian Queen* Musics (z 630/1 and 2) are to the earthier concerns of Dryden and Howard.

The same is sometimes true of Purcell's Third Musics, his overtures: pieces whose form and rhetoric often pay warm compliments to the ghost of Lully, though it is far from certain that Lully would have returned the compliment if he had heard one. (He would probably have regarded the other determining influence on them, that of the native English consort tradition, as lamentably Gothick.) In the theatre the overture seems normally to have followed the speaking of the play's prologue.[15] The prologue involved a leading actor, occasionally more than one, coming on to the deep forestage in front of the still-closed theatre curtain and wooing, lecturing, shocking, titillating, abusing and flattering the audience – almost always in polished couplets. At least, speaking before the curtain was the general rule for prologues, though it was a rule that Dryden and Howard had boldly broken back in the 1660s with their original *Indian Queen* by drawing the curtain earlier than expected to reveal an Amerindian girl and boy prologuizing in character in a picturesque tropic landscape, treating the esteemed audience out front as a vision of the benign white race fated to conquer them . . . It was a boldness Purcell made even bolder at the play's revival in 1695 by setting almost the whole of this prologue to music (airs, recitative, duets) as if it were a fragment of through-sung opera – an *Indes galantes* four decades before Rameau's. However, in shows with the much commoner spoken and curtain-closed prologue, prologue led straight to overture and overture to curtain-up. So the overture was potentially Janus-faced. Somewhat like the prologue itself, and indeed like the brightly lit forestage on which the prologue was spoken, backed by the proscenium arch and flanked by stage doors and side-boxes, it could be seen as part of the audience's world, and/or as part of the world of the drama to come.

Some overtures, notably those to *The Fairy Queen* and *King Arthur*, both of them in a bold D major and both adding a couple of trumpets to the string band, seem to point cheerfully forward to the happy and momentous outcomes that their plays' plots eventually deliver. Similarly, some tragedy overtures can be as dark as the ensuing plays' dénouements. Thus the one to Settle's ancient Persian piece *Distressed Innocence* (z 577/1) is grave and melancholic, and that to Aphra Behn's corpse-strewn Spanish-Moorish shocker *Abdelazer* (z 570/1) is at first balefully momentous, and then – in a metre of undotted quavers in duple time it shares only with *Dido* among the theatre overtures – anxious and unsettling. But it does not always happen this way. For instance, Purcell's overture to *Timon of Athens* (z 632/1: not to be confused with his edgy, impressive 'curtain-tune' for the play) has pomp and circumstance but little emotional density: it is more a reflection of the opulent proscenium than the austere script. And the overture to *The Old Bachelor* (z 607/1), the earliest comedy of Dryden's most brilliant protégé William Congreve, has an eloquent seriousness and startling richness of harmony which hardly prepare one for the exuberance, witty repartee and moments of pure farce in the play itself. If there *is* a link between play and overture here, it is the implication that, since we in the audience are about to see an especially cunning piece of literary craftsmanship, we should have, to usher it in, as fine a piece of near-abstract musical craftsmanship as our composer can contrive.

After the overture: Act I of the afternoon's tragedy, comedy, history play, farce, heroic play or 'semi-opera'; and after Act I – as after Acts II, III and IV – the remaining pieces of the set of framing music, one at each act-ending. As a rather testy prologue from the 1670s put it, this music was (at least in part)

> by Intervals design'd
> To ease the weary'd Actors voice and mind.[16]

The playhouse bandsmen, somewhat cut off from things in their gallery or music room or orchestra pit, would be attending – or possibly not attending – to the play as it progressed. As an act came to its end, the prompter might well alert them with his bell. (He had a whistle for stagehands and a bell for musicians; 'ring' is quite often written into promptbooks of the period.[17]) Invited

by the bell and/or picking up the closing words of the act –
sometimes the easier to identify because they suddenly blossomed into a rhyming couplet after an expanse of prose or blank
verse – the band would come in on cue with the proper act-tune.
In his *Comical Lovers*, Colley Cibber (husband of a pupil of
Purcell's, father of the Theophilus who liked to see full houses,
and himself a young beginner with the United Company during
the composer's most productive theatre years) describes the process as seen and heard by the audience. In Act III, two lovers in a
scene of pathetic farewells are navigating their separate ways to
the permanent doors on each side of the forestage:

> Agen they turn, still ogling as before,
> Till each gets backward to the distant Door:
> Then, when the last, last Look their Grief betrays,
> The Act is ended, and the Musick plays.

Hopefully, such Romeos and Juliets were able to go off to a slow
air or grave minuet rather than a jig or an energetic hornpipe . . .
   Did the next act begin immediately the act-tune ceased, or
were there some further minutes of interval which had no
music? No evidence to settle the issue seems to exist. The case
for interval being longer than act-tune would stress all the things
that eye-witnesses tell us Restoration audiences needed to do
at one time or another during an afternoon at the playhouse:
stretching their limbs and paying visits, primping and chatter-
ing, throwing oaths into the pit or horsing on benches there,
making assignations or forking out to Orange Moll or one of
her sisters for fruit and sweetmeats. Surely all this could not
happen during a two-minute act-tune followed non-stop by a
new act? Apart from anything else, how would anyone hear the
music? The counter-case for the interval being no longer than
the act-tune – the stronger case probably – would stress that
Dorset Garden and Drury Lane were not the darkened and rev-
erential temples of culture the twentieth century is used to; that
the audience would be as likely to do most of what it energetically did *during* the action of the play as at any other time; and
that Restoration theatre-goers probably had ears better trained
than ours to filter out what they did not want to hear and focus

on what they did, so that a music lover enjoying an act-tune could fairly cheerfully ignore such fops and gallants as would

> briskly mount a bench when th' Act is done,
> And comb their much-lov'd Periwigs to the tune

(as another irritated prologue of the 1670s put it).[18]

The cutting edge of Baroque stringed instruments could certainly ensure that they were audible; and music of real quality – Purcell's, for instance – might well compel an unusual degree of silence, as great acting certainly did. (The eighteenth-century memoir of Betterton by Anthony Aston records that 'his Voice was low and grumbling; yet he could Tune it by an artful *Climax*, which enforc'd universal Attention, even from the *Fops* and *Orange Girls*'.[19]) Certainly if act-tunes began as one act ended *and* ended as the next act began, this would give an even greater theatrical aptness to a number like the second tune in Purcell's framing set for *The Fairy Queen* (z 629/16): an energetic, hurrying piece which starts as Puck leaves the sleeping Hermia and Lysander onstage and darts off –

> Farewel Lovers, I am gone;
> I must now to *Oberon*

– and would finish as Helena hurries *on*stage in pursuit of Demetrius with the first line of Act III:

> I am out of breath with following him so fast . . .

Be that as it may, the connection of act-tunes with the ends of the acts preceding them is the crucial thing, since it seems quite often to have been a matter of act-mood at that point determining act-tune. 'Seems to have been' is as strong as one can put it, since, as is the case with the First and Second Musics, we are rather short of evidence. How good it would be, for instance, if a playhouse fiddle-part were to be found detailing just which movements of Purcell's fine set for Behn's *Abdelazer* had the job of 'tagging' – the word is John Dennis's, who had interesting ideas about act-tunes in the 1690s[20] – the strong moments which end Acts I to IV of that grim play: a summoning-up of the 'idols' Ambition, Jealousy and Revenge; an infernal oath; a resolution to conquer or perish; and the vision of a sordid death in chains. (There are several darkly energetic minor-key pieces in the set which would fill the bill admirably.) And how good it would be to know if the quartet of act-tunes required for *The Old Bachelor* are to be found among the five bright and untroubled C major numbers which Purcell includes in his diverse set of nine framing pieces to Congreve's comedy. Certainly the pieces in C major correspond well with the smiling, positive, upbeat tone of the couplets which conclude its first four acts.

We may never be able to match these things up with certainty; but it is reasonable to suggest that Purcell's act-tunes sometimes had mirroring functions of this sort, and that he would have been unlikely to allow a jaunty jig to tag an exit like that of Cibber's ogling tragical lovers. Evidence in support of this could come first from the way the words and music of the act-*songs* in his early *Theodosius* score (z 606/5–9) mirror the mood and ideas of the closing lines of the previous act in some way or other. It could also come from some cases of instrumental numbers which can be located confidently and precisely in their play texts. Take a pair of well-attested Third Act-tunes. The one in *The Fairy Queen*, which follows Queen Titania's gleeful promise to the ass-eared Bottom that they are going to have a whale of a night together, is an exhilarating hornpipe (z 629/26); the one in *Distressed Innocence*, which follows an intense conversation in a thunderstorm, is an equally intense Allegro with a tempestuous bass-line rumbling away in *moto perpetuo* (z 577/4). Mirrors both, surely.

An act-tune could also be bonded with its act by being a new version of a song sung during that act, as in Act IV of *The Indian Queen*, where 'They tell us that you mighty powers', a marvellous continuo air associated with the sad daughter of the High Inca, is put into eloquent and subtle four-part instrumental harmony to become the Fourth Act-tune. Placing a full-length string harmonization after a highly wrought sung air with continuo alone was not new to Purcell in the 1690s: he had already done it in some of his odes. ('Here the deities approve' in the Cecilian ode of 1683, 'Welcome to All the Pleasures' (z 339/3), is perhaps the most telling example.) But The *Indian Queen*'s separation of the song from the purely orchestral treatment by several pages of spoken dialogue adds an element of wistful reminiscence to the act-tune when it comes. Even the orange girls must have given at least one ear to framing music of this quality.

The 'frame' metaphor is hopefully a useful one as a way of setting such pieces back into their original contexts; but it is not 100 per cent exact, since frames tend to surround things on all sides, and there is no evidence that Purcell ever wrote instrumental music of this kind – minuet, rondeau, jig, air or whatever, played from pit or music room without stage action – to terminate a play. If he or his manager Betterton had needed a precedent for such a thing, they could have found it in the way at least one of Matthew Locke's framing sets from the 1670s is rounded off with a 'Conclusion'. It is in his *Tempest* set: a weird 'Canon 4 in 2'. Purcell appears to be emulating this movement technically with his 'Dance for the Followers of Night' in Act II of *The Fairy-Queen* (a piece as atmospheric as it is canonically rigorous); but he seems not to have emulated Conclusions *as* such. Not that there was never a little music at the end, or very near the end, of a spoken *comedy* in Purcell's time. A cheerful celebratory hop for the characters involved in the happy dénouement was quite common. 'Strike up, fiddlers! Let's have a dance!' (or words to that effect) would cue it,[21] and the tune would be provided by folk from the special tribe of onstage musicians who were employed to take the roles of serenaders, waits, fiddlers, catch-singers and the like – roles that might involve them in a bit of spoken dialogue – and who formed a separate fraternity from the players of pre-musics, overtures and act-tunes.[22] But this dance music, resourceful if not in the main hugely sophisticated stuff, seems not to have been a direct concern of Purcell's.

Still, he did tangle with these onstage musicians at other points in the show, since they were the accompanists (for such singers as did not accompany themselves) of the considerable number of Purcell songs with simple continuo support which were set into the spoken dialogue of plays of all sorts in ones and very occasionally pairs, quite often with a little dance as pen-

dant. Purcell himself composed over fifty such songs. Almost all
are solos or duets, though there is a scattering of more compli-
cated pieces, like the quartet in the form of a low-life set-to
between two housewives eventually reconciled by their husbands which is set into Edward Ravenscroft's farce *The Canterbury Guests* (z 591). In most cases the songs were sung by
professional singers attached to the playhouse and given stage-
credibility by acting the roles of waiting women, music masters
(Mr Gavot, Mr Crotchett and the like) or similar melodious bit-
parts; but once in a while a major speaking actor who had the
talent would sing songs relevant to the situation of the character
he or she was playing. The song lyrics were generally the work
of the original playwright, though they could be added by adap-
ters or donated by well-wishers. Purcell, like his Restoration
colleagues, sometimes set all the lyrics connected with a particular show, but at other times limited himself or was limited by
poet, manager or rival to just one or two. (There was apparently
no convention among song-writers equivalent to that of the
composers of framing music, that one made responsible for
everything that was needed for a given play.)

Sometimes the occasions for introducing songs of this kind
into a play plot are obviously germane and plausible. The
amused sketches of fashionable 'music meetings' and *soirées
musicales* in Thomas Southerne's *Wives' Excuse* (Act I: z 612/
1) and *Maid's Last Prayer* (Act IV: z 601/1–2) quite naturally
generate Purcell songs, as do the bizarre wedding parties in
Southerne's *Fatal Marriage* (Act III: z 595) and Dryden's *Love
Triumphant* (Act V: z 582). And the traditionally musical melan-
choly of folk crazed by love clearly justifies the sequence of
seven mad-songs for the pathetic Lyonel which runs through
Durfey's *A Fool's Preferment* (z 571) and which Purcell doubtless tailored to the talents of William Mountfort, the singing
actor who created the role. But at other times the cues for songs
by Purcell and his colleagues may at first blush seem rather
forced. Thus consequential folk in Restoration tragedy share a
suspect tendency to call on the musicians in their retinues for
therapy at moody moments.[23]

> Boy, take thy Lute, and with a pleasing ayr
> Appease my sorrows, and delude my care

says the King in Thomas Otway's *Alcibiades* (Act V). He speaks for many of his peers. Their cuings may be garrulous or peremptory, but their motives are the same, to get a lute-song – in reality more likely a theorbo-song or guitar-song – into the show. Things are similar in comedy. Of course, stage musicians vocal and instrumental could be brought into things rather more circumstantially there; but there is often still the sense of something being set up. In the plays of Congreve, for instance – Purcell wrote the songs as well as the instrumental framing sets for two of them – a lot of the action takes place in genteel homes that have 'masters of music' on their payrolls. So young Mellefont in *The Double Dealer* (Act II) can find the wooing of his somewhat reluctant mistress Cynthia interrupted by a singer passing through the hall with a continuo player or two:

> What's here, the Musick! – Oh, my Lord has promised the Company a new Song, we'll get'em to give it us by the way. [*Musicians crossing the Stage.*] Pray let us have a Favour of you, to practise the song, before the Company hear it.

And Araminta, the self-possessed heroine of *The Old Bachelor*, can find a musical remedy to hand in the second act when she does not at all like the turn that a conversation with her friends (particularly her admirer Vainlove) is taking:

> Nay come, I find we are growing serious, and then we are in great Danger of being dull – If my Musick-Master be not gone, I'll entertain you with a new Song, which comes pretty near my own Opinion of Love and your Sex – [*Calls.*] Who's there? Is Mr *Gavot* gone?

As for the rakish Valentine, hero of *Love for Love*, written in Purcell's last year, his cuing in Act V is more laconic:

> I would have Musick – Sing me the Song that I like –

But then, he *is* acting mad at the time.

Music there! Pray give us the last new song! Commands like these might seem to allow Restoration lyric writers, composers and singers *carte blanche* to come up with pretty well anything, provided it is novel and stylish. And novelty and stylishness were certainly not frowned upon by theatre managers or music lovers in the 1690s. The news that a show was to contain a number of last new songs would help fill seats; so there must have been the managerial temptation not to fret if the songs were not *over* play-specific. Besides, theatre songs of this sort, like the instrumental numbers making up a show's framing music, might well look for a profitable and independent second life through print outside their theatrical contexts, in concerts and private music-making, where their original stage-relevance or lack of it would hardly be an issue.[24] But in the case of most of Purcell's insets to a simple continuo accompaniment, this afterlife was only half the story at most, since there was much more artfulness in the songs' introduction into their original dramas than all this might suggest.

For one thing, the pleasing, rousing, soothing and mournful songs which leading characters ask for need a degree of specificity in words and music to do their jobs efficiently, and so will add to the calculated dramatic impact of the scene they figure in. For another, 'the song that I like' or the one that 'comes pretty near my own opinion of love and of your sex' will tell you quite a lot about me as a person, and so be dramatically relevant. Even an apparently quite random and accidental song like the one the musicians rehearse for Mellefont and Cynthia in *The Double Dealer* (z 592/10) may well turn out to be germane to the ideas of the play. That particular piece in fact is addressed to an unyielding beauty (called – yes – Cynthia) and makes a point with elegant musical urgency that Mellefont might be too delicate to put into plain speech:

> Prithee *Cynthia* look behind you,
> Age and Wrinkles will o'ertake you;
> Then too late Desire will find you,
> When the Power must forsake you.

Indeed, the great majority of Purcell's inset-songs which can be located precisely or fairly precisely in the plays they were composed for – about half a dozen can't – pay proper dues to their dramatic contexts, are enhanced by them, and often can be fully relished only when connected with them.[25]

Take 'I'll sail upon the Dog-star'(z 571/6). The flamboyant dottiness of the words and the tumbling, manic energy of the setting make most sense when linked with the predicament of poor Lyonel (whose song it is) in *A Fool's Preferment*. (The *dramatis personae* calls him 'a Well Bred Ingenious Gentleman: who, being hindred of his Mistress, by the King, fell distracted'.) The same is true of the time-suspending languor which bursts into hectic arousal in that other staple recital number, 'Sweeter than Roses' (z 585/1). This takes on new life when linked with its original function as mood-setter for a steamy seduction scene *chez* the courtesan Pandora in Richard Norton's tragedy *Pausanias, the Betrayer of his Country* (Act III). Context can also give edge and meaning to pieces that might seem trivial or mildly unpleasant in concert performance, as with the strophic song (z 609/11)

> Take not a woman's anger ill,
> But let this be your comfort still,
> That if one won't, another will . . .

The song's anti-sentimentality, in its text and in the brisk, chattery setting which plays fast and loose with the text's metric, is bracing enough; but there is something a bit skull-like about its grin. If we put the song back on stage, however, we can see what Purcell and his playwright Robert Gould are up to. The play is *The Rival Sisters, or The Violence of Love*, a tragical piece about forced marriages which yields four corpses before the final curtain. Light relief – if that is the word for such sourly satiric scenes – is supplied through the grotesque wooing of Ansilva, one of the rival sisters' maids, by the horny dotard Gerardo. The maid is a calculating young minx who only plays along with Gerardo for the cash prospects. At one point she seems to be yielding to him:

GERARDO: Now thou art all luscious, and season'd to the Pallat of an Epicure – There only wants the dishing up, and then –
ANSILVA: You'd fall on without saying Grace, I warrant.

GERARDO: Ay, what else? I shou'd be a Madman in such a case, to make use of a Chaplain: – But, come, now thou'rt in a good humour, I'll give thee my Favourite Song.

And he does; in person quite likely – Benjamin Johnson, who created the role, did occasionally sing on stage – or possibly cuing a musical footman (perhaps the young bass Richard Leveridge) to do the honours, so that Gerardo should not exhaust himself prematurely. In this framework, the jaunty, smug Don Juanism of 'Take not a woman's anger ill' makes excellent sense.

The songs for Gerardo in *The Rival Sisters* and Pandora in *Pausanias*, both written in Purcell's last year, show the breadth of his talent as an inset-song writer. Between their poles – of strophic elegance and flamboyant *arioso*, low cynicism and high passion – he presents a spectrum of feelings and attitudes in a wide range of telling musical forms.[26] They are feelings and attitudes largely connected with love (or with sex at least). At the extrovert, no-nonsense end of the spectrum there are energetic songs that reflect the clubby world of cavalier roisterers. Not very far from them are hard-bitten numbers proclaiming the philosophies of experienced society ladies. One example is 'Thus to a ripe consenting maid' (z 607/10), the song Congreve's Araminta tells her men-friends in *The Old Bachelor* 'comes pretty near my own opinion of love and your sex'; another is 'Pursuing beauty' (z 588/2), a song in Southerne's 'she-comedy' *Sir Anthony Love* (Act II), which compares women with guileless Amerindians who must learn to keep buccaneering European traders (men, that is to say) at arm's length. The lyrics are quite similar in their witty, gritty wisdom; but their settings, typically, differ in style. ('Pursuing beauty' is a miniature cantata complete with instrumental prelude, set largely in a super-subtle *arioso* that pays little attention to the stanza form of the text, while the song for Araminta highlights the stanza, setting it each time to the same tune: a minuet which turns roguishly into a gavotte.)

At the centre of Purcell's erotic spectrum comes a fine set of sung dialogues, comic and serious, in which nymphs and swains of various ages, classes, nationalities and dispositions consider love, and indeed sometimes marriage, and then either fall to it or back away. Beyond these, the spectrum moves towards unironic, unamused presentations of passion and devotion. Especially striking here are the intertwined high-voice duets which can suddenly add a bright intensity to some broadly comic scene or other. But there are some just as striking pieces for solo voices which deal intensely with love's perplexities. Several of them take the form of a kind of apotheosis of the Baroque minuet – grave, intimate, yet long-breathed. Thus Maximinian, the future Emperor in *Dioclesian* who is much taken with the Princess Aurelia, has an attendant sing 'What shall I do to show how much I love her?' (z 627/18) to one such minuet-melody in Act III; Princess Orazia in Act IV of *The Indian Queen* cues another (z 630/19) in 'They tell us that you mighty powers . . .' (dealing an ace which, as we have seen, is trumped by the Fourth Act-tune which soon follows); and in the preceding act the troubled Indian Queen herself, Zempoalla, sings – or has sung sympathetically for her – 'I attempt from love's sickness to fly in vain'(z 630/17): a minuet *en rondeau* in which the melody is made all the more telling by the cunning irregularity of its phrase-lengths.

Is it a limitation that the taste of the age required the great majority of Purcell's one-off continuo-based inset-numbers to be erotic in some way or another? Even the early piece of his which is overheard by King Richard in the dungeons of Pomfret Castle in the last act of Nahum Tate's 1680 version of *Richard II* is not allowed, as at the equivalent moment in Shakespeare's play, to be a symbolic fragment of instrumental music suggesting the ordered and holy cosmic harmony which the King has broken, but has to be an elegiac pastoral song – 'Retired from any mortal's sight' (z 581) – which hints, though Tate does have enough tact to make it no more than a hint, that it is for some all-too-charming nymph that its protagonist the 'pensive Damon' is dying. Yet the erotic could occasionally be transcended. This happens, in part at least, with a lively lyric of Tom Durfey's for his *Marriage-Hater Matched* (z 602/2), in which a husband-hunter is frustrated by London's obsession with 'plotting and sotting' and 'foreign affairs', and in a much longer duet – half grandiloquent, half chirpy – which two well-matched madfolk sing in Act II of *The Richmond Heiress* (z 608/1) to help cure or at least humour the seemingly mad heroine of Durfey's play. In fact these Bedlamites (*he* thinks he is a Hercules; *she* sees herself as the ultimate in *femmes fatales*) know a thing or two, not least that the outside world is no saner than they are:

> Then Mad, very Mad, very Mad, let us be,
> For *Europe* does now with our Frenzy agree . . .
>   The haughty *French* begun it,
>   The *English* Wits pursue it.
>   The *German* and *Turk* still go on with the Work,
>   And all in time will rue it.

The introduction of a little satire on public affairs here is a refreshing change from the run of Purcell's inset songs. It might even have refreshed Captain Porpuss, the bluff sea-dog in Durfey's comedy *Sir Barnaby Whigg*. 'Sing a Song that has some sense in't', he barks. 'Woon's we can get nothing now-a-days but *Phillis* and *Chloris*, and *Celia* and t'other Whore i' the *Strand*.' However, what he really wants is a sea-song:

> I shall never forget a frolick we had about Twelve years ago: I was then Captain of the *Success* . . . I had then a Lieutenant aboard, a little Dapper fellow, but as stout as *Hercules*; and when we met a-nights in the great Cabbin, over a Jolly bowl of Punch, the Rogue wou'd sing us the finest Sea-Songs, and so Roar 'em out: I think I've a fellow can remember one of 'em. Sing, sirrha.

This is the cue for Purcell's 'Blow, Boreas, blow' (z 589): a declamatory *arioso* and shantyish duet of sturdy Jack Tars dicing with death in a tempest and living to carouse another day.

Huffers and puffers like these; amorous madfolk with a taste for mocking the folly and knavery of the rest of mankind; sane (or fairly sane) lovers, rustic and urbane, comic and serious, anguished and exhilarated, cautioned and encouraged. Since these make up so great a part of the gallery of types and attitudes portrayed so variously in Purcell's inset-songs, it is apt that his biggest contribution of such songs to a single theatrical project should have been for a stage adaptation of perhaps the greatest novel to bring together swashbuckling heroism, love and lunacy: Cervantes' *Don Quixote*. It is also apt that the adaptation, staged at Dorset Garden in three parts in 1694 and 1695, should have been by Tom Durfey, since it was Durfey's lyrics in a series of plays of the 1680s and 1690s that did most to widen Purcell's range as an inset-song writer.

Purcell was only one of half-a-dozen composers involved with songs for the *Quixote* trilogy, but he did contribute six substantial pieces and two lighter ones (z 578); and together these provide quite a comprehensive tour of his particular gallery of inset-song characters and attitudes. Thus, when the Don is dubbed 'Knight of the Ill-Humoured Face' with much mock solemnity, there is a huffing – indeed rather more than huffing – duet in praise of the soldier's life: 'Sing, all ye Muses'. Later, there is a jaunty strophic celebration of universal knavery from a galley slave who has been liberated by Quixote ('Here's to his Health,' says the slave, 'and Brothers, let's entertain him with a Song') and a genially satiric dialogue in country-dance metre between a countryman who wants to try his hand at all the trades of the town and his good wife who can see the roguery of each. (Appropriately enough, this is performed to entertain Sancho Panza during his illusory governorship of Barataria.) And of course there are love-songs: a mad, tragi-comic tirade by the jilted swain Cardenio, apocalyptic rage modulating into poignant nostalgia and then into misogynistic bitterness; a simple ballad set to a 'Scotch' tune and telling of a fruitless rustic wooing; and in the last act of the last part, 'From rosy bowers', a *tour de force* of erotic yearning which is acted out by the calculating vamp Altisidora. Altisidora's plan is to jolt Quixote out of his obsession with the 'dull Dulcinea' by dazzling him with a *scena* of 'whimsical Variety, as if I were possess'd with several degrees of Passion'. Each of the degrees, from the languishing to the quite unhinged, calls for a different musical manner; so the *scena* as a whole is a complete Purcellian song-book packed into 150 bars.

However, there are two other Purcell numbers in *Don Quixote* which do not fit into his gallery of customary inset-song types. In one of them, set in a pageant scene, a swaggering St

George summons up the spirit of Albion, and the lady herself (Britannia in all but name) responds with a stirring appeal to British youth to follow the flag. In the other, a piece for three practical jokers masquerading at Quixote's expense as a sorcerer and two enchantresses, the trio boast of the power of their 'charming wand' to control the universe, prolong human love, change the face of nature for the better, and make 'a true Elizium here below'. ('Here *above*' might be more accurate in terms of mythical geography; but 'Elizium' here – the abode of blessed spirits – seems to stand for all paradisal Arcadias.) Both are odd-songs-out in several ways. They are untypical musically: one of them calls on an *obbligato* trumpet while the other is strikingly supported at the start by a string consort, and also includes some quite complex 'choruses' (albeit for three voices only). Theatrically, too, both numbers are unlike the inset as we have seen it in that they seem to call for some degree of stage spec-tacle: a splendid goddess appearing (probably through a trapdoor) in 'Genius of England'; fantasticated costumes for the magi in 'With this sacred charming wand'. Again – and this is the nub of the matter – the two pieces share a preoccupation which sets them apart from anything we have considered so far: the supernatural. However, although this isolates them from the typical one-off inset, it certainly does not marginalize them in Purcell's theatre work as a whole. They really belong in a differ-ent Purcellian category, one where musical constructs tend to be more elaborate, and/or theatrical devices more eye-catching. The category is the large and impressive one of enchantment, magic and the spirit world, of sacred rites of prayer and praise, of invocations and epiphanies, and the summoning up of a variety of earthly paradises, Arcadias, Elysiums. Framing sets, inset-songs and a few scenes of *Dido and Aeneas* apart, it is a category which accounts for 99 per cent of Purcell's theatre music.[27]

iii   Ceremonies, Masques and Magic

'The Playhouse is an enchanted island, where nothing appears in reality what it is nor what it should be.' This is Purcell's contemporary the prose-satirist Tom Brown at the beginning of the theatre-'amusement' in his *Amusements Serious and Comical*. His main target is hypocrisy and affectation in the playhouse audience, but not surprisingly he sees these things as part of a general atmosphere of artifice, make-believe and contrived magic which is just as evident on the other side of the footlights in that 'land of enchantment' and 'country of Metamorphoses'.[28] And Brown's colleagues the verse-satirists of the age make much of the appearance/reality contrasts offered by things onstage and backstage.

Actors are fair game of course, but the décor too is targeted: the muddled ranks of sliding perspective flats and shutters, the flies over the stage, the cellarage under it and the seemingly chaotic prop- and costume-stores of theatres boasting the kind of up-to-date scenery described in the last chapter. A stage of this kind figures in 'A Description of the Play-House in Dorset-Garden' from around 1700, which has traditionally but very shakily been ascribed to Joseph Addison:

> Trap-Doors and Pit-Falls form th'unfaithful Ground,
> And Magic Walls encompass it around:
> On either side maim'd Temples fill our Eyes,
> And Intermixt with Brothell-Houses rise;
> Disjointed Palaces in order stand,
> And Groves Obedient to the movers Hand
> O'ershade the Stage, and flourish at Command.[29]

In his poem 'The Stage' of 1713, one Mr Webster 'of Christ-Church, Oxon' sardonically itemizes the jumble of props, costumes and machinery in a theatrical tiring room: a jumble very like the one so vividly presented in Hogarth's engraving 'Strolling Actresses Dressing in a Barn':

> Hard by a Quart of bottled Light'ning lies
> A Bowl of double Use, and monstrous Size;
> Now rolls it high, and rumbles in its Speed,
> Now drouns the weaker Crack of Mustard-seed . . .
> Near these sets up a Dragon-drawn Calash,
> There a Ghost's Doublet delicately slash'd
> Bleeds from a mangled Breast, and gapes a frightful Gash, . . .

> Here IRIS bends her various painted Arch,
> There artificial Clouds in sullen Order march,
> Here stands a Croun upon a Rack, and there
> A WITCH's broomstick by great HECTOR's Spear.[30]

A year after 'The Stage', the young Alexander Pope takes a jumble of this sort to its surreal limit in *The Rape of the Lock*, with his phantasmagoria of the theatrical devices flitting through the mind of a stage-struck young lady afflicted with the spleen:

> Now glaring fiends, and snakes on rolling spires,
> Pale spectres, gaping tombs, and purple fires:
> Now lakes of liquid gold, Elysian scenes,
> And crystal domes, and Angels in machines.

Clearly, no one could accuse the wits of the age of being unaware that the enchantments of Baroque scenography were, on one level, just a big bag of tricks. But equally clearly they were tricks which, when properly introduced and smoothly carried out, *worked* for a very large proportion of the audience and so transcended trickery. And their complete working often involved music. At public or private theatres, Purcell himself provided pieces to go alongside many of the Baroque devices and effects alluded to in those couplets of Pope, Mr Webster and (perhaps) Addison. *Inter alia*, he has music for a change of scene *per* sliding flats and shutters from a moonlit grove to an enchanted lake, the ascent of an island through the stage traps, the beginnings of a thunderstorm, the rites of a coven of witches (possibly with broomsticks), a ceremony for the raising of a ghost, one eruption of glaring fiends and two of furies, the revelation of a false Elysian scene in a Kentish wood and a true one in a Chinese garden, the appearance over the stage of ranks of artificial clouds supporting a group of allegorical palaces, the celestial epiphanies of several spirits in machines, and the descent of an airborne goddess in a chariot drawn, if not by dragons, at least by peacocks. If you add some of the further paraphernalia strewn by Hogarth around the barn where his actresses are dressing – ancient legionary gear, a priestly crown and a pagan altar, a wave-machine and a mermaid costume –

you can find Purcell accompanying the appearance on stage of such things too, in scenes of the pagan triumphs of imperial Rome, of Aztec blood sacrifice and of the wicked ways of dark-age sirens.

All the music-linked-with-spectacle in these instances is involved with magic, with supernatural visions, or with sacred rites and ceremonies of one kind or another; and this is par for the course with Purcell. Not that the connecting of music with such things was exclusive to him or his playwrights, or indeed very new at the end of the seventeenth century. The spirit world was traditionally a world of music. Though the scenography had perhaps been less sophisticated nine or ten decades before, music had accompanied the supernatural at least as far back as the 1590s and 1600s. Think of some Shakespearian examples; for instance the hymn for the displaying of Hero's epitaph on Leonato's monument in *Much Ado About Nothing* and the 'solemn music' when the apparitions of Posthumus' family appear to him in *Cymbeline*. Theatre composers were reviving and extending this Jacobethan tradition when Purcell was a boy after the Commonwealth, while their backstage colleagues, now working in a proscenium theatre with bigger pictorial potential than the old open-air thrust stage, were making the associated visuals more striking, drawing on continental practice and on the native example of Inigo Jones's theatrical work at the Courts of James and Charles I. The result – the supernatural plus Baroque scenes-and-machines plus music – could be ravishing, as the diarist Samuel Pepys found when he went to the King's Theatre on 27 February 1668. It was a revival of *The Virgin Martyr* by Thomas Dekker and Philip Massinger, and:

> that which did please me beyond anything in the whole world was the wind musique when the Angell comes down, which is so sweet that it ravished me; and endeed, in a word, did wrap up my soul so that it made me really sick, just as I have formerly been when in love with my wife; that neither then, nor all the evening going home and at home, I was able to think of anything, but remained all night transported.[31]

On 7 November 1667, three months before that *Virgin*

Martyr, Pepys had seen another contribution to this tradition of magic plus spectacle plus music, and one that was to be of importance to Purcell's development: a new version by Dryden and Davenant of Shakespeare's *Tempest*. The original *Tempest* is of course rich in supernatural music. Its isle is full of noises, sounds and sweet airs, climaxing in Prospero's 'insubstantial pageant' of singing goddesses and dancing harvesters for the betrothal of Miranda and Prince Ferdinand. (The pageant – Ferdinand calls it 'a most majestic vision, and harmonious charmingly' – evokes the multi-media 'masques' which were such an important feature of Court life under James and Charles I, and which cast a long shadow forward over music theatre for the rest of the century, Purcell's included.) The Dryden-Davenant *Tempest*, subtitled *The Enchanted Island* (as Tom Brown presumably recalled), differs from Shakespeare's in several significant ways; but noises still fill the isle. It provides new settings for most of Ariel's original songs, gives him a couple more, one of them an echo-dialogue with Ferdinand which was set by John Banister and which Pepys understandably admired; and it turns his big recriminatory speech as a Harpy – 'You are three men of sin' – into a musical pageant of Pride, Fraud, Rapine and Murder, hosted by a pair of singing devils and finishing with an infernal dance.

Seven years later, this Restoration-style *Tempest* was revived in a revised version that was even more majestic, charmingly harmonious and full of sounds and sweet airs; and as we have seen, Purcell, 14 years old and a composition student with one of its committee of composers, may well have been backstage for the preparations. The show now had framing music by Matthew Locke (including a superb storm-tossed 'curtain-tune'), an additional inset-song for a mortal, a considerable extension in words, music and dance to the pageant-vision of avenging spirits, and a brand-new climaxing masque for the last act. The Dryden-Davenant adaptation of 1667 had left out Prospero's betrothal masque for the young lovers; but now Thomas Shadwell, as reviser and extender of the adaptation, gives him this other masque in recompense, so to speak. Promising his island guests 'calm Seas and happy Gales' for their homeward journey, Prospero volunteers a magical entertainment to embody that idea:

> I'll, by my power, transform this place, and call
> Up those who shall make good my promise to you.

Grand transformation scene; music among the rocks; appearance of sea-deities in a chariot; songs, duets, dances; wind-gods appearing aloft and flying down; fanfare and dance of Tritons; songs of peace and benediction to the voyagers. Music, the music of Purcell's teacher Pelham Humfrey in a near-continuous sequence of over fifteen minutes, is again twinned with the spectacular supernatural.[32] Clearly, young Henry took note.

Was he so impressed by all this that he resolved one day to write a *Tempest* score of his own? There is an extant late seventeenth- and/or early eighteenth-century setting of the show's lyrics which was for a long time ascribed to him. But scholars in the last few decades have tended to agree that, with the exception of one well-authenticated inset-song (z 631/10), it was Purcell's posthumous fame which led to his name being attached to the score, not a genuine link with his music desk.[33] What seems very likely, however, is that the music for the 1674 *Tempest* gave Purcell an interest in using the spectacular, visionary and supernatural scenes in any shows that might come his way as opportunities to devise musical sequences and structures more extended, elaborate, subtle in their key relationships and richly scored than would otherwise be possible in the playhouse.[34] This would enable him to transfer to the stage some of the architectural skills he was developing in his Court odes, verse anthems and trio sonatas of the 1680s without selling out to the forms and the aesthetic of full-length continental through-sung opera, to which there was a lot of rationalist and nationalist objection in public-theatre circles at the time (as well, perhaps, as hostility from a job-security point of view). Humfrey in 1674 gave him the green light for all this with the *Tempest* masques, as did his 'worthy friend' Locke in a still more elaborate score the following year for the English counterpart he and Shadwell made to the part-spoken, part-sung-and-danced *tragédie-ballet* of Molière, Corneille and Lully, *Psyche*, where, significantly, the heavenly and infernal mythological scenes for music are supplemented with musical scenes of religious ritual, as the priests and devotees of Mars sing and dance their gratitude to him and those of Apollo offer hymns and sacrifices at his altar to encourage the god to prophesy the heroine's fate.[35]

Purcell, then, had a warrant from tradition and from his musical masters to provide music for ceremonies, masques and magic on the public stage; and it must have been reassuring that the taste-making *literati* of the 1670s did not demur, not even the coolly rationalistic Charles de Saint-Evremond. As a French aristocrat living among the English, Saint-Evremond enjoyed firing cross-Channel shots at Italian and French opera, which he found grotesque in affecting to put social or intellectual conversation and discourse to music. Yet even he granted in an essay of 1678 that there were a few occasions when music might reasonably be used on stage. One of these legitimized the inset love-songs we were looking at earlier, and another allowed music for sacred rites – things like the Apollo and Mars scenes in *Psyche* – since 'vows, prayers, praises, sacrifices, and generally all that relates to the service of the gods, have been sung in all nations and in all times'.[36] So, two years later, Saint-Evremond could hardly have faulted Purcell for providing music (z 606/1–4) for a ceremony marking the initiation into monastic life of two young princesses in *Theodosius*, Lee's tragedy of love in early Christian Rome, making it a ten-minute sequence of solos, duets, trios and choruses, and involving some *obbligato* work for a pair of 'celestial' recorders at the most mystic point. As for the stage-presentation with music of the magical and pagan supernatural in an age which prided itself on its empiricism, discovered universal gravitation, set up the Bank of England and founded the Royal Society, a Purcell, Matthew Locke or Pelham Humfrey in search of theoretical justification could cite Dryden on the enriching importance of such fanciful things to a lively mind, however much that mind might revere reason and cool judgment. He put his view warmly more than once, notably in the essay 'Of Heroic Plays' and the 'Apology for Heroic Poetry' of 1672 and 1677:

> I will ask any man who loves heroic poetry (for I will not dispute their tastes who do not), if the ghost of Polydorus in Virgil, the Enchanted Wood in Tasso, and the Bower of Bliss in Spenser (which he borrows from that admirable Italian) could have been omitted without taking from their works some of the greatest beauties in them. And if any man object the impossibilities of a spirit appearing or of a palace raised by magic, I boldly answer him that an heroic poet is not tied to a bare representation of what is true, or exceeding probable: but that he may let himself loose to visionary objects, and to the representation of such things as depending not on sense, and therefore not to be comprehended by knowledge, may give him a freer scope for imagination . . . Of this nature are fairies, pigmies, and the extraordinary effects of magic; for 'tis all imitation, though of other men's fancies: and thus are Shakespeare's *Tempest*, his *Midsummer Night's Dream*, and Ben Jonson's *Masque of Witches* to be defended.

What heroic poetry could present in books, the heroic stage could present also – very often with the help of music and machines. Enchanted woods, bowers and palaces; appearing spirits, classical ghosts and Elizabethan fairies; visionary objects and the extraordinary effects of magic – Purcell would be involved with all of them in his fifteen years as a theatre composer. More specifically, although *The Tempest* may have been off-limits to him, he was to tackle a revived, revised and retitled *Midsummer Night's Dream* in the 1690s. And before that he would tangle memorably on the private stage with the subject, if not the text, of what Dryden calls Jonson's *Masque of Witches*.

Actually and significantly, Dryden gets Jonson's title wrong, and in a way which is relevant to Purcell's best-known stage work. The witches he is recalling figure in Jonson's *Masque of Queens*, performed before James I in 1609 by a cast headed by James's wife, Anne of Denmark. A Jacobean Court masque was essentially a spectacle danced by well-drilled aristocrats, either in homage to some eminent person out front or in celebration of a great occasion: the spectacle being followed by more general social dancing, 'revels' which involved both 'masquers' and Court. The masquers, wearing the most fancy of fancy dress, impersonated idealized symbolic figures in an improving imaginative fiction, the masque proper being made more splendid by sumptuous Italianate scenery and by the involvement alongside the masquers of high-toned professional singers and actors who also helped clarify to a possibly rather fuddled audience just what was going on. In the *Masque of Queens* itself, for example, the spirit of Heroic Virtue reveals that eleven illustrious and happy queens from distant times and lands have assembled to join in dancing with Bel-Anna, queen of queens (Anne of Denmark *ipsissima*), so that James's renowned Court can have still more renown. The dozen ladies have triumphed over Ignorance, Superstition, Credulity, Malice and the like; and this is symbolized by their having been able to confound and scatter a dozen witches, their anti-selves, 'faithful opposites to Fame and Glory', who had gathered at the beginning of the masque and bragged and cavorted and spun charms of such grim vigour and folkloristic vividness that it is not surprising Dryden remembered the piece as the *Masque of Witches*. Still, in Jonson's scheme of things, the witching episode was essentially an exotic, anarchic, satiric Representation of Chaos before the masque proper: an *anti*-masque in fact, to use Jonson's influential word.

The formal Court masque of James and Charles I was largely a thing of the past by Purcell's time: for one thing, the Court could rarely afford it now, and besides, the adulation and panegyric which characterized it could more cheaply and diplomatically be channelled into welcome odes, birthday odes and the occasional sung prologue to a Court entertainment. Nevertheless, 'masque' remained a word to conjure with, and many of the conventions and devices of old-time Court masquing maintained a theatrical appeal and presumably some sort of nostalgic ideological appeal too: the grotesque and/or funny visions of disorder; the heady celebrations of cosmic and national harmony; the spectacular transformations; the singing and dancing beings out of allegory and myth; the grand acts of obeisance. For instance, most of these things are in evidence on the public stage in the 1674 *Tempest*, where the pageant of devils in Act II can be read as an anti-masque to the masque-like entertainment of sea-spirits in Act V. As for Restoration reflections of Jonson's *Masque of Queens*, it is not hard to imagine Purcell happily

setting a few anti-masque-type episodes of witches singing and
dancing which would add colour to some spoken 'heroic play' in
which the queenly protagonist eventually gave the envious hags
their come-uppance, leading perhaps to a spectacular musical
Triumph of Fame and Glory. And indeed, something very like
this might seem to be going to happen with the witch music in a
major score of his of the 1680s, *Dido and Aeneas* (z 626): written to a text by Dryden's collaborator Nahum Tate and quite
possibly intended for theatricals at Charles II's Court in 1684.
There Purcell goes the whole supernatural hog theatrically
speaking, and provides wonderfully graphic and energetic
extended musical sequences (instrumental preludes, dances,
recitatives, airs, duets and choruses) for scenes of witches gathering, covening, cackling, plotting, storm-brewing, spirit-raising
and dancing: their later dances recalling the 'strange and sudden
music' that went with Jacobean anti-masques, witness the surviving sequence of satyrs' dances Robert Johnson wrote for Ben
Jonson's fairy masque *Oberon*. But Purcell's is anti-masquing
with a difference – two differences in fact. For one thing, the
supernatural sequences in *Dido* are for once not set into scenes
of spoken dialogue; the whole work is through-sung. And for
another, it is now the envious and anarchic coven which wins
out over the illustrious Queen of Carthage and not vice versa.
No Bel-Anna she. *The Masque of Queens* becomes *The Masque
of Witches*; Jonson's piece, perhaps consciously remembered,
perhaps not, but surely in the background somewhere, is stood
firmly on its head.[37] We seem to be witnessing the triumph of the
anti-masque.[38]

Dido and Aeneas is in many respects a singular work. Its
original function as a private-theatre entertainment; its enter-
prising use of theatrical and musical traditions; its dominance by
a heroine unique on Purcell's stage in that she is wholly created
through music and words-for-music; its weighty brevity and
cunning construction; the sense it gives that – *pace* Tate and
whoever it was who commissioned the piece – Purcell is for once
pretty much his own master; its status as the only through-sung
theatre piece of Purcell's that has come down to us; and the
comparative ease with which, uniquely among his stage works

so far, it has slipped into the general twentieth-century operatic repertoire: all these things make it very special. Since I write at some length about it, particularly about its structure, sources and theatrical challenges, in Chapter 11 below, I shan't dwell on that specialness here. Rather, it is worth suggesting at this point that *Dido*'s singularity *can* be over-stressed. It does belong in its period; it does chime with many other works of its composer, the dramatic ones particularly, especially in the matter of ceremonies, masques and magic.

First, that ironic inversion of an emblem out of Jacobean courtly masquing. Is it really so strange? For one thing, the myth of Dido and Aeneas as filtered through Virgil's *Aeneid* requires that the royal lovers should be separated somehow or other, and a Divine Imperial Will *à la* Virgil had maybe lost its attraction in the 1680s; would it appeal, for instance, to a Merry Monarch who saw no conflict between Eros and Empire? For another thing, the age had a great liking for a Jacobean play in which the protagonist's downfall is at least in part the result of the operations of midnight hags, Shakespeare's *Macbeth*. (Its witch scenes had been extended in the 1670s so as to include much unholy singing, dancing and – yes – flying, the dances having been choreographed by an important later colleague of Purcell's, Josias Priest.)[39] For a third thing, when writing the *Dido* libretto, Nahum Tate clearly had at the back of his mind a play he had written a few years before when Purcell was 18: *Brutus of Alba*, a tragedy with a closely related plot structure that involved witches. Dido seems almost fated to be hexed!

As for the lack of spoken dialogue, this clearly was not something Purcell encountered earlier and later when writing for public theatres which held that 'rational', 'masculine' *speech* should have a major say in full-length shows. But is it so freakish? It seems less so when one recalls that, unlike all the other theatre works of his that survive, *Dido* was not written to be performed of an afternoon in a public playhouse, and also that there was an aspect of the composer's artistic heredity and environment which arguably led both to *Dido* and away from it. Thus he had a father who had taken part in *The Siege of Rhodes*, a through-sung theatrical experiment of Davenant's.

He had a worthy friend in Matthew Locke, who in 1673 had contributed a tiny through-sung 'masque' (so-called) – a kind of opera-within-a-play – to Elkanah Settle's spoken tragedy *The Empress of Morocco*: a ten-minute Underworld scene out of the Orpheus legend treated somewhat as a continental opera composer of the time might have treated it. And he had a teacher in John Blow, who wrote a tragic 'Masque for the Entertainment of the King' in the early 1680s which recounted the myth of Venus and Adonis, was all sung, lasted about an hour and almost certainly gave Purcell several practical hints for the Court scenes in *Dido*. (A tragic Court masque would have been a contradiction in terms before the execution of Charles I, but by now the culminating dance of homage and general 'revels' were no longer thought essential to masque form. Mythology, profusion of music and some sort of Court connection were the determining elements.) *Dido and Aeneas* carries on from these pieces in blending aspects of various traditions, especially the developing native masquing tradition and some of the traditions of Continental and especially French opera. And as we have seen, it is quite reasonable to speculate that Purcell might have written several more pieces like *Dido* in the later 1680s and 1690s, had the climate at Court not changed with the death of Charles, the accession of the Italianate James and James's overthrow fairly soon afterwards by Dutch William: things which drew Purcell into Betterton's public world, where at that time there was no latitude for through-sung tragedies.[40]

So, if *Dido* is not wholly a theatrical sport or freak, are there connections in subject and treatment to be found between it and Purcell's other dramatic work? There certainly are. Its love-concerns come from much the same world as that of many of the public-theatre inset-songs. To borrow words from Saint-Evremond's 1678 essay, it is a world of 'tender and mournful passions' and 'the irresolution of a soul tossed by different motions': wholly proper subjects for stage music in his view.[41] Intriguingly, the love scenes in *Dido* also relate closely in subject to the four 'act-songs' which, along with the monastic initiation ritual, Purcell had contributed to Lee's *Theodosius* (z 606) back in 1680: a capitulation of Mars to Venus (compare Belinda's

'Pursue thy conquest, Love' in *Dido*); a celebration of happy amours in a rural setting (compare the chorus 'Thanks to these lonesome vales'); an outpouring of grief at the loss of a faithless lover (compare Dido's 'To earth and heaven I will complain'), and the narrative of a love-suicide (a prophecy of 'Remember me, but ah! forget my fate' in Dido's Lament). Did Tate see the published score of these songs in the *Theodosius* playbook and think a Dido piece might be congenial to the composer? Perhaps. Just as intriguing, there are connections between *Dido* and Purcell's only other all-sung dramatic work, the short non-theatrical oratorio for three voices and continuo, *Saul and the Witch of Endor* (z 134), its text an anonymous paraphrase of the story in the Book of Samuel which the composer probably set between 1688 and 1693, when it appeared in Playford's second book of *Harmonia Sacra*. *Saul* is a conversation-piece for three characters which Purcell puts into flexible recitative and *arioso*, framed with two highly chromatic choric trios. Reduced to its barest bones, and *mutatis mutandis*, the story it tells has striking links with *Dido*'s: a troubled monarch tangles with a witch but discovers that the spirit raised by the witch only speaks the monarch's doom. (The beginning of the closing trio of valediction in *Saul* even launches into the same Cavallian/ Lullian ground-bass phrase which underlays Dido's Lament, though it does not have the space to get very far with it.) Was Purcell especially attracted by stories in which the supernatural draws great ones towards half-anticipated downfall? Does this relate to profound movements in his own century?[42]

It is certainly in the sphere of the supernatural – in those linkings of music and spectacle with rites and ceremonies, invocations, epiphanies and visionary scenes – that *Dido and Aeneas* as a drama relates most closely to Purcell's theatre work of the 1690s. Even if one leaves aside its rather Lullian sung prologue, for which only the libretto survives but which is chock-full of the mythological, the Arcadian and the spectacular, it is remarkable how much of the *Dido* we have as set by Purcell is taken up with such matters. *Dido* is, in a sense, the neck of the hourglass between earlier spectacular musical supernaturalisms in the Restoration and that whole sphere as investigated by

Purcell in the 1690s: supernaturalisms in his *King Arthur* and *Fairy Queen*, of course – shows we will come back to later – but also in a dozen other pieces.

At the end of *Dido*, mourning courtiers call down a cloud of Cupids who scatter roses on the Queen's tomb and dance her obsequies. Earlier, the malign Sorceress chillingly calls up a coven of wayward sisters – they appear in a startling burst of musical energy – and instructs her 'trusty elf' to take the shape of Jupiter's winged messenger so he can seem to serve notice on Aeneas and hence break the Queen's heart. The elf duly delivers, and tragedy ensues. In his later involvement with spoken drama, Purcell is able to develop this line in supernatural summonses, spirit-epiphanies and messages from the beyond. His summonings-up are at their most elaborate and impressive in his scores for two tragedies from Greek mythology which had been premièred in the 1670s and were revived with new music (in part at least) almost certainly in the early 1690s: an *Oedipus* (z 583) which Dryden and Lee had adapted from Sophocles and Seneca, and which includes an elaborate sung scene (trios and solos, including the famous 'Music for a While') for calling up the ghost of Laius so that he can throw light on the sad state of his native city, and the *Circe* (z 575) of Sir William Davenant's son Charles, which had the formidable speaking actress Elizabeth Barry as its sorceress heroine when it was given around November 1690.

Circe at one point feels compelled to call up Pluto, the King of the Shades, with his demons of disorder; so she assembles her sinister retainers for incantation and oblation in a deep cave. As the recesses of the cave become visible, the orchestra plays still music reminiscent of the calm before the storm in Locke's *Tempest* curtain-tune; then solos are sung by infernal priests and attendant women; a spirit rises through the traps with appropriately noxious herbs in an urn; magicians dance in 'mystic figures, sacred to the infernal king'; Circe interrupts and stage-manages; a priestly chorus echoes and enriches. After fifteen minutes of this, '*the Earth opens, Pluto arises in a chariot drawn by black Horses*', crying: 'Why do you call me from eternal Night?' (Shades of the Shade of Samuel in *Saul and the Witch of*

Endor!) On one level it is all so much hocus-pocus to make the pit's flesh creep; but Purcell's music (especially in the final solo sung by one of the priests, 'Pluto, arise!') gives it a genuine dark intensity, embodying the serious concern of Davenant with the *vanitas vanitatum* that his infernal spirits evoke: above ground, power-crazed mischief in religion, politics and love; below ground, the eerie democracy of mankind's subjection to death.

Pluto in *Circe* and Laius in *Oedipus*, once roused and raised by music, turn out to be speaking characters. So does the Roman goddess Bellona, who gives poor Hannibal such a puzzling oracle through the mouth of her frantic priestess Cumana when he comes to consult her in Lee's tragedy *Sophonisba, or Hannibal's Overthrow*. Still, Cumana's state of possession by the goddess before the oracle actually utters – '*Enter Cumana scratching her face, stabbing a Dagger into her Armes: Spirits following her*' – is expressed through neurotically florid, unpredictable Purcellian song in 'Beneath a poplar's shadow lay me' (z 590). Equally unpredictable but a great deal funnier is 'Hark, my Damilcar', the splendidly gaga duet of Nakar and Damilcar, two rather decadent love-spirits – they admit to being 'half-tippled at a Rain-bow feast' – who '*descend in Clouds and sing*' in Dryden's *Tyrannic Love* (z 613). The conjuror Nigrinus, a speaking part, has conjured them down with a rum display of proto-rococo astral lore so that Damilcar can prophesy the outcome of the tyrant Maximin's not-so-tender passion for St Catharine of Alexandria. The words of their cloud-song are Dryden at his most wittily fantasticated;[43] and Purcell gives as good as he gets, though sadly Damilcar is reduced to speech when he eventually makes his forecast (though he does have a wonderfully intricate song in praise of Eros – 'Oh how sweet it is to love' – up his sleeve). In other plays, however, the messengers from the spirit world actually use song to deliver their riddles, exhortations, consolations, dusty answers. For instance, benign spirits appear to tragic protagonists with sung encouragements to take time by the forelock or let their consciences be their guides. Thus Kalib, the spirit most loved by Montezuma's high priest in Dryden's *Indian Emperor* (z 598), rises '*all in White in the shape of a Woman*' through the floor of a magic cave to assure the Emperor that he *can* defeat stout Cortez if only he will capitalize on a particular 'opportunity, / Which once refused will never come again'. (The 'never', with typically Purcellian emphasis, scores twenty repeats.) And in Lee's St Bartholomew's Day tragedy *The Massacre of Paris* (z 604), Charles IX's 'genius' appears to the King in a dawn reverie to dissuade him from his evil designs on the Huguenots, giving him a heady vision in song of heaven-ravishing repentance. It is a text Purcell set twice[44] to fit the abilities of two singers who performed a lot of his work and appeared in the *Massacre* at different times: the baritone John Bowman, who is given a miniature cantata in four contrasting sections, and the treble Jemmy Bowen, who gets a seamless piece of declamatory monody.[45]

Of course, as we know even while the spirits are singing in these plays, the massacre will go ahead, Hannibal will be overthrown and Montezuma will not grasp his golden opportunity. These are aspects of the irony which hangs over much of the Purcellian supernatural one way or another. It is felt especially strongly in the marvellous Act III 'cell' scene in the 1695 version of *The Indian Queen* (z 630/13–17), which brings invocation, epiphany and spirit message together, all in musical settings. The imperious Queen Zempoalla, a prey to bad dreams and perplexed as to their meaning, prevails on Ismeron, the priest of the dream-god, to call up his master in song along with the twice ten hundred deities who see men's future actions. The singing god of dreams duly materializes but declines to tell a frail mortal things that are better hidden; at which Ismeron, reverting to speech, summons the spirits of the air to try to harmonize Zempoalla's soul with instruments and voices. Alas, in the attempt, they spill the beans that her days of greatness are numbered and her love blighted. The dazzling richness and variety of Purcell's invention in all this do nothing to ensure that the Queen has a nice day.

Summoning, epiphany, spirit-message. These are not the only things to be found in *Dido and Aeneas* which are echoed, amplified and often ironized in Purcell's later theatre music. In that music there are also other sorts of ceremones and prodigies connected with the supernatural, evocations of ideal Elysian/

Arcadian lifestyles and masque-like triumph scenes involving allegorical and mythological figures: all of them things which are briefly but clearly foreshadowed (among other pre-1690 places of course) in *Dido*. Take prodigies and ceremonies. Towards the end of the scene in front of the cave in *Dido*, there is an unholy ritual to conjure up a great work of magic art: the storm that will mar the sports of the Queen and her Trojan guest. Or rather, we are assured by the witches that, when the scene is over, such a ritual *will* occur in the privacy of their 'deep-vaulted cell', it being 'too dreadful a practice for this open air'. This is a fine device on Tate and Purcell's part, ensuring that the operatic action is not slowed down by a full-dress conjur-ation-ceremony, yet at the same time allowing the black magick-ings to be sketched in, so to speak, through the unholy contrapuntal glee of two duetting witches and the sinister echoes which punctuate the coven's chorus and Furies' Dance in the music which closes the scene.

In the five-act shows of the 1690s, works of magic and sung rituals recur, and now they have space to expand a bit. Magical happenings provide arresting visual and musical moments in Acts II, III and IV of Betterton's version of *Dioclesian* (z 627/14, 17, 20). Much of the action of this chronicle of high politics and enchantment in the late Roman Empire is controlled by Delphia, a prophetess whose magic powers are directed mainly at getting her daughter married to the hero.[46] In the course of match-making, Delphia finds much inventive work for Purcell the dance-writer. She contrives to spirit up a terrifying monster which metamorphoses itself into a troupe of Furies, who dance; a troupe of grotesques who step down from wall-hangings, take chairs for partners, and dance; and an illusory royal tomb that dislimns into a cloud of butterflies – which dance.[47] As for sung rituals, there are instances at the start of the last act of *The Indian Queen* – a searching, bleak, astringent setting of the preparations for human sacrifice Aztec-style – and in the third act of *Bonduca* (z 574/11–16), Fletcher's 80-year-old play about Queen Boadicea and the invading Romans reworked for the 1690s. There the Queen, a speaking role, needs a sign as to whether her army of resistance has the active blessing and support of the ancient British gods, Andate, Tyrannes and Rugwith. Druids and priestesses pour incense on their altar fires, praying that it will kindle great answering flames. Eventually 'the oracle for war declares', but it takes its time; so that the superb ceremony of prayer and exhortation – nearly fifteen minutes of choruses, recitative, airs, duets and instrumental preludes involving strings, trumpet and recorders – is able to move from uncertainty to assurance, from 'Hear us, great Rugwith' (set like an elaborate penitential psalm for soloists, chorus and strings) to the show-stopping trumpet-song 'Britons, strike home', so much admired in the eighteenth century, a huffing song to end all huffing songs.

Earlier in *Dido*, the Court takes to the country for a *fête-champêtre*. 'Thanks to these lonesome vales,' sings Belinda, 'these desert hills and dales.' Her air and the graphic ritornello that comes before it evoke an Elysian/Arcadian vision: a pastoral world of unclouded skies, untroubled living and unspoilt love. The political and psychological complexities of Carthaginian Court life see to it, of course, that the visionary moment cannot last long. Soon, meteorologically and psychologically, 'the skies are clouded'. The pastoral vision recurs in the 1690s, however, notably in Shadwell's older Don Juan play *The Libertine*, revived around 1692 with some new Purcell settings (z 600/1). There the sordid intrigues of Seville are suddenly exchanged for a gathering of anonymous idealized country folk in 'a delightful grove'. They talk in spirited clichés about healthy rural pleasures and uncorrupted nature, and then are entertained with the 'sports' of a spring festival, to music by Purcell. It is music of a melting innocence and vivacity, not only in that school music-room war-horse 'Nymphs and shepherds, come away' but in the glee and madrigal which follow it. 'Nymphs and shepherds' itself grows in that musical context, in the context of the Edenic ideas that surround it, and in the wider context of the play too, for the madrigal's delight that 'every happy living thing/Revels in the cheerful spring' is dashed immediately by the entry of Don John and his evil associates. It is the equivalent moment to Don Giovanni's invasion of Zerlina and Masetto in the third scene of Mozart's opera; and soon there are rapes and violent revenges. The skies are indeed clouded.

A last return to *Dido*: to the end of the opening scene. When Love has pursued its conquest and the royal pair have signalled that the affair between them can be publicly acknowledged, the Carthaginian courtiers have a bright, unanimous idea –

> To the Hills and the Vales, to the Rocks and the Mountains,
> To the musical Groves and the cool shady Fountains,
> Let the Triumphs of Love and of Beauty be shown!
> Go revel, ye Cupids, the day is your own

– at which the band plays a zestful and confident 'Triumphing Dance' on a thrusty ground bass to end the scene. It is the same dramatic device that Tate and Purcell use again at the end of the 'cave' scene: the story is kept moving by postponing any formal 'triumph' sequence until the scene is over, but chorus and dance between them suggest what it will be like. If we are to take 'triumph' here not just to mean 'conquest' but also to have the sense of a Roman or Renaissance-type festive event – and the presence of a Triumphing Dance suggests this – then we might imagine Dido's composer-in-ordinary and poet laureate speedily devising an appropriate masque for performance in a particularly musical grove: calling it perhaps 'Cupid's Revels, or The Triumph of Beauty and Love'. Of course, Purcell's highly compressed opera is too fast-moving to show us how the collaboration worked out, but later spoken plays have the leisure for things of this sort.

Indeed, *Dioclesian* in 1690 can find room for two exuberant musical triumphs, in the simple sense of public celebrations at a great soldier's victories: the first in Act II celebrating Diocles' defeat of an evil regicide, the second in Act IV enrolling Dioclesian (as he has now become) in the book of fame for dispatching some invading Persians. These are triumphs with enough trumpeting and drumming to keep even William of Orange happy, though there are some striking subtleties in them as well. But there are other triumphs, including one later in *Dioclesian* itself, which are subtler in conception and musically more rewarding overall. In form they are fairly traditional masques, populated by figures of myth or allegory and performed for a select onstage audience. Thus in *The Indian Queen* (z 630/5–9) there is a Triumph of Fame over Envy (to invent a title for it) which is presented to the enthroned Queen Zempoalla.[48] Fame trumpets the Queen's glory in fine Delalandian style; the anti-masquing figure of Envy comes up from the cellarage with a well-trained consort of snakes – they hiss harmoniously on the first beats of several bars – and casts malicious aspersions; Fame rules these 'fiends of hell' out of order, and Envy sinks grumpily beneath the stage again as the trumpetings resume. And in Act II of Shadwell's 1678 version of *Timon of Athens* there is a Masque of Cupid and Bacchus, its reworked text set by Purcell, probably in 1695 (z 632/10–19). Rural nymphs in the train of Cupid sing of his power, supported by recorders; but it is a power disputed by drinkers in the train of Bacchus (anti-masquers quite possibly), supported by oboes. Each god has an air promoting his cause, and the wine-bibbers turn out not to be anti-masquers after all, since in the end there is an *entente cordiale* –

> Come let us agree, there are pleasures divine
> In wine and in love, in love and in wine

– which was even more clearly a 'triumph' in the 1678 text:

> Hold, our Forces are combin'd,
> And we together rule Mankind:

a very proper conclusion for a masque put on by the naïvely generous Timon for the guests at one of his sumptuous Athenian dinner parties.

Both these triumph masques are trenchant, vivid and good-humoured, and both in their broader contexts are deeply ironic, as the substance of the music itself (Fame's so-confident fanfares, the so-pretty twittering of Timon's recorders) seems to be hinting. The famous Zempoalla will be driven to an infamous suicide by the end of her play; and by the end of his, Timon will have renounced all sensual city pleasures and retired to live and die rough in the wilderness. But then the triumphs of love and beauty prove equally hollow in *Dido and Aeneas*; its reveling Cupids come back at the end with drooping wings. There is ultimately nothing glib or simple-mindedly frivolous about any of Purcell's masques seen as theatre pieces. Some are even manifestly in deepest earnest. The most striking of these in its context is a kind of Triumph of Nemesis as the climax of Shadwell's *Libertine*. Don John (alias Don Juan, alias Don Giovanni) has come with some evil friends to sup *chez* the Statue (Mozart's Commendatore). When they ask for wine, they are given blood to drink. When they ask for a further 'treat', the Statue spirits up an entertainment for them. First comes that 'flat-trumpet' prelude heavy with Last Things which was later to be played at Queen Mary's funeral; then a vision of singing devils kindling 'fresh flames of sulphur' to prepare a hellish welcome for especially deserving new guests. Since no repentance follows this 'treat', retribution does. '*It thunders and lightens, Devils descend and sink with* Don John, *who is cover'd with a cloud of fire as he sinks.*'

Equally earnest, but in practically every other respect the polar opposite to this *festin de pierre*, is the Triumph of Cupid very near the end of *Dioclesian* (z 627/26–39). However, it too is a 'treat'. The prophetic sorceress Delphia, having contrived to get her daughter married to the victorious Dioclesian, is present when the new emperor, Maximinian, visits the pair with his own new bride at their grange in the country. Dioclesian thinks that the meeting of four such great ones calls for a celebration. He asks Delphia if she can 'treat an emperor'. She can, and like Prospero at the end of the 1674 *Tempest* she spirits up an apposite grand concluding musical masque. Since the setting of the last act of the play is a pastoral retreat, and since the play's moral, as drawn by Dioclesian himself at the very end, is that

> Quiet, Content, and true Love, breeds more Stories,
> More perfect Joys, than Kings, and all their Glories

it is proper that the subject of the masque should be the joys of love and pleasures of contentment, and that it should be peopled largely with country folk and nature-gods, all of them eager 'to grace Love's triumphing day'.

Cupid himself leads the summoners in the impressive sequence of calls for those people to assemble on stage. The scene changes to 'a pleasant Prospect of a Noble Garden'; a grave symphony plays, and nymphs and swains, heroes and deities – soloists, chorus and dancers – make the grandest of grand entrances. So from above does a magnificent Baroque cloud-machine which 'attaches itself by two Ladders of Clouds to the Floor'. The machine holds a golden throne for Cupid. Richly decorated aerial temples for Flora, Pomona, Bacchus and the Sun seem to break through its clouds. Five dances – the music for several of them is Purcell at his most Gallic – are danced on the machine's various stages to intersperse the vocal solos and ensembles that follow this stunning *entrée*: the whole musical sequence being a dazzling and eloquent machine-in-time of finely geared forms, metres, textures and instrumentations, presenting images of pastoral contentment and the delights of wine, but principally the delicate anxieties, paradoxes and pleasures brought about by Cupid. At the climax there is a vocal chaconne to the words:

> Triumph, triumph, victorious Love;
> Triumph o'er the Universe!
> The greatest Heroes bow to thee;
> All Nature owns thy deity . . .

At which, '*Those who are on the Stage, and those who are in the several divisions of the Machine, dance a Grand Dance to the time of the Chorus.*'

The superb triumph-chaconne in *Dioclesian* is scaled to Betterton's opulent Dorset Garden in the 1690s as the Triumphing Dance in *Dido and Aeneas* (also in triple time and over a ground) was scaled to the Whitehall Palace stage in the 1680s: the *Dioclesian* dance more than twice as long as the *Dido* one,[49] richer in its intricate orchestral colouring and harmonically more daring, notably in the middle section with its spine-tingling ambiguity as to whether the harmony has or has not moved into the minor. (Not that the dance in *Dido* is any less subtle; indeed, perhaps it is rather more so, with its occasional modulation of the ground and its moment of elation when the kraken wakes and half the ground surfaces for two bars in the treble.) But the continuities between the dances, and between their masquing contexts, are as significant as the differences. The sand at the base of the hour-glass comes from its neck.

iv 'Our English Genius will not Relish that Perpetual Singing'

Oedipus, *Circe* and *Timon of Athens*; *Dioclesian*, *Theodosius* and *Tyrannic Love*; *Bonduca*, *The Indian Queen* and *The Libertine*: however great their variety of forms and textures, the extended vocal sequences Purcell contributes to these nine shows are consistent not only in quality but also in function. They lift the drama out of speech at special moments in a momentous way; they do so for quite a limited range of reasons (ceremonial, masquing, visionary, supernatural); the gear-changing between speech and music is almost always smooth; and the musical episodes always allude to dominant ideas in the spoken plays. So, with such a bonding between the nine, it is strange at first to find that two of these shows tended in Purcell's time to be given one kind of categorization and the other seven another. *Dioclesian* and *The Indian Queen* in their 1690s versions were generally labelled 'operas'. For instance, Dryden is referring to *Dioclesian* in his 1690 preface to *Amphitryon* when he praises Purcell's contribution to 'the late opera'; and a printed song collection of 1695 calls itself *The Songs in The Indian Queen: As it is now compos'd into an Opera*. The other seven shows, however, were pretty consistently known as 'tragedies', though we do find one of them, Charles Davenant's *Circe* (a 'tragedy' on its title page), being called operatic by two United Company hands: Colley Cibber, who describes it as a 'dramatick opera' in his autobiographical *Apology*, and the prompter-archivist John Downes, who simply labels it 'an opera' in his stage chronicle *Roscius anglicanus*. The double inconsistency here – tragedy/opera, opera/*dramatick* opera – is intriguing, as it suggests that 'opera' was a flexible term, or a contentious one, or both. It is certainly a term that needs looking into, not least because, for many twentieth-century music lovers, *Dioclesian* and *The Indian Queen* – and also their stable-mates *King Arthur* and

The Fairy Queen[50] – might seem at first blush not to be operas at all, however dramatic they might be.

For a long time now, people have tended to think of operas as works essentially aspiring to the condition of *The Marriage of Figaro, Aida, Bluebeard's Castle*: works, that is, of any length and any degree of opulence that take librettos and set them to continuous music (or at least to music only interrupted by applause or silence), with every utterance of every character sung. Of course, this is not a notion adequate to all the major works in the modern opera-house repertoire, since it overlooks the passages of spoken dialogue for the singer-actors in *The Magic Flute, Fidelio*, the original *Carmen* and so on. Still the notion has served, if in a rather woolly way. Not so when Purcell was young. Then, the essential idea suggested by 'opera', in England at least, was of a full-length, expensive, sophisticated theatre-piece with a considerable amount of music in addition to the expected instrumental framing set, and a lot of exciting Baroque spectacle as well. As Matthew Locke put it in his preface to *Psyche* in 1675, it was a matter of a 'Grand Design' which was put into effect with 'much consideration, industry and pains for splendid Scenes and Machines' and for 'such kinds of Musick as the Subject requires'. Did the music need to be continuous? Some people thought so; it was continuous in Continental opera after all. But others did not, Locke himself among them. As we have seen, *Psyche* has as its backbone an extensive spoken text by Shadwell, out of which grow musical epiphanies, ceremonies, 'treats' and so on. And yet when Locke printed his *Psyche* score he gave it the title *The English Opera; or The Vocal Music in Psyche, with the Instrumental Therein Intermix't*, and stressed that the piece could 'justly wear the Title, though all the Tragedy be not in Musick', because England was not like the hypermusical Italy, and so it was right to mix the music with spoken 'interlocutions, as more proper to our Genius'.

Two years later, Dryden seems to be agreeing. In 1677 he published a script for possibly the ultimate spectacular, one which (perhaps sadly, perhaps not) was never given music or staged: a rhymed version of Milton's *Paradise Lost* for speaking actors, singers, instrumentalists and a team of extremely busy machinists, which he called *The State of Innocence and the Fall of Man: an Opera written in Heroic Verse*. Yet Dryden seems to have joined the 'Continental' party seven years later when he wrote the text for an allegorical spectacular in praise of the Stuart dynasty called *Albion and Albanius: an Opera*. Set by Louis Grabu, this turned out to be the only full-length show to be through-sung in English on a public stage during Purcell's adult life, and in the preface to his libretto Dryden defines opera as 'a poetical tale or fiction, represented by vocal and instrumental music, adorned with scenes, machines, and dancing', stressing that a piece like the Restoration *Tempest* (which he might have been happy to call operatic eight years before) is not an opera proper but only 'a tragedy mixed with opera . . . because the story of it is not sung'. But yet again, as we have seen, Dryden was prepared to describe the United Company's *Dioclesian* in 1690 as 'the late opera', and the 'story' of it is not sung either!

By 1690 it seems you could pay your money and take your choice. You could stick out for through-sung full-length opera as the only true sort. (Anything less than full-length, if it was all-sung and had a mythological subject like *Dido* or *Venus and Adonis*, would very likely be called a 'masque'.[51]) Or you could give the 'opera' label to an ambitious show like *Dioclesian* or *The Indian Queen* which chose a solid backbone of spoken script and contrived its branching out into several musical scenes with a lot of scenic spectacle, the methods of relating spoken text to sung text, dance and machinery deriving from the pre-Commonwealth public theatre and/or the Court masques of James and Charles I and/or the *tragédie-* and *comédie-ballets* Molière and Lully were writing together around 1670.[52] It was essentially the high incidence and on occasion the length of such scenes and the related expense – which was often huge, needing a raising of seat-prices to come anywhere near defraying it[53] – that gave a new show the title of 'opera' *à la* Betterton in the 1690s, not a musical manner for the scenes themselves (beyond richer instrumentation occasionally) that was essentially different from their treatment in 'tragedies'. Hence *Dioclesian* and

The Indian Queen got the label because of their musical bulk, while *Tyrannic Love*, *Bonduca* and the like did not.

As we have seen, musical scenes of this kind were closely linked with ceremonies, masques and magic; and two significant things resulted from this, one in the present, one in the future. The time-present thing was that all the works from the 1670s with a quantity of music and magic – not only *Psyche* but also *Circe*, *The Tempest* and even *Macbeth* with its singing, flying witches – came often to be thought of now as 'operas', as Cibber's memoirs and Downes's *Roscius* illustrate;[54] so that the 'operatic' tradition could be seen as essentially a magic tradition. (The young George Granville, Lord Lansdowne, who was finding his way as a theatre poet in the 1690s and tried his luck with a Bettertonian opera which the great man eventually staged, trendily called it *The British Enchanters*, and went so far as to assert in the preface he wrote a few years later that the nature of opera in general 'requires the Plot to be formed upon some Story in which Enchanters and Magicians have a principal Part', since in modern work 'they supply the Place of the Gods with the Ancients'.[55]) The time-future thing – a bone buried and ready for twentieth-century contention – grew from the fact that, since extended music was exclusively associated with the visionary, the magical or the ritual, the principal actors who witnessed these episodes rarely if ever sang themselves. It is true that quite important intermediary figures linking the human and spirit worlds, Ariel in *The Tempest* or Ismeron in *The Indian Queen* for instance, do get to sing as well as speak in Restoration pieces of this sort; but Macbeth, Prospero, Circe, Psyche, Dioclesian do not, and neither does Queen Zempoalla, except perhaps in the inset-song 'I attempt from love's sickness to fly in vain' (and even that is more likely to have been sung for her by an attendant). This is all perfectly explicable in seventeenth-century terms; but it has been the last straw for many of those twentieth-century lovers of opera who see the form as always aspiring to *Figaro*, *Aida*, *Bluebeard*. They may be prepared to stretch a point with the *Flute* or *Fidelio* because Tamino and Leonora do sing as well as speak, and quite often too. But *Dioclesian* and the like! Call them *operas*??

So it has become the custom to spike the guns of these objectors by calling the pieces something else: 'English operas', 'ambigues', 'dramatick operas', 'semi-operas'. These labels are all well-intentioned and have their value, and all can quote chapter and verse in the late seventeenth or early eighteenth century. But they are hardly watertight. *Peter Grimes* too is an English opera; a lot of music theatre from all periods is 'ambigue'; all good operas arguably are dramatic operas, and all good operas before the mid-eighteenth century (by which time the 'k' was dropped) could presumably be called 'dramatick'.[56] That leaves 'semi-opera'. The term was probably invented, like 'ambigue', by the musical *savant* Roger North, who was a contemporary and admirer of Purcell's though he outlived him by more than thirty years. In his *Musicall Grammarian* of 1728, North claims that the London theatres of the late seventeenth century had to find a way to respond to the music-fever that was gripping the town:

> Therefore Mr. Betterton who was their cheif inginerr of the stage, contrived a sort of plays, which were called operas, but had bin more properly styled semioperas, for they consisted of half musick, and half drama . . . These were followed at first, but by an error of mixing 2 capitall entertainment, could not stand long. For some that would come to the play, hated the musick, and others that were very desirious of the musick, would not bear the interruption, that so much rehearsall [i.e. speech] gave.[57]

It is impossible to tell if sizeable parts of the Dorset Garden audience in the 1690s felt that way. But it seems likely that, to a large extent, North is imposing his own feelings on them (as well as being pretty insensitive to the carefully crafted dramatic aptness of the musical episodes in the best of these pieces), since he has similar things to say about the divisive alternation of recitative and formal aria in the Handelian *opera seria* which sophisticated London embraced a couple of decades after Purcell's death. North's own proto-Gluckian ideal was, as he wittily put it, to 'conduct the whole opera thro a continued current of ayre':[58] not an option open to Handel or Purcell. Still, his 'semi-opera' is as good a label as any for pieces like *Dioclesian* and *The Indian Queen* – 'operas' pure and simple to many

folk in the 1690s – until some works of this sort have so successfully entered the modern repertoire as to make such labellings
unimportant.[59]

The works most likely to get into the repertoire are the other
two semi-operas that Purcell was involved with: *King Arthur, or
The British Worthy* (z 628), the patriotic tale of Britons and
Saxons in dark-age Kent with a text by Dryden (originally written in the '80s in connection with the *Albion and Albanius*
project), which was given its première in its revised version with
Purcell's new score in 1691; and *The Fairy Queen* (z 629) of
1692, the anonymous reworking (probably by a committee led
by Betterton) of *A Midsummer Night's Dream*. Rigorous defin-
ing of terms *re* the sung and the spoken does not seem to have
been of great importance to the people promoting these works
in the 1690s. In different parts of his dedicatory preface to *King
Arthur*, Dryden can refer cheerfully both to the all-sung *Albion*
and to the half-spoken *Arthur* as 'operas';[60] and a lively puff for
The Fairy Queen in Peter Motteux's *Gentleman's Journal* for 12
February 1692 tries gamely to do justice to all views, though the
author (is it Motteux himself or one of the production team?)
can't repress his conviction – shared by Matthew Locke at the
time of *Psyche* – that overmuch recitative is somehow un-
English:

> I must tell you that we shall have speedily a New Opera, wherein
> something very surprising is promised us; Mr *Purcel* who joyns to
> the Delicacy and Beauty of the Italian way, the Graces and Gayety
> of the French composes the music, as he hath done for the *Proph-
> etess* [*Dioclesian*], and the last Opera called *King Arthur*, which
> hath been played several times the last Month. Other nations
> bestow the name of Opera only on such Plays whereof every word
> is sung. But experience hath taught us that our English genius will
> not relish that perpetual Singing . . . It is true that their *Trio's*,
> Chorus's, lively Songs and *Recits* with Accompaniments of Instru-
> ments, Symphony's, Machines, and excellent Dances make the rest
> [i.e. the expanses of plain recitative in Continental opera] to be
> born with, and the one sets off the other: But our English Gentle-
> man, when their Ear is satisfy'd, are desirous to have their mind
> pleas'd, and Musick and Dancing industriously intermix'd with
> [spoken] Comedy or Tragedy: I have often observed that the Audi-

ence is not less attentive to some extraordinary Scenes of passion or mirth [i.e. in the spoken part], than to what they call *Beaux Endroits*, or the most ravishing part of the Musical Performance.

A multi-media show that makes good tragic or comic sense in its spoken parts and includes powerful scenes for speaking actors which set off, and are set off by, the stylish musical episodes 'industriously intermix'd' with them: this concept of a Bettertonian opera fits *The Fairy Queen* quite well, and *King Arthur* too, even if it too glibly assumes that spoken drama appeals only to the mind, and music (with or without a text) only to the senses. Mind is virile, senses potentially effeminate; or so the argument ran in some London circles in the 1690s and 1700s, allowing the unknown author of a *Comparison between the Two Stages* in 1702 to stress that truly English operas should keep music in its proper place and not go overboard for it the way the Italians do:

> That which pardons the *Italian* does not pardon us: They are Idolators of Musick, an effeminate Nation, not relishing the more masculine Pleasures; their *Theatres* are meer Musick meetings, and the little hodge-podge, which is their *Drama*, is little better than a continu'd Song, without action, incident or variety: But in *England*, where Poetry has been in perfection, where our Passions are more manly, I see no more reason for following 'em in this Custom than in their Dress, or romantick way of Intriguing.[61]

The spoken parts of *King Arthur* form a heroic-chivalric blank-verse history which certainly has action, incident and variety, with the defeat by Arthur of the Saxon King Oswald blended with the enchantings and counter-enchantings of their wizards Merlin and Osmond and the several wooings of the blind Cornish Princess Emmeline. The spoken parts of *Fairy Queen* are predominantly Shakespeare: all but about 200 lines come directly from *A Midsummer Night's Dream*, though Shakespeare's text is modified quite a lot, and cut quite a lot more, to fit Restoration taste and to provide space and a proper framing for the big transformation scenes and musical sequences, which are to specially written words.[62] But there is action, incident and variety aplenty. As for the requirement of

The Gentleman's Journal that big musical episodes should be 'industriously intermix'd' with these strong scripts, all the episodes in *King Arthur* and *The Fairy Queen* do rise naturally out of the spoken drama; or rather they rise *super*naturally, since the close links we have seen elsewhere in Purcell between music, spectacle and the supernatural very much hold here too. The plots positively invite such supernaturalisms of course. Both are 'formed upon stories in which enchanters have a principal part'. Indeed, almost all the extended musical sequences of both works are involved with the spirit world in some way or other. Thus every musical episode in *The Fairy Queen* except perhaps one is a command performance for the King or Queen of the Fairies, and that one is a seemingly spontaneous epiphany by Juno, goddess of marriage. It is much the same in *King Arthur*. The antithetical wizards and their familiars Philidel and Grimbald are responsible between them for five of the eight musical sequences, fractiously sharing one of them and otherwise taking a couple each.[63] Then there is a musical ritual connected with the Saxon sacrifice of horses and humans to the gods Woden, Thor and Freya (*Bonduca* and *The Indian Queen* are not far away); which only leaves, as episodes not magical or religious, a huffing song of triumph for the victorious Britons and a pastoral homage-show of peaceful rustic life and love put on by anonymous Kentish nymphs and shepherds: a rather more knowing and *risqué* bunch than their Edenically innocent namesakes in *The Libertine*, but not the less symbolic-Arcadian for that.

Rituals, triumphs, pastorals: the categories of course are familiar from what we have seen earlier. Indeed, almost all the pieces of music-spectacle that we have glanced at in other plays have their equivalents in *King Arthur* and/or *The Fairy Queen*: ceremonies, visions (pastoral and other), triumph-masques and anti-masques, magickings, invocations and epiphanies. Not that this should suggest that the industrious intermixing of these things here is at all mechanical and off-the-peg or that the music Purcell provides for them is routine. Indeed, in the musically rich years 1691 and 1692 Purcell seems to have been incapable of writing anything routine. And the placing and musical invention of the episodes show just how well music and spectacle could set off speech, and vice versa. They show too what a range of things could be done within the semi-operatic genre.[64]

In *King Arthur*, the musical scenes are remarkably active. Almost every time the lively train of events in Arthurian Kent involves a piece of wizardry, a ceremony, a triumph or vision, music takes over without more ado and actively carries things forward. The fragment of a Saxon sacrificial ritual in Act I does not bring the show to a standstill; it is part of the 'hastening of mysterious rites' needful before a battle can begin. The pastoral entertainment in Act II put on by those Kentish lads and lasses for Emmeline is set up in part so that it can contrast dramatically with her abduction immediately afterwards. The famous Frost Scene, musically so graphic and theatrically so spectacular – a Triumph and Revels of Cupid beyond the Arctic Circle – gets in on the urgency too, in that it is placed in the middle of Osmond's attempted seduction of Emmeline. (The masque is spirited up by the wizard so as to make the point with maximum vividness that the coldest of hearts can be warmed by passion.) Even the patriotic triumph-masque Merlin devises to end *King Arthur* is active: evoking British history over a millennium from the fifth century to the seventeenth, so as to reveal 'what rolling ages shall produce: / The wealth, the loves, the glories of our isle'. Britannia rises on her island through the stage-traps. (Was James Thomson recalling this *coup de théâtre* fifty years later when he described how Britain 'rose from out the azure main' in 'Rule, Britannia!'?) Prophetic vignettes follow in a wide range of musical manners: scenes of dynamic commerce and a contented if bucolically anti-clerical peasantry; of the flourishing love-life of Venus's fairest isle, Cupid's favourite nation; and of the line of military heroes dedicated to Honour (who sings) and worthy of the Order of the Garter (which appears).

The Fairy Queen is at the opposite pole. Here the musical scenes are reflective, in the double sense that they mirror the issues of the spoken play and do so thoughtfully, unhurriedly – reflectively. Instead of blossoming, as in *King Arthur*, at any point where they might give vivid assistance to the plot, the scenes occur regularly one per act, a dozen or so lines before the act ends, at moments of repose, relaxation, celebration.

They are quite closely related to the old Stuart masque (though
with a nod here and there to the French *ballet de cour*), performed for an appreciative onstage audience: allegorical, mythological or symbolic pieces, not forwarding the story yet closely
geared to it by being concerned in their own particular way with
the ideas behind it. (This technique, which sets up a kind of
dialogue between theatrical modes, probably derives in part, via
the *comédie-ballets* of Molière and Lully, from the practice at
continental Jesuit colleges of performing a tragedy and following it with a ballet based on the concept behind the tragedy.[65])
Some of Betterton's friends held that, as well as being a major
actor and ideologue, Purcell's manager was a discerning Shakespeare critic, capable of 'searching out, and producing to Light'
the playwright's 'minute and hidden beauties'.[66] This suggests
that he was indeed the deviser of the inset-masques in *The Fairy
Queen* (though he may have had the help of – who knows –
Dryden, Durfey, the young Congreve in versifying them); for he
would understand that *A Midsummer Night's Dream* is essentially a play of ideas: ideas of the complementary worlds of
fancy-full darkness and rational daylight; of the human need to
retreat to and return from a dark region (the forest of the night);
of the workings of the poetic imagination; of the various sorts of
love and the requirements for happy marriage. So the five masques in *The Fairy Queen* reflect, and reflect on, these things, in
five formats: a celebration of retreat from the town and a mag-
icking of drunken poets (to divert the Indian boy who is the
cause of Oberon and Titania's quarrel); a purification of Titania's bower and pageant of the spirits of the night (to lull the
fairy queen to sleep); a kind of erotic revue in dance and song,
including a nicely contrasting anthology of inset-type love-songs
(to entertain and rouse Bully Bottom); a homage of the four
seasons (to welcome the return at dawn of Phoebus, the ordering and life-giving sun god); and a benediction and triumph of
Juno and Hymen, the symbols of married constancy and joy (to
delight the reconciled lovers). Much of this last masque takes
place in a fantastic *chinoiserie* garden: an ideal otherwhere, an
enlightened Arcadia-beyond-Arcadia where the natives are able
to do what Shakespeare's comedy is arguably trying to get its

audience to do, to reconcile reason and love.[67] (They 'keep little Company together now a days', as Bottom observes.)

The sung episodes of *The Fairy Queen*, then, are all quite Shakespearian 'philosophically' speaking. And if in a dramaturgical way they seem very un-Shakespearian at first blush, then so be it. This is a Baroque show devised before the birth of Bardolatry. Yet for all that, there are connections. For one thing, four out of five of its musical masques occur at or near points where there were cues for musical entertainments or celebrations in Shakespeare's original; and several other Shakespeare plays (*As You Like It, The Merry Wives of Windsor, Timon of Athens* and of course *The Tempest*) have masquing episodes which suggest that the Bard would not have been wholly out of sympathy with the masquing proclivities of Betterton and his team. Prospero's masque in Act IV of *The Tempest* is particularly relevant. Molière, Lully and the Jesuits may well be influences, but there is a sense in which the strategy of *The Fairy Queen* is simply to take what Prospero does – which is to allegorize his current preoccupations with Miranda and Ferdinand in a spectacle-to-music, a Triumph of Fertile Chastity – and to multiply it by five so that each act of the semi-opera shall have its pertinent masque. *The Fairy Queen* is *A. Midsummer Night's Dream* rewritten by a Restoration Prospero.

So, though the anti-masque triumphs in *Dido and Aeneas*, the masque triumphs in *The Fairy Queen* and *King Arthur*. Yet Dorset Garden audiences in the 1690s were clearly not meant to be more than half seduced by these Triumphs of Hymen and Britannia. Not that such anti-masquing elements as appear in the two semi-operas pose any great threats. Their drunken poets and harvest revellers, savage 'green men' and groping clowns, human icicles and naked sirens are either figures of indulgent fun or offer bluffs that can be called without enormous effort. Rather it is that the masques themselves are presented as fine imaginings that do not quite square with reality: inspiring dreams at best. The last words of both shows emphasize this. Dryden, not the most contented man with the state of the nation in the 1690s, has Arthur say to Merlin after the Britannia masque:

Wisely you have, whate'er will please, revealed:
What would displease, as wisely have concealed:
Triumphs of war and peace, at full ye show,
But swiftly turn the pages of our woe . . .

And in *The Fairy Queen*, the sturdy chaconne and prophetic
chorus which climax the Triumph of Hymen are followed by an
in-character spoken epilogue which undercuts them. Taking
their ideas largely from the final speeches of Shakespeare's
Oberon and Puck but with some of Mercutio's more deflating
fairy lore from the 'Queen Mab' speech in *Romeo and Juliet*
perhaps borrowed too, the Fairy King and Queen begin by
addressing the onstage lovers in properly high style; but their
style soon changes to an urbane, barbed knowingness as they
turn to pit, box and gallery and offer their audience various
bribes to applaud the show, ending:

OBERON: We'll try a Thousand charming Ways to win ye.
TITANIA: If all this will not do, the Devil's in ye.

And what are the bribes? Phantasms, delusive hopes, wish-
fulfilling dreams, fairy gold . . . The imagination, properly
indulged, is as properly put in its place.

In *King Arthur* and *The Fairy Queen* themselves, of course,
many of the most winning ways are Purcell's. The individual
musical numbers are all strong, and they are masterfully various: from the swaggering pop-style of the trumpet-song 'Come
if you dare' which celebrates Arthur's Kentish victory to the
erudition of the instrumental 'Canon four in two' hinting at
cabbalistic mysteries with which the dancing Followers of Night
give Titania strange dreams; from the lyric eloquence-in-a-nut-
shell of Secrecy's song in Titania's nocturne-masque ('One
charming night') to the extended mosaic of varying solos,
ensembles and ritornellos which makes up the Lully-with-a-dif-
ference passacaglia in Osmond's magic wood ('How happy the
lover'). But as much mastery is shown in the way particular
numbers interlink either with other numbers or with other
aspects of the playhouse. Cross-musical linkages can be 'operatic' in the Continental sense, as with *The Fairy Queen*'s all-

sung anti-masque of frisky sprites tormenting a stammering poet: a fine structure of interlocking metres which is a pendant to the celebration of forest-retreat; or in something *close* to the Continental sense, as with the scene of King Arthur's soldiers at a loss between marsh and *terra firma* when blandished out of their way by the evil Grimbald, where the action is propelled by solo songs and choruses but with spoken interjections. Or the linkages can be more pageant-like. For instance, there is the rich conjunction of the four songs, each with a wonderfully graphic instrumental prelude, which make up the homage the seasons present to Phoebus in *The Fairy Queen*. And sudden *dis*junctions, when anti-masquing elements give way to masquing ones or vice versa, can be just as rich. The funniest example perhaps is the way the solemn invocation of Hymen for two sopranos and chorus near the end of *The Fairy Queen* leads to an instrumental epiphany-prelude which suggests that the old boy himself is mischievous, eccentric, capricious and no stuffed shirt.[68] The most moving is the way the drunken hoe-down song and dance of the peasantry in *King Arthur* –

> We'll toss off our ale till we cannot stand;
> And heigh for the honour of old England

– is followed by a minuet-prelude for the epiphanizing Venus ('Fairest isle') of the most tender poise and elegant gravity.

Purcell does not only liaise with himself, so to speak, but with his Dorset Garden colleagues too. For the design team there is some vivid scene-and-machine music: the sixfold fanfare in Act IV of *The Fairy-Queen* which explodes in response to the duet 'Let the Fifes, and the Clarions, and shrill Trumpets sound' and which accompanies the stage direction '*A machine appears, the Clouds break from before it, and Phoebus appears in a Chariot drawn by four Horses*'; and the sharp-edged, crystalline prelude in Act III of *King Arthur* when '*Osmond strikes the ground with his wand: the scene changes to a Prospect of Winter in Frozen Countries.*' There are highly theatrical dances for Josias Priest to choreograph: the quivering dance of the near-frozen Hyperboreans in that Frost Scene for instance, and in *The Fairy Queen* the *pas d'action* in three movements for swans who become fairies but are scattered by wild woodwoses during the revue for Titania and her Bottom. There is music which serves to complement vivid stage costume – as with the hayseed, straw-hatted prelude to the seduction dialogue of Corydon and Mopsa in the same scene – and to complement no costume at all: as in the startlingly languorous Monteverdian duetting (canonic but decidedly uncanonical) of the two sirens Arthur encounters in the magic wood, a pair of Dalilas who do their best to ensure he never becomes 'the British Worthy'. And crucially there is music which meshes with speech. A lot does this of course, but there are especially telling moments, as when Oswald in *King Arthur* speaks a withering self-appraisal ('Ambitious fools we are') just after a chorus of Saxon priests has sung bumptious encouragements to a group of holy victims who are going to be sacrificed to Woden and the rest to help the war effort. Or when Titania speaks the last orders of the day to her elves, and adds:

> Each knows her Office. Sing me now to Sleep;
> And let the Sentinels their Watches keep.

At which, '*Enter* Night, Mystery, Secresie, Sleep; *and their Attendants*' to a slow, soft tread of regular minims for muted *fugato* violins and violas – no bass instruments or continuo – which eventually provide the un-earthed, unearthly accompaniment to Night's long lullaby. It is as if music as an art were being invented afresh for that moment.

Certainly *King Arthur* and *The Fairy Queen*, however unlike each other they are, share an interwoven, seamless quality across a wide range of modes and means. It is a quality George Granville stressed in his preface to *The British Enchanters*:

> The several Parts of the Entertainment should be so suited to relieve one another, as to be tedious in none; and the connexion should be such, that not one should be able to subsist without the other; like Embroidery, so fixt and wrought into the Substance, that no part of the Ornament could be removed, without tearing the Stuff.

Granville hoped that care in the making and the use of the best stuffs would give semi-opera a bright future:

If the Splendor of the *French* Opera, and the Harmony of the *Italian*, were so skilfully interwoven with the Charms of Poetry, upon a regular Dramatick Bottom, as to instruct, as well as delight, to improve the Mind, as well as ravish the Sense, there can be no doubt that such an Addition would entitle our *English* Opera to the Preference of all others.[69]

Alas for hopes. A dozen years after Purcell's death the form itself was as good as dead.[70] But three centuries later its masterpieces of the 1690s surely deserve to be given with proper attention to all the several parts of the entertainment, with their interweaving displayed, and with no tearing of the stuff.

NOTES

1 Reproduced as part of a useful 'iconography' in *Zimmerman II*, 358.

2 *Humours and Conversations* (1693, R 1961), 105–6.

3 Anon., 'A Poem Occasioned on the Death of Mr. Henry Purcell', in *Zimmerman II*, 297; Lansdowne, Epilogue to *The Jew of Venice*, in Christopher Spencer, ed., *Five Restoration Adaptations of Shakespeare* (Urbana, Ill., 1965), 401.

4 *Letters from the Dead to the Living* (1702), in A. L. Hayward, ed., *Amusements Serious and Comical* (London , 1927), 434.

5 H. C. de Lafontaine, *The King's Musick* (London, 1909), 485. See 271 for a royal countermand. The original order was a reaction against the boom in choirboy companies (Hamlet's 'little eyases') acting in public *c*1600.

6 For musico-theatrical activities from the 1650s to the 1670s, see Eric Walter White, *A History of English Opera* (London, 1983), chapters 4–6.

7 See Bruce Wood and Andrew Pinnock, ' "Unscarr'd by turning times"? The Dating of Purcell's *Dido and Aeneas*', *Early Music*, xx (1992), 372–90. (The famous performance at Josias Priest's school in 1689 was most likely a revival.) Wood and Pinnock's essay started a debate which continued on and off in issues of *Early Music* in 1993–4.

8 For Betterton, see P. Highfill, K. Burnim and E. Langhans, *A Biographical Dictionary of Actors . . . in London, 1660–1800* (Carbondale, Ill., 1973), II, 73–96.

9 There is a good deal in J. A. Winn, *'When Beauty Fires the Blood': Love and the Arts in the Age of Dryden* (Ann Arbor, 1992), especially chapters 3–5, to suggest the sort of conversations on artistic matters they might have had.

10 The script of *The Gordian Knot*, alone among those Purcell was involved with, has disappeared, and there is not even total certainty as to who wrote it.

11 For such music in the 1630s, see Chapter 2 of Julia Wood, 'Music in Caroline Plays' (Ph.D. diss., U. of Edinburgh, 1991); for the 1660s and early 1670s, see Peter Holman's introduction to Locke, *The Rare Theatrical* (facsimile, London, 1989), xii–xvi.

12 Compare bars 9–24 of Purcell's Hornpipe with the central 2/4 section of Holst's 'Ostinato'. (*The Married Beau* was one of four framing sets from which Holst selected and arranged movements for school-orchestra use.)

13 Quoted by Curtis A. Price, *Music in the Restoration Theatre* (Ann Arbor, 1979), 259, note 5. Price's second chapter is a useful discussion of framing music generally.

14 Quoted by Montague Summers in his eccentric but indispensable *Restoration Theatre* (London, 1934), 109; cf. 45–51.

15 On occasion, overture may have come first and prologue second. The slender surviving evidence for both arrangements (and the use of the phrase 'curtain-tune') is considered in Curtis A. Price, op. cit., 55–7.

16 See R. G. Noyes, 'A Manuscript Restoration Prologue for *Volpone*', *Modern Language Notes*, lii (1937), 198–200. The prologue objects to theatrical music-rooms 'outvying' the efforts of playwrights and actors, vividly reflecting a strain of Restoration rationalism which connects music with mere feeling and speech with superior intellect.

17 See Edward Langhans, *Restoration Promptbooks* (Carbondale, Ill., 1981), xix–xx, xxvii and Index s.v. 'Ring notes'.

18 Prologue to *The Ordinary*, c1671; see W. Van Lennep *et al.*, ed., *The London Stage 1660–1800: Part I 1660–1700* (Carbondale, Ill., 1965), clxviii. Roger North, however, did object forcibly to philistine elements in the audience 'disturb[ing] those who do attend' to the musicians and reacting with 'demmy it's a dirge' should the music attempt 'anything great and pompous'; in Mary Chan and Jamie Kassler, eds., *Cursory Notes of Musicke* (Kensington, N.S.W., 1986), 228. For intervals earlier in the century, see Gary Taylor and John Jowett, *Shakespeare Reshaped* (Oxford, 1993), 3–50, especially 6–16 and 49–50.

19 *Supplement to Colley Cibber*, in Cibber, *Apology*, ed. R. W. Lowe, (London, 1889), II, 300. For the concept of riding an audience's responses, see Jocelyn Powell, *Restoration Theatre Production* (London, 1984), 13–23.

20 Dennis connects act-tunes with Greek tragic choruses in *The Impartial Critick* (1693): E. N. Hooker, ed., *Critical Works* (Baltimore, 1939), I, 32, 39–40. In his pamphlet *The Musical Entertainments in the Tragedy of Rinaldo and Armida* (1699) he maintains that 'all the Musick in this Play, even the Musick between the Acts, is part of the Tragedy', and requires of the First Act-tune that it 'continues very softly the first Ten or Twelve Lines of the Second Act'. (See C. H. Wilkinson, ed., *Theatre Miscellany* (Oxford, 1953), 105, 109.)

21 Montague Summers, op. cit., 165–70, gives many instances.

22 See Curtis A. Price, op. cit., 72–81, and his 'Restoration Stage Fiddlers and their Music', *Early Music*, vii (1979), 315–22.

23 For these and other cues for tragic music, see R. G. Noyes, 'Conventions

of Song in Restoration Tragedy', *Publications of the Modern Language Association*, liii (1938), 162–88.

24 They might appear in show-specific collections like *The Songs to the New Play of Don Quixote* (1694), or in *The Gentleman's Journal*, or as individual song-sheets, or in song-books assembling 'the newest songs now in use' (or some such formula): *Joyful Cuckoldom*, *Thesaurus Musicus* and the like.

25 One of the strengths of Curtis A. Price's admirable *Henry Purcell and the London Stage* (Cambridge, 1984) is its thorough and vivid placing of these pieces (and of Purcell's more extended theatre sequences too) in the contexts of their play scripts. Price is also illuminating in his pursuit of Purcellian key symbolism and in his harmonic analyses of individual songs.

26 For an overview of Purcell's technical resources and development as a song writer, see Ian Spink, *English Song: Dowland to Purcell* (London, 1974), 208–40. (With the exception of the extended 'Plaint' in *The Fairy Queen* (z 629/40) – rather a special case – none of the one-off inset-songs takes the form of an invention on a 'ground', which is interesting considering the form's memorable frequency in the rest of Purcell's secular vocal music: in *Dido and Aeneas*, the odes, the non-theatrical songs and some of the more extended musical sequences in spoken plays.)

27 The 100th per cent is the occasional beery catch, e.g. 'Jack, thou'rt a toper', the ancient Roman footsloggers' celebration of after-hours drinking in the 1695 version of Fletcher's *Bonduca* (z 574/10), and also perhaps the occasional symphony of wind instruments such as the 'Composition in Imitation of Hunting' called for in Act V of *The Fairy Queen* though not figuring in Purcell's extensive score for that show as it has come down to us.

28 A. L. Hayward, ed., *Amusements*, op. cit., 31, 35.

29 For 'The Play-House', see C. N. Greenough, *Harvard Studies and Notes*, xvii (1935), 55–65.

30 Quoted in Montague Summers, op. cit., 253.

31 *Pepys*, ix, 94.

32 Jocelyn Powell, op. cit., Chapter 4, is a vivid evocation of a performance of *The Tempest* in 1674.

33 The current of opinion was changed by Margaret Laurie, 'Did Purcell set *The Tempest*?', *Proceedings of the Royal Musical Association*, xc (1963–4), 43–57.

34 For the musical architecture of Purcell's extended stage sequences, see pp. 331–6 of Margaret Laurie's chapter in Ian Spink, ed., *The Seventeenth Century*, Blackwell History of Music in Britain (Oxford, 1992), III. Purcell did not always feel himself bound to follow the stated or implied intentions of his poets as to who should sing what in these sequences. Compare, e.g., the original text with Purcell's setting in 'Music for a while' (z 583/2: Dryden-Lee, *Oedipus*) or in 'Now join your warbling voices all' (z 629/9–10: Anon., *The Fairy Queen*).

35 The musical impact of *Psyche* is usefully explored in Jennifer McDonald,

'Matthew Locke's *The English Opera*, and the Theatre Music of Purcell', *Studies in Music* [W. Australia], xv (1981), 62–75.

36 'Upon Operas', in S. Elledge and D. Schier, ed., *The Continental Model: Selected French Critical Essays of the Seventeenth Century* (Minneapolis, 1960), 165.

37 As Steven Plank points out in a wide-ranging essay, the celebrated 'Ho! ho!' choruses of the *Dido* coven are pre-echoed by the witches' cries of 'Hoo! Har!' (footnoted by Jonson with references to the best demonological authorities) in *The Masque of Queens*; ' "And Now About the Cauldron Sing": Music and the Supernatural on the Restoration Stage', *Early Music*, xviii (1990), 397. (In *Brutus of Alba*, his earlier version of the Dido myth, Tate already has his witches gleefully ho-hoing.)

38 Cf. Wilfred Mellers, *Harmonious Meeting* (London, 1965), 205, 209.

39 For Priest's career, see S. J. Cohen's piece in I. K. Fletcher, S. J. Cohen and R. Lonsdale, *'Famed for Dance': Essays on the Theory and Practice of Theatrical Dancing in England, 1660–1740* (New York, 1960), 22–33. His Court and theatre connections in the 1670s and his Purcellian ones in the 1690s make it likely that he choreographed *Dido* – at Court probably and later at his own girls' school – in the 1680s.

40 All-sung mythological 'masques' do appear on the public stage later in the 1690s; see Lucyle Hook, 'Motteux and the Classical Masque', in S. S. Kenny, ed., *British Theatre and the Other Arts, 1660–1800* (Washington, DC, 1984), 105–15.

41 'Upon Operas', in S. Elledge and D. Schier, eds., *The Continental Model*, op. cit., 165.

42 For associations of the *Saul* text (some decades old by the time Purcell set it) with current religious and political issues, see Mary Chan, 'The Witch of Endor and Seventeenth-century Propaganda', *Musica Disciplina*, xxxiv (1980), 205–14.

43 Dryden considered that in this episode he had 'allow'd his Fancy the full scope and swing', as he put it in his prologue to *Tyrannic Love*. For his pains he found his song brilliantly travestied in Buckingham's *The Rehearsal* (1671): a play which is a vivid reminder, as are Thomas Duffett's *Mock-Tempest* and *Psyche Debauch'd* of 1674 and 1675, that not all Restoration wits relished fanciful spectacle-to-music.

44 His justly celebrated sensitivity to words clearly did not involve the feeling that a particular text could only be set one way, as is shown away from the theatre in his radically different settings of a little meditation by Henry Heveningham on Shakespeare's phrase 'If music be the food of love . . .' (z 379 A and C).

45 Beyond Bowen and Bowman, the eight playhouse singers and musically gifted actors with whom Purcell seems to have worked most closely were Mrs Ayliff, Charlotte Butler, Letitia Cross, Mrs Hodgson, Thomas Doggett, William Mountfort, Mr Pate and John Reading. For their careers, see P. Highfill, K. Burnim and E. Langhans, op. cit.; for their Purcellian connections, see Curtis A. Price, *Henry Purcell and the London Stage*, via the index.

46 Indeed, *The Prophetess* was the title of the original play, which in Better-ton's version became *The Prophetess, or The History of Dioclesian*. The contraction to just *Dioclesian*, which has stuck, dates from around 1700.

47 For these and other magic effects, see Chapter 5 of Julia Muller, *Words and Music in Henry Purcell's First Semi-Opera, 'Dioclesian': an Approach to Early Music through Early Theatre* (Lewiston, NY, 1990), and Frans Muller, 'Flying Dragons and Dancing Chairs at Dorset Garden: Staging *Dioclesian*', *Theatre Notebook*, xlvii (1993), 80–95.

48 In which of her Court scenes it is presented is not wholly clear: one of the difficulties of marrying script to music which Andrew Pinnock addresses in 'Play into Opera: Purcell's *The Indian Queen*', *Early Music*, xviii (1990), 3–21.

49 In the interim, Purcell must have heard the mammoth vocal-instrumental chaconne at the end of Act II of the Grabu-Dryden *Albion and Albanius*.

50 For full and valuable accounts of these four 'operas', see Curtis A. Price, *Henry Purcell and the London Stage*, 125–43, 263–357.

51 Thus *Venus* is called 'a Masque for the Entertainment of the King' in an early manuscript score and *Dido* is called 'a Mask' when inserted into a version of Shakespeare's *Measure for Measure* in 1700; but terminology is fluid: the libretti printed for performances of both works at Josias Priest's school in the 1680s describes them as 'operas'. See Richard Luckett, 'A New Source for *Venus and Adonis*', *Musical Times*, cxxx (1989), 76–9.

52 The all-sung *tragédies lyriques* which Lully went on to write are relevant too. Not only did Purcell arguably know the musical substance of some of them; the very clear distinction they make between sung declamation and balletic *divertissement* is analogous to the speech/'masque' distinction in Bettertonian opera.

53 For finances, logistics etc., see Judith Milhous, 'The Multimedia Spectacu-lar on the Restoration Stage', in S. S. Kenny, op. cit., 41–66.

54 Cibber, *Apology*, Everyman's Library edn (London, 1914), 54, 99; Downes, *Roscius anglicanus*, ed. Judith Milhous and R. D. Hume (London, 1987), 71–7; cf. 89, 102.

55 George Granville, Lord Lansdowne, *The Genuine Works in Verse and Prose* (1732), I, 196.

56 This isn't to say that valuable studies have not been written by scholars who prefer one or other of these terms. Especially acute on the ideas behind the genre is Richard Luckett, 'Exotick but Rational Entertain-ments: the English Dramatick Operas', in M. Axton and R. Williams, eds., *English Drama: Forms and Development* (Cambridge, 1977), 123–41.

57 M. Chan and J. Kassler, eds., *Musicall Grammarian* (Cambridge, 1990), 266–7. Cf. North's *Cursory Notes of Musicke* of c1700, ed. cit., 230–31: 'I know for my own part I went for the music . . . It's possible some untun-able people might have the same respect for the play, and then the music must needs be cartwheels.'

58 Ibid., 215–16. The early operas of Cavalli probably come as close as anything in the seventeenth century to North's ideal.

59 *Dioclesian* and *The Indian Queen* themselves are perhaps more likely to

become 'festival' pieces than repertory ones, *Dioclesian* mainly because its fifth-act masque is disproportionate to the rest of the show, *The Indian Queen* because *its* fifth-act masque is by Henry Purcell's brother Daniel (Henry's own score ending with the ritual at the start of Act V).

60 Pressed on this, Dryden might have clarified things by contrasting *Arthur* the 'dramatick opera' (the formula he uses on its title page) with *Albion* the 'singing opera', a phrase he used in a letter of 1684: *Letters*, ed. C. E. Ward (Durham, NC, 1942), 23.

61 Anon., *Comparison*, ed. S. B. Wells (Princeton, 1942), 30–31. John Dennis amplifies these points with a fine truculence in his 1706 *Essay on the Operas after the Italian Manner*; *Critical Works*, I, 382 ff. For thoughts in the previous generation on speech, music and gender, see J. A. Winn, op. cit., 8–13, 136–46 etc.

62 For details of cutting, reworking etc., see Roger Savage, 'The Shakespeare-Purcell *Fairy Queen*: a Defence and Recommendation', *Early Music*, i (1973), 200–21. More recent work on the text is to be found in Bruce Wood and Andrew Pinnock, '*The Fairy Queen*: a Fresh Look at the Issues', *Early Music*, xxi (1993), 44–62.

63 According, that is, to the play text as it has come down to us. One of the Merlin-Philidel episodes, a celebration of Emmeline's restored sight, has either lost its musical setting or never had one. For an interpretation of Dryden's and Purcell's dramaturgies, see David Charlton, '*King Arthur*: Dramatick Opera', *Music and Letters*, lxiv (1983), 183–92.

64 As a species of public-stage Restoration drama, the genre naturally admitted instrumental framing sets, and sometimes a one-off inset-song or two as well. Love-songs in the inset manner also feature prominently in some of the extended musical sequences. Earnest sung dialogues between lovers who eventually reach a good mutual understanding are an especially important feature of the last-act masques in *Dioclesian* and *King Arthur*; and the scene of the Chinese Man and Woman near the end of *The Fairy Queen* is arguably in the same mould.

65 For Jesuit concept-linking, see Philippe Beaussant, *Lully, ou Le Musicien du Soleil* (Paris, 1992), 278–9; for linkings in Molière, see Robert McBride, 'Ballet: a Neglected Key to Molière's Theatre', *Dance Research*, ii (1984), 3–18.

66 Anon., *An Account of the Life of . . . Betterton* (1749), 33; quoted in J. Muller, op. cit., 316.

67 On the *chinoiserie*, see Roger Savage, op. cit., 211, note 22, and 217, note 35.

68 Assuming, that is, that it is played with some briskness, at a tempo similar to the one required by the solo plus trio in *Oedipus*, 'Come away, do not stay' (z 583/3).

69 George Granville, Lord Lansdowne, op. cit., I, 197–8.

70 For a lively account of its final years (which in theatrical terms were more of a bang than a whimper), see R. D. Hume, 'Opera in London, 1695–1706', in S. S. Kenny, op. cit., 67–91.

V

PURCELL IN PERFORMANCE

10

Performing Purcell

ANDREW PARROTT

The anniversary in 1959 of Purcell's birth was also that of Handel's death, and for any assessment of the current state of our knowledge of Purcellian performance practice Handelian scholarship provides a useful yardstick. As a result particularly of further Handelian celebrations in 1985, a great deal of detailed research was undertaken that can now assist the performer and thereby illuminate in performance the music of England's great adopted son, while even with plans for 1995 firmly in place, it is clear that the pace of equivalent research into our Orpheus Britannicus has been decidedly slower. It may be argued, though, that substantial advances in understanding, while perhaps not yet reflected in musicological literature, are evident in live performances and recordings, especially in those involving period instruments. Yet it is not long since, in a prestigious London concert of Purcell's church music, given by an all-male choir and a period-instrument band, oboes were unapologetically added to Purcell's strings and several pieces tacitly transposed. More disturbingly, these and other questionable decisions seem to have passed entirely without comment. The example – by no means isolated – serves to illustrate two general points. First, that in the absence of any sophisticated appreciation of Purcellian conventions, performers will tend to fall back on more familiar Handelian practices. Second, that details of performance practice can rarely be viewed in isolation: dubious instrumentation, for instance, may lead to the adoption of an inappropriate pitch standard, and in turn to wholesale transpositions, both of which will influence intonation, colour and balance.

In short, much work lies ahead if full justice is to be done in performance to Purcell's rich legacy, and in this chapter I can only hope to take the process a few steps further. A straight-forward summary of published research would achieve little; instead I have chosen to concentrate on issues that seem to me to be of critical importance and to demand particular attention, ignoring other broad areas of performance practice (notably rhythm[1] and tempo[2]) and also many very specific ones. I have also aimed to draw together as much of the available evidence as possible and to allow it to speak for itself.

It should be said at the outset that the sources for such a study as this are for the most part frustratingly disparate and inadequate. Purcell's own work on the 12th edition (1694) of Playford's *An Introduction to the Skill of Musick* is disappoint-ingly unenlightening in matters of performance practice,[3] and, after Christopher Simpson's *The Division-Viol*, first published in the year of Purcell's birth, and Thomas Mace's conservative *Musick's Monument* (1676[4]), no major practical treatises were published in England in the course of Purcell's lifetime. On the other hand, Roger North's voluminous manuscript writings begun around the time of Purcell's death are perhaps ample compensation and are extensively quoted here. North was just a few years older than Purcell, was acquainted with him, lived in London from 1669 until the early 1690s, was 'a medler with most sorts of instruments'[5] (harpsichord, organ, violin, bass viol), sang a little, and, above all, possessed a keen ear and a lively pen. Also invaluable are the organographical data col-lected some time in the 1690s by the Cambridge scholar James Talbot, a 'friend & admirer' of Purcell's.[6] But in general we must rely on the musical sources themselves (and in particular on performance materials), on Court archives, on a whole range of isolated documents, on diaries (especially Evelyn's), and on a handful of surviving instruments.

As a composer Purcell himself knew that 'after all the learned Encomions that words can contrive [Musick] commends itself best by the performances of a skilful hand, and an angelical voice',[7] and throughout his short life he was intimately involved in practical music-making at the highest professional level. Versatility was commonplace and many of his contemporaries doubled as singer/instrumentalist, wind/string player, performer/ composer, or player/maker. As an executant Purcell was presumably best known in his own day as an organist, both at Westminster Abbey (from 1679) and with the Chapel Royal (from 1682). But the instruments he would have played are remarkably poorly documented: we know little more than that Robert Dallam's 'faire Double Organ for the use of his Ma^ts Chappel in Whitehall'[8] was ready for use in 1664 and survived until the Palace fire of 1698,[9] and that the Abbey's organ was overhauled and enlarged by Bernard Smith in 1694–5.[10] (Purcell himself provided an additional instrument for the coronations of 1685 and 1689.[11]) Moreover, although there are a few stop-lists, not a single contemporary church organ survives intact.

From 1681 Bernard Smith ('Father' Smith) held the post of organ-maker to the Court,[13] and as part of the protracted and very partisan contest between him and Renatus Harris in the 1680s to build an organ for the Temple Church[14] Draghi evidently played for Harris (a fellow Catholic), while both Purcell and Blow publicly showed off (the Protestant) Smith's 23-stop instrument (see Table 1),[15] with its '3 full setts of keyes and quarter notes'.[16] The half-dozen extant organ pieces by Purcell scarcely hint at such an elaborate instrument; only the Voluntary for Double Organ (z 719) demands more than one manual, and the Cornet solos of the Voluntary on the Old Hundredth (z 721) – by Blow? – were probably intended for a single manual with divided stops. Sweet and brilliant wooden pipes were evidently a hallmark of Father Smith's work and the Temple organ's 'sweetnes and fulnes of Sound' drew comment;[17] apart from a few domestic instruments, the most reliable witness now is perhaps the restored 1698 organ in the University Church, Cambridge.[18]

Towards the end of 1685 Purcell added to his two positions as organist that of 'harpsicall' player in James II's private music.[19] While his first published keyboard music was 'for the Virginals, Harpsichord, and Spinet' (*The Second Part of Musick's Handmaid*, 1689), that of the posthumous *A Choice Collection of Lessons* (1696/3, rev. 1699) specifies just harpsichord and

TABLE I

Specification of Bernard Smith's organ for the Temple Church

Great Organ

Prestand of mettle	12'
Holflute of wood and mettle	12'
Principall of mettle	6'
Quinta of mettle	4'
Super octavo	3'
Cornett of mettle	2'
Sesquialtera of mettle	3'
Gedackt of wainescott	6'
Mixture of mettle	3'
Trumpett of mettle	12'

Choir Organ

Gedackt wainescott	12'
Holflute of mettle	6'
A Sadt of mettle	6'
Spitts flute of mettle	3'
A Violl and Violin of mettle	12'
Voice humane of mettle	12'

Ecchos

Gedackt of wood	6'
Sup. Octavo of mettle	3'
Gedackt of wood	
Flute of mettle	
Cornett of mettle	
Sesquialtera	
Trumpett	

Source: Edmund Macrory, *Notes on the Temple Organ* (London, 3/1911), 33–4.

spinet, reflecting a shift in fashion away from the rectangular virginal and towards the tonally very different wing-shaped spinet.[20] At Purcell's death 'the organ, the double spinet, the single spinet'[21] in his possession passed to his son, but again, little is known about the particular instruments he would have played. While Purcell was assistant keeper of the King's instruments, the purchase (for £30) was recorded of 'a greate Harpsichord with 3 ranks of strings for his Ma^{ts} musick in ye hall and in ye privy lodgings'.[22] The maker of what was almost certainly still a single-manual instrument is not named, but around the same time Charles Haward, 'ye virginall maker', had been brought in by Hingeston to repair 'ye Harpsicords & pedalls'.[23] As it happens, an instrument by Hawood, altered in the eighteenth century but dated 1683 and now at Hovingham Hall, is the only fully attested English harpsichord to have survived from the second half of the seventeenth century. Its original specification was an Italianate 8'8' with, perhaps surprisingly, a lute stop. The case for associating Hawood more closely with the Court and thus with Purcell is strengthened by two further details: Queen Anne is known to have owned a virginal by him,[24] and recurrent references in Court documents to 'pedalls' lead indirectly to the elder Hawood, John, himself a distinguished maker.[25]

Two years after Purcell's death a modest volume of 'ye newest Aires & Song Tunes' was published by Walsh under the title *The Harpsichord Master*.[26] Its interest for us here lies in the prefatory material, some 'plain & easy Instructions for Learners on ye Spinnet or Harpsicord', and especially in the portion on ornament signs and fingering; this is pictured in Plate 14. (These instructions were reprinted in the 1699 edition of *A Choice Collection of Lessons* but without attribution.) Moreover, the first item purports to be a 'Prelude for ye fingering by M^r H: Purcell' (Example 1). The style of fingering matches at least three Italian sources of the seventeenth century[27] and suggests a possible link with Italian players such as Draghi and Bartolomeo Albrici, who were both in England from *c*1666.

The ornament signs that abound in both the organ and harpsichord sources are inherited directly from Locke (*Melothesia*, 1673) and others. All are included in the *Rules for Graces*, and only three require any comment. The explanation of the *battery* sign (= modern }) is surely just a garbled attempt to notate a simple arpeggiated chord, whereas both the *beat* and the *plain note & shake* really do deserve to be taken at face value: the latter does not require a tie between the first two notes[28] and,

EX. 1   Henry Purcell: 'Prelude for yᵉ fingering' from *The Harpsichord Master* (1697)

* The fingering for the LH in the original used the system in which the thumb is 5, the little finger is 1, and so on.

tempting though it may be to regard the *beat* simply as a mordent (♩), the presence of an initial lower auxiliary is implied by Carr (1686) and specified by Blakeston (1694), Prendcourt (*c*1700) and North (*c*1710).[29] (Perhaps surprisingly, there is no contemporary evidence for the simple mordent in English keyboard music.) The compound ornament ⨏ , found quite frequently in Purcell's solo keyboard music, would thus sound ⨏, with a reiterated lower auxiliary.

Many other keyboard ornaments were, of course, 'seldome or never exprest in wrighting, for they are in the hand and the player takes them of course'.[30] North's writings on 'The Art of Gracing', while not confined to keyboard matters, are a salutary reminder of this hidden world.[31] 'A Table of Graces proper to the Viol or Violin', more or less identical to Simpson's, is found in *An Introduction to the Skill of Musick*,[32] and a pithy and informative set of 'Rules for gracing on the flute' survives from the 1690s.[33]

A passing observation by North on ornaments serves to raise the issue of keyboard tuning systems: 'Another use of the semitonian temperings is to abate the rancor of the scismes'[34] – in other words, an ornament involving a neighbouring semitone can help to disguise out-of-tune intervals. What temperament(s) then did Purcell favour for his instruments?

The source closest to Purcell himself is Dr William Holder's *A Treatise of the Natural Grounds, and Principles of Harmony* (1694), written 'for the Sake and Service of all Lovers of Musick, and particularly the Gentlemen of Their Majesties Chapell Royal'. Holder, Purcell's senior by fifty years and himself a competent composer, had been Sub-Dean of the Chapel (from 1674 until *c*1688) and his explanation of how 'to put an Organ or Harpsichord into more general usefull Tune'[35] is explicitly not innovative: his aim was rather to describe actual practice in physical terms. What emerges is a meantone with the fifths (up to) a $\frac{1}{4}$ comma narrow and with the 'Anomalies ... thrown upon such Chords as are least used for the Key: as $^{\#}$G, $^{\flat}$E, *&c*' (i.e. with the 'wolf' between G$^{\#}$ and E$\flat$). Interestingly, Holder goes on to comment that, except at cadences, even these bad chords 'the Ear will bear with, as it doth with other Discords in binding [= chromatic] passages'. North, who later (1726) described an irregular meantone, argued that the 'bad' keys 'by meer out-of-tuned-ness have certein caracters, very serviceable to the various purposes of Musick', and warned against the use of more 'equal' temperaments.[36]

It has been shown that, with some retuning, all of Purcell's solo harpsichord music is playable in meantone temperament;[37] apart from C$^\sharp$, E$^\flat$, F$^\sharp$, G$^\sharp$ and B$^\flat$, the only chromatic notes to occur are A$^\flat$ (but never in conjunction with G$^\sharp$) and D$^\sharp$ (never with E$^\natural$). In most circumstances such retuning is obviously out of the question for an organ (or, at least, for all but a modest domestic instrument), yet of Purcell's six surviving organ pieces three require D$^\sharp$ (z 719, which also uses E$^\flat$, z 720 and z 721), and one of these (z 721) the even more problematic A$^\sharp$ and E$^\sharp$. The 'quarter notes' on Smith's Temple organ, mentioned above, were split keys (and additional pipes) for G$^\sharp$/A$^\flat$ and D$^\sharp$/E$^\flat$, and were considered a novelty.[38] But although John Player and others are also said to have built harpsichords and spinets with quarter-notes,[39] split keys were only one (partial) solution: an experienced keyboard player would probably instinctively release 'bad' notes early wherever possible or, in realizing a basso continuo, perhaps avoid them altogether. Or when G$^\sharp$ was too low to function as a reasonable A$^\flat$, for example, the player could 'favor', or ornament, it 'by a mixture with the note above (that is with $\natural$A), be it a back-fall or slight trill'; this would 'make the pipe or string sound as being a little sharper'.[40]

An understanding of the niceties of tuning was, of course, not confined to keyboard players. Indeed, Purcell's contemporary Pier Francesco Tosi would later argue that keyboard instruments tended to undermine a singer's proper understanding of the different sizes of semitone:

> Every one knows not that there is a Semitone Major and Minor, because the Difference cannot be known by an Organ or Harpsichord, if the Keys of the Instrument are not split ... this Knowledge ... [in] Songs accompanied with Bow Instruments ... becomes so necessary, that if a *Soprano* was to sing *D* sharp, like *E* flat, a nice Ear will find he is out of Tune, because this last rises.[41]

Tosi goes on to advise his readers to 'consult the best Performers on the Violin' on the matter. Woodwind fingering charts, such as that for 'the Hoboy' in *The Second Book of Theatre Music* (1699), similarly show alternatives for D$^{\#}$/E$^{\flat}$ and G$^{\#}$/A$^{\flat}$ which imply that the flats sounded higher than the sharps.[42] And although equal temperament was a natural system for fretted instruments, which 'all our Violls, Lutes, Gitares, and the like instruments do follow',[43] there was considerable interest in setting such instruments unequally.[44]

These matters of tuning have interesting implications for continuo practice, especially in Purcell's extended works. The title page of *Orpheus Britannicus* (1698) informs us that the songs 'are placed in their several Keys according to the Order of the *Gamut*' – surely a convenience for performers rather than a theoretical scheme. But it is highly unlikely that a harpsichordist would have been expected to retune in the course of 'Hail! Bright Cecilia!' (1692), which uses nine keys, or between the two scenes of *Dido*'s Act II, which require E$^{\flat}$, A$^{\flat}$, D$^{\flat}$ and C$^{\#}$, G$^{\#}$, D$^{\#}$ respectively. In the absence of split keys, might two instruments with complementary tunings have been used, by one or two players? (There are records from the early 1670s of London theatres hiring two harpsichords, and in the early eighteenth century two instruments were normally used for English dialogues.[45]) Was the harpsichord indeed the predominant continuo instrument of the time? And is it even correct always to assume the presence of a chordal instrument?

There are no definitive answers to most of these questions, but the performer will perhaps be better equipped to find reasonable conjectural solutions with a fuller understanding of English continuo practice in general. In particular, it is well worth asking whether the presence of a keyboard instrument is justified in the first place. Table 2 lists the various continuo options given on the title pages of extant song publications issued during Purcell's lifetime.[46] Theorbo(-lute) is named in all but one.[47] Bass viol is absent only once, but is absent, too, from the posthumous *Orpheus Britannicus*, with its bass 'Figur'd for the *Organ, Harpsichord,* or *Theorbo-Lute*'. Only from 1687 does harpsichord occur consistently (and Book IV of *The Theater of Music*

TABLE 2

Continuo options from song publications issued during
Purcell's lifetime

NB only first editions and the first volumes of series are included

B-V = Bass-Viol
H = Harpsichord
O = Organ
T(-L) = Theorbo(-Lute)

1673	[John Playford]: *Choice Songs and Ayres*	T-L or B-V
1678	John Banister and Thomas Low: *New Ayres, Dialogues, and Trialogues*	T-L or B-V
1685	[Henry Playford and Richard Carr]: *The Theater of Music*	T or B-V
1685	John Blow *et al.*: *A Third Collection of New Songs*	T *and* B-V
1687	[John Carr and Samuel Scott]: *Comes amoris*	H T or B-V
1687	[John Carr and Samuel Scott]: *Vinculum societatis*	H T or B-V
1687	[John Crouch]: *A Collection of the Choyest* [sic] *and Newest Songs*	H T or B-V
1688	[Henry Playford]: *The Banquet of Musick*	T-L B-V H or O
1688	[Henry Playford]: *Harmonia sacra*	T-L B-V H or O
1690	John Wolfgang Franck: *Remedium melancholiae*	H T or B-V
c1692	Robert King: *Songs for One Two and Three Voices*	O or H
1693	[John Hudgebut]: *Thesaurus musicus*	H T or B-V
1695	[Henry Playford]: *Deliciae musicae*	T-L B-V H or O
1695	[Henry Playford]: *The New Treasury of Musick***	T-L or B-V, H or Spinnet

*A compilation from *The Theater of Musick*, I, II and IV, and *Choice Ayres*, IV and V.

from that year expands to include harpsichord[48]), while organ
appears fairly regularly from the following year.[49] Despite a
rather narrower range of comfortable keys than on keyboard
instruments, the theorbo was undoubtedly the most flexible and
subtle instrument of vocal accompaniment through most of this
period, and it is presumably the theorbo that is generally to be
understood in connection with those singers known to have
accompanied themselves on the 'lute' – John Abell, Arabella
Hunt,[50] and Mrs Knepp[51] among them.[52] For Mace the norm
was a double-strung instrument in G (or, if necessary, A),
whereas for Talbot it could be either single- or double-strung, in
either tuning.[53] The archlute, which seems to have come to
England from Italy very late in the century and which in a short
space of time largely displaced the theorbo,[54] does not appear in
these title pages at all, nor in Court documents, nor among the
instruments to be taught at the proposed 'Royal Academies' in
1695,[55] but it was known to Talbot, who measured an instrument belonging to 'Mr [John] Shores'.[56] The suspicion that the
instrument established itself just too late to have influenced
Purcell's music-making is reinforced by its absence from (and
the theorbo's presence in) the intended 'Accompaniment' to Talbot's 'An Ode for the Consort at York Buildings upon the death
of Mr. H. P.'.[57]

These song-book title pages also make no mention of the
fashionable guitar,[58] which, especially among actor-singers,
remained a popular instrument of self-accompaniment, being
relatively easy both to play (especially the 'brushing way') and
to carry.[59] As Purcell's apparently limited use of the instrument
suggests, it was regarded very much as a dance instrument and
traditionally had erotic associations. In 'Hail! Bright Cecilia!' a
guitar's participation is implied by the text of the duet (with
recorders), 'In vain the am'rous flute and soft guitar, / Jointly
labour to inspire wanton heat and loose desire'; but only in
Dido and Aeneas is the instrument expressly called for by
Purcell, where the 1689 libretto specifies 'A Dance Gittars
Chacony' (at the end of Act I) and 'Gitter Ground a Dance' (in
the middle of Act II).[60] (There is surely no 'missing' music at
these points, as has commonly been supposed; rather, the dances

would have been improvised above Purcell's given ground basses, that of the Triumphing Dance and that of 'Oft she visits this lone mountain'.[61])

The harpsichord, too, was used by singers to accompany themselves. Evelyn heard the castrato Siface at Pepys's home in 1687 and observed: 'He touch'd the Harpsichord to his Voice rarely well.'[62] Similarly, Evelyn's daughter Mary often 'play'd a through-base on the Harpsichord' to her own 'incomparable sweete Voice'.[63] These reports share an interesting feature with others of the period – of John Abell 'being accompanied with Signor *Francesco* on the *Harpsichord*' in 1682 and Mr Pordage singing with 'Signor Jo: Baptist [Draghi], playing to it on the Harpsichord' in 1685[64] – and with Hawkins's anecdotal description of Purcell accompanying Gostling and Mrs Hunt on the harpsichord at Court in 1691 or 1692:[65] in none is any mention made of a supporting bowed string instrument. This accords with the clear implications of the information in Table 2, that in the song repertoire a bass viol was intended invariably not as a supplementary instrument to a chordal one but as a self-sufficient alternative. The possible objection that this is too literal an interpretation of a casual turn of phrase must vanish when we find certain songs described as 'Composed to be sung either to the Theorbo-Lute, or Bass-Viol'.[66] A viol can, of course, play occasional chords, and Roger North used to accompany his elder brother Francis's singing in this fashion:

> And it being necessary to the sound of a voice, whatever it is, to have an instrument to accompany, and I being well habituated to the viol and the fingering, I used to touch the principall notes as well as I could, and by degrees to putt in cords, and at last to full harmony, as the instrument would afford.[67]

This form of accompaniment probably became less fashionable with time but apparently persisted even after Purcell's death (see, for example, Matteis's *A Collection of New Songs*, 1696).

Does this preference for a single continuo instrument apply also in purely instrumental chamber music? In his preface to the *Sonnata's of III Parts* for 'TWO VIOLLINS And BASSE:/To the Organ *or* Harpsecord' (1683), Purcell attributes a delayed publication date to the fact 'that he has now thought fit to cause the whole Thorough Bass to be Engraven, which was a thing quite besides his first Resolutions'.[68] In other words, a generously figured 'Basso Continuo' part is given in addition to the original unfigured 'Basso' partbook. That two bass instruments are required is clear from the title of the posthumous *Ten Sonatas of Four Parts* (1697), with its 'Through Bass for the *Harpsichord, or Organ*', which is presented in the same way. Moreover, a uniquely documented performance of (presumably) the earlier works (*c*1683) points, albeit somewhat ambiguously, to four players: Francis North, who was also a keen viol player, 'caused the devine Purcell to bring his Itallian manner'd compositions [to his home]; and with him [Purcell] on his harpsicord, my self [Roger North] and another violin, wee performed them more than once'.[69] The possibility nevertheless remains that instrumental chamber works with a single bass part may require just a single bass instrument, and not necessarily a chordal one.[70]

In an orchestral context the harmonic need for a chordal instrument is often slight. Is the High Baroque norm of an ever-present chordal continuo necessarily appropriate in Purcell's case? An engraving of the 1685 coronation feast in Westminster Hall affords a rare glimpse of the royal violin band ('ye Musick') in action – twenty players and apparently no continuo instruments.[71] At the start of Locke and Shadwell's version of *The Tempest* (1674) we read of 'the Band of 24 Violins, with the Harpsicals and Theorbo's which accompany the Voices'.[72] The wording seems exactly to describe the Lullian operatic model, in which continuo instruments were usually reserved for vocal sections (including choruses); *airs de ballet* and many other independent *symphonies* (including overtures) contain no figuring.[73] But the picture is less clear with Restoration theatre music where conventions were more fluid and evidence is limited. In a few individual cases the presence in the sources of autograph or early contemporary figuring can settle the matter: the 1691 printed score of *Dioclesian*, for example, contains two revealing bars of figuring in the overture. But this need not imply the same practice for a slightly earlier work such as *Dido* (before 1689?[74]) or for non-theatrical works. Furthermore, it seems that even 'in early eighteenth-century London theatres the harpsichord was used exclusively to accompany the voices'.[75] (But by the second decade of the eighteenth century North was writing of the harpsichord that 'in a great consort, tho' struck full at every note, it is lean and soundless. If one can but say there is such an instrument heard amongst them, it is all.'[76])

The figuring of bass parts from Purcell's time is in general very sparse and frequently non-existent.[77] Consequently, writers on continuo practice concentrate on harmonic matters: Locke's *Melothesia, or, Certain General Rules for Playing upon a Continued-Bass* (1673) and Blow's manuscript 'Rules for playing of a Through Bass upon Organ & Harpsicon' do just that.[78] But, 'whether figured or not, it is certein, a thro-base part may best be played from the score: and if there were nothing else to recomend it but the capacity of a nicer waiting on the parts then displayed, by seeing their movement, it's enough'.[79]

Organ parts copied by Blow for three of Purcell's anthems arranged without strings and those of a dozen collected by Gostling[80] adopt a quite plain style and the fairly familiar two- or three- (and occasionally four-) part texture of other late seventeenth-century organ books, with occasional harmonic enrichment. But what of stylistic matters in theorbo and harpsichord realizations? While admitting 'That the *Greatest Excellency* in *This Kind* of *Performance*, lies beyond whatever *Directions* can be given by *Rule*', Mace provides twenty-one useful examples of how to 'Amplifie your Play' on the theorbo, by '*Breaking* your *Parts*, or *Stops*, in way of *Dividing-Play* upon *Cadences*, or *Closes*'.[81] Handwritten realizations of five songs including Purcell's 'How pleasant is This flowry Plain and Grove!' are found in a copy of *The Banquet of Musick* (1688–92), but they are undated and may well have been intended for archlute; their style is quite active and melodic.[82] Specifically for harpsichord is the simple realization in a contemporary source of a three-bar modulatory continuo phrase in the ode 'From Hardy Climes' (1683; Example 2). But rather more revealing are two short solo harpsichord pieces (z T681 and T682), both grounds, derived from vocal models (Example 3). Both alternate a simple melodic line (at the higher octave) with a

EX. 2 Henry Purcell: 'From Hardy Climes' (z 325/4a), bars 1–3

For the Harpsecard

written-out continuo part essentially in two parts (occasionally three) in the middle register, and use 'broken' rhythms and more or less exact repetitions. This style would seem to have much more in common with North's view (*c*1710–20) that the harpsichord excelled in 'humouring a solo or single voice, where there is much of interlude, which lets that instrument in to shew itself':

> For the sprinkling or *arpeggio*, the proper genius of it, must have pauses, for liberty of that kind, which hath an egregious effect, as either in leading the air, to possess a voice with its key, [or] to enter *petit* fuges or intersperse *ritornello's*.[83]

North goes on to emphasize the need to be 'a master of composition in generall':

> For there is occasion of so much management in the manner of play, sometimes striking onely the accords, sometimes *arpeggiando*, sometimes touching the air, and perpetually observing the emphatick places, to fill, forbear, or adorne with a just favour, that [anyone who is only] a thro-base master, and not an ayerist, is but an abcdarian . . .

He also maintains that:

> It is not allow'd a thro-base part to break and adorne while he accompanys, but to touch the accords onely as may be figured, or [as] the composition requires. Yet there is a difference in the management when the upper parts move slow, and when they devide, or when they are full, or pause. In that latter case, somewhat more airey may be putt in, and often there is occasion to fill more or less.[84]

EX.   3a   Henry Purcell: *Ground* (z T681), bars 1–6

EX.   3b   Henry Purcell: *A New Ground* (z T682), bars 1–5

As a continuo instrument the 'Noble Base Viol' seems, for the most part, to have held its own against 'the harsh volon' (bass violin).[85] We have already seen that a viol very probably played in a contemporary performance of the earlier trio sonatas, and a subsequent advertisement for the set confirms this scoring;[86] the undesignated bass of the later collection, similarly, is labelled 'Viol di gambo' in an early eighteenth-century source.[87] But Purcell's later years may well have been a period in which the virtual monopoly of the bass viol as a bowed string continuo instrument began to be challenged by the bass violin. The latter, generally bowed underhand, was for a long time associated exclusively with professional musicians, often 'some hireling drudge' (like the 'Fat-Red-Fac'd-Fidler that plays upon the Base' in Otway's *Friendship in Fashion*, 1678), and was considered 'a cours instrument': 'as then used [in the 1670s], [it] was a very hard and harsh sounded base, and nothing so soft and sweet as now [*c*1726]'.[88]

By 1692 Purcell could confidently specify a bass violin to support two violins in the duet 'Hark! each tree' ('Hail! Bright Cecilia!'), and at a private gathering in Oxford the following year, in the company of 'Mr Shore [and] Monseur la Rich', Francis Withey observed that 'Monse Diseb plais on ye Base Violin Ex[cellently]'.[89] Two tell-tale *BB*♭s occur in the bass (bars 10 and 46) to the bass solo (again with two violins) 'The father's brave . . .' ('A Song for the Duke of Gloucester's Birthday', 1695), as does a *BB* in the D major '3 parts upon a Ground' (z 731). (Talbot gives the lowest note of the bass violin as *BB*♭, without mentioning C as an alternative; the lower note appears in Purcell's orchestral music – for example, in the overture to *The Indian Queen* and in the symphony to 'A Song for the Duke of Gloucester's Birthday' – but only seldom.[90]) In the anthems with strings it would seem that, as a rule, the (unspecified) bowed string bass played only with the upper strings, in purely instrumental sections and tuttis, and that the continuo for solo sections was provided by organ, often with theorbo(s). In addition, viols may have doubled the choral bass.[91]

Before turning from matters of continuo practice, it may be worth asking whether an 8′ 'great' bass viol, like Orlando Gibbons's 'great Dooble Basse', survived in use from the earlier part of the century.[92] Certainly, the 'Double Base' writing in Blow's 'Lord, who shall dwell in thy tabernacle?' (from the late 1680s?) need not imply a 16′ instrument.[93] The six-string 'Violone or Double Bass' viol '(German)' mentioned by Talbot has its lowest string tuned to low *GG*,[94] and, like the theorbo, would be capable of occasionally dropping an octave to enrich a bass line. The advantage of such a viol as continuo instrument would be not so much its range as the quality of sound in the bass register:

> Lent the noble *viola* or double base viol: the strings have length in proportion to their magnitude and tension, which makes the tone sweet and loud. The base-violin is too short and strong, therefore harsh, whatever of organ or harpeggia there is. Let the double base viol governe the *basso continuo*, and if one be not enough let there be more.[95]

Was this 'double bass' viol the 8′ instrument which survived, at least in Germany and Austria, into the eighteenth century,[96] and might such an instrument therefore have had a place in Purcell's music?[97] Specifically, might this have been the type of viol employed by the Chapel Royal to support the choral voices? 'I cannot but commend the double base, or standing viol, for plaine bases,' wrote North (*c*1695), 'especially for accompanying voices, because of its softness joyned with such a force as helps the voice very much.'[98]

Only two aspects of Purcell's string orchestra need special attention here: its bass line and its strength. As we have seen, a bass violin tuned a tone below the cello is implied even in music from the composer's last year. But what of a 16′ bass? Convincing evidence for the use of any form of 16′ orchestral bass seems to be wholly absent from the music of Purcell and his immediate contemporaries. Anthony à Wood, noting the rise of the violin band in the 1650s, wrote: 'only violins used, as treble, tenor, and bass-violin',[99] and Court archives for the remainder of the century record the purchase of 'Base violins' (and strings for them), but of nothing obviously larger.[100] Even in post-Purcellian Italian operas 'the instrumental part' was, at least in retrospect, considered 'under based', because bassoons failed to 'urge the other instruments, as the [new 16'?] double violls doe'.[101] On the other hand, a 'double bass' by Edward Lewis, dated 1695, has survived, and Talbot measured a five- or six-string fretted 'double bass viol' with a body-length of over five feet, belonging to Gottfried Finger. As far as I can ascertain, the first known specialist double-bass player in England was probably Giuseppe Fedeli, known as Joseph Saggione, a composer and member of Christopher Rich's Drury Lane company orchestra in the early 1700s.[102] Significantly, it was Saggione, together with Montéclair, who was later credited with having introduced the instrument to the Paris Opéra *c*1701.[103]

It would seem then that, in this one respect at least, orchestras in England mirrored the French model throughout Purcell's lifetime.[104] At Whitehall the full body of the Twenty-four Violins may occasionally have taken part in the various birthday and welcome odes, but from 1668 the players were organized into two groups to 'wait & attend upon his Ma[ty] ... twelve one moneth & twelve ye other'.[105] Also, when the Court was at Windsor only twelve players were usually available.[106] For the 1685 coronation there were some thirty-five instrumentalists (in addition to the trumpeters)[107] and Staggins received payment for 'faire writeing of a composition for his Majesty's coronation day from the originall in score the 6 parts, for drawing ye said composition into forty severall parts for trumpetts, hautboyes violins, tennors, bases'.[108] (Staggins's bills for music-copying in 1675–6, incidentally, confirm that his players did not normally share copies but that 'every man [had] a part to himselfe'.[109]) In theatres such a large group would have been almost unheard of.[110] At Wren's Dorset Garden theatre, which probably accommodated 700 or 800 spectators, the 'musick room' above the proscenium arch perhaps measured roughly 25' by 8'.[111] Nor would other buildings associated with the performances of Purcell's odes and secular public pieces generally have demanded large forces. Although the brief reduction to two violins and violas per part in the opening chorus of the richly scored 'Hail! Bright Cecilia!'[112] suggests at least fourteen string players for the first performance in Stationers' Hall, a repeat given in York Buildings in 1693 cannot have involved more than twenty or so performers *in toto*: there 'the Great Room' seems to have been just 32' 4" long, 31' 6" broad, 21' high, with 'a Semicircle of Seats, and stands for Musick' in a raised alcove 15' 9" deep and 17' in diameter.[113]

While coronation verse anthems such as 'My Heart is Inditing' (for James II) and 'Praise the Lord, O Jerusalem' (for William and Mary) would have been played by the full Twenty-four Violins, it may well have been simple lack of space in the chapel at Whitehall Palace that led to the 'orchestrally' accompanied anthems by Purcell and others being played there by a mere handful of players, situated probably in the music room that opened on to the chapel at first-floor level. (The choir was in stalls below, but verse sections may usually have been sung from the gallery.[114]) The chapel itself, 'panelled round almost up to the roof', cannot have measured much more than 75' by 30' or so.[115] Four to six 'violins' plus two viols – 'a *select number* of his [Majesty's] private music'[116] – served there on a rota system, and the almost inescapable conclusion is that they played with just one player per part.[117]

From 1674 and for the remainder of Purcell's lifetime, the Court band was in the charge of the violinist Nicholas Staggins, who had travelled in 'France . . . Italy, & other Forrin Parts, to capacitate & make my self fit for ye Service of His Late Ma^{ty} Kg Charles ye Second'.[118] And among the Court violinists from 1681 was John Lenton, whose modest *The Gentleman's Diversion, or the Violin explained* (1693) apparently has the distinction of being the first extant violin tutor in any language.[119] Rejecting both the older example of Matteis, who 'rested his instrument against his short ribbs',[120] and the newer chin-on technique, Lenton considered that 'the best way of commanding the instrument will be to place it something higher than your Breast'.[121]

Christopher Simpson's instructions (1659) for holding and using a viol bow (including gracing 'by the bow') were echoed by both Playford and Mace[122] and seem to have been regarded as models through the remainder of the century. Comparably detailed information for violin bowing is harder to find. Lenton scarcely gives any on the grounds that 'The humours of Masters

being very Various . . . what is approved by one would be condemned by another',[123] but the instructions he does give match
the Rule of the Down Bow, and include the characteristically
French [ꜰᵛꜰ|ꜰ] for triple time.[124] The 'bipedalian' bow used by
Matteis North considered 'very long' and 'as for a base violl',[125]
but Talbot gives two feet as the 'usual length of the Consort
Bow' (in line with Lenton's view that 'your Bow be as long as
your Instrument') and an extra two or three inches as the 'length
of the Bow for Solo's or Sonata's'.[126] Lenton recommends that
the elbow is held no higher 'than necessity requires' and
describes a bow grip with the thumb on the hair at the frog,[127]
despite North's assertion that Matteis had 'taught the English to
hold the bow by the wood onely and not to touch the hair,
which was no small reformation'.[128]

Certainly, Matteis's playing seems to have epitomized the
refinement that well-modulated bowing could achieve; in 1674
Evelyn

> heard that stupendious Violin Signor *Nicholao* . . . whom cer-
> tainly never mortal man Exceeded on that Instrument: he had a
> stroak so sweete, & made it speake like the Voice of a man; &
> when he pleased, like a Consort of severall Instruments . . .[129]

These expressive skills and vocal qualities bring us to the
matter of vibrato. It was doubtless with Matteis again in mind
that North wrote:

> The Italians have brought the bow to an high perfection, so that
> nothing of their playing is so difficult as the *arcata* or long bow,
> with which they will begin a long note, clear, without rubb, and
> draw it forth swelling lowder and lowder, and at the ackme take a
> slow waiver; not [a] trill to break the sound or mix 2 notes, but as
> if the bird sat at the end of a spring [and] as she sang the spring
> waived her up and downe, or as if the wind that brought the sound
> shaked, or a small bell were struck and the sound continuing
> waived to and againe – so would I express what is justly not to be
> shewn but to the ear by an exquisite hand.[130]

This form of vibrato was evidently quite new to English players at the time, and even *c*1715–20 North was writing of 'the
late invention they call a wrist-shake'.[131] Its function was, he

wrote, 'that the sound may waive, but not stopp or vary its tone'
(i.e. pitch). The point is amplified elsewhere:

> It is rarely observed, but lett it pass for a truth upon my word, that
> the greatest elegance of the finest voices is the prolation of a
> clear plain sound. And I may add, that in voice or instrument
> (where the hand draws the sound) it is the most difficult part to
> performe . . .
>
> Therefore as to the *pratique*, I would have a voice or hand
> taught, first to prolate a long, true steddy and strong sound . . . to
> superinduce [on a plain note] a gentle slow wavering, not into a
> trill, upon the swelling the note; such as trumpetts use, as if the
> instrument were a litle shaken with the wind of its owne sound,
> but not so as to vary the tone [i.e. pitch], which must be religiously
> held to its place, like a pillar on its base, without the least loss of
> the accord. This waving of a note is not to be described, but by
> example. But as wee often use odd similes to express our meaning
> and help the imagination, take these images of sound by lines,
> which represent the humour of sound judiciously mannaged:

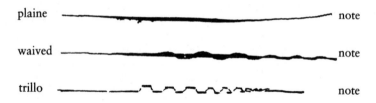

> The latter is the trill, which, as you see, breaking the tone [i.e.
> pitch] and mixing with another, is dangerous for a scollar to medle
> with, till he hath the mastery of the sound, else it will make him
> apt to loose the principall tone: and that spoiles all.[132]

Vibrato was clearly regarded as an ornament (or grace), and
one especially associated in instrumental use with the violin:

> There is another sort of trill, which varyeth not the tone, but
> sounds as if the air shakt, as when an upright tree plays a litle in
> the air. Few instruments [have it] except the violin, upon which it
> is used to perfection. The trumpet hath it also, and the viol in some
> degree; the rowl of the finger without stop, gives it upon the violin,
> but upon the viol gentle touches very neer the stop, but that is not
> so perfect as the other. It is rather a soft and lowd then a trill, but

extraordinary gratefull, and setts off a plaine tone to a wonder as may be heard but not described.[133]

The analogous form of vibrato for woodwind instruments is the finger-vibrato, found in Hudgebut's *Vade mecum* (1679), Salter's *Genteel Companion* (1683) and *The Compleat Flute-Master* (1695), where it is called 'an open shake or sweetning', achieved by 'shaking your finger over the half hole immidiately below yᵉ note to be sweetned ending with it off'.[134]

A different form of vibrato, explicitly called for in Purcell's music as a special effect, is the easily misinterpreted *tremolo* (𝅘𝅥𝅯𝅘𝅥𝅯𝅘𝅥𝅯), which occurs in writing both for bowed strings and for voices (Example 4), and which 'resembles the shaking stop of an organ'.[135] For string players, the 'Italians *tremolo*', probably learnt from Matteis, was not a *tremolando* (𝅘𝅥) but a bow

EX. 4 Henry Purcell: *King Arthur, or the British Worthy* (z 628)

EX. 4a Prelude while the Cold Genius rises (z 628/20a), bars 1–3

EX. 4b 'What power art thou' (z 628/20b), bars 1–5

EX.   4c   'See, we assemble thy revels to hold' (z 628/24b), bars 1–3

vibrato made by playing an even rhythm 'with the same bow, but distinguishing the notes' (♩♩♩♩).[136] For voices it was presumably an equivalent gentle re-articulation (from the diaphragm or throat) or rhythmic pulsation, on a single pitch and syllable. A further occurrence of 'Tremulo' (but without its symbol) seems to have attracted little attention: the canzona for flat trumpets that concludes the Funeral Music for Queen Mary (1695) appears as in Example 5 in Oxford, Oriel College (MS U a 37). Here a breath vibrato in all parts is surely implied for groups of repeated notes (starting ♩ ♩ ♩ ♩), the first notes tongued, the remainder articulated from the diaphragm or throat.

EX. 5 Henry Purcell: Canzona from the Music for Queen Mary's Funeral (z 860/2), bars 1–8

Tremulo

Early in 1690 Purcell found himself in a position to draw on an orchestra that had expanded from a string group, with occasional 'flutes' (recorders)[137] and on just one brief occasion a single oboe,[138] to one which could normally include both oboes and trumpet(s). Clearly trumpet playing had reached a new level of sophistication:

> While the company is at table the hautboys and trumpets play successively. Mr Showers [Shore] hath taught the latter of late years to sound with all the softness imaginable.[139]

This 'softness' was no doubt a principal reason for the trumpets' gaining admission to an orchestral context, and the development of the 'flat' trumpet, which Purcell called on twice in his last year or so, was itself a reflection of a new sophistication.

This instrument, by means of a double-slide which draws back towards the player's head (rather than away from it, as on the trombone), could play certain 'exotick notes'[140] and thus in minor ('flat') keys, 'it being a thing formerly thought impossible upon an instrument designed for a sharp [major] key'.[141] It has even been argued that these 'flat trumpets were used routinely in the English orchestra of the Purcell period', in normal ('sharp') trumpet music,[142] thereby facilitating quick changes – from C to D tuning (or *vice versa*) as in all four semi-operas – or obviating any such necessity – as in *The Libertine* where only some of the writing is obviously for flat trumpets. More important, the occasional prominent non-harmonic note such as that marked with an asterisk in Example 6 would cease to be problematic.[143]

EX.   6   Henry Purcell: 'Hail! Bright Cecilia!' (z 328/11b), bars 71–3

Purcell's earliest notated kettle-drum parts are those of *The Fairy Queen* (1692), and, while it is possible that the earlier use of trumpets implies the presence of drums too, Purcell's writing is rarely so formulaic or so simple harmonically for a part to have been easily improvised. (The notion that kettle-drums would have played in the March and Canzona for flat trumpets at Queen Mary's funeral cannot be sustained, but it seems that the March was performed in procession to the sound of side drums.[144])

The possibility of unnotated parts, or rather of unspecified instruments, arises in several further cases. Trumpet writing from the last year and a half or so of the composer's life almost always lacks a second trumpet part, which could perhaps be merely a notational quirk of the surviving sources.[145] Within works which use oboes, there are also occasional ambiguities over their possible involvement in string-only movements; but certainly the addition of oboes to the string writing of, for example, *Dido and Aeneas* is gratuitous and anachronistic. Similarly, the appearance of a bassoon (with an independent part) in *Dioclesian* (1690) – together with a 'tenor hautboy' – may mark Purcell's first use of the instrument[146] and its first occurrence in an English score[147] but should not be taken to imply its presence alongside oboes on every occasion, least of all perhaps in non-orchestral movements.

These woodwind instruments would have been of the new 'Baroque' type developed in France in the 1650s and 1660s and evidently first heard in England in 1673.[148] The players, too, were mostly from France: the group of five 'Hooboys that were in Holland' with William III in 1691 consisted of George Sutton (the first known English player) and four Frenchmen, among them François Le Riche and Paisible's 'good friend, Peter Bressan, the instrument maker'.[149] It was Le Riche who supplied Talbot with a tablature of oboe fingerings and also, quite probably, the 'French hautbois' which Talbot measured; the oboe itself was by Bressan (1663–1731), as were other woodwind instruments Talbot inspected. At least thirty-six recorders and three flutes by this maker are known to survive, and a recent tentative suggestion that the 'Galpin' oboe (now in the Bate Collection, Oxford[150]) could be an early instrument of his[151] leads directly to discussion of a central issue in Purcellian performance practice: that of pitch.

Practically all Purcell's large-scale compositions from 1690 onward make use of the oboe. (The instrument was presumably still unavailable in 1694 in Dublin where 'Great Parent, Hail!' was first performed, and, for the *Te Deum* and *Jubilate*, first heard at St Bride's, Fleet Street, later the same year, it may have been ruled out by an incompatible organ pitch or by the players' Catholicism.) As there is no reason to believe that the oboe was treated as a transposing instrument, it follows that the pitch standard for these works would have been dictated by the new 'French' woodwind instruments. Whatever its precise origin, the 'Galpin' oboe seems to be a unique survival from the seventeenth century and is generally agreed to date from the 1680s or 1690s and to play at approximately $a' = 392$,[152] a well-documented contemporary 'French' pitch. It is certainly the longest instrument known, together with one of a similar date by Naust which plays at the same pitch (more or less exactly an equal tone beneath $a' = 440$). Furthermore, although Talbot's Bressan was shorter, the difference is mainly in the bell and the sounding length does not suggest that the pitch was different; in any event, 'it is likely that it played at something considerably lower than the usual "Baroque" standard of the present'[153] ($a' = 415$).

Low pitches ($a' = 390$–98) were by no means exclusive to France and are found both where the influence of the new French woodwind instruments was felt (as in some German circles) and also, for example, in Rome, quite independently. Nor were they confined to the seventeenth century: Brook Taylor's calculations (1713) reliably show that his harpsichord sounded just above $a' = 390$ or even lower,[154] and later still Robert Smith (1749) reported that the 1708 organ of Trinity College, Cambridge (by Bernard Smith and Christopher Shrider), stood at approximately $a' = 393$, having at some stage been lowered (by a tone?) 'to the Roman pitch, as I judge by its agreement with that of the pitch-pipes made above 30 years ago'.[155] And at a time when pitches in the region of $a' = 420$–26 may have become reasonably standard, William Tansur (1746) observed that 'our new *Consort-Pitch* is more fitter for *Vocal Performance* than the *old Consort Pitch*, which is half a *Tone* lower'.[156] This eighteenth-century evidence points to an earlier 'consort pitch' below $a' = 400$. In practice, the low French-influenced standard seems to have risen slowly in the early years of the new century[157] and a fascinating letter (dated January 1712) from a French oboist working in London reveals that a pitch almost a quarter of a tone higher than at the opera in Paris was by then in use: this suggests a level of $a' = 400$–406,[158] which matches several instruments both by Bressan and by Thomas Stanesby senior (c1668–1734). It must be emphasized, though, that the evidence for this slightly higher 'low' pitch seems to come entirely from after Purcell's death.[159] For a precise definition of orchestral pitch in the 1690s, then, there seems to be no more tangible evidence than that of the 'Galpin' oboe, corroborated by Talbot's measurements of a Bressan oboe. (And, as we shall see, written vocal ranges support the idea that the advent of such instruments caused a substantial shift in orchestral pitch.) For clues about church pitch(es), we must turn first to organs.

From extant pipework and recorded measurements of pipes it can be shown that (in terms of 'quire pitch') four important organs built in the 1660s, at Exeter, Gloucester and Worcester Cathedrals and at New College, Oxford, played at levels from roughly $a' = 440$ to a semitone higher.[160] This 'high' pitch, most probably echoing a pre-Commonwealth standard, came to be regarded as too high for convenience, and both Smith and Harris are known to have lowered the pitch of older instruments: in the 1670s Smith was responsible 'for taking half a note lower the Organ in ye Chappell' at Whitehall,[161] and in 1684 he undertook 'to take down sink and Reduce the said halfe note throughout the whole Organ' at Canterbury, too,[162] while, for his part, Harris agreed with Magdalen College, Oxford, in 1690 to 'alter the pitch of the said organs half a note lower than they now are', and again, significantly, with New College in 1713 'to make ye Organ one note lower'.[163] In general, Harris seems to have favoured a standard lower than Smith's, one which may, incidentally, be seen as an important antecedent of the more familiar mid-eighteenth-century 'consort' pitch (see above). But the majority of Purcell's church music was tailor-made either for Whitehall Chapel or for Westminster Abbey, and he would almost certainly have regarded the pitch of Smith's organs as normal and appropriate. This has often been described as 'high',[164] yet in 1847 Sutton observed that 'Schmidts's Organs were generally below concert pitch, and great numbers have been altered by cutting the pipes'.[165] The better documented instruments by Smith suggest a norm of approximately $a' = 442$ (see Table 3).[166]

If organs and woodwind instruments can provide some firm evidence of pitch standards, it is clearly for vocal music that an understanding of pitch is most critical. And vocal ranges

TABLE 3
Approximate pitches of organs by Bernard Smith and Renatus
Harris*

Bernard Smith	1683–7	London, Temple Church	$a' = 442$
	1690	Hampton Court	$a' = 442$
	[1690	London, St Mary at Hill	'Common Church']
	1708	Cambridge, Trinity College	$a' = 442$
Renatus Harris	1670	Newcastle, St Nicholas	$a' = 429$
	(?) 1689	Norwich Cathedral	$a' = 427$
	1696	London, St Andrew's, Undershaft	$a' = 428$

Talbot's (slightly ambiguous) organ-pipe measurements, which come
perhaps from the St Paul's Cathedral instrument by Smith (1694–9),
may suggest a pitch of $a' = 428$–37, intermediate between these two.
(See Peter Williams, 'The First English Organ Treatise', *The Organ*,
xliv (1964), 20–22, 27–9, 32.)

* This table is based primarily on the data given in Alexander J. Ellis, 'On the
History of Musical Pitch', *Journal of The Society of Arts*, 5 March 1880,
293–336, but presents only the most reliable of the relevant measurements and
calculations found there.

themselves can in turn add to this understanding. Table 4 shows
the choral ranges of datable works by Purcell. The similarity of
(a) and (b) suggests that the string group at the Chapel Royal
tuned to the organ. Though the wider ranges of the secular
works make exact comparisons with the anthems difficult, (c),
despite its low bass notes, seems overall to imply a very similar
(or perhaps a slightly lower) pitch standard. The clearest point
to emerge is that the presence of woodwind instruments from
1690 onwards must have required strings to play at a substantially lower pitch – in the region of a tone lower – than formerly.
Confirmation of this shift of pitch standard is to be found in
Purcell's writing for William Turner, practically the only solo
singer named in works from both before and after the introduction of oboes; the later writing lies exactly a tone higher.[167] The
shift also offers an explanation for Gostling's apparent loss of
low notes around this time.[168]

TABLE 4

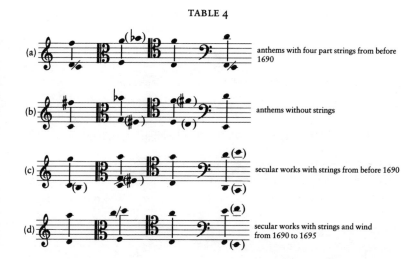

(a)   anthems with four part strings from before 1690

(b)   anthems without strings

(c)   secular works with strings from before 1690

(d)   secular works with strings and wind from 1690 to 1695

In broad terms, we may be reasonably confident that there are at least two pitch standards implicit in Purcell's music: an organ pitch very close to modern pitch and, from 1690 onward, an orchestral pitch the best part of a tone beneath it. (The higher and lower organ pitches also in use may not have influenced his compositional practice.) Before 1690 orchestras may normally have played either at (Smith's) 'organ' pitch, as did the strings at the Chapel Royal, or possibly somewhat lower, perhaps at the pitch used by Harris.

With this framework in mind we are in a better position to understand the types of voice for which Purcell wrote. Solos for soprano rarely rise higher than their choral counterparts, and then only by a step, and never in a way that would be likely to jeopardize either tonal or verbal delivery. Bass solos, whether or not intended for 'That stupendious Base' John Gostling,[169] tend to have much wider ranges and often require an agility not always associated with basses (Example 7). Solo writing for tenor is comparatively rare, and it is the much misunderstood Purcellian countertenor that merits most attention here.

The 1680s and 1690s seem to mark an historical mid-way point in the evolution of the countertenor, with the emergence of the later, and indeed current, falsettist countertenor overlapping

EX. 7a Henry Purcell: 'I will give Thanks unto Thee, O Lord' (z 20/10), bars 244–6

as for the proud He be-hold-eth them a - far off.

EX. 7b Henry Purcell: 'Hail! Bright Cecilia!' (z 328/2a), bars 1–6

Hail! Hail_____ bright Ce - ci - lia, Hail! Hail_____

bright Ce - ci - lia, Hail! Hail!

with the glorious last years of an earlier tradition in which – contrary to popular belief – the voice was, in modern terms, essentially a (high) tenor.[170] In his solo writing Purcell appears to differentiate between the two types, while his choral parts tend to amalgamate them. The generally quite high tessitura of these choral lines often suggests falsetto singing, but the frequent low phrases within them surely demand some use of chest voice (Example 8).

While a choral texture helps to disguise any necessary mixing of techniques, a solo context is much less accommodating. Consequently most of Purcell's solo writing divides fairly clearly into high or low parts. Most are low and, after allowances for any differences of pitch standard, have every appearance of being suited to today's (high) tenors – and of being implausibly low for even the most accomplished of today's (falsettist) counter-tenors. Example 9 gives just a few of the many conspicuously low-lying phrases.

By writing in a higher clef than usual (C2 rather than C3) and by using an exceptional designation ('High Contra tenor for Mr Howel'), Purcell himself seems to be differentiating the upper

EX. 8a   Henry Purcell: *Funeral Sentences*, second working (z 17b), bars 49–51

de - li-ver us not in - to the bit - ter pains of e - ter - nal death.

EX. 8b   Henry Purcell: 'Bow Down Thine Ear, O Lord' (z 11/6), bars 98–101

and   will praise   thy   name   for   e - ver - more,

EX. 8c   Henry Purcell: *Dido and Aeneas* (z 626/7b), bars 65–72

Cu - pids strew your paths with flowers,   Ga - ther'd from E - ly - sian bowers.

EX. 8d   Henry Purcell: *Dido and Aeneas* (z 626/27), bars 11–12

Haste, haste to   town,   haste, haste to town,

EX. 8e   Henry Purcell: 'Hail! Bright Cecilia!' (z 328/5), bars 30–31

made   up   of   va   -   rious parts,

part of the duet 'Hark! hark! each Tree' ('Hail! Bright Cecilia!') from these normal 'low' countertenor solos (Example 10).[171] In the duet 'Sound the trumpet' ('Come Ye Sons of Art', 1694), where the text justifies both countertenors singing at the very tops of their voices, Purcell arguably parades the two types side by side: the written ranges lie a third apart ($c\#'-e''$ and $a-b'$ plus a single brief $c\#''$). Evelyn apparently chose to describe the higher type not as a countertenor at all but as a 'treble':

> After supper, came in the famous Trebble *Mr. Abel* newly return'd from *Italy*, & indeede I never heard a more excellent voice, one would have sworne it had ben a Womans it was so high, & so well & skillfully manag'd . . .[172]

(Purcell's writing in the 1687 welcome song for James II, 'Sound the Trumpet', takes Abell up to written b' and down only to a, while the song 'Aloud proclaim', 'set and sung by Mr. Abell' himself and published in 1702, rises to a d'', a sounding difference of perhaps only a semitone.)

But are there reasons of a less subjective nature for viewing so much of Purcell's countertenor writing as not having been intended for falsettists? (This of course begs the question of exactly what reasons there may be, apart from the word's subsequent connotations, for taking the still conventional opposite view.) Although Burney's later testimony may not be wholly reliable, he felt confident to write that William Turner 'was sworn in gentleman of the Royal Chapel 1669, as a countertenor singer, his voice settling to that pitch; a circumstance which so seldom happens, naturally, that if it be cultivated the possessor is sure of employment';[173] from a later eighteenth-century perspective a non-falsettist countertenor was indeed a rarity. Certainly the oft-repeated notion that Purcell himself was a (falsettist) countertenor who also sang bass does not stand up to scrutiny. According to an account in *The Gentleman's Journal*, the second stanza (''Tis Nature's voice') of 'Hail! Bright Cecilia!' 'was sung with incredible Graces by Mr. *Purcell* himself';[174] did he actually sing, or merely compose, the ornamentation? Despite the presence of Mr Pate's name against the line in the autograph score,[175] Purcell probably really did sing this

EX. 9a Henry Purcell: 'O Lord', first working of the second verse (z 13a), bars 13–17

EX. 9b Henry Purcell: *King Arthur* (z 628/30bc), bars 60–69

EX. 9c Henry Purcell: 'Hail! Bright Cecilia!' (z 328/4), bars 27–9

EX. 9d Henry Purcell: 'Who Can from Joy Refrain?' A Birthday Song for the Duke of Gloucester (z 342/7), bars 9–13

EX. 10   Henry Purcell: 'Hail! Bright Cecilia!' (z 328/3b), bars
136–43

When   to   the Thra - cian lyre,   with   lea - fy wings they

flew, ———————————————————— with lea - fy they flew,

exceptionally florid (low) countertenor solo at its first performance (to his own accompaniment?) in 1692.[176] But his place
among the basses in the 1685 coronation procession was surely
a matter of pure convenience, 'simply to make up a complete
file';[177] indeed, the last file of 'basses' consisted of four senior
musicians, Blagrave, Staggins, Blow and Child.[178] On the other
hand, the case of Mr Pordage, whom Evelyn recorded as singing
'with an excellent voice both Treble and Base' in 1685[179] may
well be an exception – that is, unless Evelyn simply meant that
Pordage had an unusually wide vocal range. Interestingly, it is
not the term 'countertenor' but 'treble' that is again being used
to describe what may have been falsetto singing, and indeed
Locke had earlier associated the use of 'Mens feigned Voices'
with 'superiour Parts' ordinarily sung by boys.[180] In either case,
the notion of countertenor/bass interchangeability being a
common occurrence cannot be sustained.

If the (low) countertenor corresponded to today's (high) tenor,
what was the nature of the tenor voice? The modest upper limits
of Purcell's tenor parts, and perhaps also the relative scarcity of
solo writing for that voice, imply in turn that it was thought
of as a more baritonal 'second' tenor rather than as an equivalent of the modern tenor. But although Reggio had 'a perfect
good tenor & base &c',[181] and John Bowman, Purcell's favourite high bass, may have also sung a tenor part in *King Arthur*,[182]
tenor and countertenor voices, interestingly enough, seem generally to have enjoyed a much closer relationship than bass and
tenor.[183] In an affidavit of 1664 Thomas Richardson refers to

'the next place of a lay tenor or counter tenor that shall be voyd', and the following year Andrew Carter was sworn in as a Gentleman of the Chapel Royal 'to come into pay in [*sic*] the next tenor or counter tenor's place shalbe voyde'.[184] These may have been purely administrative manoeuvres, but they are wholly exceptional in mentioning two voice types. (In practice, both Carter and Richardson, who is elsewhere listed as a countertenor, evidently succeeded countertenors.[185]) Thomas Heywood, who had entered the Chapel Royal in 1678 'in place of Cha: Husbands', a countertenor,[186] was listed among the countertenors in the 1685 coronation procession,[187] although at the same time he held a place as tenor in the Private Musick (alongside Abell, Turner, Gostling and Bowman).[188]

The case for believing countertenor and tenor voices to have been almost indistinguishable on occasion is further strengthened by the evidence of several musical sources. In an early manuscript source of Purcell's 1687 Welcome Song for King James the name [Anthony] Robert appears against a tenor solo,[189] while in three other works from the 1690s the same singer is allocated (low) countertenor parts. (Ironically, the tenor solo may well in practice have been the highest of these parts.) The actor-singer John Pate is known to have sung both a tenor role (Kalib) in *The Indian Emperor* in 1692 and two countertenor roles (Mopsa and Summer) in the 1693 revival of *The Fairy Queen*. Furthermore, in Purcell's autograph score of 'Hail! Bright Cecilia!' Pate's name is found against not only ''Tis Nature's voice' (a countertenor solo) but also the tenor part of a brief duet within the opening chorus.[190] (It may be worth pointing out that Pate's singing of the roles of Kalib 'in the shape of a Woman' and of the rustic Mopsa 'in Woman's habit' – and subsequently of 'a Lusty Strapping Middle ag'd Widdow all in Mourning' – no more demands the use of falsetto than does the role of the Sorceress in *Dido and Aeneas* when taken by a man.[191]) 'Celebrate this Festival' (1693), similarly, contains both a countertenor and a tenor solo evidently sung by the French-born Alexander Damascene; in four other works by Purcell Damascene sang countertenor solos. Of all Purcell's countertenor soloists the most frequently named is John Freeman; an isolated tenor part sung by him in 1694 (as St George) in the duet 'Genius of England' from *Don Quixote* part II lies no lower than many of his other solos and is identical in range with three sung by him the following year in *The Indian Queen*.[192] (He was also named as a tenor in Draghi's 1687 St Cecilia's Day Ode.) This tenor/countertenor connection continued throughout Purcell's lifetime: John Church, who as a 19- or 20-year-old took a tenor role (Second Aerial Spirit) in *The Indian Queen* (1695), sang as a countertenor later the same year in a *Te Deum* by Blow and again in Clarke's 'A Song on New Year's Day 1706'.[193]

In at least one respect the comparison of the (low) counter-tenor with today's tenor is perhaps misleading: the physical stamina and sheer power that enable some of today's singers to project successfully over a symphony orchestra are never demanded by Purcell's music. Indeed, a big voice was sometimes considered a liability: after listening to a French boy with 'a delicate voice', Evelyn

> also heard Mrs Packer (daughter to my old friend) sing before his Majestie & the Duke privately, That stupendious Base *Gosling*, accompanying her, but hers was so lowd, as tooke away much of the sweetnesse; certainly never woman had a stronger, or better [voice] could she possibly have govern'd it: She would do rarely in a large Church among the Nunns.[194]

Many singers specialized in this 'private' singing:[195] Arabella Hunt, who possessed a voice 'like the pipe of a bullfinch',[196] moved exclusively in Court circles and among her wealthy friends, never appearing on the public stage.[197] For women, this was largely a matter of social decorum, but even in private there were strict codes of behaviour that affected performance. Evelyn admired his daughter Mary's poise:

> the sweetnesse of her voice, and manegement of it, adding such an agreablenesse to her Countenance, without any constraint and concerne, that when she sung, it was as charming to the Eye, as to the Eare . . . [198]

In the louder singing that theatres required, such facial control was more difficult to maintain, and when in *King Arthur* that 'capital, and admired Performer' Mrs Butler 'in the person of

Cupid' chose to ignore stage convention and 'turne her face
to the scean, and her back to the theater', North ascribed the
admirable results ('even beyond any thing I ever heard upon
the English stage') 'to nothing so much as the liberty she had of
concealing her face, which she could not endure should be so
contorted as is necessary to sound well, before her gallants, or at
least her envious sex'.[199]

An inhibited delivery may well have been a common failing
among female singers; in North's view 'The English have generally voices good enough, tho' not up to the pitch of warmer
countreys', 'But come into the theater or musick-meeting, and
you shall have a woman sing like a mouse in a cheese, scarce to
be heard, and for the most part her teeth shutt.'[200] He was
also critical of singing masters who 'begin to teach with tunes,
whereas they should begin with pronunciation'.[201]

In the theatres, actor-singers performed alongside more
specialist singers. The leading actress of her day, also admired
for her singing, was Mrs Bracegirdle, and it was a mad-song by
Eccles 'so incomparably well sung, and acted' by her that was
the inspiration for Purcell's song upon 'Mrs Bracegirdle Singing
(I burn &c) in ye play of Don Quixote'.[202] Indeed, Dryden's
verdict on the music in *The Richmond Heiress* (1693) was that
Mrs Bracegirdle and Thomas Doggett 'sung better than Redding
and Mrs Ayloff, whose trade it was'.[203] Mrs Butler, Purcell's leading soprano for three years from 1689, similarly 'prov'd not
only a good Actress, but was allow'd, in those Days, to sing
and dance to great Perfection'.[204] More remarkable still was the
actress-singer for whom Purcell wrote so many fine soprano
songs during the last eight months of his life: Miss Cross claimed
to be only 12 years old in 1695 and was in any case no more
than 14.[205] (The other singers in the company were the countertenor Freeman and the bass Leveridge, both in their 20s, and the
boy Jemmy Bowen.)

In contrast to Bracegirdle, Butler and Cross, Mrs Ayliff was
primarily a singer, though she did occasionally take acting
roles.[206] Possibly the finest of Purcell's sopranos (*pace* Dryden),
she is also the only female singer named in the odes: she sang
'Thou tun'st this world' in 'Hail! Bright Cecilia!' and both a solo

and a duet (with 'the Boy') in 'Celebrate this Festival'. Of the song 'Ah me! to many deaths decreed', 'set by *Mr. Purcell* the *Italian* way' in Crowne's *Regulus* (1692), *The Gentleman's Journal* wrote: 'had you heard it sung by Mrs *Ayliff* you would have own'd that there is no pleasure like that which good Notes, when so divinely sung, can create'.[207]

While there have always been those who 'despair of ever having as good Voices among us, as they have in *Italy*',[208] 'the *Italian* way' of singing was certainly cultivated by many. Reggio, who settled in London in 1664, taught singing there for over twenty years (young Mary Evelyn was one of his pupils[209]), but, sadly, there are no known extant copies of his *The Art of Singing* (*c*1678). The castrato Siface (Giovanni Francesco Grossi), who 'came over from Rome, esteemed one of the best voices in *Italy*',[210] made quite an impression on London society, although he seems to have spent just five months in England (in 1687). His 'holding out & delicatenesse in extending & loosing a note with that incomparable softnesse, & sweetenesse' Evelyn found admirable,[211] while Tosi commented that, although he had 'the most singular Beauty' of voice, his 'Manner of Singing was remarkably plain [unembellished], consisting particularly in the *Messa di Voce*, the putting forth his Voice, and the Expression'.[212] Tosi was himself a castrato, who arrived in London in 1692 and soon began giving weekly concerts and teaching singing;[213] his use of *rubato* ('The Breaking and yet Keeping Time') particularly impressed North,[214] and his 'Observations on the Florid Song', dedicated to the Earl of Peterborough, is perhaps the single most valuable treatise on mid-Baroque Italian vocal style. But then, as now, the best way of assimilating an Italian style of singing was to visit Italy. John Abell was 'newly return'd from Italy' when Evelyn heard him in 1682[215] (and after the revolution he spent more than a decade abroad). Three years later Evelyn was 'invited to heare that celebrated voice of Mr. *Pordage*, newly come from *Rome*',[216] and later still, in 1698, he 'dined at Mr Pepyss, where I heard that rare Voice of Mr. *Pate*, who was lately come from *Italy*, reputed the most excellent singer, ever England had: he sang severall compositions of the last Mr. Pursal, esteemed the best composer of any Englishman hitherto'.[217]

Where modern practice for large-scale vocal works is to use the minimum practicable number of soloists, Purcell clearly revelled in opportunities to display as many different voices as possible – in 'Hail! Bright Cecilia!' at least a dozen, half of them countertenors, and in 'Celebrate this Festival' a similar number. (Most, if not all, probably sang in the choruses, too.) Almost invariably, these will have been close colleagues whose voices he knew intimately.[218] Certainly Purcell understood better than anyone that 'the compass of a good tone, and extent in the scale, are very different',[219] and the two versions of 'You twice ten hundred deities' (*The Indian Queen*) show the lengths to which he could go to accommodate different singers.[220] It is hardly surprising therefore that, apart from an occasional 'loud' or 'soft', the vocal music generally lacks expressive directions.[221] Several ornaments familiar from keyboard practice – the shake (✐), beat (✝), forefall (╱) and backfall (╲) – were part of a singer's vocabulary too, and their signs appear from time to time in the sources, but, although Purcell's vocal lines incorporate much ornamentation, further embellishment would often have been added as a matter of course. (The composer's own G minor version of 'If music be the food of love' (setting 1) reveals a particular fondness for backfalls, but interestingly this may pre-date the plainer, A minor, version (Example 11).[222]) It is difficult to gauge the exact relevance to Purcell's music of Caccini's instructions given in translation in all editions of Playford's *Brief Introduction to the Skill of Musick* from 1664 to 1694 and summarized in the *Synopsis of Vocal Musick* (1680):

> An Exclamation is a slacking of the voice to reinforce it afterwards . . . A Trillo is a shaking of the Uvula on the Throat in one Sound or Note, as the Gruppo is in two Sounds or Notes, the one being by one degree higher than the other, and are commonly used in cadences and closes. These Ornaments are not to be used in Airy Songs . . . but in Passionate Musick, wherein . . . the ordinary measure of Time is here less regarded, for many times is the value of the Notes made less by half, and sometimes more, according to the conceit of the words, with a graceful neglect.[223]

EX. 11 Henry Purcell: 'If music be the food of love' (z 379c), bars
14–18

The Gentleman's
Journal,
June 1692 (p. 27)

Your eyes, your mien, your tongue de-clare That

Comes Amoris IV,
1693 (p. 15)

you are mu - sic— ev' - ry - where

(Caccini's *trillo* was eventually replaced in Playford's 1697 edition: 'Of the TRILL or SHAKE, Directions for learning it is only this, To move your Voice easily upon one Syllable the distance of a Note . . . SLOW, then *faster* by degrees.'[224])

A common failing among those 'who court a voice' was that 'in learning they have cheif regard to ornaments, such as are called graces, and pretty devisions, which makes them neglect the art of sounding full and true, and that onely renders a voice musicall'.[225] The young Jemmy Bowen was presumably well past this stage when he sang as a boy for Purcell:

> He, when practising a Song set by Mr. *Purcell*, some of the Music told him to grace and run a Division in such a Place. *O let him alone*, said Mr. *Purcell*; *he will grace it more naturally than you, or I, can teach him.*[226]

(By 1698 Bowen was singing as a countertenor and one can only guess at his age. Purcell's own voice seems to have broken relatively early, when he was 13 or 14; Blow was evidently 15 and Humfrey 17, while in France around the same time Bacilly observed that the change 'usually comes about between the ages of fifteen and twenty in males'.[227])

Most of Purcell's male soloists also sang as members of the

Chapel Royal. At full strength this choir, which sang not only for services but in the various Court odes, consisted of ten or twelve boys and between twenty and thirty men.[228] But these numbers are perhaps deceptive and ignore in particular a rota system for the Gentlemen in operation on 'working days'.[229] A more typical strength for a Sunday or major feast day would perhaps have been eight or ten boys and fifteen to twenty men, facing each other in Decani and Cantoris stalls.[230] Westminster Abbey supported eight 'Quiristers' and twelve or sixteen 'Quire-men',[231] and a reduced section in the opening chorus of 'Hail! Bright Cecilia!' for '4 trebles' and two of each other part may imply a similar body of twenty or more singers. But undoubt-edly in humbler institutions and on lesser occasions choirs would often have been smaller still: in the early 1670s Mace was lamenting the fact that 'in most [*cathedrall*] *Quires* there is but allotted *One Man to a Part*'.[232] Furthermore, some works often assumed to be choral – notably Purcell's two Latin psalm set-tings, '*Beati omnes*' and '*Jehovah, quam multi sunt hostes mei*' – were surely intended as vocal chamber music, for private or devotional rather than church performance, and thus by one voice to a part.[233]

If I have chosen to end this survey of issues of Purcellian performance practice with a discussion of vocal matters, it is with these that most performers of Purcell's music must nor-mally begin. Yet for the most part scholars and performers have scarcely begun to address the subject, partly perhaps because of a natural scepticism that anything of substance awaits discovery. Of course, none of the practical issues touched on in this chapter will on their own lead us to the heart of Purcell's music, but cumulatively the fragments of information that have come down to us can enable performances to develop from a starting-point nearer to that of the close circle of professional musicians for whom Purcell wrote. And – at least in my own view – a deeper understanding of the supreme craftsmanship which informs his work will almost inevitably assist today's performers in releas-ing the essence of Purcell's glorious music to the full.

NOTES

1   For Roger North's observations on the use of dotted rhythms ('tho Not Expres't') to give 'a life and spirit' to passages written 'plaine', see *Works II*, v, xiii.

2   See Purcell's address 'To the Reader' in the *Sonnata's of III Parts* (1683), his discussion 'of the Moods, or Proportions of the Time or Measure of Notes' in Chapter IX of *An Introduction to the Skill of Musick* (London, 12/1694), and the 'Instructions for Learners' in *The Harpsichord Master* (1697). See also Klaus Miehling, 'Das Tempo bei Henry Purcell', *Basler Jahrbuch für historische Musikpraxis*, xv (1991), 117–47.

3   See W. Barclay Squire, 'Purcell as Theorist', *Sammelbände der Internationalen Musik-Gesellschaft*, vi (1904/5), 521–67.

4   Evidently 'wholly *Compos'd*' in 1672; see Thomas Mace, *Musick's Monument* (London, 1676), 45.

5   John Wilson, ed., *Roger North on Music* (London, 1959), xxii; hereinafter cited as *North I*.

6   Robert Unwin, ' "An English Writer on Music": James Talbot 1664–1708', *Galpin Society Journal*, xl (1987), 59.

7   *Sonnata's of III Parts* (1683), Preface.

8   Andrew Ashbee, *Records of English Court Music* (Snodland, 1986–1993), I, 69–70. At an early stage Dallam made 'an Addition to the said Organ and a new Stopp with Conveyances and another sett of keyes'.

9   Peter Williams, *A New History of the Organ* (London, 1980), 135. In 1687 Purcell claimed that 'The organ is at present so out of repair that to cleanse, tune and put in good order will cost £40 . . .' J. A. Westrup, *Purcell* (London, 1937; rev. 4/1980), 57.

10 J. A. Westrup, op. cit., 79–80, and James Boeringer, *Organa Britannica*, (Lewisburg/London/Toronto, 1989), III, 256–9.

11 Andrew Ashbee, op. cit., V, 273, 276. In 1685 'A little Organ for the Kings Choir' was placed in a gallery overlooking the Abbey's high altar on the south side (see the 'Ground-Plot' given in Francis Sandford, *The History of the Coronation of James II and Queen Mary* (London, 1687)).

12 See Stephen Bicknell, 'English Organ-Building 1642–1685', *Journal of the British Institute of Organ Studies*, v (1981), 19–21, etc.

13 Andrew Ashbee, op. cit., I, 195. He had been described as 'the King's organ maker' at least a decade earlier and had built a one-manual instrument for the King's private chapel at Windsor in 1673.

14 See *North I*, 354.

15 According to Thomas Tudway, quoted in Sir John Hawkins, *A General History of the Science and Practice of Music* (London, 1875), II, 691.

16 William Leslie Sumner, *The Organ* (London, 4/1973), 158–9.

17 Edmund Macrory, *Notes on the Temple Organ* (London, 3/1911), 24.

18 Nicholas Thistlethwaite, 'ORGANO PNEUMATICO: The Construction and Design of Bernard Smith's Organ for the University Church, Cambridge, 1698', *Journal of the British Institute of Organ Studies*, ii (1978), 31–62.

19 Andrew Ashbee, op. cit., II, 3–4.

20 This shift had begun *c*1670. Stephen Keene's two known virginals are dated 1668 and 1675, while from 1685 onwards only spinets by him survive.

21 *Zimmerman II*, 314.

22 Andrew Ashbee, op. cit., I, 157.

23 Ibid., 156–7. Pepys in 1668 'called upon one Haywood that makes virginalls, and did there like of a little Espinettes and will have him finish them for me; for I had mind to a small Harpsicon, but this takes up less room . . .' (4 April 1668; IX, 148–9. See also 10, 13 and 15 July 1668; IX, 259, 261, 262.)

24 E. F. Rimbault, *The Pianoforte: Its Origin, Progress and Construction* (London, 1860), 68.

25 Andrew Ashbee, op. cit., V, 125; I, 209. Said by Mace, op. cit., 235–6, to have been 'of a *Late Invention*, contriv'd (as I have been inform'd) by one Mr. *John Hayward* of *London*', the instrument was 'in *Shape and Bulk* just like a Harpsicon', but with 'several *Various Stops* at Pleasure; and all *Quick and Nimble*, by the *Ready Turn* of the Foot . . . *Wonderfully Rare, and Excellent*: So that doubtless It *Excels* all *Harpsicons*, or *Organs* in the World, for *Admirable Sweetness and Humour, either for a Private, or a Consort use*.' A quarter of a century later another commentator observed that 'The *Harpsicon* is of late mightily Improved, by the Invention of the Pedal, which brings it so near to the Organ, that it only seems to come short of it in Lungs' (Michael Tilmouth, 'Some Improvements in Music noted by William Turner in 1697', *Galpin Society Journal*, x (1957), 58). A 'Fantasia for one Violin, Base Viol, a Pedall Harpsicord, or Organ' by Hingeston survives (*GB-Ob* MS Mus. Sch. e 382).

26 1697 (R/1980).

27 Banchieri (1611), Penna (1672) and Bismantova (1677); see Maria Boxall, ' "The Harpsichord Master 1697" and its Relationship to Contemporary Instruction and Playing', *The English Harpsichord Magazine*, ii (1981), 178–83. See also *North I*, 57 for examples of Prendcourt's fingering.

28 Ferguson renames this '*backfall and shake*' and adds a tie, by analogy with the French *tremblement appuyé* (Howard Ferguson, *Keyboard Interpretation* (London, 1975), 150).

29 H. Diack Johnstone, 'The English Beat', in Robert Judd, ed., *Aspects of Keyboard Music* (Oxford, 1992), 34–44. Howard Ferguson (op. cit., 148–52), writing before the rediscovery of *The Harpsichord Master* (1697), argued that the printer may accidentally have jumped from this sign to the next explanation but one, thereby omitting such an interpretation of the *beat*, together with a following term and its sign; in other words, that the explanation shown was intended for a missing ♩ (*forefall and beat*).

30 *North I*, 155.

31 *North I*, 149–73.

32 See also Peter Holman, *Four and Twenty Fiddlers: The Violin at the*

English Court, 1540–1690 (Oxford, 1993), 377, for an illustration of ornaments from John Lenton's violin tutor, *The Gentleman's Diversion* (London, 1694).

33   GB-*Lbl* Add. MS 35043, f. 125, 'Never shake first nor last [note]. Never shake nor beat 2 notes in the same place. all Ascending Prick't notes are Beaten. all Descending are shaked; all sharpes are shaked ascending or falling. Never shake a quaver nor Semiquaver. – Take breath after all Long notes; Prepare all Longe shakes; Raise all Long Beats afterwards Sweeten – ; if you meet wth 3 Crotchetts Descending Beat ye first shake ye second & play the third plaine. – The Note before a Close is to be shaked; Double Relish all Long Shakes if ye Note after ascend but not if it descend – where there is a Prickt Crotchett quaver & Crotchett stay Long upon ye Prickt Crotchet. If y be 3 Crocthets [*sic*] ascending Divide ye first into 2; Double rellish the 2, & play the 3^d plaine. – If 2 thirds Descending shake the one & Leave ye other; if but one Either shake or Slur. Shake no Ascending flatts. all Descending flatts are to be shaked – Naturall sharpes when they are made flatt must be raised when they are beaten – all shakes are taken from ye Note above, after a Shake keep ye finger, downe, All Beats are taken from ye Note below, after a beat keep the finger up. F.Fa.Ut & G.Sol, Re, Ut in alt are allwaies Beaten wth the forefinger; There are but 3 notes Naturally sharp. Viz. A La.Mi Re. B.fa Bi Mi & E.La. A Prick behind a Note makes it half as Long againe.' See Thurston Dart, 'Recorder "Gracings" in 1700', *Galpin Society Journal*, xii (1959), 93–4. See also Peter Holman, *Four and Twenty Fiddlers*, op. cit., 375–6, for ornament signs used in the 'Tune for the flutes' from John Blow's *Venus and Adonis*, Act I.

34   *North I*, 155.

35   William Holder, *A Treatise of the Natural Grounds, and Principles of Harmony* (London, 1694), 180–82.

36   *North I*, 208–12. See also the 'Rules for Tuning a Harpsicord or Spinnett' in Godfrey Keller's *A Compleat Method for attaining to play Thorough Bass upon either Organ, Harpsicord or Theorbo-Lute* (London, 1705), and Peter Williams, 'Equal Temperament and the English Organ, 1675–1825', *Acta Musicologica*, xl (1968), 53–65.

37   John Meffen, 'A Question of Temperament: Purcell and Croft', *Musical Times*, cxix (1978), 504–6. For a different view, see J. Murray Barbour, 'Bach and the Art of Temperament', *Musical Quarterly*, xxxiii (1947), 77–8.

38   'The Organ at the Temple hath quarter notes, which no organ in England hath, and can play any tune; as, for instance, ye tune of ye 119 Psalm [in F minor], and severall other services set by excellent musicians, which no [other] organ will do.' (Edmund Macrory, op. cit., 35; see also North I, 212.)

39   Ambrose Warren, *The Tonometer* (London, 1725), 7.

40   *North I*, 155.

41   Pier Francesco Tosi, *Opinioni de' cantori antichi e moderni, o sieno Osservazioni sopra il canto figurato* (Bologna, 1723; trans. J. E. Galliard,

Observations on the Florid Song (London, 2/1743), 19–21; see also 36–7).

42 See Bruce Haynes, 'Beyond Temperament: Non-keyboard Intonation in the 17th and 18th Centuries', *Early Music*, xix (1991), 359–61. See also the tablature by 'Mr La Riche' reproduced in Anthony Baines, 'James Talbot's Manuscript', *Galpin Society Journal*, i (1948), 14.

43 *GB-Lbl* Add. MS 4388, 42–3. See Mark Lindley, *Lutes, Viols & Temperaments* (Cambridge, 1984), 45; see also 33–6.

44 See Thomas Salmon, *A Proposal to perform Musick in Perfect & Mathematical Proportions* (London, 1688). The following year Richard Meares (the elder) advertised that he would fret instruments according to Salmon's system, 'approved by the Mathematical Professors of both Universities' (Michael Tilmouth, 'A Calendar of References to Music in Newspapers Published in London and the Provinces, 1660–1719', *Royal Musical Association Research Chronicle*, i (1961), 8). See also Mark Lindley, op. cit., 68–9.

45 Andrew Ashbee, op. cit., I, 156, and Judith Milhous and Curtis A. Price, 'Harpsichords in the London Theatres, 1697–1715', *Early Music*, xviii (1990), 38–46.

46 The information is drawn principally from Cyrus Lawrence Day and Eleanore Boswell Murrie, *English Song Books 1651–1702* (London, 1940).

47 The implications of the various terms are still not fully understood, partly because no English lutes survive from this period, but the English theorbo differed from the Italian *tiorba/chitarrone* in having shorter diapasons and a more lute-like body and perhaps tone. For Mace, 'The Theorboe, is no other, than *That* which we call'd *the Old English Lute* ... [but] *is Principally us'd in Playing to the Voice, or in Consort; It being a Lute of the Largest Seize; and we make It much more Large in Sound*, by contriving unto *It a Long Head, to Augment and Increase that Sound, and Fulness of the Basses, or Diapasons, which are a great Ornament to the Voice, or Consort.*' Thomas Mace, op. cit., 207.

48 Earlier, William King's *Songs and Ayres* (1668) had added 'Harpsecon' to the otherwise standard alternatives of theorbo/bass viol.

49 Chamber organs were to be found not only at Court and in grand houses, but occasionally even in taverns; John Harley, *Music in Purcell's London: the Social Background* (London, 1968), 138. Purcell owned one (see above), and John North as a Cambridge student in the 1660s had 'got a small organ into his chamber at Jesus Colledge' (*North I*, 252).

50 The mezzotint made by John Smith in 1706, a year after her death, from a portrait by G. Kneller depicts her playing 'an 11-course French lute', which is essentially a solo instrument.

51 Curtis A. Price, *Music in the Restoration Theatre* (Ann Arbor, Mich., 1979), 78.

52 See also *North I*, 16, note 15. According to Pepys (22 July 1664; V, 217), Reggio 'sings Italian songs to the Theorbo most neatly'.

53 For a discussion of the use of fingernails or flesh for plucking, see Peter

Walls, 'The Baroque Era: Strings', *Performance Practice – The New Grove Handbooks in Music* (London, 1989), 74.

54　See Robert Spencer, 'Chitarrone, theorbo and archlute', *Early Music*, iv (1976), 417. An isolated early appearance of the term archlute is found in the 'Advertisements to the Reader' of Matthew Locke's *Melothesia* (London, 1673), which mention 'Rules for Playing on a *Continued Bass* . . . equally fit the *Theorbo, Arch-Lute, Harp*, or any other Instrument capable of performing Duplicity of Parts . . .'

55　'Mr Purcell' was one of four listed teachers of organ and harpsichord, while 'Lute, Guittar and Theorbo' were to be taught by 'Mr De la Tour, Mr Dupre, Mr Crevecoeur'; see Michael Tilmouth, 'The Royal Academies of 1695', *Music and Letters*, xxxviii (1957), 327.

56　Michael Prynne, 'James Talbot's Manuscript; *IV.* Plucked Strings – The Lute Family', *Galpin Society Journal*, xiv (1961), 60. Not long after Purcell's death one commentator observed that 'The *Theorbo*, which is no other than an Arch-Lute, keeping to the old Tuning, is still generally made use of in Consorts'; see Michael Tilmouth, 'Some Improvements in Music noted by William Turner in 1697', *Galpin Society Journal*, x (1957), 58. In the late 1720s North wrote of 'Dr. Walgrave [*c* 1636–1701] a prodigy of an archlutinist', but Evelyn in 1685 described Walgrave's accompanying Mr Pordage 'with his *Theorba Lute*'; Mary Chan and Jamie C. Kassler, eds., *Roger North's 'Cursory Notes of Musicke' (c.1698–c.1703): A Physical, Psychological and Critical Theory* (Kensington, N.S.W., 1986), 269, hereinafter cited as *North II*; *Evelyn*, 27 January 1685; IV, 403. Elsewhere North described 'Dr. Waldegrave' as one of 'a set of men who advanced much the Italian way, and slighted the French' (*North II*, 285; see also *North I*, 308). According to Pepys, he was 'an Englishman bred at Rome' (*Pepys*, 12 April 1664; V, 119).

57　US-NH (K. Foxwell/26835d); see Robert Unwin, op. cit., 67–9.

58　'The guitarre was never so much in use & credit as it is at this day' (Nicola Matteis, *The False Consonances of Musick* (1682), 2). In 1680 Reggio 'sung *admirably* to a *Guitarr*' at Evelyn's home (*Evelyn*, 23 September 1680; IV, 220), and in 1686 Abell received £10 'for a Gittarr by him bought for his Ma^ts service in his Bed-Chamber' (Andrew Ashbee, op. cit., II, 17, 38). According to Hawkins, op. cit., 693, the Duke of York would accompany the singing of Charles II and Gostling on the guitar. In 1690 Benjamin Garrot offered instruction in 'playing upon the Gittar, either by Letters or Notes' (*The London Gazette*, 10 November; see Michael Tilmouth, 'A Calendar', op. cit., 10).

59　See Curtis A. Price, *Restoration Theatre*, op. cit., 78. The guitar was played either the 'brushing way' (i.e. strummed) or the 'pinching way'; see Michael Tilmouth, 'Some Improvements in Music noted by William Turner in 1697', *Galpin Society Journal*, x (1957), 58.

60　One guitar or several? In Staggins's and Crowne's *Calisto* (1674) four guitars were involved, probably playing onstage for dances (Andrew Ashbee, op. cit., I, 146). See also Peter Holman, *Four and Twenty Fiddlers*, op. cit., 368–9.

61 The 1981 recording by Andrew Parrott with the Taverner Choir and
    Players of *Dido and Aeneas*, CHAN 8306, adopts this solution.

62 *Evelyn*, 19 April 1687; IV, 547.

63 *Evelyn*, 14 March 1685; IV, 421. Also, Catherine Shore, said by Burney
    to have been 'a scholar of Purcell in singing and playing of the harpsi-
    chord', appeared in her husband Colley Cibber's *Woman's Wit: or The
    Lady in Fashion* (1697), first playing and then singing, presumably to her
    own accompaniment (Curtis A. Price, *Restoration Theatre*, op. cit., 80).

64 *Evelyn*, 27 January 1682; IV, 270 and 28 January 1685; IV, 404.

65 John Hawkins, op. cit., 564.

66 John Banister and Thomas Low, *New Ayres, Dialogues, and Trialogues*
    (1678), 1. Almost twenty years earlier, John Gamble's *Ayres and Dia-
    logues* (1659) were similarly intended 'To be Sung either to the THEORBO-
    LUTE or BASSE-VIOL'.

67 *North I*, 26.

68 *The London Gazette* (28 May 1682) had announced that copies of
    Purcell's 'Sonata's of three Parts for two Violins and Base to the Harpsi-
    cord or Organ' were 'compleately finished' (Michael Tilmouth, 'A Calen-
    dar', op. cit., 5).

69 *North I*, 47.

70 *The Loyal Post* (28 October 1682) announced Gerhard Diessener's
    recently published 'consort of Musick for three parts (*viz*). Two Violins,
    and a Base Viol' (Michael Tilmouth, 'A Calendar', op. cit., 5).

71 Francis Sandford, op. cit., plate 4, 'A Prospect of the Inside of Westmins-
    ter Hall'. Reproduced in Peter Holman, *Four and Twenty Fiddlers*, op.
    cit., as fig. 13.3.

72 Curtis A. Price, *Restoration Theatre*, op. cit., 79.

73 Graham Sadler, 'The role of the Keyboard Continuo in French Opera
    1673–1776', *Early Music*, viii (1980), 148–57; see also Peter Holman,
    Four and Twenty Fiddlers, op. cit., 384–5.

74 Bruce Wood and Andrew Pinnock, ' "Unscarr'd by turning times"?: the
    Dating of Purcell's *Dido and Aeneas*', *Early Music*, xx (1992), 372–90,
    and Curtis A. Price, 'Dido and Aeneas: Questions of Style and Evidence',
    Early Music, xxii (1994), 115–25; continuing.

75 Judith Milhous and Curtis A. Price, op. cit., 43. See also Peter Holman,
    'Reluctant Continuo', *Early Music*, ix (1981), 75–8.

76 *North I*, 248.

77 Curtis A. Price, *Henry Purcell and the London Stage* (Cambridge, 1984),
    243.

78 See Franck Arnold, *The Art of Accompaniment from a Thorough-Bass*
    (London, 1931), 154–63, 163–72. (Blow's instructions are from *GB-Lbl*
    Add. MS 34072, ff. 1–5.) See also Godfrey Keller, *A Compleat Method for
    attaining to play a Thorough Bass upon either Organ, Harpsicord or
    Theorbo-Lute* (London, 1705), described by Arnold, op. cit., 247–50,
    and Prendcourt's 'The treatis of the continued or through basse' (*GB-Lbl*
    Add. MS 32549, ff. 17–30ᵛ).

79 *North I*, 249.

80 See *Works II*, xiii, 69–87, 133–41.

81 Thomas Mace, op. cit., part II, Chapter 43, esp. 217, 221–4. An early example of a written-out accompaniment for theorbo is found in Lady Ann Blount's Song Book, for the anonymous 'Sing aloud harmonious spheres'. Locke points out that 'When a *Bass* hathe many swift Notes running one after another . . . for the *Theorbo* &c. it is sufficient to Play single Notes' (Franck Arnold, op. cit., 157). Matteis's 'Instructions for playing a true Base upon the Guitarre' and other instruments include a brief discussion of the rate of chord-playing (*The False Consonances of Musick* (1682), 19–20; cf. Mace, op. cit., 229); this matches Blow's advice to keyboard players that: 'If your Bass move by Quavers or Semiquavers, you need not play wth your right hand more than on[ce] to four quavers, or once to two quavers, being the same as if your Bass had been Minums or Crochets' (Arnold, op. cit., 166). See also Nigel North, *Continuo Playing on the Lute, Archlute and Theorbo* (London, 1987), 196.

82 *GB-Ob* Mus. 8 c.2. See Peter Holman, 'Continuo Realizations in a Playford Songbook', *Early Music*, vi (1978), 268–9. For the opening of the Purcell song, see Ian Spink, *English Song: Dowland to Purcell* (London, 1974), 216.

83 *North I*, 247–8.

84 *North I*, 249.

85 *North I*, 227. Of viol-only accompaniments there appear to be no written-out examples from so late in the century.

86 'Sonnata's of three Parts, for two *Violins* and *Bass-Viol*, with a Through-Bass for the *Organ* or *Harpsichord*', in [J. Playford], *Choice Ayres, and Songs and Dialogues* (1684), V, 63.

87 Low C occurs in IV (2, bar 38) of the 1683 set, but nowhere in the 1697 set. It was not uncommon for the bass viol to tune its lowest string down a tone; see Christopher Simpson, *The Division-Viol* (London, 1667), 8, and Robert Donington, 'James Talbot's Manuscript II: Bowed Strings', *Galpin Society Journal*, iii (1950), 33.

88 Curtis A. Price, *Restoration Theatre*, op. cit., 266, *North I*, 304. Mary Chan and Jamie C. Kassler, eds., *Roger North's The Musicall Grammarian 1728* (Cambridge, 1990), 265, hereinafter cited as North III.

89 Robert Thompson, ' "Francis Withie of Oxon" and his commonplace Book, Christ Church, Oxford, MS 337', *Chelys*, xx (1991), 11. 'Diseb' was probably Desabay(e); see Andrew Ashbee, op. cit., II, 16, 19, 91, 102.

90 See also Peter Holman, *Four and Twenty Fiddlers*, op. cit., 406–7

91 Ibid., 318–19.

92 In his family portrait (*c* 1650) Sir Peter Lely, a close friend and benefactor of Roger North's, depicts himself playing a large viol of a size intermediate between that of the normal bass and a 16' violone. See Peter Holman, *Four and Twenty Fiddlers*, op. cit., plate 5a.

93 Similarly, the 'Great Basse' in George Jeffreys' 'Felice Pastorella'; see also Peter Holman, *Four and Twenty Fiddlers*, op. cit., 216–17. In the case of

some sonatas by Keller the term 'double basses' appears merely to indicate the inclusion of a pair of (identical) bass parts, specifically for 'Organo e Violoncello' (Godfrij Keller, *Six Sonatas/The First Three/For a Trumpett, Houbois or violins/with Doubble Basses. The Other Three/ For two flutes, and two Haubois/or two violins with Doubble Basses* (Amsterdam, 1699 or 1700)).

94   Robert Donington, op. cit., 33.

95   *North I*, 274 (written some time in the six years after Purcell's death).

96   Peter Walls, op. cit., 46.

97   Two German viol players who worked in England were Theodore Steffkin (until 1673) and (from *c*1685) Gottfried Finger. The viol teachers at the proposed Royal Academies in 1695 were to have been Finger and 'Mr Stephkins', presumably either Frederick or Christian, the sons of Theodore (Michael Tilmouth, 'The Royal Academies of 1695', *Music and Letters*, xxxviii (1957), 327).

98   *North I*, 16.

99   *GB-Ob* MS Wood D. 19 (4), f. 32ᵛ.

100 See also Michael Tilmouth, 'Some Improvements in Music Noted by William Turner in 1697', *Galpin Society Journal*, x (1957), 58, and Talbot's 'tuning of the violins' (Robert Donington, op. cit., 29), where the double bass is conspicuous by its absence.

101 *North I*, 274.

102 See also Andrew Ashbee, op. cit., II, 102, where 'Sigʳ Sajony' is listed with the 'Instrumentall Musick' of the Queen's Theatre, Haymarket, in 1710.

103 Michel Corrette, *Méthode pour apprendre à jouer de la contre-basse . . .* (Paris, 1773), 1. See also Mary Cyr, '*Basses* and *basse continue* in the Orchestra of the Paris Opéra 1700–1764', *Early Music*, x (1982), 155–70.

104 Whatever the French influences on the early Restoration Court string band, it was 'Cremona' instruments that were occasionally imported (Andrew Ashbee, op. cit., I, 15, 37, 60, and V, 110, 112, 133), although from Purcell's time at Court we know of only 'a Cremona Base Violin' bought for £20 in 1680 (Ashbee, I, 92). In 1692 'a number of Curious Violins, Cremonia and others' were advertised for sale (*The London Gazette*, 15 December; see Michael Tilmouth, 'A Calendar', op. cit., 13). Later, North commented: 'some say England hath dispeopled Italy of viollins' (*North III*, 272). Talbot's measurements of a violin lent by 'Banister' apparently resemble those of the 'grand pattern' Amati (Robert Donington, op. cit., 27, 29, 30; David D. Boyden, *The History of Violin Playing from its Origins to 1761* (London, 1965), 202), but surviving English instruments show more Northern European influences. Notable contemporary makers were William Baker of Oxford (*c*.1645–85), Edward Pamphilon (*fl. c*1670–1695), Thomas Urquhart (*c*1650–80) and the young Barak Norman (*c*1670–1740). Both gut and silk strings overwound with 'Small Wire' were known in England since at least 1664 but were not necessarily in common use; their increased density enabled thinner and therefore tonally 'better and lowder' strings to be used in the

bass of an instrument (Michael G. Lowe, 'The Historical Development of the Lute in the 17th Century', *Galpin Society Journal*, xxix (1976), 24).

105 Andrew Ashbee, op. cit., I, 83. See also Peter Holman, *Four and Twenty Fiddlers*, op. cit., App. D; and Thomas Mace, op. cit., 233.

106 See Andrew Ashbee, op. cit., I, 184, 187, etc.

107 Peter Holman, *Four and Twenty Fiddlers*, op. cit., 401.

108 Andrew Ashbee, op. cit., II, 12. Note again the absence of a double bass.

109 Ibid., I, 155–6.

110 Curtis A. Price, *Restoration Theatre*, op. cit., 81, 82, 267; and *North I*, 274.

111 Mark A. Radice, 'Theater Architecture at the Time of Purcell and Its Influence on His "Dramatick Operas" ', *Musical Quarterly*, lxxiv (1990), 111, 126, 129.

112 *Works II*, viii, 13–14. A comparable reduction from 'full' to 'single' strings is indicated in an early score of *King Arthur* (see *Works* II, xxvi, 18–20); and in Grabu's 'From harmony, from heavenly harmony' 1687, see Peter Holman, *Four and Twenty Fiddlers*, op. cit., 427–8.

113 *North I*, 306. Mace gives a plan for an 18-foot square 'Musick-Roome, w^ich would have none in It besides the Performers', surrounded by twelve galleries which, 'though but little, will (I believe) hold 200 *Persons* very well, without *Crowding*' (op. cit., 239, 241). Advertisements for weekly music-making in the Great Room, Lambeth Wells, in 1697 mention 'Vocal and Instrumental Musick, consisting of about Thirty Instruments and Voices, after the method of the Musick meeting in York Buildings' (Michael Tilmouth, 'A Calendar', op. cit., 19); such a total need not imply the simultaneous involvement of all performers.

114 Peter Holman, *Four and Twenty Fiddlers*, op. cit., 398–9, 404–5. For the 1685 coronation in Westminster Abbey the spatial separation between the three special galleries accommodating the musicians was considerable. The 'Kings Choir' and the 'Master and Kings Choir of Instrumental Musick' were diagonally across from each other near the high altar, while the Abbey's own choir was just west of the transepts, next to 'The Great Organ' on the north side of the choir. The 'whole *Consort* of *Voices* and *Instruments*' performed Blow's 'God Spake Sometimes in Visions' and Purcell's 'My Heart is Inditing' (see Francis Sandford, op. cit., 99, 101, etc.).

115 Peter Holman, *Four and Twenty Fiddlers*, op. cit., 389, 391.

116 Thomas Tudway, *GB-Lbl* MS Harleian 7338, ff. 2v–3.

117 See also Peter Holman, *Four and Twenty Fiddlers*, op. cit., 397–400, and Andrew Ashbee, op. cit., I, 108–9, 113.

118 Andrew Ashbee, op. cit., V, 91.

119 Two earlier English tutors, from the 1680s, are apparently not extant; see Malcolm Boyd and John Rayson, 'The Gentleman's Diversion; John Lenton and the First Violin Tutor', *Early Music*, x (1982), 329–32.

120 *North I*, 309 and note 63.

121 John Lenton, op. cit., 11; see Boyd and Rayson, op. cit. According to Playford, the violin was 'rested on the left breast, a little below the

shoulder' (*An Introduction to the Skill of Musick* (London, 7/1674), 114).

122 Playford, op. cit., 101–4; and Thomas Mace, op. cit., 248.
123 Peter Walls, op. cit., 45.
124 Ibid., 51.
125 *North I*, 168, 309.
126 Robert Donington, op. cit., 29.
127 Peter Walls, op. cit., 49. The title page of John Playford's *The Division – Violin* (London, 2/1685) clearly illustrates bow shapes.
128 *North I*, 309.
129 *Evelyn*, 19 November 1674; IV, 48.
130 *North I*, 164.
131 *North I*, 167. Later still, around 1726, he complained of its overuse (*North I*, 164–5).
132 *North I*, 17–18 and plate II; see also *North I*, 128.
133 *North II*, 223. The viol's equivalent to which North refers was a two-finger vibrato, described by Simpson: '*Close-shake* [Tremor pressus] is that when we shake the Finger as close and near the sounding Note as possible may be, touching the String with the Shaking finger so softly and nicely that it make no variation of Tone [i.e. pitch]. This may be used where no other Grace is concerned . . .' This 'explanation' is effectively identical with one given earlier by Playford; Simpson classifies it as one of the 'more smooth and Feminine' graces, 'which are more natural to the *Treble*, or upper parts' (Simpson, op. cit., 11–12). (However popular the ornament may have been among viol players – and it is mentioned in connection with the bass viol as late as c1726 by North, who calls it a 'close beat' – the sign itself is not known to occur in contemporary musical sources.) The now normal one-finger vibrato, found alongside the close shake in French sources (de Machy, 1685; Marais, 1686; and Rousseau, 1687) is not mentioned by the English viol players, but the apparent familiarity of the English lutenists with it may suggest that it was not unknown in English viol technique of the period. Mace (op. cit., 109) informs us that in lute playing: 'The *Sting*, is another very *Neat, and Pritty Grace*; (But not *Modish* in *These Days*) . . . first strike your *Note*, and so soon as It is struck, *hold your Finger (but not too Hard) stopt upon the Place* (letting your *Thumb loose*) and *wave your Hand, (Exactly) downwards, and upwards, several Times, from the Nut, to the Bridge*; by which *Motion*, your *Finger will draw, or stretch the String a little upwards, and downwards, so*, as to make the Sound seem to *Swell*.'
134 See Greta Moens-Haenen, *Das Vibrato in der Musik des Barock* (Graz, 1988), 88–93, and Bruce Dickey, 'Untersuchungen zur historischen Auffassung des Vibratos auf Blasinstrumenten', *Basler Jahrbuch für historische Musikpraxis*, ii (1978), 88–91.
135 *North I*, 186. See also Simpson, op. cit., 10.
136 *North I*, 22–3, 227, 355. See also Stewart Carter, 'The String Tremolo in the 17th Century', *Early Music*, xix (1991), 53–5; and Lionel Sawkins,

'Trembleurs and Cold People: how should they shiver?', in Michael Burden, ed., *Performing the Music of Henry Purcell* (Oxford, 1995).

137   The 'bass flute' that makes an appearance in 'Hark! each tree' from the 1692 ode 'Hail! Bright Cecilia!' must be Talbot's 'pedal or double bass' recorder (in C), as the part descends beneath (written) F, as does the 'bass flute' part in Blow's 'Lord, who shall dwell in thy tabernacle?'. Some figuring in the part shows that this very delicate instrument (and effect) would have been supported by a continuo instrument.

138   In 'Swifter, Isis' (1681).

139   *The Gentleman's Journal*, January 1692. In 1699 Godfrey Keller wrote that the 'Trumpet [is] an Instrument formerly practis'd in ye rough Consorts of ye Field but now instructed in gentler Notes, it has learnt to accompany ye softest Flutes and can join with the most charming Voices' (dedication to an 'English Princess' of three trumpet sonatas; see Edward Tarr, *The Trumpet* (London, 1988), 135).

140   *North II*, 119.

141   *The Gentleman's Journal*, January 1692. The instrument was a particular speciality of John Shore's and of perhaps a small handful of his close colleagues'. In the March and Canzona the three upper parts use only slide positions 1–3, while the bass, which lies fairly high, goes as far as position 5 and may have been played (on a flat trumpet) by a sackbut player. The simple homophonic anthem 'Thou knowest Lord', which according to Tudway in 1717 (*GB-Lbl* Harleian MS 7340) was 'accompanied wth flat Mournfull Trumpets', would, if played, take the bass to position 6 and tenor to 4; what was meant, almost certainly, was not that trumpets doubled the voices but simply that the anthem was sung *in conjunction with* the brass pieces.

142   Andrew Pinnock, 'A Wider Role for the Flat Trumpet', *Galpin Society Journal*, xlii (1989), 107.

143   See Peter Downey, 'What Samuel Pepys Heard on 3 February 1661: English Trumpet Style under the Later Stuart Monarchs', *Early Music*, xviii (1990), 417–28; Andrew Pinnock and Bruce Wood, 'A Counterblast on English Trumpets', *Early Music*, xix (1991), 437–43; Peter Holman, 'English Trumpets – a Response', *Early Music*, xix (1991), 443. See also Crispian Steele-Perkins, 'Practical Observations on Natural, Slide and Flat Trumpets', *Galpin Society Journal*, xlii (1989), 122–6; David Rycroft, 'Flat Trumpet Facts and Figures,' *Galpin Society Journal*, xlii (1989), 134–42; and Frank Tomes, 'Flat Trumpet Experiments', *Galpin Society Journal*, xliii (1990), 164–5.

144   See Bruce Wood, 'The First Performance of Purcell's Funeral Music for Queen Mary', in Michael Burden, ed., *Performing the Music of Henry Purcell* (Oxford, 1995).

145   Peter Downey, private communication.

146   David Lasocki, 'The French hautboy in England, 1673–1730', *Early Music*, xvi (1988), 341.

147   Curtis A. Price, *Henry Purcell*, op cit., 263.

148 David Lasocki, 'Professional Recorder Playing in England 1500–1740 II: 1640–1740', *Early Music*, x (1982), 183; and op. cit., 339.

149 Andrew Ashbee, op. cit., II, 35–6, 38–41; *Grove VI*, III, 263.

150 See no. 200, Anthony Baines, *The Bate Collection of Historical Musical Instruments: Catalogue of the Collection* (Oxford, 1976), 18.

151 Bruce Haynes, op. cit., 112.

152 Players who have found this the instrument's most likely intended pitch include Paul Goodwin, Bruce Haynes, Michel Piguet and Anthony Robson.

153 Bruce Haynes, op. cit., 117.

154 Cary Karp, 'Pitch', *Performance Practice – The New Grove Handbooks in Music* (London, 1989), 160.

155 Robert Smith, *Harmonics, or The Philosophy of Musical Sounds* (Cambridge, 1749), 221; the second edition (1759), 208 reads: 'about the year 1720'.

156 William Tansur, *A New Musical Grammar* (London, 1746), 57.

157 French pitch itself also rose in due course, according to Quantz (1752) and Agricola (1757); see Arthur Mendel, 'On the Pitches in Use in Bach's Time, Part II', *Musical Quarterly*, xli (1955), 469–70.

158 Tula Giannini, 'A Letter from Louis Rousselet, 18th-century French Oboist at the Royal Opera in England', *Newsletter of the American Musical Instrument Society*, xvi/2 (June 1987), 10–11.

159 A possible exception is the 15-stop, 2-manual house organ at Adlington Hall, Cheshire, believed to have been built around 1693, which now plays at about $a' = 407$ (John Mander, 'Some Notes on the Organ in Adlington Hall', *Journal of the British Institute of Organ Studies*, x (1986), 68).

160 Dominic Gwynn, 'Organ Pitch in Seventeenth-century England', *Journal of the British Institute of Organ Studies*, ix (1985), 65–78.

161 Andrew Freeman, *Father Smith otherwise Bernard Schmidt, being an account of a Seventeenth Century Organ Maker* (London, 1926), 13.

162 Sidney W. Harvey, 'Two Unpublished Records of Father Smith', *The Organ*, i (1921), 98.

163 Dominic Gwynn, op. cit., 76, notes 20 and 21.

164 Edward John Hopkins and E. F. Rimbault, *The Organ: Its History and Construction* (London, 3/1877), 107.

165 Sir John Sutton, *A Short Account of Organs Built in England* (London, 1847), 37. Sutton's 'concert pitch' could have been anything from $a' = 433$ to $a' = 453$ (see Alexander J. Ellis, 'The History of Musical Pitch', *Journal of the Society of Arts*, 5 March 1880, 305).

166 Discrepancies of pitch between organs are undoubtedly the reason for similar discrepancies of notation among contemporary sources. Most anthems with organ accompaniment would have worked reasonably well at either Harris's or Smith's pitch, but a handful would not. In these instances, an organist playing on an instrument tuned in 1/4-comma meantone, or in most other unequal temperaments, can almost never risk transposition by a semitone, whereas a shift of a tone is quite often

for example, was probably written originally in A minor (three sources) for Smith's (high) pitch but then put into B minor (five sources) for lower-pitched organs, the intermediate B♭ minor being both practically and notationally out of the question. Similarly, the Richard Ayleward Organ Book, associated with Norwich Cathedral (and therefore with Harris's 1689 instrument), includes upward transpositions as alternatives for five of its nineteen anthems. *GB-Wc* MS A.3.10, an organ score, has Purcell's 'Blessed is the Man' ('Composed for the Charter House') in D minor, a tone higher than in eleven other sources, and 'Thy way, O God, is Holy' in C minor, a tone lower (surprisingly) than in seven other sources.

167   Three works from the period 1685–7 have the range *g–b♭'*, and three from 1690–93 *a–c"*.

168   See Chapter 6, above.

169   *Evelyn*, 28 January 1685; IV, 404. See also J. A. Westrup, op. cit., 5 (quoted in note 218 below), 196; and Hawkins, op. cit., 693.

170   The first unequivocal reference to falsetto singing in England appears to be in Matthew Locke's comment that 'for above a Year after the Opening of His Majesties Chappel, the Orderers of the Musick there, were necessitated to supply the superiour Parts of their Musick with Cornets and Mens feigned Voices' (*Present Practice of Musick Vindicated* (London, 1673), 19).

171   There are similar solos specifically for Howell in 'Love's Goddess' (1693) and 'A Song for the Duke of Gloucester's Birthday' (1695).

172   *Evelyn*, 27 January 1682; IV, 270.

173   Charles Burney, *A General History of Music* (London, 1776–89), ed. F. Mercer, (London, 1935), II, 36.

174   November 1692, 19.

175   *GB-Ob* MS Mus. c. 26; this was probably used for at least one repeat performance.

176   Two early printed sources (London, *c*1693) present Purcell's song as 'sung by himself at St. Cecilia's Feast'.

177   Jeremy Noble, 'Purcell and the Chapel Royal', in Imogen Holst, ed., *Henry Purcell 1659–1695: Essays on his Music* (London, 1959), 62.

178   Francis Sandford, op. cit., 71.

179   *Evelyn*, 27 January 1685; IV, 403.

180   Matthew Locke, *Present Practice*, op. cit., 19.

181   *Evelyn*, 23 September 1680; IV, 220.

182   Curtis A. Price, *Henry Purcell*, op. cit., 299.

183   See Jeremy Noble, op. cit., 62–4. Also, the tenor cantoris 1 of 'Blow up the Trumpet in Sion' is notated in the C3 clef with the instruction, 'The contratenor & tenor for this anthem are here to sing together' (*Works II*, xxviii, 193).

184   *Old Cheque-Book*, 14, 112.

185   Andrew Ashbee, op. cit., I, 136.

186   Ibid., V, 73; and *Old Cheque-Book*, 13, 16, 112.

187   Francis Sandford, op. cit., 70.

188   Andrew Ashbee, op. cit., II, 3, 122.

189 *Works I*, xii, xviii.

190 *Works II*, viii, 17, bars 43–7.

191 Olive Baldwin and Thelma Wilson, 'Alfred Deller, John Freeman and Mr. Pate', *Music and Letters*, l (1969), 107; Curtis A. Price and Irena Cholij, 'Dido's Bass Sorceress', *Musical Times*, cxxvii (1986), 615–18.

192 *Works II*, xvi, 178; and xix, 12, 34, 67.

193 *GB-Lbl* Add. MS 31457 and Add. MS 31813.

194 *Evelyn*, 28 January 1685; IV, 404.

195 *The London Gazette* for 11 June 1694 announced a 'consort' in which 'a Gentlewoman Sings that hath one of the best Voices in England, not before heard in publick' (Michael Tilmouth, 'A Calendar', op. cit., 15).

196 John Hawkins, op. cit., 761.

197 Olive Baldwin and Thelma Wilson, 'Purcell's Sopranos', *Musical Times*, cxxiii (1982), 602.

198 *Evelyn*, 14 March 1685; IV, 421–2.

199 *North I*, 217–18.

200 Ibid., 215; see also 216, and John Playford, *An Introduction to the Skill of Musick*, op. cit., 20.

201 *North I*, 216.

202 Curtis A. Price, *Henry Purcell*, op. cit., 215.

203 Letter to William Walsh, 9 May 1693, in Charles E. Ward, ed., *The Letters of John Dryden* (Durham, North Carolina, 1942), 52–3.

204 Colley Cibber, *An Apology for the Life of Mr. Colley Cibber* (London, 1740), 97.

205 Olive Baldwin and Thelma Wilson, 'Purcell's Sopranos', op. cit., 607. *The London Gazette* (26 November 1694) announced 'the Addition of two new Voices' to the Charles Street consort, 'one a young Gentlewomans of 12 years of Age' (Michael Tilmouth, 'A Calendar', op. cit., 15).

206 Olive Baldwin and Thelma Wilson, 'Purcell's Sopranos', op. cit., 603.

207 *The Gentleman's Journal*, August 1692.

208 Preface to *The Fairy Queen*.

209 *Evelyn*, 14 March 1685; IV, 421, 427, 428.

210 Ibid., 30 January 1687; IV, 537.

211 Ibid., 19 April 1687; IV, 547.

212 Pier Francesco Tosi, op. cit., 102

213 Michael Tilmouth, 'A Calendar', op. cit., 13.

214 *North I*, 151.

215 *Evelyn*, 27 January 1682; IV, 270.

216 Ibid., 27 January 1685; IV, 403.

217 Ibid., 30 May 1698; V, 289.

218 A letter from Thomas Purcell to Gostling in 1679 reports that 'my sonne is composing wherein you will be chiefly concern'd' (J. A. Westrup, op. cit., 5).

219 *North I*, 262.

220 Curtis A. Price, *Henry Purcell*, op. cit., 130.

221 Exceptions include 'sighing and languishing by degrees' in "'Tis Nature's voice' from 'Hail! Bright Cecilia!'.

222 *Works II*, xxv, 157–61, 300.

223 *Synopsis of Vocal Musick . . . By A. B. Philo-Mus* (London, 1680), 44.

224 John Playford, op cit., 31.

225 *North III*, 99.

226 Anthony Aston, quoted in Robert W. Lowe, ed., *A Brief Supplement to Colley Cibber, An Apology* (London, 1889, rev. 2/New York, 1966), 312.

227 Bénigne de Bacilly, *Remarques curieuses sur l'art de bien chanter* (Paris, 1668), 36.

228 The full group of thirty-two Gentlemen of the Chapel Royal listed by Francis Sandford, (op. cit., 70–71) includes five who in 1685 were almost certainly non-singing members – Blagrave, Staggins, Blow, Child and Purcell himself ('Organist of Westminster').

229 Christopher Dearnley, *English Church Music 1650–1750* (London, 1970), 32. A Memorandum of 5 April 1693 established a fining system for 'whatever Gentleman of the Chappell in waiting should absent himself from the practice of the Anthem on Saturdays or other holiday eves, when the King or Queen were to bee present on the morrow, or upon any other occasions before the Wednesdays and Fridays in Lent, being thereto ordered by the Subdean to appear' (*Old Cheque Book*, 86). Court Odes, incidentally, appear to have had three 'practices' prior to performance; see J. A. Westrup, op. cit., 57.

230 Andrew Ashbee, op. cit., I, 136 and *passim*. The 5th edition of Edward Phillips's *The New World of Words* (London, 1696), to which Purcell contributed, defines an anthem as 'a divine Song consisting of Verses sung alternatively by the two opposite Quires, and Chorus's'.

231 Francis Sandford (op. cit., 70) lists sixteen men for James II's coronation (1685), but there were twelve for that of William and Mary (1689); see Franklin B. Zimmerman, 'Purcell and the Dean of Westminster – Some New Evidence', *Music and Letters*, xliii (1962), 13.

232 Thomas Mace, op. cit, 23.

233 The autograph manuscript (*GB-Lbl* Add. MS 30930) of these two works contains no verse/chorus indications.

Producing Dido and Aeneas:
An Investigation into Sixteen Problems[1]

ROGER SAVAGE

Mounting any opera presents a number of problems. Mounting pre-Mozartian opera doubles the number. When the producer and conductor have agreed about the casting, pacing and general feel of the piece, the conductor must wrestle with all sorts of issues: vocal/instrumental timbre and balance, continuo realization, tempi, decoration, double dots and so on. And the producer has not only to face the normal challenges of his or her craft: achieving a good rapport with the designer and choreographer; sensitizing the singers to dramatic values; devising a chain of stage images which seemingly provoke the words of the libretto and the notes of the music; establishing a rate of eventuation in stage business which is appropriate to the kind of score in hand. With opera before the 1780s there are further problems to solve, created by the lapse or loss over the last two centuries of performance conventions, audience expectations, areas of shared knowledge, sometimes even of crucial documents. The sixteen paragraphs which follow are one producer's account of the problems of this sort raised by Dido and Aeneas (z 626). Some of them are typical, others less so, but in this case the untypical ones are not unimportant. They arise from Dido's being such a short piece – barely an hour in length in the musical form that has come down to us – and from the relative simplicity of its resources, which makes it quite easy to perform with some degree of adequacy and which has long been connected with its reputation as a work premièred by largely amateur forces: 'Perform'd at Mr. Josias Priest's Boarding-School at Chelsey. By Young Gentlewomen,' as the 1689 libretto has it. These things, together with its superb musical quality, have led to *Dido*'s becoming very popular since the turn of this century, especially with amateurs. Hence it has to be well, not just adequately, done, and here its highly charged brevity makes life very difficult from the producer's point of view. Once the curtain is up there is no time to waste and no room for by-play. Each tableau, step, gesture, prop and lighting-cue must arise from necessity and have its effect at once, and yet there must be no point-making which draws attention to itself and so distracts from the depth and flow of the music. *Dido* is in fact a tall order for a producer. Schoenberg on Webern comes to mind: it is easy enough to turn a sigh into a novel, less so to convey a novel in a sigh.

i   How does one programme Dido?

With only sixty minutes' worth of music and no real opportunity for an interval, *Dido and Aeneas* needs to be paired with another work to make an evening, preferably an evening that is in some way integrated overall. There are several possibilities:

(1) *The original prologue*: a masque-like piece for which the libretto but no music survives. Reconstructions using music from elsewhere in Purcell are possible, however, and one has been published by Thurston Dart and Margaret Laurie in their edition,[2] though even this would not very much increase the length of the evening, being twenty minutes long at most. It might valuably be combined with (2), (3) or (4), however.

(2) *A curtain-raiser*: something perhaps of roughly the same age and mood as *Dido* and calling for similar resources, e.g. the *Ballo delle ingrate* or *Combattimento di Tancredi e Clorinda* of Monteverdi, or Act I of Cavalli's *La Didone* (a *Prise de Troie* to go with Purcell's *Troyens à Carthage*), or Marc-Antoine Charpentier's '*opéra de chasse*', *Actéon*, which has the same physical setting as the Grove scene in *Dido* ('Here Actaeon met his fate . . .').

(3) *An afterpiece*: a short, light work from roughly the same period as *Dido* with some connections (perhaps parodic) in subject or treatment, such as Lampe's *Dragon of Wantley* or his *Pyramus and Thisbe*; or – if money allows – a contrasting work

which overlaps *Dido* in some way, e.g. Weill's *Seven Deadly Sins*, which also presents a woman's destruction by worldly experience and also juxtaposes song and dance.

(4) *A modern complement*: there is a one-act opera *Fanny Robin* written by Edward Harper specifically as a companion-piece for *Dido*, which it quotes, parallels and consciously differs from in various ways, notably by using the English ballad-motif of the Soldier Who Rode Away rather than the classical epic one. Harper's opera[3] calls for a professional in the lead but can otherwise be managed by amateur forces. (Though based on Thomas Hardy's *Far from the Madding Crowd* and quoting English folksong, its musical idiom is very much of the 1970s.)

ii *Is there a reliable performing edition of the opera?*

If that means a *definitive* edition, the answer is no, since no autograph score or contemporary printing of the music is known to survive, only the printed libretti from 1689 and 1700 which do not always agree with each other and which depart in various ways from a group of eighteenth-century manuscript copies of the original score which quite often differ among themselves. Still, each of the editions of the work now available – Dent's for Oxford University Press (revised in 1987 by Ellen Harris), Britten and Holst's for Boosey & Hawkes, and Laurie/ Dart's for Novello (which first saw the light of day as a performing edition by both of them in 1961 and later became the Purcell Society scholarly edition by Laurie) – is responsible and respectable; and it is worth the producer's while to establish all his options among the surviving music, words and stage directions by looking at all of them carefully. It is best to look at the miniature score rather than the vocal score in the case of Britten/ Holst, but to look at both Novello scores, since they complement each other. Do not feel that as producer you have to leave all such matters to your conductor. (For instance, from a producer's point of view there is much to be said for the Ohki manuscript's[4] variant setting of the words 'Our next motion / Must be to storm . . .' in the Sorceress's last aria, as given in the appendix to Britten/Holst; and I prefer the 1689 libretto's 'Let

Jove say what he will' in Aeneas' last recitative to the various manuscripts' limp-wristed 'say what he please'.) With such a brief piece as *Dido*, the common question in opera of 'What can we cut?' becomes for once 'What can we add?' The answer depends on what one takes to be the relation between the score as it survives and the surviving libretti. To Dent's original edition I am convinced one should add witching music for the end of the Grove scene ('Then since our charms have sped . . .'), which the manuscripts lack though the 1689 libretto includes the words, and possibly one should add the two guitar dances that the 1689 libretto mentions (the Hughes revision suggests music which could be used for the dances); to Britten/Holst (which has witches' music for 'Since our charms' arranged from other Purcell works) one may want to add the guitar dances; while the Laurie/Dart 1961 performing edition is pretty well 'complete', though its guitar numbers in the appendix are only bases for improvisation and its continuo realization throughout is – for better or worse – not as striking as Dent's or Britten's. However, be warned: some of the end-of-Grove-scene music which is supplied in Britten/Holst has the disadvantage of now being perhaps too well known from its original context in *The Indian Queen* (z 630/7), while the Laurie/Dart solution to the problem at this point, though also using 'real' Purcell, is somewhat untheatrical in that it allows the poor witches no time to get on stage before flinging them into solid four-part harmony, though an extended continuo flourish might solve the problem. An effective 'new' setting of the words, a skilful piece of unashamed Purcellian pastiche by Michael Tilmouth, can be found in *Early Music*, iv (1976), 405–6.

iii   Is there anything good to read before rehearsals begin?

Perhaps the three best things from Purcell's own age are a seventeenth-century English version of Book IV of Virgil's *Aeneid* (the most thorough classical treatment of the Dido myth), Sir William Davenant's Restoration adaptation of *Macbeth* (first printed in 1674 and a source of the opera's witches), and Nahum Tate's *Brutus of Alba, or The Enchanted Lovers* (1678, a tragedy loosely based on the Dido myth by Purcell's future librettist). The outstanding Virgil version is Dryden's, which first appeared in 1697 and is to be found in all good editions of his poems. This has a fine Restoration-classical flavour, and it is immaterial that it postdates *Dido and Aeneas*, since (as far as I know) Tate did not make consistent or extensive use of any specific translation while writing his text. (His reliance on the Latin original, on the other hand, is often marked. For instance, Dido's odd rhetorical question about Aeneas in the first scene – 'What battles did he sing?' – is not so much a suggestion that characters in tragical operas never merely *speak* as a translation of *Aeneid* IV.14: *'quae bella exhausta canebat'*; and Aeneas' 'What language can I try / My injured queen to pacify?' in the Grove scene is very close to Virgil at IV.283–4.) Davenant's *Macbeth* version appears in Christopher Spencer's admirable *Five Restoration Adaptations of Shakespeare* (1965), but *Brutus of Alba* will be found only in big learned libraries (either in its original printing or in the 1987 scholarly edition by R. R. Craven which appears in Stephen Orgel's 'Satire and Sense' series published by Garland). *Brutus*'s rarity is no great loss to the world at large, considering its general awfulness – Tate wrote much better when obliged by Purcell to cramp his verses into something singable – though it is a very interesting play for its formidable Sorceress and its hints of appropriate business and décor for *Dido*. (Craven's edition has a useful appendix of verbal parallels between tragedy and libretto.) As for preparatory reading from the last forty years, there have been quite a lot of generally illuminating things, but specifically from a producer's point of view, two of the most worthwhile are, I think, Eric Walter White's scholarly essay, 'New Light on *Dido and Aeneas*', in *Henry Purcell 1659–1695* (a tercentenary *Festschrift* edited in 1959 by Imogen Holst), and Graham Sheffield's survey of the recordings of *Dido* in *Opera on Record 2* (ed. Alan Blyth, 1983). Elsewhere there are insights to be had from Selma Cohen's account of *Dido*'s probable choreographer and godfather Josias Priest in her essay on Restoration theatrical dancing in the *Bulletin of the New York Public Library*, lxiii (1959), reprinted the following year in *Famed For Dance* by Cohen,

I. K. Fletcher and Roger Lonsdale, and from a just and lively defence of Tate as librettist by Imogen Holst in her collection mentioned above, still perhaps necessary to counter his die-hard reputation as a comical incompetent. (I myself believe that his libretto has only one real lapse, which is that Dido's important sentence beginning 'Mean wretches' grief can touch . . .' in the opening scene is syntactically too obscure for singing. Equally there is, I think, only one solecism in Purcell's setting: Dido's crucial phrase 'To death I'll fly' in her quarrel with Aeneas is set in such a way that it is normally inaudible. The other moment of obscurity in most performances, and it needs strong production to clarify it, is the Sorceress's sentence beginning, 'But when they've done, my trusty elf . . .' where perhaps Tate and Purcell should share the blame.)

More recently, Curtis A. Price has anthologized some lively views of the work in the 'Criticism and Analysis' section of his *Dido* volume for the Norton Critical Scores series (1986). This also includes the Laurie edition of the surviving music and the Tilmouth witching scene I mentioned earlier, as well as useful things on backgrounds and on performance history by Price and Laurie themselves. Ellen Harris's book *Henry Purcell's 'Dido and Aeneas'* (1987) is also interesting on performance history, and a fascinating piece by Bruce Wood and Andrew Pinnock in *Early Music*, xx (1992), ' "Unscarr'd by turning times"?', is pretty convincing in its hypothesis that the opera was not, as so long held, written *for* Priest's Chelsea school in 1689 but only revived *by* it, having its true première about five years before, most likely in a professional performance at Charles II's Court. Producers of the opera tempted to think of it as conceived for amateurs and redolent of the Restoration equivalent of hockey-sticks and gym-slips will find food for thought here.

iv   How far should a production exploit the connection with Virgil's Aeneid?

Here a little learning is a dangerous thing. It tempts us to rap Purcell and Tate over the knuckles for 'getting Virgil wrong' and set out to correct them in production. This is counterproductive, however. Certainly any intelligent member of the audience at the première would have seen *Dido and Aeneas* as a creative interpretation, a reworking of episodes in the *Aeneid*, not as a simple, straightforward setting of Virgil. And this was quite acceptable Baroque practice: Busenello was just as cavalier with Virgil in his text for Cavalli's *La Didone* in 1641, and so was Metastasio in his *Didone abbandonata* libretto, first set by Domenico Sarro in 1724 and all the rage for some years afterwards. What Tate and Purcell do is to leave out all references to Aeneas' son and Dido's former husband, turn her sister Anna into a warm-hearted but rather flighty confidante called Belinda, consummate the lovers' passion well before the celebrated storm and not during it, have Aeneas dispatched from Carthage by an evil trick rather than the will of Rome-creating providence, and suggest that Dido simply dies of a broken heart without wild cries of revenge and the need for a funeral pyre. As if this were not enough, they allow Aeneas a final (though rejected) surrender to love rather than duty, and give a third or so of their opera to the Iago-like plottings of a coven of Gothic spirits who have no original in Virgil at all (where the malign Juno of the *Aeneid* would certainly disown them) and who derive pretty clearly from the Davenant *Macbeth* which superseded Shakespeare's in the Restoration and for which (coincidentally or not) Josias Priest devised the dances. (Put a few lines of Davenant's additions to Shakespeare –

> At the night-Raven's dismal voice,
> Whilst others tremble, we rejoyce;
> And nimbly, nimbly dance we still
> To th'Ecchoes from an hollow Hill . . .
> Let's to the Cave and our dire Charms prepare

– beside Tate's Cave scene in *Dido* and you will see what I mean.) What is more, Tate and Purcell are clearly much more interested in Dido than in the Trojan hero. Indeed, it might have saved a lot of misunderstanding if they had called their opera *The Tragedy of Dido Queen of Carthage*, as Marlowe did his play a century before. But none of this is to imply that their work is anything other than quite consistent in itself. It is simply to suggest that, in our age of classical illiteracy, a producer should call on Virgil only with a lot of circumspection, except of course where the poet can help to explain small obscurities in the libretto such as the reference in the first scene to that 'tale so strong' sung offstage by Aeneas. (The listeners needed to be strong too, since the tale consisted of the equivalent of the 1500 hexameters which make up Books II and III of the *Aeneid*.) Tate and Purcell are really writing an opera on Dido and *fate*, a word which appears no fewer than ten times in the libretto, and using *what* they please *how* they please from the *Aeneid*, *Macbeth*, *Brutus of Alba* (of which the *Dido* libretto is no carbon copy), and so on.

v   Is there a proper décor for the opera?

I can see no reason for setting the opera in a Trojan-Punic world either of neo-classical imagination or of accurate archaeology. There might be room for both in a décor for *The Trojans* of Berlioz (which, incidentally, is much more straightforwardly Virgilian, and in places Shakespearian, than *Dido*); but both would be anachronistic to a tragedy of the 1680s: neo-classicism by 100 years and 'correct historical detail' by about 150. Edward Gordon Craig wrote in the programme for the epoch-making production of *Dido* he designed and produced in 1900 that he had 'taken particular care to be entirely incorrect in all matters of detail'; and Craig is often a good example to follow. After all, the opera is essentially a study of the conflicting emotions of an archetypal woman of social and psychological stature. It could be argued in fact that, leaving aside Aeneas and his *buffo* counterpart the tenor-solo sailor, all the characters in the opera are really personified aspects *of* Dido: Belinda and the Second Woman projections of her yearning towards erotic fulfilment, the Sorceress a formidable anti-self embodying all her insecurities and apprehensions of disaster contingent on her involving herself in any deep personal relationship, and the two solo witches nightmarish shadows of Belinda and the Second Woman. If this is so, it is tempting and perhaps desirable to set the opera now – as one might set a similar Baroque psycho-tragedy dominated by one woman, Racine's *Phèdre* (1677) – in a post-naturalistic *lieu vague* created purely by light, with abstract costumes and symbolic props (cf. that memorable modernistic line from Guillaume de Vere-Tipple's *Aeneas on the Saxophone*, 'And Dido on her lilo *à sa proie attachée*', as preserved for us by Osbert Lancaster in *Drayneflete Revealed . . .*). This was something of Craig's approach in the 1900 production: a poetic exploitation of coloured light and sheer space which is vividly described in Edward Craig's life of his father (1968) and in the 1983 monograph on him by Christopher Innes. Far better this, certainly, than designing *Dido* as a chunk of Carthaginian history. Better still though, perhaps, to set it *à l'antique* in the seventeenth-century sense, with flats and shutters representing grand vistas which change by unseen hands from colonnades to cliffs to trees in full view of the audience (not as expensive to rig up as they might sound), with flamboyant Roman-Baroque tragic costumes for hero and heroine (cuirasses, plumes and such) and perhaps a flying 'machine' to allow the false Mercury and drooping Cupids to descend properly. (The Cupids are cousins to those in Shadwell's *Psyche* of 1675, the décor for which is discussed in the Restoration chapter of Sybil Rosenfeld's *Short History of Scene Design in Great Britain*, 1973.) Again, one could derive the costumes for the witches from the *Macbeth* engraving in Nicholas Rowe's early eighteenth-century edition of Shakespeare, and one might find hints for the courtly costumes in the detailed records of the staging of the Court masque *Calisto* (given in the Hall Theatre at Whitehall Palace in 1675) which are to be found in Eleanore Boswell's *The Restoration Court Stage* of 1932. Wood and Pinnock's speculation that *Dido* was premièred at Court only nine years later makes Boswell's book an intriguing resource. For a designer to do all this – always provided it is without olde worlde quaintness – is no more 'merely antiquarian' than for the musical director to use a harpsichord as a continuo instrument or a countertenor for his false Mercury. Besides, it provides a visual style which complements the musical-verbal style and so helps the audience to focus with the necessary speed on the real issues of the opera: passion, duty and the human condition (or 'Cupid', 'empire' and 'fate', to use Tate's language).

vi Should there be a double chorus?

A remarkably large slice of *Dido*'s musical cake is given to the chorus. (It has as many bars to sing as Dido, Aeneas and the Sorceress put together.) However, speculation can point both ways when it comes to considering whether Purcell intended there to be one chorus-group playing Dido's courtiers and another the witches and sailors, or whether he expected the same group to play all the choral parts. Certainly if there is enough singing talent and costume cash available, the two-group arrangement is easier on the wardrobe-mistress and stage-manager, since it cuts out a series of frantic backstage costume changes; yet I am not sure that it is really preferable. The easy-going sensuality of Dido's Court and the bitchiness of the witches are equally inimical to the Queen's happiness, and this comes over very clearly if it is evident to an audience that the same troupe of talented masqueraders is playing both. There is a corollary to this which is on the face of it absurd, that the same singer should play both Dido and the Sorceress. But even here the absurdity would be one of over-emphasis rather than perversity. And is it *so* absurd? Janet Baker has played the Sorceress in the Banqueting Hall at Hampton Court and Dido in the Baroque theatre at Drottningholm, and recently Della Jones has on occasion actually taken both roles – Odette/Odile-fashion – in the same show, in *one* show compounding the doubling by doing it as one of the group of 'pit' singers supporting a danced performance of the opera by the Mark Morris Dance Group in which Morris played both Queen and Sorceress while his *corps de ballet* doubled courtiers and witches with panache. (While on gender-bending, Irena Cholij and Curtis A. Price have assembled a strong case that the Sorceress was performed by a man at the 1700 revival, five years after Purcell's death.[5] And in his life-time? The jury is still out on that.)

vii   The evil sisters: are they comic or sinister?

The Sorceress, her two attendants and the ho-hoing chorus do not take part in a detachable sub-plot of light relief. They are essential to the idea-pattern of the opera in that they embody the Spirit That Denies, and justify, or perhaps represent, the heroine's insecurity. Also they are essential to the intrigue in that it is they who create the false Mercury and who trick Aeneas into leaving Dido. The divergence from Virgil here is especially significant. Virgil's heroic Aeneas needs to be rescued by the good gods from his Carthaginian enchantress because she is, among other things, a Circe-figure and the embodiment of Rome's traditional enemy across the Mediterranean. Granted Tate and Purcell's Aeneas is also destined to found Rome; but it is a coven of evil sisters who maliciously set the founding of Rome in direct opposition to continuing a love affair with a never-less-than-sympathetic Dido; and it is they, not Jove, who contrive to have the affair snapped off the first night after its consummation. They *deceive* Aeneas into thinking that Love and Empire are irreconcilable. This is behaviour worthy of their close relations, Shakespeare's Weird Sisters. (The Sorceress in *Dido* even 'quotes' *Macbeth* – I.3.32, I.5.8 or II.1.20 – with her very first words by calling up her 'wayward sisters', this being the phrase used in all seventeenth-century texts of Shakespeare and Shakespeare/Davenant: it was later editors who changed the adjective to 'weird'.) The motiveless malignity of *Macbeth*'s hags relates them to Iago in *Othello*, and Iago's aside at the climax of Othello and Desdemona's happiness –

> O, you are well tuned now!
> But I'll set down the pegs that make this music

– anticipates the Sorceress's

> The Queen of Carthage, whom we hate,
> As we do all in prosperous state,
> Ere sunset shall most wretched prove,
> Deprived of fame, of life and love

just as her coven's 'Destruction's our delight, / Delight our greatest sorrow' is anticipated by the 'Fair is foul, and foul is fair' of the *Macbeth* witches. To bring in one more big Restoration gun to stress the diabolic connections of Purcell's witches, compare their 'Destruction's our delight' chorus with

> To do aught good never will be our task
> But ever to do ill our sole delight

which is Satan in *Paradise Lost*, no less (I.159–60). Given all this, I see no reason for making the witches in *Dido* anything other than menacingly sinister, though their energy and glee may well exhilarate and fascinate us. A way to realize this in production is to take a leaf out of Franz Liszt's book. His way of solving the problem of presenting the Spirit That Denies in the *Faust Symphony* is to make the Mephistopheles scherzo a black parody of the opening Faust movement; and this can be applied usefully to production of the witch scenes in *Dido*. After all, Tate and Purcell provide the structure: their courtly scenes have a female protagonist singing mainly slow music, two girl attendants with more animated music, a cheerful but hardly sensitive chorus which sings simple dance numbers in the main, and one male soloist – a voyager who loves and leaves. If you look at the witch scenes (including the one with the sailors) you will find this structure repeated exactly, which can hardly be accidental. Hence it posits an icy dignity for the Sorceress (no pantomime wicked fairy she) and means that in production the sentiments and rituals of the Court can be grotesquely guyed by the witches (widdershins dances, sick-caricature mimes to accompany the Sorceress's prophecies and provoke those ho-ho outbursts etc.), a process to which Purcell's music gives warrant in the Sailor's Song, where that lover-leaver's cynical libertinism at

> And silence their mourning
> With vows of returning
> But never intending to visit them more

is accompanied by a jaunty pre-echo of the familiar ground bass which will support Dido's aria of mourning at the climax of the opera. (By the way, I am not sure that Purcell and Tate meant their evil sisters to be the disadvantaged harridans, sluts and crones of downtown Carthage that some socially minded producers choose nowadays to make them. Is there anything really demotic or *demi-mondaine* about their music? And you only have to compare the words they sing with those of Davenant's witches, or even those of Tate's own Mediterranean coven in *Brutus of Alba*, to realize that the sisters in *Dido*, however wayward, have definite class.)

viii   Are there four scenes in Dido *or five?*

The division into acts in *Dido and Aeneas* does not seem to me to be very helpful, and besides, the manuscripts and 1689 libretto differ over where the divisions come. It is better, I think, to conceive of the piece in four scenes – (1) 'The Palace'; (2) 'The Cave'; (3) 'The Grove'; and (4) 'The Ships' – each with its single inexorable line. Between scenes – always after some sort of triumphing dance and at least twice with the possibility of thunder and lightning from backstage – there should be at most a half-minute pause for the painted wings and shutters to change before the audience's eyes and for the audience to get a little of its breath back. Or are there five scenes? A footnote to the Laurie/Dart performing editions says of the moment before Dido's final entry ('Your counsel all is urged in vain'), 'the scene should change back to the Palace here, evidently'. While granting that such a change could be made on the Restoration stage in a few seconds, I do not find it evident that it should happen at all, for two reasons. First, each new scene up to now has been preceded by an instrumental prelude and there is none (or at least none survives) at this point; second, there is a powerful theatrical irony if Dido and Aeneas quarrel grandly over parting on the same wharf on which the sailors and their witching molls have just been taking their 'boozy short leave'. Again, one can argue that it is quite wrong for the audience to be able to regain any breath here; and besides, running the action on allows the producer, if so minded, to keep the Sorceress on stage until the end of the Witches' Dance, then have her dismiss her sisters and for a split second share the stage with her anti-self the

Queen, who has come on to face her lover for the last time and then her death.

ix   Is Aeneas a complete booby?

If having Dido and the Sorceress twist eyebeams for an instant is allowable in an opera which has very little room for such production 'points', so perhaps is encouraging the Sorceress and her two attendants to come gloating on stage (far *up*stage) half a minute early for their cue at 'Then since our charms have sped' in the Grove scene, early enough to be visible to the audience while Aeneas, in soliloquy down front, is blaming the gods for his having to desert Dido. This emphasizes the extent to which Aeneas is a puppet in the witches' hands and, paradoxically perhaps, helps to maintain the audience's sympathy for him. Still, I would hesitate before telling an Aeneas that he is being literally upstaged during his climactic high F: the role has a pronounced enough reputation among baritones for unrewardingness as it is. Joseph Kerman speaks for the baritones in the often perceptive section on *Dido* in his *Opera as Drama* (1956), where he describes the Trojan prince as 'a complete booby'. But this is unjust, I think. True, Aeneas has no arias, not even a proper duet, and he does let the witches ride roughshod over him. But then it is Dido's opera and Aeneas is significant only as her loved seducer. There is no call for us to look at his head from within, as it were, as an aria would allow us to. Indeed, there is interesting evidence in the Eric Walter White essay I mentioned above that Purcell may perhaps have been offered the text for an Aeneas aria beginning

> Direct me, friends, what choice to make
> Since love and fame together press me

and either set it and then discarded the setting or declined to set it at all. As for letting the witches ride roughshod, it must be said in Aeneas' defence that he thinks that it is the *gods* he is letting subdue him, which is, after all, very pious. (There is nothing in the actual ultimatum of the false Mercury to suggest its falsity.) Then again, Aeneas is as handsome, brave and amorous as he is pious. So far, so positive. And he is the more interesting as a dramatic character because he is, in addition, so self-absorbed that he cannot see the complexities of others, certainly not of Dido. I suspect too that he is a rather selfish love-maker ('one night enjoyed . . .'), certainly too animal for the sensitive Queen. How else is one supposed to take the monster's head on the bending spear (the only obligatory prop in the whole opera), which so troubles her that it beclouds her day?

x   Is there a clear time-scheme in the opera?

The four lines 'Go revel, ye Cupids, the day is your own', 'Charge him sail tonight with all his fleet away', 'Ere sunset shall most wretched prove', and 'One night enjoyed, the next forsook' between them determine a time-scheme: the Palace scene takes place 'once upon a time', the Cave scene in the early hours of the following morning, the Grove scene around the middle of the same day as the Cave scene, and the Ships scene that night. A few hours before curtain-up Aeneas has 'sung' his 'tale so strong and full of woe' to Dido and her Court (another sore point with the baritones!). A vivid but simple lighting plot could present Scene 1 in an ever-increasing indoor daylight (*petite levée*, *grande levée*, diplomatic reception, cheerful festivity); Scene 2 as starting in the half-light of a chilly dawn and ending with something bright enough to drive the witches into their cave to avoid the glare of 'this open air'; Scene 3 as an afternoon *fête-champêtre* bathed in sunlight until the storm-clouds build up at the reference to the monster's head and then dominate and darken the grove till the end; and Scene 4 as leading from a lurid post-storm sunset for the 'boozy short leave' to moonlight ('Phoebe's pale deluding beams') at the unfurling of the sails. (Through the moonlight scurries the libretto's 'Jack of the Lanthorn': presumably the Sorceress's Puck/Ariel-like 'trusty elf', who has exchanged the disguise of Mercury in which he has perplexed Aeneas for that of a will-o'-the-wisp to perplex Aeneas' ship-men. Ideas for staging this scene might well be provoked by looking at the quite detailed stage directions of the Jack o'Lantern masque in Robert Stapylton's

Slighted Maid of 1663, which Dennis Arundell describes in Chapter 6 of *The Critic at the Opera* (1957).)

xi How far should electricity be used?

For sound effects, the electrical should and can be avoided. The thunder the manuscripts call for at the beginning and end of the Cave scene must be of the same order as the orchestral thunder in the middle of the Grove scene, which is to say Baroque-artificial – for preference made by cannon-balls in a thunder-run (see *The Oxford Companion to the Theatre* on this). For lighting effects the problem is greater. It is tempting to insist that the electrical should be avoided here too, and the whole thing lit with candles. But unless the venue is one where public fire regulations do not apply one cannot avoid electricity. So the person on the board needs to be constrained to work within the limits of simulating what a well-equipped private Restoration theatre that inherited the masquing traditions of the Stuart Court could do, which means in effect simple pre-sets, perhaps some atmospheric colouring and a limited amount of general fading; but next-to-no isolated spots and no aspiring to Broadway-musical virtuosity.

xii What does one do with the chorus?

I am tempted to ignore my own advice about lighting during Dido's two great arias over a ground bass, which seem to be directed at Belinda and perhaps at the Second Woman but hardly at the Court *en masse*. Surely there is a case here for bringing the follow-spot up on the heroine and fading the courtiers down very low. Maybe; but it is not an impressive case, just a weak *ad hoc* solution to one part of the general problem of *Dido*'s almost omnipresent chorus. It is a problem which has been variously tackled. You can read in the columns of *Opera* of the chess-game that once went on at Cambridge during Dido's 'Peace and I are strangers grown', and of the Kabuki stylization for a stationary chorus at Tokyo, and of the producer at Dallas who chose to banish the chorus to the pit.[6] I would suggest that a more moderate course is more satisfying and apropos. Take the case of Dido's Lament. The music earlier in this scene has unfortunately not given any signal for the entry of the courtiers, yet they need to be on stage in time for their 'Great minds against themselves conspire' and hence they are present when the Queen dies. Their arrival, I think, needs to be tactful, unobtrusive and piecemeal: some with Belinda and the Second Woman at Dido's own entry; others with Aeneas when he makes his crest-fallen appearance (which must surely mirror his more cocksure arrival in Scene 1); the rest – individually cued and always with somewhere to go – between that entry and 'Great minds' itself. Such comings and goings of Dido's Court can be easily achieved if the most authoritative of the chorus men is given the role of Dido's chamberlain or major domo, her equivalent of the Sorceress's 'trusty elf'; so all that needs to happen at 'Thy hand, Belinda' is for the chamberlain to avert his head and the rest of the Court will follow suit: there is no need for general fades. (It helps too if two other chorus men are cast as confidant-lieutenants to Aeneas. On a level of symmetry this gives the Prince a similar retinue to those of Dido and the Sorceress, and it also allows a boyfriend apiece to Belinda and Second Woman in the Grove scene.) Just as it is the musical director's problem to balance the necessity for each scene in *Dido* to be as ongoing as a symphonic movement with the other necessity that every dramatic moment he put across with maximum intensity, so it is the producer's problem to achieve a clear, unfussy line for each scene while at the same time ensuring that the figures on stage are never just standing about (something the music never does). Court protocol, together with a carefully worked out demeanour for the heroine and the principle that the activity of the witches is a deadly mockery of both, will provide a reliable source for all needful business.

xiii Monsters and fountains: how much does one stress the symbols?

My facetious mention of Osbert Lancaster's *Waste Land* parody earlier has its serious point. After all, the *Vénus tout entière à sa proie attachée* of Racine's *Phèdre* could almost be the motto of Purcell's opera. In a rather different sense from Charpentier's *Actéon*, *Dido* too is an '*opéra de chasse*': the symbolism of erotic pursuit and capture is central to it. 'Pursue thy conquest, Love!' says Belinda in Scene 1, and 'Fate forbids what you pursue' are Dido's first words when Aeneas comes courting. The loving pursuit find its emblem in a courtly hunting party ('The Queen and he are now in chase . . . So fair the game, so rich the sport'), during which one of Dido's women sings of a virgin goddess's lover fatally 'pursued by his own hounds' and Aeneas compares the boar he has caught to the one which gored to death the boy the goddess of love doted on. These are bad omens which, with the sexual roles reversed, are soon fulfilled: it is Dido who is the Actaeon/Adonis trapped and destroyed ('One night enjoyed, the next forsook'). And as soon as the quondam virgin queen, resting during the chase near Diana's fountain after a night of love with Aeneas, sees the bleeding monster's head on the Prince's spear, she 'discovers too, too late' what has happened to her. At that moment someone walks over her grave:

> The skies are clouded. Hark, how thunder
> Rends the mountain oaks asunder!

I would not suggest that the symbolism of *Vénus et sa proie* is very clearly worked out in Tate's libretto. But I do think that it would be as unwise to pooh-pooh it altogether as to turn the Grove scene into an expressionist jamboree on the strength of it. The producer must be tactful. Until the weather breaks, the gathering at the grove is a civilized rite-cum-entertainment, as the Sorceress – called there Ragusa – makes clear in Act III of Tate's *Brutus of Alba*:

> When the sports are done
> The Court repairs to the *Diana* Fountain,
> To worship there the Goddess of the Woods,
> And drink of the cool Stream . . .
> When they have drunk, an entertainment follows . . .
> Heark, the Stagg's faln, and now the Court comes on
> To th'Fountain to perform the *Sylvan* Rites;
> 'Tis time we were preparing for the Storm.

The *Dido* gathering should be suave and elegant but not prettified or frivolous. Actaeon's pain is still in the air, and the climax of the Second Woman's marvellous aria makes us feel it. (In another sense John Blow's *Venus and Adonis*, only a few years old when *Dido* was given, is still in the air too: Aeneas' recitative about the boar is surely on one level an allusion to it.) Beyond this, two things are worth noting where staging is concerned. First, the couplet beginning 'the skies are clouded' is the only thing Dido sings in the whole scene; so it must be carefully prepared for if it is not to seem a very English conversation-filler. Second, the couplet is soon followed by her leaving the grove without Aeneas, which probably means that she has avoided him since the couplet and that any attempts he may have made to come to her side have been thwarted by the jostling of the town-bound crowd (rather as in the final reel of *Les enfants du paradis*). Hence a lot of dramatic emphasis is thrown on to that boar's head on the bending spear, which must be Baroque-heraldic, sinister, mildly phallic and quite unfunny. Rule one for *Dido*-producers is 'Find a good maker of boars' heads.' If you can't, do *The Seagull* instead . . .

xiv   Who dances what?

The music of *Dido* is very gestural. (If you feel no muscular response to the four orchestral bars in the middle of the chorus 'To the hills and the vales' or to the viola line under the Sorceress's phrase 'whom we *hate*' in the Cave scene or to the Queen's 'No repentance shall reclaim' in her quarrel with Aeneas, think even more seriously about switching to Chekhov.) Hence the opera will support expansive and eloquent movement, from which various formal measures such as the Triumphing Dance and antic pantomimes such as the Jack o'Lantern episode can take off. The libretto and manuscripts do not make it clear who among the performers did the dancing in the original performances. I see no reason why the Queen and Prince should not dance a private 'Gittars Chacony' and 'Gitter Ground a Dance' in the Palace and Grove scenes (if those numbers are going to be included), and it is effective if they join publicly in the Court's

Triumphing Dance after the two rogue bars in the middle of the number when the first violins start to play the ground bass. For the rest, in the Chelsea production Mr Priest probably taught the many dances called for to some of his young gentlewomen and their gentlemen friends, but whether those gentlefolk were, or should be, the same girls and boys who sing the choruses is not clear. Perhaps the likelihood is a separate dance troupe: this would certainly have been likely at a Court première with professional performers. Records of the elaborate Court entertainment *Calisto* in 1675 (which Priest was also involved in) make it clear that singers and dancers were distinct teams in that; and besides, in *Dido* itself a separation is implied by the request of the full coven that 'Nymphs of Carthage' should lead the pleasing, easing dance at the end of the Grove scene and by the libretto's stage direction that the Cupids who appear in the clouds after the chorus 'Great minds against themselves conspire' should dance either during or after the chorus 'With drooping wings you Cupids come'. What *is* clear is that the dancing should be Baroque-based – Priest, not Petipa. Young Pavlovas need not apply, though applicants will need to be pretty versatile to cope with the 'masquing' and 'anti-masquing' dance styles called for.

xv   Is Dido a virgin queen at the start and when does intimacy take place?

Forgive the forensic questions in what, after all, is a very discreet opera, but the producer and principals presumably do need to know the answers. If I read the libretto aright, with its wholesale modifications of Virgil and partial modifications of Tate's earlier *Brutus* too, the opera gives us a study of a virgin queen married to her nation and suppressing the urge to personal fulfilment through love because of an awareness that it might be divisive of her country or of her attention to her country. In spite of this she chooses, blamelessly but self-laceratingly, to accept a dashing young nobleman as her lover. (The closeness of so much of this to the Britten/Plomer *Gloriana* is intriguing, and I doubt it is wholly coincidental, since Britten started to compose *Gloriana* the year after he had made his edition of *Dido* and conducted several performances of it. In some of these, the tragic lovers were played by Joan Cross and Peter Pears, who went on to create the roles of Elizabeth and Essex in *Gloriana*. The fact that the former addresses her sage counsellor Robert Cecil at one point as her 'trusty elf' is the least of the parallels between the two operas.) It is perhaps a flaw in Purcell's opera – it certainly makes it difficult for the performers – that the precise moment of Dido's acceptance of Aeneas' love near the end of the first scene is not made musically clear, though one must admit that it is hard to imagine any words on the subject by the Queen, and a love duet (something remotely related to the finale of *L'Incoronazione di Poppea*) would give too much parity of interest to Aeneas. The moment of acceptance has to come somewhere between Belinda's observation that the Queen's 'eyes / Confess the flame her tongue denies' and the chorus's 'Let the triumphs of love and of beauty be shown' about thirty seconds later, which does not give much time for the necessary piece of simple but eloquent mime. There is more time, of course, if one inserts 'A Dance Gittars Chacony' at this point – something the 1689 libretto asks for but Purcell's surviving score does not provide. Could it be that at the first performance Aeneas led Dido in a formal courtship-and-acceptance dance here, accompanied by a much scaled-down band to suggest the intimacy of the moment and, since so accompanied, not needing the composer to write the part out beforehand? Support for this would come from the fact that the only other unsurviving guitar dance, the 'ground' in the Grove scene, also comes at a point where the now united royal lovers could aptly execute a stately but private *pas de deux*, i.e. just before the Second Woman's Actaeon aria. Certainly without these guitar movements the hero and heroine are allowed puritanically little *tendresse* on stage. The *tendresse* offstage follows Scene 1. When the lovers leave after 'Go revel, ye Cupids', it is to set out for some notional hunting lodge where they spend the night, their love-making coinciding with the announcement by the Sorceress that she has devised 'a mischief that shall make all Carthage flame'. (It is, by the way, an interesting example of the opera's wry use of Virgil that the first scene's Triumphing Dance should immediately be followed by thunder and lightning and a scene-change to a secluded cave. Every Restoration schoolboy would know that Dido and Aeneas were about to enter and take shelter together. Instead we are presented with the Sorceress, Dido's destructive anti-self.)

xvi   How does Dido die?

Dido's death for Metastasio and Sarro in *Didone abbandonata* (1724) is almost as histrionic and spectacular as Brünnhilde's for Wagner in *Götterdämmerung*: she throws herself frantically into the burning ruins of her palace just before it is overwhelmed by a raging sea. But Dido's dying for Tate and Purcell is almost as ambiguous as Isolde's in *Tristan*. With Isolde it is not so much death as transfiguration. With Dido the chorus's references to her tomb and drooping-winged Cupids assure us that death has come, but when and how is not definite. 'When' is something a sensitive producer and his or her leading lady will have virtually to choreograph to relate to the two final statements of the ground bass of her Lament. 'How' is more problematical. She is clearly resolved to die and her heart is near breaking-point. But earlier in the scene she seems to have threatened suicide ('To death I'll fly if longer you delay'), and earlier still the Sorceress has prophesied that she will 'bleed'. The only consistent and tactful solution, I think, is that she should produce or find a small dagger and pierce her breast with it firmly but unmelo-dramatically during the orchestral conclusion to the Lament, acting the scene as if the tiniest physical wound would be sufficient to dispatch someone whose vitality has been almost drained away by emotional suffering. The music will do the rest. As for the dagger, it is worth noting that it breaks the rule that there are no essential props in *Dido*, with the grand exception of the monster's head on the bending spear. I have found it effective in production – and a way to maintain that austerity, as well as to provide Dido with a kind of tomb to die on and perhaps have roses scattered over – if, during the antic Jack o'Lantern dance earlier in the Ships scene, some of Aeneas' sailors bring in the hero's spear, helmet, breastplate and sea-chests *en route* for his ship, but are scared away by the witches before they can take them off again. This means that the Queen can take a dagger from the breastplate, then sink on to the chests (less far to fall than the floor in very slow, quiet music) and die beneath a hollow Aeneas-image. It happens that such a piece of business is also fairly faithful to Virgil's account of Dido's death, for what that is worth.

> Purcell's opera is capable of being presented on the stage in very many different ways. It can be given with the singers seated on chairs and making but few movements; or it can be mounted as they mount the operas of Gluck in Paris. And then there is another way of mounting it; that is in the more modern and up-to-date manner. And then there is the way of the individualist. This is Mr Craig's way. It is always different, and when he produces a play or an opera he follows no old-fashioned manner, and no up-to-date manner; he does it in a manner which is personal and which is not to be imitated and which cannot be imitated.

This is 'Allen Carric' (alias Gordon Craig) in *The Mask* for January 1909 praising his own production of *Dido* nine years after the event. And though my way with the opera is clearly very different from his – when W. B. Yeats celebrates 'Gordon Craig's purple backcloth that made Dido and Aeneas seem wandering on the edge of eternity', I want to replace the lovers with Pelléas and Mélisande – the terms of his discussion seem to me sound. I certainly agree that the producer must do things 'in a manner which is personal', but I doubt whether the personalness need or should be as private, intransigent, perhaps irresponsible, as Craig implies. My personal manner, as I hope these sixteen investigations have shown, springs from an attempt to marry two beliefs: first, that if an 'early' opera is any good, it is because it is a memorable embodiment in sound and gesture of something important for us as an audience now; second, that the intent of a seventeenth- or eighteenth-century opera composer in providing his blueprint of notes was inextricably and happily bound up with the resources and conventions of the librettists, choreographers, scenographers and stage-managers he worked with, and may best come alive when they do. I recommend these beliefs with an assurance that their marriage, if achieved by sixty-nine different producers working with different companies in different theatres, would not lead to productions which were carbon copies of each other or of that unrepeatable first night at Whitehall, Windsor or wherever. What it would do would be to give every single one of those nine-and-sixty productions a better chance of being *right* than many an early opera we see around nowadays.

NOTES

1 This essay, which supplements the discussion of *Dido and Aeneas* on pp. 352–6 above, first appeared in *Early Music*, iv (1976), and was reprinted with some revisions in the Norton Critical Scores *Dido* volume edited in 1986 by Curtis A. Price. There are some further revisions here, principally about a dozen additional or rewritten sentences to take account of significant developments in Didonian scholarship and performance between 1986 and 1993. (I was tempted also to substitute 'directing' and 'director' for 'producing' and 'producer' *passim*, but decided it was better to let sleeping terminology lie.)

2 Published by Novello (London, 1961, rev. 2/1966).

3 Edward Harper, *Fanny Robin* (Oxford University Press, 1979).

4 Nanki Music Library, Japan.

5 Irena Cholij and Curtis A. Price, 'Dido's Bass Sorceress', *Musical Times*, cxxvii (1986), 615–18.

6 These examples are from *Opera*, xvii (1966) and xxiv (1973).

Bibliography

The purpose of the following bibliography is to provide an overview of Purcell's life and career, and to present material relevant to the main areas covered by the contributors. It is, therefore, divided into six sections: I General Studies of Purcell's Life, Times, Works and Reputation; II Biographical; III Purcell's Contemporaries; IV Purcell's Works – (i) Church music, (ii) The odes, (iii) Instrumental music; V Purcell and the Theatre – (i) The London theatres during Purcell's time, (ii) Purcell's music for the stage; and VI Performing and Recording Purcell. It is a selective bibliography emphasizing publications appearing after 1945; readers requiring a more comprehensive survey of material on Purcell are referred to Franklin B. Zimmerman's *Henry Purcell: A Guide to Research* which they will find listed in Part I of the bibliography.

I General Studies of Purcell's Life, Times, Works and Reputation

Adams, Martin, *Henry Purcell: The Origins and Development of His Musical Style* (Cambridge, 1995)

Arundell, Denis, *Henry Purcell* (London, 1927; rev. 2/1971)

—— 'Purcell and Natural Speech', *Musical Times*, c (1959), 323

Ayers, J. C., *The Influence of French Composers on the Work of Purcell* (London , 1964)

Burden, Michael, *Purcell Remembered* (London, 1995)

Campbell, Margaret, *Henry Purcell, the Glory of his Age* (London, 1993)

Cogan, R., 'Towards a Theory of Verbal Timbre and Vocal Line in Purcell, Sessions, and Stravinsky', *Perspectives of New Music*, viii (1969–70), 75–81

Cox, David, 'Henry Purcell, the British Orpheus (1659–1695)', *Gramophone*, xxxvii (1959), 1–2

Demarquez, Susan, *Purcell: la vie, l'oeuvre* (Paris, 1951)

Dupré, H., *Purcell* (Paris, 1927, Eng. trans. 1928; rev. 1975)

Flothuis, Marius, 'Purcell, Strawinsky en de Vooruitgang', *Mens en Melodie*, iv (1949), 82–4

Fortune, Nigel, 'A New Purcell Source', *Music Review*, xxv (1964), 109–13

Grennhalgh, Michael J., *The Music of Henry Purcell: A Guide for Librarians, Listeners and Students* (Eastcote, 1982)

Herissone, Rebecca, 'Purcell's Revisions of His Own Works', in Curtis A. Price, ed., *Purcell Studies* (Cambridge, 1995)

Holland, A. K., *Henry Purcell: The English Musical Tradition* (London, 1932; rev. 2/1948)

Holman, Peter, *Henry Purcell* (Oxford, 1995).

Holst, Imogen, ed., *Henry Purcell (1659–1695): Essays on his Music* (London, 1959)

King, A. Hyatt, 'The First "Complete Edition" of Purcell', *Monthly Musical Record*, lxxxi (1951), 63–9; rev. as 'Benjamin Goodison and the First "Complete Edition" of Purcell', in Richard Baum and Wolfgang Rehm, eds., *Musik und Verlag: Karl Votterle zum 65. Geburtstag* (Kassel, 1968), 391–6

Klessmann, E., 'Von wesen der musik Henry Purcells', *Musica*, xiii (1959), 634–6

Legany, Dezso, *Purcell* (Budapest, 1959)

Luckett, Richard, ' "Or Rather our Musical Shakespeare": Charles Burney's Purcell', in Richard Luckett and Christopher Hogwood, eds., *Music in Eighteenth-century England: Essays in Memory of Charles Cudworth* (Cambridge, 1983), 59–77

Marco, Guy, 'The Variety in Purcell's Word-painting', *Music Review*, xviii (1957), 1–3

Meinardus, W., 'Die Technik des Basso Ostinato bei Henry Purcell' (Ph.D. diss., U. of Cologne, 1950)

Mellers, Wilfrid, 'The Heroism of Henry Purcell: Music and Politics in Restoration England', in Christopher Norris, ed., *Music and the Politics of Culture* (London, 1989), 20–40.

—— 'Purcell's Ceremonial Elegy: *Four-part Fancy no. 4 in C minor, Hear my Prayer, Welcome to all the Pleasures*', in *Harmonious Meeting* (London, 1965), 194–202

Miller, Hugh M., 'Henry Purcell and the Ground Bass', *Music and Letters*, xxix (1948), 340–47

Pears, Peter, 'Homage to the British Orpheus', in Imogen Holst, ed.,

Henry Purcell 1659–1695: Essays on his Music (London, 1959), 1–6

Price, Curtis A., 'Purcell's Character and a Re-assessment of his Keyboard Music', in Curtis A. Price, ed., *Purcell Studies* (Cambridge, 1995)

—— ed., *Purcell Studies* (Cambridge, 1995)

Ravenzwaij, G. van, 'Henry Purcell's muzikale synthese in Engelands Restauratie-periode', in J. Van Nuffel, ed., *Miscellanea musicologie Floris van der Mueren* (Ghent, 1950), 201–7

—— *Purcell* (Haarlem and Antwerp, 1954)

Rohrer, Katherine, 'The Energy of English Words: Text and Expression in Purcell's Vocal Music' (Ph.D. diss., Princeton U., 1980)

Schjelderup-Ebbe, D., *Purcell's Cadences* (Oslo, 1962)

Sietz, Reinhold, *Henry Purcell: Zeit, Leben, Werk* (Leipzig, 1955)

Smith, Alan, *An Index of the Works of Henry Purcell, as Published by the Purcell Society* (London, n.d. [1970?])

Thomson, Robert, 'Purcell's Great Autographs', in Curtis A. Price, ed., *Purcell Studies* (Cambridge, 1995)

Vipont, E., *Henry Purcell and his Times* (London, 1959)

Westrup, J. A., 'Das Englische in Henry Purcell's Musik', *Musica*, xiii (1959), 170–73

—— *Purcell* (London, 1937; rev. 4/1980)

—— 'Purcell and Handel', *Music and Letters*, xl (1959), 103–8

—— 'Purcell's Reputation', *Musical Times*, c (1959), 318–20

Zimmerman, Franklin B., 'Handel's Purcellian Borrowings in his Later Operas and Oratorios', in Walter Gerstenberg, Jan LaRue and Wolfgang Rehm, eds., *Festschrift Otto Erich Deutsch* (Kassel, 1963), 20–30

—— *Henry Purcell: A Guide to Research* (New York, 1989)

—— *Henry Purcell 1659–1695: An Analytical Catalogue of his Music* (London, 1963)

—— *Henry Purcell 1659–1695: his Life and Times* (London, 1967; rev. 2/Philadelphia, 1983)

—— *Henry Purcell 1659–1695: Melodic and Intervallic Indexes to his Complete Works* (Philadelphia, 1975)

—— 'Monteverdi and Purcell', *Musical Times*, xcix (1958), 368–9

—— 'Poets in Praise of Purcell', *Musical Times*, c (1959), 526–8

—— 'Purcellian Passages in the Compositions of G. F. Handel', in Richard Luckett and Christopher Hogwood, eds., *Music in Eighteenth-century England: Essays in Memory of Charles Cudworth* (Cambridge, 1983), 49–58

II *Biographical*

Bergmann, Walter, 'Three Pieces of Music on Henry Purcell's Death',
  The Consort, xvii (1960), 13–19

Boston, John L., 'Purcell's Father', *Music and Letters*, xxxvi (1955),
  408–10 [letter]

Burden, Michael, ' "He had the honour to be your master"; Lady
  Rhoda Cavendish's music lessons with Henry Purcell', *Music and
  Letters*, lxxvi (1995)

Buttrey, John, 'Did Purcell go to Holland in 1691?' *Musical Times*, cx
  (1969), 929–31

Squire, W. Barclay, 'Purcell as Theorist', *Sammelbande der
  Internationalen Musick-Gesellschaft*, vi (1904–5), 521–67

Tilmouth, Michael, 'Henry Purcell, Assistant Lexicographer', *Musical
  Times*, c (1959), 325–6

Westrup, J. A., 'Purcell's Parentage', *Music Review*, xxv (1964),
  100–103

Zimmerman, Franklin B., 'Purcell and the Dean of Westminster –
  Some New Evidence', *Music and Letters*, xliii (1962), 7–15

—— 'Purcell Iconography: Missing Items', *Musical Times*, ci (1960),
  369; with supplementary letter from the author, 499

—— 'Purcell Portraiture', *Hinrichsen's Music Book*, x (1958),
  136–49

—— 'Purcell's Family Circle Revisited and Revised', *Journal of the
  American Musicological Society*, xvi (1963), 373–81

—— 'Purcell's Handwriting', in Imogen Holst, ed., *Henry Purcell
  1659–1695: Essays on his Music* (London, 1959), 103–5

III *Purcell's Contemporaries*

Baldwin, Olive and Wilson, Thelma, 'Alfred Deller, John Freeman
  and Mr Pate', *Music and Letters*, l (1969), 103–10

—— 'Musick Advanced and Vindicated', *Musical Times*, cxi (1970),
  148–50

John Blow

  Lewis, Anthony, 'Purcell and Blow's *Venus and Adonis*', *Music and
    Letters*, xliv (1963), 266–9

  Luckett, Richard, 'A New Source for *Venus and Adonis*', *Musical
    Times*, cxxx (1989), 76–9

  McGuinness, Rosamond, 'The Chronology of John Blow's Court
    Odes', *Music and Letters*, xlvi (1965), 102–21

Ruff, Lillian M., 'Dr Blow's "Rules for Composition" ', *Musical Times*, civ (1963), 184–5

Shaw, Watkins, 'John Blow', *Musical Times*, xcix (1958), 542–4

Wood, Bruce, 'John Blow's Anthems with Strings' (Ph.D. diss., U. of Cambridge, 1977)

—— ' "Only Purcell e're shall equal Blow" ', in Curtis A. Price, ed., *Purcell Studies* (Cambridge, 1995)

Charteris, Richard, 'Some Manuscript Discoveries of Henry Purcell and his Contemporaries in the Newberry Library, Chicago', *Notes*, xxxvii (1980–81), 7–13

William Child

Hudson, Frederick, and Large, Roy W., 'William Child (1606/7–1697) – a New Investigation of Sources', *Music Review*, xxxi (1970), 265–84

Henry Cooke

McGrady, Richard, 'Captain Cooke: a Tercentenary Tribute', *Musical Times*, cxiii (1972), 659–60

Colles, H. C., 'Lully and Purcell', in H. J. Colles, ed., *Essays and Lectures* (London, 1945), 50–51

Covell, Roger, 'Seventeenth-century Music for *The Tempest*', *Studies in Music* [W. Australia], ii (1968), 43–65

Dart, Thurston, 'The Cibell', *La Revue Belge de Musicologie*, vi (1952), 24–30

—— 'Purcell and Bull', *Musical Times*, civ (1963), 30–31

Fiske, Roger, 'The *Macbeth* Music', *Music and Letters*, xcv (1964), 114–25

Ford, Wyn K., 'The Chapel Royal in the Time of Purcell', *Musical Times*, c (1959), 592–3

Foster, Myles Birket, *Anthems and Anthem Composers* (London, 1901)

Harley, John, 'Music and Musicians in Restoration London', *Musical Quarterly*, xl (1954), 509–20

Holman, Peter, 'Bartholomew Isaack and "Mr Isaack" of Eton: a Confusing Tale of Restoration Musicians', *Musical Times*, cxxviii (1987), 381–5

—— 'Purcell and Roseingrave: a new autograph', in Curtis A. Price, ed. *Purcell Studies* (Cambridge, 1995)

—— '*Valentinian*, Rochester and Louis Grabu', in John Caldwell, Edward Olleson and Susan Wollenberg, eds., *The Well Enchanting Skill: Music, Poetry and Drama in the Culture of the Renaissance: Essays in Honour of F. W. Sternfeld* (Oxford, 1990), 127–41

Pelham Humfrey

Dennison, Peter, 'The Church Music of Pelham Humfrey', *Proceedings of the Royal Musical Association*, xcviii (1971–2), 65–71

—— *Pelham Humfrey* (Oxford, 1986)

Ford, Robert, 'Henman, Humfrey and "Have Mercy" ', *Musical Times*, cxxvii (1986), 459–62

Klakowich, Robert, '*Scocca pur*: Genesis of an English Ground', *Journal of the Royal Musical Association*, cxvi (1991), 63–77; see also letter 'Cavalli and Purcell' from F. W. Sternfeld, 324–5

Matthew Locke

Dennison, Peter, 'The Sacred Music of Matthew Locke', *Music and Letters*, lx (1979), 60–75

Field, Christopher D. S., 'Matthew Locke and the Consort Suite', *Music and Letters*, li (1970), 15–25

Lefkowitz, Murray, 'Shadwell and Locke's *Psyche*: the French Connection', *Proceedings of the Royal Musical Association*, cvi (1979–80), 42–55

MacDonald, Jennifer, 'Matthew Locke's *The English Opera*, and the Theatre Music of Purcell', *Studies in Music* [W. Australia], xv (1981), 62–75

Tilmouth, Michael, 'Revisions in the Chamber Music of Matthew Locke', *Proceedings of the Royal Musical Association*, xcviii (1971–2), 89–100

Mabbett, Margaret, 'Italian Musicians in Restoration England (1660–90)', *Music and Letters*, lxvii (1986), 237–47

Rimbault, E. F., ed., *The Old Cheque Book or Book of Remembrance of the Chapel Royal from 1561 to 1744* (London, 1872)

Roger North

Roger North's The Musicall Grammarian 1728, ed. Mary Chan and Jamie C. Kassler (Cambridge, 1990)

Roger North on Music, ed. John Wilson (London, 1959)

Ruff, Lillian, M., 'The 17th-Century English Music Theorists' (Ph.D. diss., U. of Nottingham, 1962)

—— 'The Music Lectures at Gresham College in the 17th Century', *The Consort*, xxiii (1966), 89–99

—— 'Thomas Salmon's "Essay to the Advancement of Musick" ', *The Consort*, xxi (1964), 266–75

Westrup, J.A., 'Foreign Musicians in Stuart England', *Musical Quarterly*, xxvii (1941), 70–89

Michael Wise

Smith, Michael J., 'The Church Music of Michael Wise', *Musical Times*, cxiv (1973), 69–73, and supplementary transcription of the anthem 'Christ Arising from the Dead'

Wood, Bruce, 'Cavendish Weedon: Impresario Extraordinary', *The Consort*, xxxiii (1977), 222–4

—— 'A note on Two Cambridge Manuscripts and Copyists', *Music and Letters*, lvi (1975), 308–12; [John Walter and *GB-Cf* Mus. MS 117; Bartholemew Isaack and *GB-Ckr* MS 22]

IV   *Purcell's Works*

(i)   CHURCH MUSIC

Cutts, John P., 'An Unpublished Purcell Setting', *Music and Letters*, xxxviii (1957), 1–13; see also letter from Nigel Fortune and editor's response, 207–8

Dennison, Peter, 'The Stylistic Origins of the Early Church Music [of Purcell]', in F. W. Sternfeld, Nigel Fortune and Edward Olleson, eds., *Essays in Honour of Sir Jack Westrup* (Oxford, 1975), 44–61

Ford, Anthony, 'A Purcell Service and its Sources', *Musical Times*, cxxiv (1983), 121–2

Ford, Robert, 'Purcell as his own Editor: The Funeral Sentences', *Journal of Musicological Research*, vii (1986), 47–67

—— 'A Sacred Song not by Purcell', *Musical Times*, cxxv (1984), 45–7

Fortune, Nigel, 'The Domestic Sacred Music [of Purcell]', in F. W. Sternfeld, Nigel Fortune and Edward Olleson, eds., *Essays in Honour of Sir Jack Westrup* (Oxford, 1975), 62–78

Hardwicke, Peter, 'Foreign Influences in the Verse Anthems of Henry Purcell' (MM diss., U. of Alberta, 1973)

Howard, Michael, 'An Anthem by Henry Purcell', *Monthly Musical Record*, lxxxiii (1953), 66–9

Klenz, William, 'The Church Sonatas of Henry Purcell' (Ph.D. diss., U. of North Carolina, 1948)

Noble, Jeremy, 'Purcell and the Chapel Royal', in Imogen Holst, ed., *Henry Purcell 1659–1695: Essays on his Music* (London, 1959), 52–66

Shay, Robert, 'Purcell as Collector of 'Ancient' Music: Fitzwilliam MS 88', in Curtis A. Price, ed., *Purcell Studies* (Cambridge, 1995)

Theile, Eugen, 'Die Kirchenmusik Henry Purcells', *Musik und Gottesdienst*, xxii (1958), 97–105

Van Tassel, Eric, 'Two Purcell Discoveries – 1: Purcell's "Give Sentence" ', *Musical Times*, cxviii (1977), 381–3

Wood, Bruce, 'A Newly Identified Purcell Autograph', *Music and Letters*, lix (1978), 329–32

—— 'Two Purcell Discoveries – 2: A Coronation Anthem Lost and Found', *Musical Times*, cxviii (1977), 466–8

Zimmerman, Franklin, B., *The Anthems of Henry Purcell* (New York, 1971)

—— 'Anthems of Purcell and Contemporaries in a Newly Rediscovered "Gostling Manuscript" ', *Acta Musicologica*, xli (1969), 55–70

—— 'A Newly Discovered Anthem by Purcell', *Musical Quarterly*, xlv (1959), 302–11

—— 'Purcell's "Service Anthem", *O God, Thou Art my God* and the B-flat major Service', *Musical Quarterly*, c (1964), 207–14

(ii)   ODES AND OCCASIONAL MUSIC

Adams, Martin, 'Purcell, Blow and the English Court Ode', in Curtis A. Price, ed., *Purcell Studies* (Cambridge, 1995)

—— 'Purcell's *Laudate Ceciliam*', in *Irish Musical Studies* (Dublin, 1990), 227–47

Baldwin, Olive and Wilson, Thelma, 'Who Can from Joy Refraine?; Purcell's Birthday Song for the Duke of Gloucester', *Musical Times*, cxxii (1981), 596–9

Gordon, Lewis W., 'The Odes of Henry Purcell', *American Choral Review*, xxvi (1984), 33

Leininger, George, 'The Odes of Henry Purcell: a Stylistic Survey' (Ph.D. diss., U. of Pennsylvania, 1976)

McGuinness, Rosamond, *English Court Odes, 1660–1820* (Oxford, 1971)

—— 'The Ground-bass in the English Court Ode', *Music and Letters*, li (1970), 118–40; 265–78

Pohlenz, Michael, 'A Performance Analysis of "Come Ye Sons of Art" by Henry Purcell' (DMA diss., U. of Oklahoma, 1983)

Spink, Ian, 'Purcell's Odes: Propaganda and Panegyric', in Curtis A. Price, ed., *Purcell Studies* (Cambridge, 1995)

(iii)   INSTRUMENTAL MUSIC

Arnold, Cecily and Johnson, Marshall, 'The English Fantasy Suite', *Proceedings of the Royal Musical Association*, lxxxii (1955–6), 1–14

Boal, Ellen TeSelle, 'Purcell's Clock Tempos and the Fantasias', *Journal of the Viola da Gamba Society of America*, xx (1983), 24–39

Browning, Alan, 'Purcell's Stairre Case Overture', *Musical Times*, cxxi (1980), 768–9

Bucht, Gunnar, 'Purcell och den engelske fancyn. Till 300-araminnet av tonsattarens fodelse', *Musikrevy*, xxiii (1958), 233–5, 245

Conley, Philip R., 'The Use of the Trumpet in the Music of Purcell', *Brass Quarterly*, iii (1959), 3–11

Cooper, Barry, 'Did Purcell Write a Trumpet Voluntary?', *Musical Times*, cxix (1978), 791–3, 1073–5

Cudworth, Charles, 'Some New Facts about the Trumpet Voluntary', *Musical Times*, xciv (1953), 401–3

—— and Zimmerman, Franklin B., 'The Trumpet Voluntary', *Music and Letters*, xci (1960), 342–8

Dart, Thurston, 'Purcell's Chamber Music', *Proceedings of the Royal Musical Association*, lxxxv (1958–9), 81–93

Faure-Lingorow, S., *Der Instrumentalstil von Purcell* (Berne, 1950)

Ford, Robert, 'Osborn MS 515, a Guardbook of Restoration Instrumental Music', *Fontes Artis Musicae*, xxx (1983), 174–84

Holman, Peter, *'Four and Twenty Fiddlers': The Violin at the English Court 1540–1690* (Oxford, 1993)

—— 'The Trumpet Sonata in England', *Early Music*, iv (1976), 424–9

Illing, Robert, *Henry Purcell's Sonata in G minor for Violin and Continuo: an Account of its Survival from both the Historical and Technical Point of View* (Adelaide, 1975)

Koeltzsch, Hans, 'Henry Purcell's gambenfantasien', *Musica*, ix (1955), 364–6

Meyer, E. H., *English Chamber Music : the History of a Great Art from the Middle Ages to Purcell* (London, 1946); rev. E. H. Meyer and Diana Poulton as *Early English Chamber Music from the Middle Ages to Purcell* (London, 1982)

Rawlinson, H., 'Fantasia upon One Note for Strings', *Strad*, lviii (1948), 202–4

—— 'Purcell's Music for String Orchestra', *Strad*, lxx (1959), 49–53

Shaw, H. Watkins, 'Purcell's Trio Sonatas', *Musical Times*, cxx (1979), 495–6

Stevens, Denis, 'Purcell's Art of Fantasia', *Music and Letters*, xxxiii (1952), 341–5

Tilmouth, Michael, 'The Technique and Forms of Purcell's Sonatas', *Music and Letters*, xl (1959), 109–21

Wailes, Marylin, 'Four Short Fantasies by Henry Purcell', *Score*, no. 20 (1957), 59–65

Wessely-Kropik, Helene, 'Henry Purcell als Instrumentalkomponist', *Studien zur Musikwissenschaft*, xxii (1955), 85–141

V *Purcell and the Theatre*

(i) THE LONDON THEATRES DURING PURCELL'S TIME

Avery, Emmet L., 'The Restoration Audience', *Philological Quarterly*, xlv (1966), 54–61

Baur-Heinhold, Margarete, *The Baroque Theatre: a Cultural History of the 17th and 18th Centuries* (Munich, 1966; trans. Mary Whitall, New York, 1967)

Boswell, Elenore, *The Restoration Court Stage 1660–1702* (Cambridge, Mass., 1932)

Downes, John, *Roscius Anglicanus* (1708), ed. Judith Milhous and Robert D. Hume (London, 1987)

Freehafer, John, 'The Formation of the London Patent Companies in 1660', *Theatre Notebook*, xx (1965), 6–30

Langhans, Edward A., 'A Conjectural Reconstruction of the Dorset Garden Theatre', *Theatre Survey*, xiii (1972), 74–93

—— *Restoration Promptbooks* (Carbondale, 1981)

Moore, Robert E., *Music in the Restoration Theatre* (London, 1961)

Price, Curtis A., *Music in the Restoration Theatre with a Catalogue of Instrumental Music in Plays 1665–1713* (Ann Arbor, 1979)

—— 'Restoration Theatre Music Restored', *Musical Times*, cxxiv (1983), 344–7

Radice, Mark A., 'Theatre Architecture at the Time of Purcell and its Influence on his "Dramatick Operas" ', *Musical Quarterly*, lxxiv (1990), 98–130

Roberts, David, *The Ladies: Female Patronage of Restoration Drama 1660–1700* (Oxford, 1989)

Rosenfeld, Sybil, *Georgian Scene Painters* (Cambridge, 1981)

Saunders, George, *A Treatise on Theatres* (London, 1790; *facs.* New York, 1968)

Sorelius, Gunnar, 'The Early History of the Restoration Theatre: some Problems Reconsidered', *Theatre Notebook*, xxxiii (1979), 52–61

Southern, Richard, *Changeable Scenery* (London, 1952)

Spring, John R., 'The Dorset Garden Theatre: Playhouse or Opera House?', *Theatre Notebook*, xxxiv (1980), 60–69

Visser, Colin, 'French Opera and the Making of Dorset Garden Theatre', *Theatre Research International*, vi (1981), 163–71

(ii) PURCELL'S MUSIC FOR THE STAGE

Baldwin, Olive and Wilson, Thelma, 'Purcell's Sopranos', *Musical Times*, cxxiii (1982), 602–9

—— 'Purcell's Stage Singers', in Michael Burden, ed., *Performing the Music of Henry Purcell* (Oxford, 1995)

—— 'Richard Leveridge, 1670–1758: 1: Purcell and the Dramatic Operas', *Musical Times*, cxi (1970), 592–4

Bicknell, Joan Colleen, 'Interdependence of Word and Tone in the Dramatic Music of Henry Purcell' (Ph.D. diss., Stanford U., 1960)

Burden, Michael, 'Purcell Debauch'd; the Dramatick Operas in Performance', in Michael Burden, ed., *Performing the Music of Henry Purcell* (Oxford, 1995)

—— ed., *Henry Purcell's Operas: The Complete Texts* (Oxford, 1995)

Buttrey, John, 'The Evolution of English Opera between 1656 and 1695: A Reinvestigation' (Ph.D. diss., U. of Cambridge, 1967)

Dent, Edward J., *Foundations of English Opera* (Cambridge, 1928)

Dido and Aeneas

Buttrey, John, 'Dating Purcell's *Dido and Aeneas*', *Proceedings of the Royal Musical Association*, xciv (1967–8), 51–62

Chan, Mary, 'The Witch of Endor and Seventeenth-century Propaganda', *Musica Disciplina*, xxxiv (1980), 205–14

Charteris, Richard, 'Newly Discovered Sources of Music by Henry Purcell', *Music and Letters*, lxxv (1994), 16–32

Craven, Robert A., 'Nahum Tate's Third *Dido and Aeneas*: the Sources of the Libretto to Purcell's Opera', *World of Opera*, i (1979), 65–78

Eastman, Holly, 'The Drama of the Passions: Tate and Purcell's Characterization of Dido', *Musical Quarterly*, lxxiii (1989), 364–81

Falconer, David, 'The Two Mr Priests of Chelsea', *Musical Times*, cxxviii (1987), 263

Godt, Irving, 'Purcell and Dido (and Aeneas)', *Studies in the History of Music*, ii (1988), 60–82

Goldie, Mark, 'The Earliest Notice of Purcell's *Dido and Aeneas*', *Early Music*, xx (1992), 392–400

Harris, Ellen T., *Henry Purcell's Dido and Aeneas* (Oxford, 1987)

—— 'Recitative and Aria in *Dido and Aeneas*', *Studies in the History of Music*, ii (1988), 31–59

Holst, Imogen, 'A Note on the Nanki Collection of Purcell's Works', in Imogen Holst, ed., *Henry Purcell 1659–1695: Essays on his Music* (London, 1959), 127–30

—— 'Purcell's Librettist, Nahum Tate', in Imogen Holst, ed., *Henry Purcell 1659–1695: Essays on his Music* (London, 1959), 35–41

Mann, William, 'Dido and Aeneas', *Opera*, ii (1951), 657–61

Mellers, Wilfrid, 'The Tragic Heroine and the Un-hero; Henry Purcell: *Dido and Aeneas*', in *Harmonious Meeting* (London, 1965), 203–14

Mullally, Robert, 'A female Aeneas?', *Musical Times*, cxxx (1989), 80–82

Price, Curtis A., '*Dido and Aeneas*: Questions of Style and Evidence', *Early Music*, xii (1994), 115–25; with letter from Bruce Wood, "Singin' in the Rain': Yet More on Dating *Dido*', *Early Music*, xxii (1994), 365–7

—— and Cholij, Irena, 'Dido's Bass Sorceress', *Musical Times*, cxxvii (1986), 615–18

Purcell, Henry, *Dido and Aeneas*, ed. Curtis A. Price (New York, 1986)

Radice, Mark A., 'Tate's Libretto for *Dido and Aeneas*: a Revaluation', *Bach: The Quarterly Journal of the Riemenschneider-Bach Institute*, vii (1976), 20–26

White, Eric Walter, 'New Light on Purcell's *Dido and Aeneas*', in Imogen Holst, ed., *Henry Purcell 1659–1695: Essays on his Music* (London, 1959), 14–34

Walkling, Andrew, 'Politics and the Restoration Masque: The Case of *Dido and Aeneas*', in G. Maclean, ed., *Literature, Culture and Society in the Stuart Restoration*

Wood, Bruce and Pinnock, Andrew, '*Unscarr'd by Turning Times?*: The Dating of Purcell's *Dido and Aeneas*', *Early Music*, xx (1992), 372–90; with letter from Martin Adams, 'More on Dating *Dido*', *Early Music*, xxi (1993), 510, and a response by Andrew Walkling, ' "The Dating of Purcell's *Dido and Aeneas*"?', *Early Music*, xxii (1994), 469–81

Yamamoto, H., 'The Dramaturgy of Purcell's "Dido and Aeneas" ' (Ph.D. diss., Tokyo, 1967)

Dioclesian

Ham, Roswell, G., 'Dryden's Dedication for *The Music of the Prophetesse*, 1691', *Publications of the Modern Language Association*, l (1935), 1065–75

McCutcheon, R. P., 'Dryden's Prologue to *The Prophetess*', *Modern Language Notes*, xxxix (1924), 123–4

Muller, Frans and Julie, 'Purcell's *Dioclesian* on the Dorset Garden Stage', in Michael Burden, ed., *Performing the Music of Henry Purcell* (Oxford, 1995)

Muller, Julie, *Words and Music in Henry Purcell's First Semi-opera Dioclesian* (Lewiston, 1990)

Dugaw, Dianne, ' "Critical Instants": Theatre Songs in the Age of Dryden and Purcell', *Eighteenth-Century Studies*, xxiii (1989–90), 157–81

The Fairy Queen

Burden, Michael, ' "Gallimaufry at Covent Garden"; Purcell's *The Fairy-Queen* in 1946', *Early Music*, xxiii (1995)

Colles, H., 'Purcell Restored', in H. J. Colles, ed. *Essays and Lectures*, (London, 1945), 47–9

Dunkin, Paul S., 'Issues of *The Fairy Queen*, 1692', *The Library*, 4th series, xxvi (1945–6), 297–304

Lewis, Anthony, 'Notes and Reflections on a New Edition of Purcell's *The Fairy Queen*', *Music Review*, xxv (1964), 104–8

—— 'Purcell and Blow's "Venus and Adonis" ', *Music and Letters*, xliv (1963), 266–9

Savage, Roger, 'The Shakespeare-Purcell *Fairy Queen*: a Defence and Recommendation', *Early Music*, i (1973), 200–21

Wood, Bruce and Pinnock, Andrew, '*The Fairy Queen:* A Fresh Look at the Issues', *Early Music*, xxi (1993), 44–62

Fletcher, I. K., Cohen, Selma Jeane, and Lonsdale, Roger, eds., *Famed for Dance: Essays on the Theory and Practice of Theatrical Dance in England, 1660–1740* (New York, 1960)

The Indian Queen

Pinnock, Andrew, 'Play into Opera: Purcell's *The Indian Queen*', *Early Music*, xviii (1990), 3–21

King Arthur

Altieri, Joanne, 'Baroque Hieroglyphics: Dryden's *King Arthur*', *Philological Quarterly*, lxi (1982), 431–51

Asslid, Michael, 'The Impossible Form of Art: Dryden, Purcell and *King Arthur*', *Studies in the Literary Imagination*, x (1977), 125–44

Charlton, David, '*King Arthur*: Dramatick Opera', *Music and Letters*, lciv (1983), 183–92

Dent, Edward J., 'Purcell's *King Arthur*', in F. Aprahamian, ed., *Essays on Music* (London, 1967), 179–83

Dircks, P. T., 'Thomas Arne to David Garrick: an Unrecorded Letter', *Theatre Notebook*, xxx (1976), 87–90

Farnsworth, Rodney, ' "Hither, this way": A Rhetorical-musical Analysis of a Scene from Purcell's *King Arthur*', *Musical Quarterly*, lxxiv (1990), 83–97

Graham, C., 'King Arthur Revised and Revived', *Opera*, xxi (1970), 904–10

Harris, Ellen T., '*King Arthur's* Eighteenth-Century Journey', in
    Curtis A. Price, ed., *Purcell Studies* (Cambridge, 1995)
Pinnock, Andrew, '*King Arthur* Expos'd: A Lesson in Anatomy', in
    Curtis A. Price, ed., *Purcell Studies* (Cambridge, 1995)
Sawkins, Lionel, '*Trembleurs* and Cold People: How Should They
    Shiver?', in Michael Burden, ed., *Performing the Music of
    Henry Purcell* (Oxford, 1995)
Tiggers, Piet, '*King Arthur* van Henry Purcell', *Mens en Melodie*, ix
    (1954), 47–51
Laurie, Margaret A., 'Purcell's Stage Works' (Ph.D. diss., U. of
    Cambridge, 1962)
Luckett, Richard, 'Exotick but Rational Entertainments: The English
    Dramatick Operas', in Marie Axton and Raymond Williams, eds.,
    English Drama: Form and Development (Cambridge, 1977),
    123–41
McDonald, Jennifer, 'English Masque, English Opera, and Purcell:
    Two Traditions and their Bearing on the Major Dramatic Works
    of Henry Purcell' (Ph.D. diss., U. of Melbourne, 1988)
—— 'Matthew Locke's *The English Opera*, and the Theatre Music of
    Purcell', *Studies in Music* [W. Australia], xv (1981), 62–75
Mellers, Wilfrid, 'Purcell and the Restoration Theatre: *The Fairy
    Queen, The Tempest*', in *Harmonious Meeting* (London, 1965),
    215–25
Moore, Robert E., *Henry Purcell and the Restoration Theatre*
    (Cambridge, Mass., 1961)
Plank, Steven, E., ' "And Now About the Caldron Sing": Music and
    the Supernatural on the Restoration Stage', *Early Music*, xviii
    (1990), 392–407
Pinnock, Andrew, and Wood, Bruce, *The Operas of Henry Purcell*
    (Cambridge, 1995)
Price, Curtis A., *Henry Purcell and the London Stage* (Cambridge,
    1984)
—— 'Political Allegory in Late-Seventeenth-century English Opera',
    in Nigel Fortune, ed., *Music and Theatre: Essays in Honour of
    Winton Dean* (Cambridge, 1987), 1–29
Rose, G., 'A New Purcell Source', *Journal of the American
    Musicological Society*, xxv (1972), 230–36
Rumery, L. R., 'Choral Music in Purcell's Dramatic Works', *American
    Choral Review*, xxvi (1984), 5–11
Savage, Roger, 'Calling up Genius', in Michael Burden, ed.,
    Performing the Music of Henry Purcell (Oxford, 1995)
Semmens, Richard, 'Dancing and Dance Music in Purcell's Operas',

in Michael Burden, ed., *Performing the Music of Henry Purcell* (Oxford, 1995)

The Tempest

Laurie, Margaret A., 'Did Purcell set *The Tempest?*', *Proceedings of the Royal Musical Association*, xc (1963–4), 43–57

Lewis, Anthony, 'Purcell's Music for *The Tempest*', *Musical Times*, c (1959), 321–2

Rylands, George and Lewis, Anthony, 'The Tempest or The Enchanted Island', *Musical Times*, c (1959), 320–22

Timon of Athens

Swalin, B. F., 'Purcell's Masque in Timon of Athens', *American Musicological Society Papers*, Oberlin 1946

Westrup, J. A., 'Purcell's music for "Timon of Athens" ', in Heinrich Huschen, ed., *Festschrift Karl Gustav Fellerer* (Regensburg, 1962), 573–8

Tippett, Michael, 'Our Sense of Continuity in English Drama and Music', in Imogen Holst, ed., *Henry Purcell 1659–1695: Essays on his Music* (London, 1959), 42–51

Walkling, Andrew, 'Performance and Political Allegory: what to interpret and when on the Restoration Stage', in Michael Burden, ed., *Performing the Music of Henry Purcell* (Oxford, 1995)

Walls, Peter, 'The Origins of English Recitative', *Proceedings of the Royal Musical Association*, cx (1983–4), 25–40

White, Eric Walter, 'Early Theatrical Performances of Purcell's Operas, with a Calendar of Recorded Performances, 1690–1710', *Theatre Notebook*, xxiii (1958–9), 43–65

VI *Performing and Recording Purcell*

Arundell, Dennis, 'New Light on *Dido and Aeneas*', *Opera*, xiii (1962), 445–8; with letter from Margaret Laurie and reply by Dennis Arundell, 765–6

Bergmann, Walter, 'Henry Purcell's Use of the Recorder', *Recorder and Music*, vii (1983), 310–13

Bicknell, Joan Colleen, 'On Performing Purcell's Vocal Music: Some Neglected Evidence', *Music Review*, xxv (1964), 27–33

Boal, Ellen TeSelle, 'Purcell's Clock Tempos and the Fantasias', *Journal of the Viola da Gamba Society of America*, xx (1983), 24–39

Britten, Benjamin, 'On Realizing the Continuo in Purcell's Songs', in Imogen Holst, ed., *Henry Purcell 1659–1695: Essays on his Music* (London, 1959), 7–13

Burden, Michael, ed., *Performing the Music of Henry Purcell* (Oxford, 1995)

Burkart, R. E., 'The Trumpet in England in the Seventeenth Century with Emphasis on its Treatment in the Works of Henry Purcell' (Ph.D. diss., U. of Wisconsin, 1972)

Dilworth, John, 'Violin Making in England in the Age of Purcell', in Michael Burden, ed., *Performing the Music of Henry Purcell* (Oxford, 1995)

Donington, Robert, 'Further Seventeenth- and Eighteenth-century Evidence Bearing on the Performance of Purcell's Works', in Imogen Holst, ed., *Henry Purcell 1659–1695: Essays on his Music* (London, 1959), 122–6

—— 'Performing Purcell's Music Today', in Imogen Holst, ed., *Henry Purcell 1659–1695: Essays on his Music* (London, 1959), 74–102

Downey, Peter, 'Performing Mr Purcell's "Exotick" Trumpet Notes', in Michael Burden, ed., *Performing the Music of Henry Purcell* (Oxford, 1995)

—— 'What Samuel Pepys Heard on 3 February 1661: English Trumpet Style under the Stuart Monarchs', *Early Music*, xviii (1990), 417–28

Gwynne, Dominic, 'The English Organ in Purcell's Lifetime', in Michael Burden, ed., *Performing the Music of Henry Purcell* (Oxford, 1995)

Holman, Peter, 'English Trumpets – a Response', *Early Music*, xix (1991), 443

—— 'Original Sets of Parts for Restoration Concerted Music at Oxford', in Michael Burden, ed., *Performing the Music of Henry Purcell* (Oxford, 1995)

Johnstone, H. Diack, 'Ornamentation in the Keyboard Music of Henry Purcell and His Contemporaries', in Michael Burden, ed., *Performing the Music of Henry Purcell* (Oxford, 1995)

Laurie, A. Margaret, 'Continuity and Tempo in Purcell's Vocal Works', in Curtis A. Price, ed., *Purcell Studies* (Cambridge, 1995)

Mahy, K. W., 'The Problem of Thorough-bass Realization in Selected Songs of Henry Purcell: a Critical Comparison of Available Editions' (DMA diss., Indiana U., 1974)

Meffen, John, 'A Question of Temperament: Purcell and Croft', *Musical Times*, cxix (1978), 504–6

Miehling, Klans, 'Das Tempo bei Henry Purcell', *Basler Jahrbuch fur historische Musikpraxis*, xv (1991), 117–47

Morris, Timothy M., 'Voice Ranges, Voice Types and Pitch in Purcell's Concerted Works', in Michael Burden, ed., *Performing the Music of Henry Purcell* (Oxford, 1995)

Phillips, Gordon, 'Purcell's Organs and Organ Music', *Hinrichsen's Music Book*, x (1958), 133–5

Pinnock, Andrew and Wood, Bruce, 'A Counterblast on English Trumpets', *Early Music*, xix (1991), 436–43

Price, Curtis A., 'Purcell's Theatre Music on Record', *Early Music*, xii (1984), 85–90

Ronen, Ruth-Eva, 'Of Costume and Etiquette: Staging in the Time of Purcell', in Michael Burden, ed., *Performing the Music of Henry Purcell* (Oxford, 1995)

Rose, Bernard, 'Some Further Observations on the Performance of Purcell's Music', *Musical Times*, c (1959), 385–6

Roseberry, Eric, 'Britten's Purcell Realizations and Folksong Arrangements', *Tempo*, lvii (1961), 7–28; rev. as 'The Purcell Realizations' in Christopher Palmer, ed., *The Britten Companion* (London, 1984), 356–66

Semmens, Richard, 'Dancing and Dance Music in Purcell's Operas', in Michael Burden, ed., *Performing the Music of Henry Purcell* (Oxford, 1995)

Shaw, H. Watkins, 'Purcell's "Bell" Anthem and its Performance', *Musical Times*, c (1959), 285–6

Stevens, Denis, 'Purcell on the Gramophone', *Music and Letters*, xl (1959), 166–71

Van Tassel, Eric, 'English Church Music c. 1660–1700', *Early Music*, vi (1978), 572–8; vii (1979), 85–8

Wood, Bruce, 'The First Performance of Purcell's Funeral Music for Queen Mary', in Michael Burden, ed., *Performing the Music of Henry Purcell* (Oxford, 1995)

The Contributors

Michael Burden is Lecturer in Music at New College, Oxford, and Director of the New Chamber Opera. He has a special interest in the history of the masque, and is engaged in a study of dramatick opera and on a new edition of the text and music of *The Fairy Queen* which will be the first full publication of any of Purcell's semi-operas.

Graham Dixon is a Senior Producer at BBC Radio 3, and has written extensively on Baroque music, including articles on Monteverdi and Handel and a monograph on Carissimi. He is musicological adviser to the York Early Music Festival.

Peter Holman is Director of The Parley of Instruments, Musical Director of Opera Restor'd, and Senior Associate Lecturer at Colchester Institute, School of Music. His book *'Four and Twenty Fiddlers': the Violin at the English Court 1540–1690* was published in 1993 by The Clarendon Press.

Edward A. Langhans is Professor Emeritus of Drama and Theatre at the University of Hawaii and has published extensively on Restoration and eighteenth-century British theatre.

Andrew Parrott is a conductor and is director of the Taverner Choir, Consort and Players. Among his many recordings are several of music by Purcell, including *Dido and Aeneas*, odes and works for the church, theatre and chamber.

Andrew Pinnock is the Arts Council's Musical Officer with special responsibility for early music. He founded the Early English Opera Society in 1987, and has written articles on early English opera and the history of the trumpet. He is currently working on the new Purcell Society edition of *The Indian Queen*.

Roger Savage is Senior Lecturer in English Literature at the University of Edinburgh. He has research interests in Restoration drama and, as a producer, was responsible for one of the first complete stagings of *The Fairy Queen* given since Purcell's death.

Eric Van Tassel is a freelance editor and writer specializing in early music. He was formerly Editorial Director for BMG Classics in New York, and has been an editor with Cambridge and Princeton University Presses and recording reviews editor for *Early Music*. With Edward Higginbottom, he published a completion of Purcell's anthem 'Give Sentence with Me'.

Jonathan P. Wainwright is Lecturer in Music at St Catherine's and Pembroke Colleges, Oxford, and has research interests in sixteenth- and seventeenth-century English and Italian music, particularly musical patronage and music collections.

Bruce Wood, a Senior Lecturer in Music at the University of Wales, Bangor, is the editor of five volumes of royal and Cecilian odes in the new Purcell Society Edition.

General Index

Index of Works

Note: Songs are indexed under their full titles; plays etc are indexed under the first significant word in the title, ignoring articles